ETS® TOEIC®

JN120915

公式 TOEIC®
Listening & Reading
問題集
6

IIBC
一般財団法人 国際ビジネスコミュニケーション協会

ETS TOEIC®
OFFICIAL TEST PREPARATION AND LEARNING

はじめに

本書は『公式 *TOEIC*® Listening & Reading 問題集』シリーズの第6弾です。2016年5月実施の公開テストから加わった新しい出題形式に対応し、実際と同じテスト形式で2回分の問題を掲載しています。*TOEIC*® Listening & Reading Test の受験準備にお使いください。

本シリーズの特長

- 問題は全て、ETSが実際のテストと同じプロセスで制作しています。
- サンプル問題とテスト2回分の問題(200問×2回、計400問)を掲載し、リスニングセクションは*TOEIC*®公式スピーカーによる音声が収録されています。
  - ＊実際のテストでは、担当スピーカーや発音の種類(どの国の発音か)の割合が変更される場合があります。
- 素点から参考スコア範囲が算出可能です。
- 正解を導くための詳しい解説の他、学習の助けとなる語注「Words & Phrases」(Part 3、4、6、7)や表現紹介のコーナー「Expressions」(Part 6、7)を掲載しています。

付属CD・特典の音声について

- CDは一般的なプレーヤーで再生できます。また、CDの音声をパソコンなどの機器に取り込んで再生することもできます。
- 特典として、TEST 1、2のリーディングセクションの以下の音声をダウンロードすることができます。問題に解答した後の学習用教材としてご活用ください。
  - 正解が入った問題音声(Part 5、6)
  - 文書の音声(Part 7)

＊株式会社 Globee が提供するサービス abceed への会員登録(無料)が必要です。

音声ダウンロードの手順：

1. パソコンまたはスマートフォンで音声ダウンロード用のサイトにアクセスします。
(右の QR コードまたはブラウザから https://app.abceed.com/audio/iibc-officialprep へ)
2. 表示されたページから、abceed の新規会員登録を行います。既に会員の場合は、ログイン情報を入力して上記1. のサイトへアクセスします。
3. 上記1. のサイトにアクセス後、本教材の画像をクリックします。クリックすると、教材詳細画面へ遷移します。
4. スマートフォンの場合は、アプリ「abceed」の案内が出ますので、アプリからご利用ください。パソコンの場合は、教材詳細画面の「音声」のアイコンからご利用ください。

＊音声は何度でもダウンロード・再生ができます。ダウンロードについてのお問い合わせは下記へ
　Eメール:support@globeejphelp.zendesk.com (お問い合わせ窓口の営業日：祝日を除く月～金曜日)
＊特典音声は、必ず一度TEST 1、2 のリーディングセクションの問題に解答した後に、ご利用ください。詳しい使い方は、別冊『解答・解説』p.200をご参照ください。

本書が、*TOEIC*® Listening & Reading Testの出題形式の理解と受験準備、そして皆さまの英語学習のお役に立つことを願っております。

2020年2月
一般財団法人 国際ビジネスコミュニケーション協会

目　次

本誌

＊解答用紙は112ページの後ろに綴じ込まれています。

別冊 『解答・解説』

TOEIC® Listening & Reading Testについて

TOEIC® Listening & Reading Testとは？

TOEIC® Listening & Reading Test（以下、*TOEIC*® L&R）は、*TOEIC*® Programのテストの一つで、英語におけるListening（聞く）とReading（読む）の力を測定します。結果は合格・不合格ではなく、リスニングセクション5～495点、リーディングセクション5～495点、トータル10～990点のスコアで評価されます。スコアの基準は常に一定であり、 英語能力に変化がない限りスコアも一定に保たれます。知識・教養としての英語ではなく、オフィスや日常生活における英語によるコミュニケーション能力を幅広く測定するテストです。特定の文化を知らないと理解できない表現を排除しているので、誰もが公平に受けることができる「グローバルスタンダード」として活用されています。

問題形式

- リスニングセクション（約45分間・100問）とリーディングセクション（75分間・100問）から成り、約2時間で200問に解答します。
- テストは英文のみで構成されており、英文和訳や和文英訳といった設問はありません。
- マークシート方式の一斉客観テストです。
- リスニングセクションにおける発音は、米国・英国・カナダ・オーストラリアが使われています。

＊テスト中、問題用紙への書き込みは一切禁じられています。

リスニングセクション（約45分間）

パート	name of each part	パート名	問題数
1	Photographs	写真描写問題	6
2	Question-Response	応答問題	25
3	Conversations	会話問題	39
4	Talks	説明文問題	30

リーディングセクション（75分間）

パート	name of each part	パート名	問題数
5	Incomplete Sentences	短文穴埋め問題	30
6	Text Completion	長文穴埋め問題	16
7	• Single passages • Multiple passages	1つの文書 複数の文書	29 25

開発・運営団体について

TOEIC® L&Rは、Educational Testing Service（ETS）によって開発・制作されています。ETSは、米国ニュージャージー州プリンストンに拠点を置き、*TOEIC*® ProgramやTOEFL、GRE（大学院入学共通試験）を含む約200のテストプログラムを開発している世界最大の非営利テスト開発機関です。

日本における*TOEIC*® L&Rを含む*TOEIC*® Programの実施･運営は、一般財団法人 国際ビジネスコミュニケーション協会（IIBC）が行っています。IIBCは、公式教材の出版やグローバル人材育成など､「人と企業の国際化」の推進に貢献するための活動を展開しています。

本書の構成と使い方

本書は、本誌と別冊に分かれています。それぞれの主な内容は以下の通りです。

- 本誌 ……「サンプル問題」「TEST 1」「TEST 2」「解答用紙」
- 別冊『解答・解説』……「参考スコア範囲の算出方法」「正解一覧」「解答・解説」「CDトラック・特典音声ファイル 一覧表」「音声を使った学習例の紹介」

本誌

サンプル問題（29問）[本誌p.8-27]

全パートから合計29問を掲載しています。

CD 1 02-10

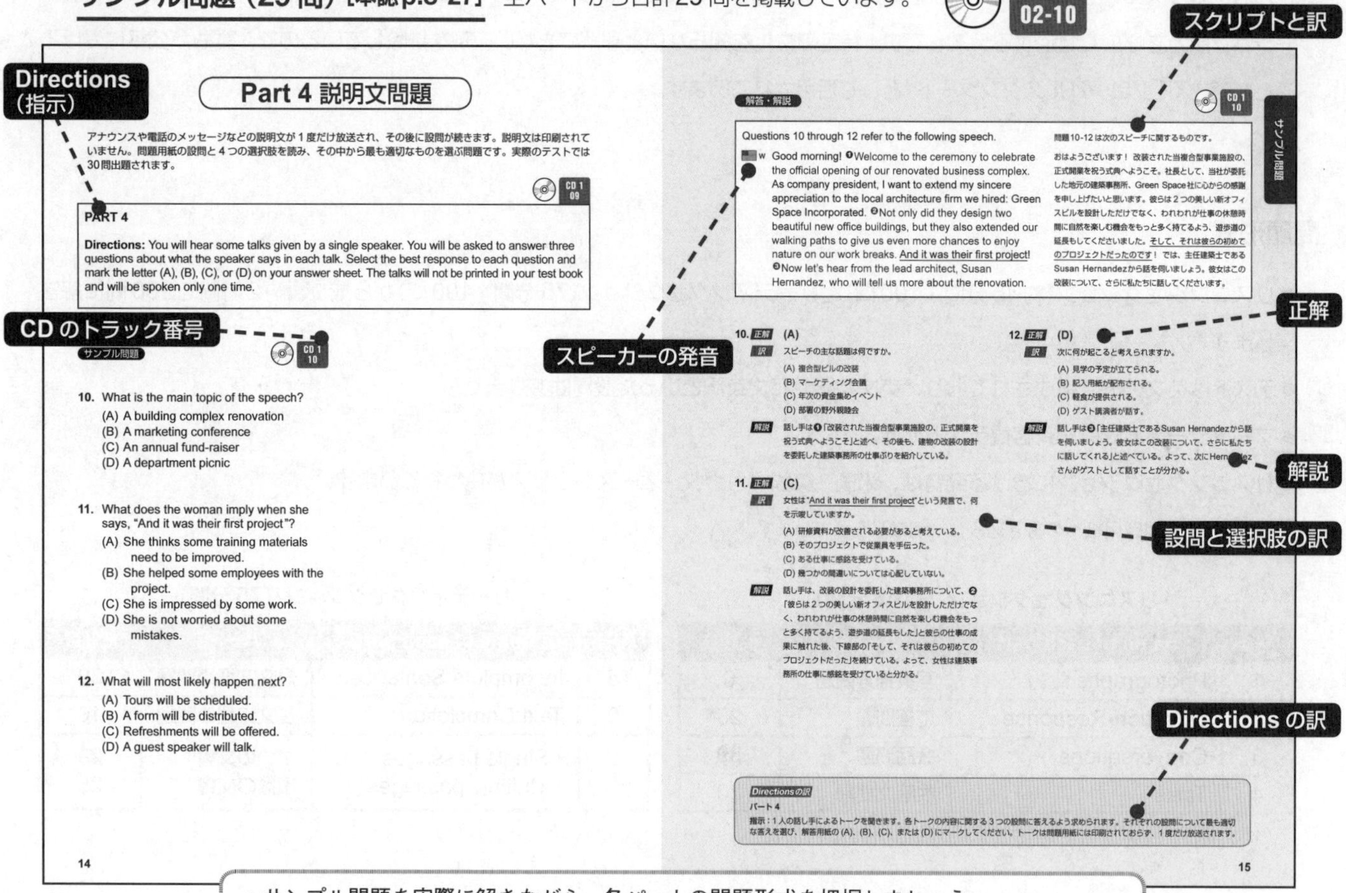

Part 4 説明文問題

アナウンスや電話のメッセージなどの説明文が1度だけ放送され、その後に設問が続きます。説明文は印刷されていません。問題用紙の設問と4つの選択肢を読み、その中から最も適切なものを選ぶ問題です。実際のテストでは30問出題されます。

CD 1 09

PART 4

Directions: You will hear some talks given by a single speaker. You will be asked to answer three questions about what the speaker says in each talk. Select the best response to each question and mark the letter (A), (B), (C), or (D) on your answer sheet. The talks will not be printed in your test book and will be spoken only one time.

サンプル問題 CD 1 10

10. What is the main topic of the speech?
(A) A building complex renovation
(B) A marketing conference
(C) An annual fund-raiser
(D) A department picnic

11. What does the woman imply when she says, "And it was their first project"?
(A) She thinks some training materials need to be improved.
(B) She helped some employees with the project.
(C) She is impressed by some work.
(D) She is not worried about some mistakes.

12. What will most likely happen next?
(A) Tours will be scheduled.
(B) A form will be distributed.
(C) Refreshments will be offered.
(D) A guest speaker will talk.

14

解答・解説 CD 1 10

Questions 10 through 12 refer to the following speech.

W Good morning! ❶Welcome to the ceremony to celebrate the official opening of our renovated business complex. As company president, I want to extend my sincere appreciation to the local architecture firm we hired: Green Space Incorporated. ❷Not only did they design two beautiful new office buildings, but they also extended our walking paths to give us even more chances to enjoy nature on our work breaks. And it was their first project! ❸Now let's hear from the lead architect, Susan Hernandez, who will tell us more about the renovation.

問題10-12は次のスピーチに関するものです。

おはようございます！ 改装された当複合型事業施設の、正式開業を祝う式典へようこそ。社長として、当社が委託した地元の建築事務所、Green Space社に心からの感謝を申し上げたいと思います。彼らは2つの美しい新オフィスビルを設計しただけでなく、われわれが仕事の休憩時間に自然を楽しむ機会をもっと多く持てるよう、遊歩道の延長もしてくださいました。そして、それは彼らの初めてのプロジェクトだったのです！ では、主任建築士であるSusan Hernandezから話を伺いましょう。彼女はこの改装について、さらに私たちに話してくださいます。

サンプル問題

10. 正解 (A)
訳 スピーチの主な話題は何ですか。
(A) 複合型ビルの改装
(B) マーケティング会議
(C) 年次の資金集めイベント
(D) 部署の野外親睦会
解説 話し手は❶「改装された当複合型事業施設の、正式開業を祝う式典へようこそ」と述べ、その後も、建物の改装の設計を委託した建築事務所の仕事ぶりを紹介している。

11. 正解 (C)
訳 女性は"And it was their first project"という発言で、何を示唆していますか。
(A) 研修資料が改善される必要があると考えている。
(B) そのプロジェクトで従業員を手伝った。
(C) ある仕事に感銘を受けている。
(D) 幾つかの間違いについては心配していない。
解説 話し手は、改装の設計を委託した建築事務所について、❷「彼らは2つの美しい新オフィスビルを設計しただけでなく、われわれが仕事の休憩時間に自然を楽しむ機会をもっと多く持てるよう、遊歩道の延長もした」と彼らの仕事の成果に触れた後、下線部の「そして、それは彼らの初めてのプロジェクトだった」を続けている。よって、女性は建築事務所の仕事に感銘を受けていると分かる。

12. 正解 (D)
訳 次に何が起こると考えられますか。
(A) 見学の予定が立てられる。
(B) 記入用紙が配布される。
(C) 軽食が提供される。
(D) ゲスト講演者が話す。
解説 話し手は❸「主任建築士であるSusan Hernandezから話を伺いましょう。彼女はこの改装について、さらに私たちに話してくれる」と述べている。よって、次にHernandezさんがゲストとして話すことが分かる。

Directionsの訳
パート4
指示：1人の話し手によるトークを聞きます。各トークの内容に関する3つの設問に答えるよう求められます。それぞれの設問について最も適切な答えを選び、解答用紙の (A)、(B)、(C)、または (D) にマークしてください。トークは問題用紙には印刷されておらず、1度だけ放送されます。

15

- サンプル問題を実際に解きながら、各パートの問題形式を把握しましょう。
- リスニングセクションでは、CD の音声を聞き、スピードや発音を確認しましょう。

＝米国の発音　＝英国の発音　＝カナダの発音　＝オーストラリアの発音
M ＝男性（Man）　W ＝女性（Woman）

TEST 1 [本誌p.29-70]

CD 1 11-92

TEST 2 [本誌p.71-111]

CD 2 01-82

TEST 1、2 ともに、実際のテストと同じ、合計 200 問で構成されています。

リスニングセクション	100 問	約 45 分間
リーディングセクション	100 問	75 分間

予行演習として時間を計って解答し、時間配分の参考にしたり、伸ばしたい分野や弱点を把握したり、使い方を工夫してみましょう。

別冊『解答・解説』

参考スコア範囲の算出方法［別冊 p.4］

正解数を基に、参考スコア範囲を算出できます。

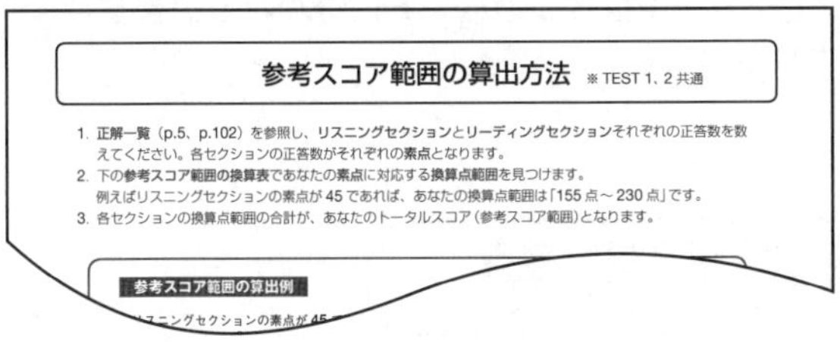
参考スコア範囲の算出方法 ※TEST 1、2 共通

1. 正解一覧（p.5、p.102）を参照し、リスニングセクションとリーディングセクションそれぞれの正答数を数えてください。各セクションの正答数がそれぞれの素点となります。
2. 下の参考スコア範囲の換算表であなたの素点に対応する換算点範囲を見つけます。例えばリスニングセクションの素点が45であれば、あなたの換算点範囲は「155点～230点」です。
3. 各セクションの換算点範囲の合計が、あなたのトータルスコア（参考スコア範囲）となります。

参考スコア範囲の算出例

正解一覧［TEST 1 ➡ 別冊 p.5　TEST 2 ➡ 別冊 p.102］

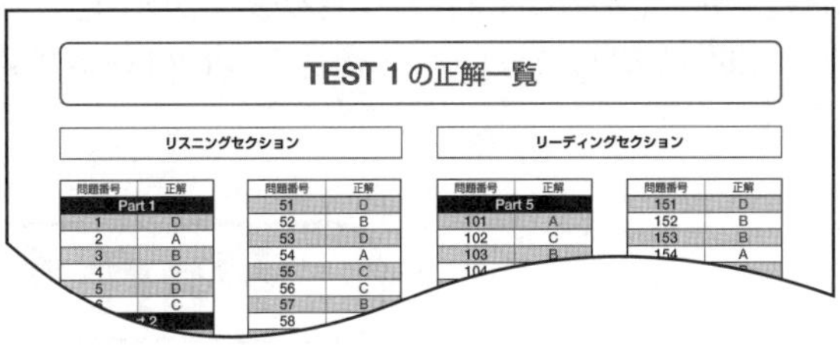
TEST 1 の正解一覧

リスニングセクション　リーディングセクション

問題番号	正解	問題番号	正解	問題番号	正解	問題番号	正解
Part 1		51	D	Part 5		151	D
1	D	52	B	101	A	152	B
2	A	53	D	102	C	153	B
3	B	54	A	103	B	154	A
4	C	55	C				
5	D	56	C				
6	C	57	B				
		58					

解答・解説［TEST 1 ➡ 別冊 p.6-101　TEST 2 ➡ 別冊 p.103-197］

表記の説明は、別冊 p.2-3 をご覧ください。

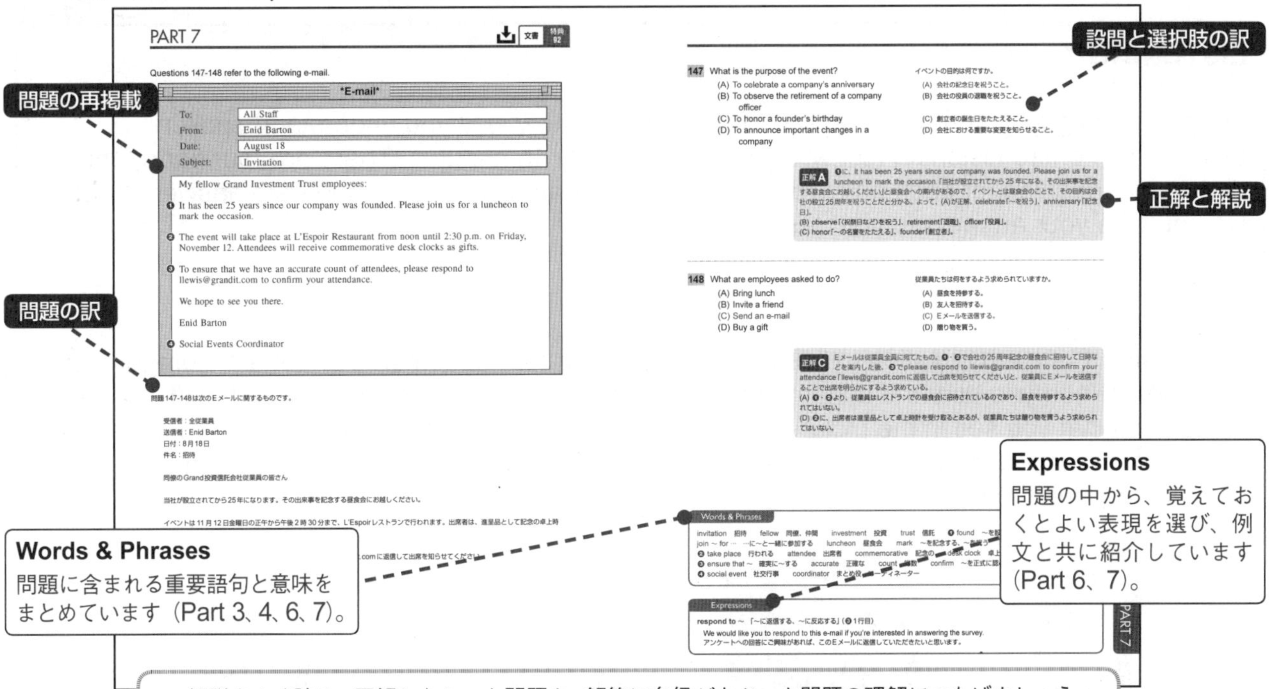

- 解説をよく読み、正解しなかった問題や、解答に自信がなかった問題の理解につなげましょう。
- Words & Phrases や Expressions を利用して語句の理解を深め、表現の幅を広げましょう。
- リスニングセクションで聞き取りが難しかった問題は、スクリプトや訳を参照しながら何度も音声を聞いて確認してみましょう。

CD トラック・特典音声ファイル 一覧表
［別冊 p.198-199］

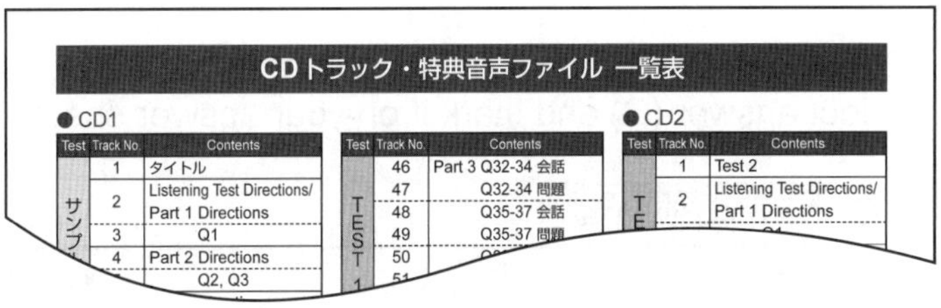
CD トラック・特典音声ファイル 一覧表

● CD1

Test	Track No.	Contents
	1	タイトル
サンプル	2	Listening Test Directions/ Part 1 Directions
	3	Q1
	4	Part 2 Directions
		Q2, Q3

Test	Track No.	Contents
TEST 1	46	Part 3 Q32-34 会話
	47	Q32-34 問題
	48	Q35-37 会話
	49	Q35-37 問題
	50	

● CD2

Test	Track No.	Contents
	1	Test 2
TE	2	Listening Test Directions/ Part 1 Directions

サンプル問題

TOEIC® Listening & Reading Test (以下、*TOEIC*® L&R)の問題形式を、サンプル問題を使ってご紹介します。サンプル問題は、全部で29問(リスニングセクション12問、リーディングセクション17問)です。問題の番号は連番になっており、実際のテストの問題番号とは異なります。

TOEIC® L&Rのリスニングセクションは4つ、リーディングセクションは3つのパートに分かれています。問題用紙には、各パートの最初にDirectionsが英文で印刷されています。

Part 1 写真描写問題

1枚の写真について4つの短い説明文が1度だけ放送されます。説明文は印刷されていません。4つのうち写真を最も適切に描写しているものを選ぶ問題です。実際のテストでは6問出題されます。

CD 1 02

LISTENING TEST

In the Listening test, you will be asked to demonstrate how well you understand spoken English. The entire Listening test will last approximately 45 minutes. There are four parts, and directions are given for each part. You must mark your answers on the separate answer sheet. Do not write your answers in your test book.

PART 1

Directions: For each question in this part, you will hear four statements about a picture in your test book. When you hear the statements, you must select the one statement that best describes what you see in the picture. Then find the number of the question on your answer sheet and mark your answer. The statements will not be printed in your test book and will be spoken only one time.

Look at the example item below.

Now listen to the four statements.
(A) They're moving some furniture.
(B) They're entering a meeting room.
(C) They're sitting at a table.
(D) They're cleaning the carpet.

Statement (C), "They're sitting at a table," is the best description of the picture, so you should select answer (C) and mark it on your answer sheet.

Now Part 1 will begin.

＊上記枠内の網掛けの部分は音声のみで、問題用紙には印刷されていません。

1.

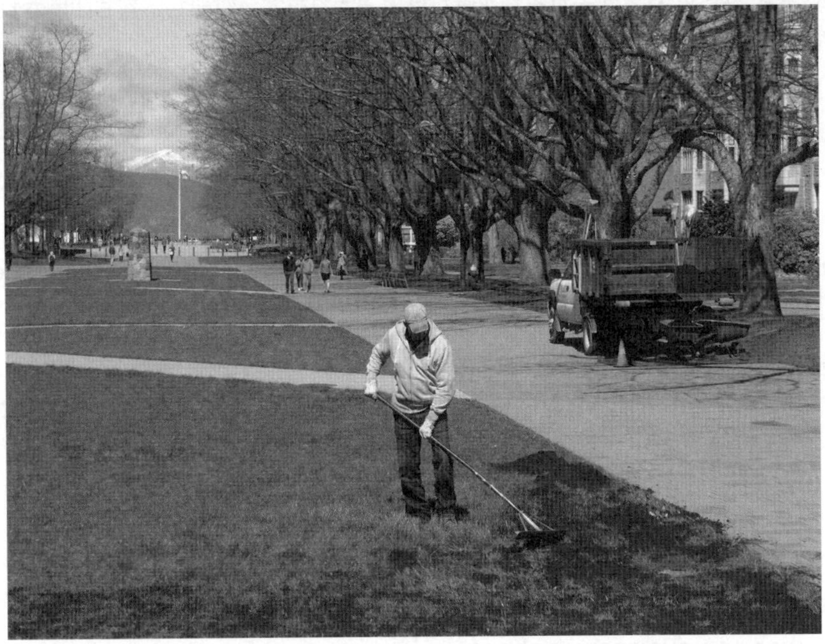

解答・解説

1. Look at the picture marked number 1 in your test book.

M (A) A truck is stopped at a stoplight.
(B) A man is using a gardening tool.
(C) Some people are sitting on the grass.
(D) Some workers are cutting down a tree.

訳 問題用紙にある問題1の写真を見てください。

(A) トラックが停止信号で止まっている。
(B) 男性が造園用具を使っている。
(C) 何人かの人々が芝生の上に座っている。
(D) 何人かの作業員が木を切り倒している。

正解 **(B)**

解説 gardeningは「造園、園芸」、toolは「用具、道具」という意味。

Directionsの訳

リスニングテスト

リスニングテストでは、話されている英語をどのくらいよく理解しているかが問われます。リスニングテストは全体で約45分間です。4つのパートがあり、各パートにおいて指示が与えられます。答えは、別紙の解答用紙にマークしてください。問題用紙に答えを書き込んではいけません。

パート1

指示：このパートの各設問では、問題用紙にある写真について、4つの説明文を聞きます。説明文を聞いて、写真の内容を最も適切に描写しているものを選んでください。そして解答用紙の該当する問題番号にあなたの答えをマークしてください。説明文は問題用紙には印刷されておらず、1度だけ放送されます。

下の例題を見てください。

では4つの説明文を聞きましょう。
(A) 彼らは家具を動かしている。
(B) 彼らは会議室に入ろうとしている。
(C) 彼らはテーブルのところに座っている。
(D) 彼らはカーペットを掃除している。

(C)の文、“They're sitting at a table”(彼らはテーブルのところに座っている)がこの写真を最も適切に描写しているので、(C)を選び、解答用紙にマークします。

ではパート1が始まります。

Part 2 応答問題

1つの質問または発言と、3つの応答がそれぞれ1度だけ放送されます。質問も応答も印刷されていません。質問に対して最も適切な応答を選ぶ問題です。実際のテストでは25問出題されます。

CD 1 04

PART 2

Directions: You will hear a question or statement and three responses spoken in English. They will not be printed in your test book and will be spoken only one time. Select the best response to the question or statement and mark the letter (A), (B), or (C) on your answer sheet.

Now let us begin with question number 2.

＊上記枠内の網掛けの部分は音声のみで、問題用紙には印刷されていません。

サンプル問題

CD 1 05

2. Mark your answer on your answer sheet.

3. Mark your answer on your answer sheet.

解答・解説

2. W Are you taking an international or a domestic flight?

M (A) I'd prefer a window seat.
(B) He moved there last year.
(C) I'm flying internationally.

訳 あなたは国際線の便に乗りますか、それとも国内線の便ですか。

(A) 私は窓側の席を希望します。
(B) 彼は昨年、そこへ引っ越しました。
(C) 私は国際線の飛行機で行きます。

正解 **(C)**

解説 *A* or *B*?の形で、国際線と国内線のどちらの便に乗るのかを尋ねているのに対し、「国際線の飛行機で行く」と答えている(C)が正解。

3. M Shouldn't we hire more salespeople?

W (A) I'm glad they went.
(B) A higher profit.
(C) Let's look at the budget.

訳 私たちはもっと販売員を雇った方がいいのではありませんか。

(A) 私は、彼らが行ってうれしいです。
(B) より高い利益です。
(C) 予算を見てみましょう。

正解 **(C)**

解説 「もっと販売員を雇った方がいいのではないか」という男性の発言に対し、「予算を見てみよう」と雇用の検討を示唆している(C)が正解。

Directionsの訳

パート2

指示：英語による1つの質問または発言と、3つの応答を聞きます。それらは問題用紙には印刷されておらず、1度だけ放送されます。質問または発言に対して最も適切な応答を選び、解答用紙の(A)、(B)、または(C)にマークしてください。

では、問題2から始めましょう。

問題の訳

答えを解答用紙にマークしてください。

Part 3 会話問題

会話が１度だけ放送され、その後に設問が続きます。会話は印刷されていません。問題用紙の設問と４つの選択肢を読み、その中から最も適切なものを選ぶ問題です。実際のテストでは39問出題されます。

CD 1 06

PART 3

Directions: You will hear some conversations between two or more people. You will be asked to answer three questions about what the speakers say in each conversation. Select the best response to each question and mark the letter (A), (B), (C), or (D) on your answer sheet. The conversations will not be printed in your test book and will be spoken only one time.

サンプル問題

CD 1 07

4. Which department is the man most likely calling?
(A) Receiving
(B) Catering
(C) Security
(D) Finance

5. Why does the man apologize?
(A) He has forgotten his badge.
(B) His report will be late.
(C) A meeting location has to be changed.
(D) A shipment must be delivered after business hours.

6. What does the woman say she will do?
(A) Arrange additional workspace
(B) Publish some materials
(C) Issue a temporary pass
(D) Ask staff to work late

CD 1 08

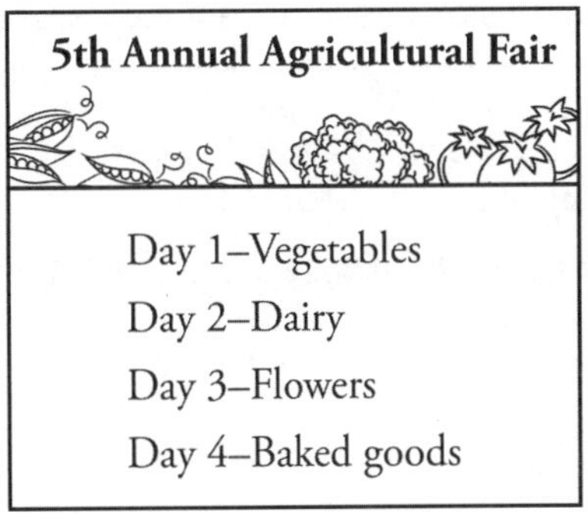

7. Why do the speakers want to attend the fair?
(A) To advertise a new business
(B) To find local food suppliers
(C) To sell some products
(D) To participate in a workshop

8. What does the man say he has downloaded?
(A) An electronic book
(B) A mobile phone application
(C) Some photographs
(D) Some tickets

9. Look at the graphic. Which day do the speakers decide to attend the fair?
(A) Day 1
(B) Day 2
(C) Day 3
(D) Day 4

CD 1 07

Questions 4 through 6 refer to the following conversation.

問題4-6は次の会話に関するものです。

M Hello. ❶I'm expecting an extra-large load of clothing racks delivered to the store today, and they'll arrive after business hours. Are you the person I should inform about this?

もしもし。今日お店に、洋服ラックの特大の積み荷が配達される予定ですが、それらは営業時間の後に着きます。あなたがこの件についてお知らせすべき方でしょうか。

W Yes, ❷I'm head of Receiving. But ❸you're supposed to have suppliers make deliveries during business hours.

はい、私が荷受け部門の責任者です。でも、供給業者には、営業時間中に配達してもらうことになっているはずですが。

M ❹I'm sorry, but this is the only time the supplier can deliver them, and we need the racks for a fashion show we're having tomorrow.

申し訳ありません。しかし、これが、供給業者がそれらを配達できる唯一の時間帯で、私たちが明日開催するファッションショーには、そのラックが必要なんです。

W I understand. ❺I'm not sure which of my staff members is working tonight, but I'll ask one of them to stay late to accept the delivery.

分かりました。今夜うちのスタッフの誰が勤務するのか定かではありませんが、配達物を受け取るために遅くまで残るよう、彼らのうちの1人に頼みます。

4. 正解 **(A)**

訳 男性はどの部署に電話をかけていると考えられますか。

(A) 荷受け
(B) ケータリング
(C) 警備
(D) 財務

解説 男性からの電話に応答した女性は❷「私が荷受け部門の責任者だ」と答え、その後も2人は配達物の受け取りについて話をしている。

5. 正解 **(D)**

訳 男性はなぜ謝罪していますか。

(A) 自分のバッジを忘れたから。
(B) 報告書が遅れるから。
(C) 会議の場所が変更されなければならないから。
(D) 荷物が営業時間の後に配達されざるを得ないから。

解説 ❶「積み荷が配達される予定だが、それらは営業時間の後に着く」という男性の報告に対し、女性が❸「供給業者には、営業時間中に配達してもらうことになっているはず」と指摘している。それに対して男性は❹で、「申し訳ない」と謝罪後「これが、供給業者がそれらを配達できる唯一の時間帯で、私たちが明日開催するファッションショーには、そのラックが必要だ」と事情を説明している。よって、正解は(D)。

6. 正解 **(D)**

訳 女性は何をすると言っていますか。

(A) 追加の作業スペースを手配する。
(B) 資料を公表する。
(C) 臨時の通行証を発行する。
(D) スタッフに遅くまで勤務するよう頼む。

解説 女性は❺「今夜うちのスタッフの誰が勤務するのか定かではないが、配達物を受け取るために遅くまで残るよう、彼らのうちの1人に頼む」と述べている。stay lateをwork late「遅くまで勤務する」と表した(D)が正解。

Directionsの訳

パート3

指示：2人あるいはそれ以上の人々の会話を聞きます。各会話の内容に関する3つの設問に答えるよう求められます。それぞれの設問について最も適切な答えを選び、解答用紙の(A)、(B)、(C)、または(D)にマークしてください。会話は問題用紙には印刷されておらず、1度だけ放送されます。

Questions 7 through 9 refer to the following conversation and schedule.	問題7-9は次の会話と予定表に関するものです。
W Pedro, ❶I know we're still looking for local fresh food suppliers for our new restaurant. We should check out the Agricultural Fair next month.	Pedro、私たちはまだ、うちの新しいレストランのために、地元の生鮮食品の供給業者を探しているわよね。来月の農業フェアを見てみるべきだわ。
M That's a good idea. It's a major event, so many local farmers will be there. ❷I downloaded the fair's mobile phone application. The app has a lot of helpful information, including a schedule. Which day do you think we should go?	それは良い考えだね。大きなイベントだから、多数の地元の農業経営者たちがそこにいるだろう。僕はフェアの携帯電話用アプリをダウンロードしたよ。このアプリには、予定表を含め、役立つ情報がたくさんあるんだ。僕たちはどの日に行くべきだと思う？
W Well, it looks like they'll have dairy vendors on the second day.	そうね、乳製品の販売業者は2日目にいるみたいね。
M Hmm, I just contacted a dairy company that might work for us. ❸We really need a vegetable supplier though…	うーん、僕はうちに合いそうな乳製品会社に連絡を取ったばかりなんだ。僕たちには野菜の供給業者がぜひとも必要だけど…。
W Oh, OK. ❹They have a day for showcasing vegetable farmers. Let's go then.	ああ、分かったわ。野菜農家の出展日があるわ。そのときに行きましょう。

7. 正解 **(B)**

訳 なぜ話し手たちはフェアに行きたいと思っていますか。

(A) 新しい店を宣伝するため。
(B) 地元の食品供給業者を見つけるため。
(C) 製品を販売するため。
(D) 講習会に参加するため。

解説 女性は❶「私たちはまだ、うちの新しいレストランのために、地元の生鮮食品の供給業者を探している。来月の農業フェアを見てみるべきだ」と提案し、男性もそれに同意している。よって、(B)が適切。

8. 正解 **(B)**

訳 男性は何をダウンロードしたと言っていますか。

(A) 電子書籍
(B) 携帯電話用アプリ
(C) 数枚の写真
(D) 数枚のチケット

解説 男性は❷「僕はフェアの携帯電話用アプリをダウンロードした」と述べている。

9. 正解 **(A)**

訳 図を見てください。話し手たちはどの日にフェアへ行くことに決めますか。

(A) 1日目
(B) 2日目
(C) 3日目
(D) 4日目

解説 ❸「僕たちには野菜の供給業者がぜひとも必要だ」という男性の発言に対し、女性は❹「野菜農家の出展日がある。そのときに行こう」と提案している。予定表から、野菜農家が集まる日は1日目だと分かる。予定表のbaked goodsはクッキーやパンなどのオーブンで焼いた食品を指す。

図の訳

第5回　年次農業フェア
1日目 ── 野菜
2日目 ── 乳製品
3日目 ── 花
4日目 ── パン・焼き菓子

Part 4 説明文問題

アナウンスや電話のメッセージなどの説明文が１度だけ放送され、その後に設問が続きます。説明文は印刷されていません。問題用紙の設問と４つの選択肢を読み、その中から最も適切なものを選ぶ問題です。実際のテストでは30問出題されます。

CD 1 09

PART 4

Directions: You will hear some talks given by a single speaker. You will be asked to answer three questions about what the speaker says in each talk. Select the best response to each question and mark the letter (A), (B), (C), or (D) on your answer sheet. The talks will not be printed in your test book and will be spoken only one time.

サンプル問題

CD 1 10

10. What is the main topic of the speech?

(A) A building complex renovation
(B) A marketing conference
(C) An annual fund-raiser
(D) A department picnic

11. What does the woman imply when she says, "And it was their first project"?

(A) She thinks some training materials need to be improved.
(B) She helped some employees with the project.
(C) She is impressed by some work.
(D) She is not worried about some mistakes.

12. What will most likely happen next?

(A) Tours will be scheduled.
(B) A form will be distributed.
(C) Refreshments will be offered.
(D) A guest speaker will talk.

Questions 10 through 12 refer to the following speech.

W Good morning! ❶Welcome to the ceremony to celebrate the official opening of our renovated business complex. As company president, I want to extend my sincere appreciation to the local architecture firm we hired: Green Space Incorporated. ❷Not only did they design two beautiful new office buildings, but they also extended our walking paths to give us even more chances to enjoy nature on our work breaks. And it was their first project! ❸Now let's hear from the lead architect, Susan Hernandez, who will tell us more about the renovation.

問題10-12は次のスピーチに関するものです。

おはようございます！ 改装された当複合型事業施設の、正式開業を祝う式典へようこそ。社長として、当社が委託した地元の建築事務所、Green Space社に心からの感謝を申し上げたいと思います。彼らは2つの美しい新オフィスビルを設計しただけでなく、われわれが仕事の休憩時間に自然を楽しむ機会をもっと多く持てるよう、遊歩道の延長もしてくださいました。そして、それは彼らの初めてのプロジェクトだったのです！ では、主任建築士であるSusan Hernandezから話を伺いましょう。彼女はこの改装について、さらに私たちに話してくださいます。

10. 正解 **(A)**

訳 スピーチの主な話題は何ですか。

(A) 複合型ビルの改装
(B) マーケティング会議
(C) 年次の資金集めイベント
(D) 部署の野外親睦会

解説 話し手は❶「改装された当複合型事業施設の、正式開業を祝う式典へようこそ」と述べ、その後も、建物の改装の設計を委託した建築事務所の仕事ぶりを紹介している。

11. 正解 **(C)**

訳 女性は"And it was their first project"という発言で、何を示唆していますか。

(A) 研修資料が改善される必要があると考えている。
(B) そのプロジェクトで従業員を手伝った。
(C) ある仕事に感銘を受けている。
(D) 幾つかの間違いについては心配していない。

解説 話し手は、改装の設計を委託した建築事務所について、❷「彼らは2つの美しい新オフィスビルを設計しただけでなく、われわれが仕事の休憩時間に自然を楽しむ機会をもっと多く持てるよう、遊歩道の延長もした」と彼らの仕事の成果に触れた後、下線部の「そして、それは彼らの初めてのプロジェクトだった」を続けている。よって、女性は建築事務所の仕事に感銘を受けていると分かる。

12. 正解 **(D)**

訳 次に何が起こると考えられますか。

(A) 見学の予定が立てられる。
(B) 記入用紙が配布される。
(C) 軽食が提供される。
(D) ゲスト講演者が話す。

解説 話し手は❸「主任建築士であるSusan Hernandezから話を伺いましょう。彼女はこの改装について、さらに私たちに話してくれる」と述べている。よって、次にHernandezさんがゲストとして話すことが分かる。

Directionsの訳

パート4

指示：1人の話し手によるトークを聞きます。各トークの内容に関する3つの設問に答えるよう求められます。それぞれの設問について最も適切な答えを選び、解答用紙の(A)、(B)、(C)、または(D)にマークしてください。トークは問題用紙には印刷されておらず、1度だけ放送されます。

ここからはリーディングセクションです。
実際のテストでは、リスニングセクションの終わりに"This is the end of the Listening test. Turn to Part 5 in your test book."(これでリスニングテストは終了です。問題用紙のパート5に進んでください。)というアナウンスがありますので、それが聞こえたらリーディングセクションの解答を始めます。

Part 5 短文穴埋め問題

4つの選択肢の中から最も適切なものを選び、不完全な文を完成させる問題です。実際のテストでは30問出題されます。

READING TEST

In the Reading test, you will read a variety of texts and answer several different types of reading comprehension questions. The entire Reading test will last 75 minutes. There are three parts, and directions are given for each part. You are encouraged to answer as many questions as possible within the time allowed.

You must mark your answers on the separate answer sheet. Do not write your answers in your test book.

PART 5

Directions: A word or phrase is missing in each of the sentences below. Four answer choices are given below each sentence. Select the best answer to complete the sentence. Then mark the letter (A), (B), (C), or (D) on your answer sheet.

サンプル問題

13. Before ------- with the recruiter, applicants should sign in at the personnel department's reception desk.
(A) meets
(B) meeting
(C) to meet
(D) was met

14. Stefano Linen Company suggests requesting a small fabric ------- before placing your final order.
(A) bonus
(B) sample
(C) feature
(D) model

13. 正解 **(B)**

訳 採用担当者と会う前に、応募者の方々は人事部の受付で署名して到着を記録してください。

(A) 動詞の三人称単数現在形
(B) 動名詞
(C) to不定詞
(D) 受動態の過去形

解説 選択肢は全て動詞meet「会う」の変化した形。文頭からカンマまでの部分に主語と動詞がないため、Beforeは前置詞と考えられる。前置詞に続く空所には名詞の働きをする語句が入るので、動名詞の(B) meetingが適切である。sign in「署名して到着を記録する」。

14. 正解 **(B)**

訳 Stefanoリネン社は、お客さまが最終的な注文をなさる前に、小さな布地見本をご要望になることをお勧めしています。

(A) 特別手当
(B) 見本
(C) 特徴
(D) 模型

解説 選択肢は全て名詞。空所の後ろは「お客さまが最終的な注文をする前に」という意味。(B) sample「見本」を空所に入れるとsmall fabric sample「小さな布地見本」となり、注文前に要望するものとして適切で、意味が通る。

Directionsの訳

リーディングテスト

リーディングテストでは、さまざまな文章を読んで、読解力を測る何種類かの問題に答えます。リーディングテストは全体で75分間です。3つのパートがあり、各パートにおいて指示が与えられます。制限時間内に、できるだけ多くの設問に答えてください。

答えは、別紙の解答用紙にマークしてください。問題用紙に答えを書き込んではいけません。

パート5

指示：以下の各文において語や句が抜けています。各文の下には選択肢が4つ与えられています。文を完成させるのに最も適切な答えを選びます。そして解答用紙の (A)、(B)、(C)、または (D) にマークしてください。

Part 6 長文穴埋め問題

4 つの選択肢の中から最も適切なものを選び、不完全な文書を完成させる問題です。実際のテストでは 16 問出題されます。

PART 6

Directions: Read the texts that follow. A word, phrase, or sentence is missing in parts of each text. Four answer choices for each question are given below the text. Select the best answer to complete the text. Then mark the letter (A), (B), (C), or (D) on your answer sheet.

サンプル問題

Questions 15-18 refer to the following article.

❶ SAN DIEGO (May 5)—Matino Industries has just bolstered its image with environmentally conscious customers thanks to its ------- (**15.**) to reduce its use of nonrenewable energy to less than 20 percent within five years. -------. (**16.**) Best practices guidelines are already being revised ------- (**17.**) powering down and disconnecting equipment when not in use. In addition, solar-panel arrays are slated for installation on-site as early as next year. When weather ------- (**18.**) are clear, these panels will offset Matino's reliance on the power grid, as they already do for a growing list of companies.

＊❶は解説の中で説明している文書中の段落番号等を示しています。問題用紙には印刷されていません。

15. (A) product
(B) commitment
(C) contest
(D) workforce

16. (A) Discounts on all its products have increased Matino's customer base.
(B) Management predicts that the takeover will result in a net financial gain.
(C) To achieve this goal, the company will begin by improving its energy efficiency.
(D) The initial step will involve redesigning the company's logo and slogans.

17. (A) been encouraging
(B) have encouraged
(C) encourages
(D) to encourage

18. (A) conditions
(B) instructions
(C) views
(D) reports

問題15-18は次の記事に関するものです。

サンディエゴ（5月5日）――Matino産業社は、同社の再生不能エネルギーの使用を5年以内に20パーセント未満に削減するという公約のおかげで、環境意識の高い顧客にとっての同社のイメージを強化したところである。*この目標を達成するために同社は、自社のエネルギー効率を改善することから始める予定だ。機器を使用していないときには電源を落として接続を切ることを推奨するために、最良実践ガイドラインがすでに改定されているところである。さらに、早くも来年には、ソーラーパネルの列が構内に設置される予定である。天候条件が晴れのときには、これらのパネルが、増え続ける多くの企業に対してすでにそうしているように、Matino社の送電網依存を弱めることになる。

*問題16の挿入文の訳

15. 正解 **(B)**

訳
(A) 製品
(B) 公約
(C) 競争
(D) 全従業員

解説 ❶の1～3行目は「Matino産業社は、同社の-------のおかげで、同社のイメージを強化したところだ」というのが、文の中心の意味。空所の後ろの「同社の再生不能エネルギーの使用を5年以内に20パーセント未満に削減すること」は、空所に入る名詞の内容を示していると考えられるので、文意から(B) commitment「公約」が適切。

16. 正解 **(C)**

訳
(A) 全ての自社製品に対する割引が、Matino社の顧客基盤を拡大してきた。
(B) 経営陣は、その企業買収は財務上の純利益をもたらすと予測している。
(C) この目標を達成するために同社は、自社のエネルギー効率を改善することから始める予定だ。
(D) 第1段階には、会社のロゴとスローガンを作り直すことが含まれる予定だ。

解説 空所の前の文では、Matino産業社が同社の再生不能エネルギーの使用を5年以内に20パーセント未満に削減することが述べられている。この内容をthis goalで受けて、目標達成のために同社がこれから取り組むことを挙げている(C)が流れとして適切。

17. 正解 **(D)**

訳
(A) 〈be動詞の過去分詞＋現在分詞〉
(B) 現在完了形
(C) 動詞の三人称単数現在形
(D) to不定詞

解説 選択肢は全て動詞encourage「～を推奨する」が変化した形。空所の前に〈主語＋動詞〉の形があり、andやorなどの接続詞もないことから、空所に動詞は入らない。空所には、to不定詞の(D) to encourageが適切。

18. 正解 **(A)**

訳
(A) 条件
(B) 指示
(C) 見解
(D) 報道

解説 空所を含む文の、文頭からカンマまでは「天候-------が晴れのときには」という意味。these panels以降では、その際にソーラーパネルがもたらす効果について述べられている。「天候条件が晴れのときには」とすると意味が通るため、(A) conditions「条件」が適切。

Directionsの訳

パート6

指示：以下の文書を読んでください。各文書の中で語や句、または文が部分的に抜けています。文書の下には各設問の選択肢が4つ与えられています。文書を完成させるのに最も適切な答えを選びます。そして解答用紙の(A)、(B)、(C)、または(D)にマークしてください。

Part 7 読解問題

いろいろな形式の、1つもしくは複数の文書に関する問題が出題されます。設問と4つの選択肢を読み、その中から最も適切なものを選ぶ問題です。実際のテストでは1つの文書に関する問題が29問、複数の文書に関する問題が25問出題されます。

PART 7

Directions: In this part you will read a selection of texts, such as magazine and newspaper articles, e-mails, and instant messages. Each text or set of texts is followed by several questions. Select the best answer for each question and mark the letter (A), (B), (C), or (D) on your answer sheet.

サンプル問題

Questions 19-20 refer to the following text-message chain.

❶ **Jen Bosco [1:31 P.M.]**
Can you look in the kitchen and see if I left behind a large warming tray?

❷ **Jim Dumas [1:32 P.M.]**
Hold on, I'll check.

❸ **Jim Dumas [1:35 P.M.]**
Found it. It's on the prep table.

❹ **Jen Bosco [1:36 P.M.]**
Can you bring it here? The wedding starts in less than an hour.

❺ **Jim Dumas [1:37 P.M.]**
Sure. But you should know that the new refrigeration unit still hasn't arrived.

❻ **Jen Bosco [1:38 P.M.]**
Are you kidding? They promised we'd have it first thing in the morning!

❼ **Jim Dumas [1:39 P.M.]**
What should I do?

❽ **Jen Bosco [1:40 P.M.]**
Just make sure to leave instructions with Ms. Francis about where it should be placed.

❾ **Jim Dumas [1:41 P.M.]**
Will do. I'll see you in about 40 minutes with the tray.

19. For whom do the writers most likely work?

(A) A catering company
(B) A home-improvement store
(C) A kitchen-design company
(D) An appliance manufacturer

20. At 1:38 P.M., what does Ms. Bosco most likely mean when she writes, "Are you kidding"?

(A) She thinks Mr. Dumas is exaggerating.
(B) She knew she would have to wait a long time.
(C) She expects the refrigeration unit to arrive soon.
(D) She is upset that a delivery has not been made.

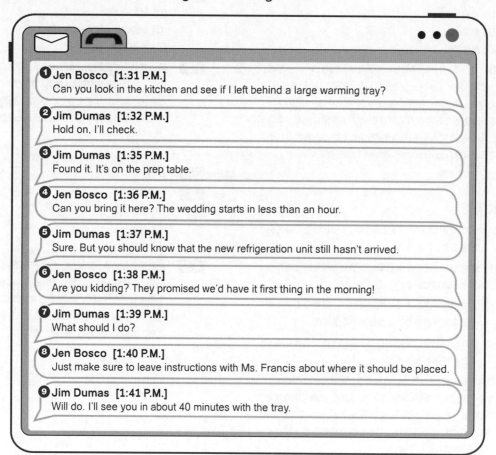

解答・解説

問題19-20は次のテキストメッセージのやり取りに関するものです。

Jen Bosco [午後1時31分]
調理場の中をのぞいて、私が大きな保温トレーを置き忘れたかどうかを確かめてくれるかしら。

Jim Dumas [午後1時32分]
待ってて。確認するよ。

Jim Dumas [午後1時35分]
見つけた。調理台の上にあるよ。

Jen Bosco [午後1時36分]
それをここに持ってきてくれる？ 結婚式が1時間足らずで始まるの。

Jim Dumas [午後1時37分]
もちろん。でも、新しい冷蔵装置がまだ届いていないことを知っておいた方がいいよ。

Jen Bosco [午後1時38分]
冗談でしょう？ 朝一番には私たちにそれを届けてくれると、彼らは約束したのよ。

Jim Dumas [午後1時39分]
僕はどうしたらいい？

Jen Bosco [午後1時40分]
とにかく、どこにそれを置けばいいか、Francisさんに必ず指示を残しておいて。

Jim Dumas [午後1時41分]
そうするよ。約40分後にトレーを持って君に会うね。

19. **正解** **(A)**

訳 書き手たちはどこに勤めていると考えられますか。

(A) ケータリング会社
(B) ホームセンター
(C) キッチン設計会社
(D) 電化製品メーカー

解説 ❶と❷のやり取りから、書き手たちの職場には調理場があることが分かる。また❹で、BoscoさんがDumasさんに保温トレーを結婚式の場に持ってくるよう伝えていることから、書き手たちは料理を作り配達を行っていると考えられる。よって、(A)が適切。

20. **正解** **(D)**

訳 午後1時38分にBoscoさんは、"Are you kidding"という発言で、何を意味していると考えられますか。

(A) Dumasさんが誇張していると思っている。
(B) 長い間待たなくてはならないことを知っていた。
(C) 冷蔵装置がもうすぐ届くだろうと見込んでいる。
(D) 配達が行われていないことに動揺している。

解説 Dumasさんが❺「新しい冷蔵装置がまだ届いていないことを知っておいた方がいい」と伝えたのに対して、Boscoさんは「冗談でしょう？」と驚きを示し、「朝一番には私たちにそれを届けてくれると、彼らは約束した」と続けている。つまり、Boscoさんは配達が約束通りに行われていないことに動揺していると考えられる。

Directionsの訳

パート7

指示：このパートでは、雑誌や新聞の記事、Eメールやインスタントメッセージなどのさまざまな文書を読みます。1つの文書または複数の文書のセットにはそれぞれ、幾つかの設問が続いています。各設問について最も適切な答えを選び、解答用紙の (A)、(B)、(C)、または (D) にマークしてください。

サンプル問題

Questions 21-24 refer to the following Web page.

http://straubuniversityschoolofmedicine.edu/vendors/rfp0023

❶ Straub University School of Medicine is currently seeking a vendor to provide surgical gloves, laboratory coats, and protective goggles. The university requires high-quality, hospital-grade equipment for its students and faculty and is especially interested in providers who currently work with local hospitals and clinics.

❷ You can download the complete Request for Proposal (RFP) instructions from our Web site. Below is a summary of the proposal requirements. — [1] —.

- A standard proposal form, which can be downloaded from our Web site
- A general description of the provider and its experience in the industry
- Product descriptions with a complete list of specifications and prices
- Contact information of three current or recent clients who are able to speak to the quality of the provider's products or services

❸ If you have any questions about the RFP, please submit them in writing to queries@straub.edu by July 20. — [2] —. Responses to questions will be posted publicly on the Straub University School of Medicine's Web page on August 4.

❹ Proposals must be received no later than August 15. — [3] —. All submissions will be thoroughly reviewed, and the winning proposal will be announced on September 10. A contract will be finalized with the strongest candidate that same month, and the agreement will take effect starting October 1. — [4] —.

21. Who are the instructions intended for?
(A) Sellers of medical supplies
(B) Applicants for hospital jobs
(C) Hospital administrators
(D) Medical students

22. What are candidates required to submit?
(A) Questions about the proposal
(B) Professional references
(C) An application fee
(D) Product samples

23. When will candidates learn if they have been selected?
(A) In July
(B) In August
(C) In September
(D) In October

24. In which of the positions marked [1], [2], [3], and [4] does the following sentence best belong?

"All documentation must arrive by this date in a sealed envelope addressed to the School of Medicine's Purchasing Department."

(A) [1]
(B) [2]
(C) [3]
(D) [4]

解答・解説

問題21-24は次のウェブページに関するものです。

http://straubuniversityschoolofmedicine.edu/vendors/rfp0023

Straub大学医学部は現在、手術用手袋、白衣、保護用ゴーグルを供給してくれる業者を求めています。本学は、学生と教授陣向けの、高品質で病院仕様の備品を必要としており、特に、地元の病院や診療所と現在取引をしている販売会社に関心があります。

本学のウェブサイトから、提案依頼書（RFP）の指示一式をダウンロードすることができます。以下は提案要件の概略です。

・定型の提案書式。本学のウェブサイトからダウンロード可能
・販売会社の概要および業界における同社の経験
・仕様および価格の全一覧を付した、製品の説明
・販売会社の製品あるいはサービスの質について述べることのできる、現在もしくは最近の顧客3社の連絡先

RFPについて何かご質問がございましたら、それらを文書で7月20日までにqueries@straub.edu宛てにご提出ください。ご質問に対する回答は、8月4日にStraub大学医学部のウェブページ上で公開されます。

提案書は8月15日必着です。*全ての書類は、封書でこの日付までに医学部の購買部宛てに到着しなければなりません。全ての提出物は入念に検討され、採用された提案書は9月10日に発表されます。契約書は最有力候補業者とその同月に最終的な形にされ、契約は10月1日より発効します。

*問題24の挿入文の訳

21. 正解 **(A)**

訳 この指示は誰に向けられていますか。

(A) 医療用品の販売会社
(B) 病院の職への応募者
(C) 病院の管理者
(D) 医学生

解説 ❶1～2行目に「Straub大学医学部は現在、手術用手袋、白衣、保護用ゴーグルを供給する業者を求めている」とあり、❷では提案要件の概略について、❹では提出期日や選考過程などについて説明されている。よって、この指示は医療用品の販売会社に向けたものだと分かる。

22. 正解 **(B)**

訳 候補者は何を提出することを求められていますか。

(A) 提案書に関する質問
(B) 取引上の照会先
(C) 申込金
(D) 製品の見本

解説 ❷で提案要件の概略として挙げられている箇条書きの4点目に、「販売会社の製品あるいはサービスの質について述べることのできる、現在もしくは最近の顧客3社の連絡先」とある。

23. 正解 **(C)**

訳 候補者はいつ、自分が選出されたかどうかを知りますか。

(A) 7月
(B) 8月
(C) 9月
(D) 10月

解説 ❹2行目に、the winning proposal will be announced on September 10「採用された提案書は9月10日に発表される」とある。

24. 正解 **(C)**

訳 [1]、[2]、[3]、[4]と記載された箇所のうち、次の文が入るのに最もふさわしいのはどれですか。

「全ての書類は、封書でこの日付までに医学部の購買部宛てに到着しなければなりません」

(A) [1]
(B) [2]
(C) [3]
(D) [4]

解説 挿入文は書類の提出方法と宛先を伝えている。(C) [3]に入れると、挿入文中のthis date「この日付」が❹1行目のAugust 15を指し、提案書の提出期日に続けて提出方法と宛先を伝える自然な流れとなる。

サンプル問題

Questions 25-29 refer to the following article, e-mail, and Web page.

❶ (November 6)—The Rudi's store at 47 Kask Highway in Glencoe Park will shut its doors next Saturday, adding another empty building to the local landscape. The shutdown is one of a rash of store closings in the greater Billington area and is a result of two major forces. First, Rudi's has changed its business plan, relying increasingly on online sales. Second, much of the traffic on Kask Highway has been rerouted to the recently completed bypass, resulting in fewer potential customers passing through Billington.

❷ Other Rudi's closings over the past two years include the store at 38 Quail Hill Road, the store at 21 Lowell Boulevard, and the downtown megastore at 59 Claremont Street on the banks of the Corks River. A Rudi's spokesperson stated that no further closures are expected.

To:	nathanpaugh@ioscodesign.com
From:	ccovey@tedesintl.com
Subject:	Tedes Building
Date:	January 25

Dear Mr. Paugh,

❶ The preliminary drawings you sent are right on target. I think your proposal to demolish most of the east wall and install floor-to-ceiling windows is terrific. If we were to leave everything as it now is, we would end up with a rather somber interior.

❷ Let's keep the current stairway where it is so that people can walk straight through the entrance and up to the second floor meeting rooms. We can configure the remaining area in the center of the first floor as open work space, with the executive offices off to the left side against the west wall. Including a large picture window at the entrance to the fitness center in the back of the first floor space is also a good idea.

❸ Please move forward with drawing up draft plans for our board's approval.

Thank you,

Cynthia Covey

http://www.buildingmonthly.com/readersreviews

HOME | LATEST ISSUE | **READERS' REVIEWS** | ADVERTISERS

The new Tedes corporate building
Posted by Monty K.

❶ Tedes International has opened its corporate headquarters in a former Rudi's megastore building. In an area with many vacated retail buildings, one is now a workplace for over 400 Tedes employees. Corporations looking for prime real estate should take notice.

❷ The interior design of the Tedes Building is notable for its mixed use of open and closed space. The entrance is open and inviting and leads to a wide staircase up to the second floor, which houses offices for upper management. Large windows installed as one of the exterior walls create a bright atmosphere in the open work space and nearby meeting rooms, while boats glide by on the river right in front of them. On my visit, several employees were exercising on fitness bikes in full view at the rear of the first-floor space.

25. What is the purpose of the article?
(A) To notify readers of recent job openings
(B) To publicize an online sale
(C) To report on a store closing
(D) To alert motorists to changing traffic patterns

26. Who most likely is Mr. Paugh?
(A) An artist
(B) An architect
(C) A real estate agent
(D) A reporter

27. Which former Rudi's location did Tedes International choose for its headquarters?
(A) 47 Kask Highway
(B) 38 Quail Hill Road
(C) 21 Lowell Boulevard
(D) 59 Claremont Street

28. What aspect of the design suggested by Ms. Covey was ultimately rejected?
(A) The replacement of a wall with windows
(B) The layout of the entrance
(C) The inclusion of a fitness center
(D) The location of the offices

29. What is implied by the reviewer?
(A) Tedes International is planning to expand.
(B) Tedes International wants to sell its property.
(C) Vacant buildings have great potential.
(D) Local businesses may experience reduced profits.

解答・解説

問題25-29は次の記事、Eメール、ウェブページに関するものです。

1. 記事

（11月6日）――グレンコーパークのカスク街道47番地にあるRudi's社の店舗は、次の土曜日に扉を閉ざし、その地域の風景にもう1棟空きビルを加えることになる。この閉店は、ビリントン広域圏で頻発する店舗の閉鎖の1つであり、2つの大きな影響力によるものである。第1に、Rudi's社が事業計画を変更し、オンライン販売に一層依存するようになったこと。第2に、カスク街道の交通の大部分が、最近完成した迂回路の方へ流れ、ビリントンを通る潜在顧客が減少する結果となったことだ。

過去2年間のRudi's社の他の閉店には、クウェイルヒル通り38番地の店舗、ローウェル大通り21番地の店舗、そしてコークス川岸のクレアモント通り59番地にあった中心街の超大型店舗が含まれる。Rudi's社の広報担当者は、これ以上の閉店は一切予定されていないと明言した。

2. Eメール

受信者：nathanpaugh@ioscodesign.com
送信者：ccovey@tedesintl.com
件名：　Tedes ビル
日付：　1月25日

Paugh様

お送りくださった仮の図面は、まさに期待通りのものです。東側の壁の大半を取り壊し、床から天井までの窓を設置するという貴殿のご提案は素晴らしいと思います。もし何もかも現状のままにしておいたとしたら、最終的にかなり陰気な内装になってしまうでしょう。

今の階段は、そのままの場所で残しましょう。そうすれば人々が入り口をまっすぐ通り抜け、2階の会議室に歩いて上がっていけます。1階の中央にある残りの区域は開放的な作業スペースとし、重役の執務室を左側へ、西の壁際に配置することができます。1階スペースの奥にあるフィットネスセンターへの入り口に大きな一枚ガラスの窓を入れることも良いアイデアです。

当社役員会の承認に向けて、設計図の草案の作成を進めてください。

よろしくお願いいたします。

Cynthia Covey

3. ウェブページ

http://www.buildingmonthly.com/readersreviews

ホーム　　最新号　　読者レビュー　　広告主

Tedes 社の新しいビル
Monty K. 投稿

Tedesインターナショナル社は、かつてRudi's社の超大型店舗だった建物に本社を開設した。空き家となった小売店のビルが多数ある地域において、1棟は今や400名超のTedes社の従業員の職場である。優良な不動産を求めている企業は注目すべきである。

Tedes ビルの内部設計は、開放的スペースと閉鎖的スペースを取り混ぜて使用していることで注目に値する。入り口は広々として、いざなうようであり、2階に至る広い階段に通じている。2階には、経営上層部のための執務室が入っている。外壁の一部として設置された大型の窓は、開放的な作業スペースと近くの会議室に明るい雰囲気を作り出し、他方で、すぐ目の前にある川をボートが滑るように進む。私の訪問時には、数名の従業員が1階スペースの奥で、よく見える所でフィットネスバイクで運動をしていた。

25. 正解 **(C)**

訳 記事の目的は何ですか。

(A) 読者に最近の求人を知らせること。
(B) オンラインのセールを宣伝すること。
(C) 店舗の閉鎖を報道すること。
(D) 車を運転する人に、交通パターンの変化について注意を喚起すること。

解説 1の記事の❶ 1〜3行目に、「グレンコーパークのカスク街道47番地にあるRudi's社の店舗は、次の土曜日に扉を閉ざす」とあり、その後も閉店の要因などが述べられている。よって、記事の目的はRudi's社の店舗の閉鎖を報道することだと分かる。

26. 正解 **(B)**

訳 Paughさんとは誰だと考えられますか。

(A) 芸術家
(B) 建築家
(C) 不動産仲介人
(D) 記者

解説 Paughさんは2のEメールの受信者。Eメールの本文では、❶ 1行目で「お送りくださった仮の図面は、まさに期待通りのものだ」と伝えられ、建物の設計についての話が続いている。さらに、❸で「設計図の草案の作成を進めてほしい」と依頼を受けていることから、Paughさんは建築家と考えられる。

27. 正解 **(D)**

訳 Tedesインターナショナル社は、かつてのRudi's社のどの場所を本社に選びましたか。

(A) カスク街道47番地
(B) クウェイルヒル通り38番地
(C) ローウェル大通り21番地
(D) クレアモント通り59番地

解説 3のウェブページの❶ 1〜2行目に、「Tedesインターナショナル社は、かつてRudi's社の超大型店舗だった建物に本社を開設した」とある。1の記事の❷ 3〜5行目に、閉店したRudi's社の店舗の1つとして、「コークス川岸のクレアモント通り59番地にあった中心街の超大型店舗」が挙げられているので、(D)が正解。

28. 正解 **(D)**

訳 Coveyさんによって示された設計のどの点が、最終的に不採用とされましたか。

(A) 壁を窓で置き換えること
(B) 入り口の配置
(C) フィットネスセンターを含めること
(D) 執務室の位置

解説 Coveyさんは2のEメールの送信者。仮の図面を作ったPaughさんに対して、❷ 2〜4行目で「1階の中央にある残りの区域は開放的な作業スペースとし、重役の執務室を左側へ、西の壁際に配置することができる」と述べている。一方、完成したビルの読者レビューを載せた3のウェブページには、❷ 2〜3行目に「入り口は広々として、いざなうようであり、2階に至る広い階段に通じている。2階には、経営上層部のための執務室が入っている」とあることから、重役の執務室はCoveyさんが提案した1階ではなく、2階に配置されたと分かる。

29. 正解 **(C)**

訳 レビュー投稿者によって何が示唆されていますか。

(A) Tedesインターナショナル社は拡大する予定である。
(B) Tedesインターナショナル社は同社の不動産を売却したいと思っている。
(C) 空きビルは大きな可能性を持っている。
(D) 地元の企業は減益を経験するかもしれない。

解説 3のウェブページの読者レビューの❶ 1〜3行目で、Tedesインターナショナル社がかつてRudi's社の超大型店舗だった建物に本社を開設したことで、空きビル1棟が今や多数の従業員の職場へと変化したことが述べられている。続けて「優良な不動産を求めている企業は注目すべきだ」とあることから、レビュー投稿者は空きビルに大きな可能性があることを示唆していると考えられる。

採点・結果について

TOEIC® Listening & Reading Test のテスト結果は合格・不合格ではなく、リスニングセクション 5〜495 点、リーディングセクション 5〜495 点、トータル 10〜990 点のスコアで、5 点刻みで表示されます。このスコアは、常に評価基準を一定に保つために統計処理が行われ、英語能力に変化がない限りスコアも一定に保たれる点が大きな特長です。

テスト結果は Official Score Certificate（公式認定証）として、試験日から 30 日以内に発送されます。また、インターネットからお申し込みいただく際、「テスト結果のインターネット表示」で「利用する」を選択すると、試験日から 17 日後にインターネットでスコアを確認することが可能です。（日米の祝日の影響により、遅れる場合がございます。）

Official Score Certificate（公式認定証）のサンプル

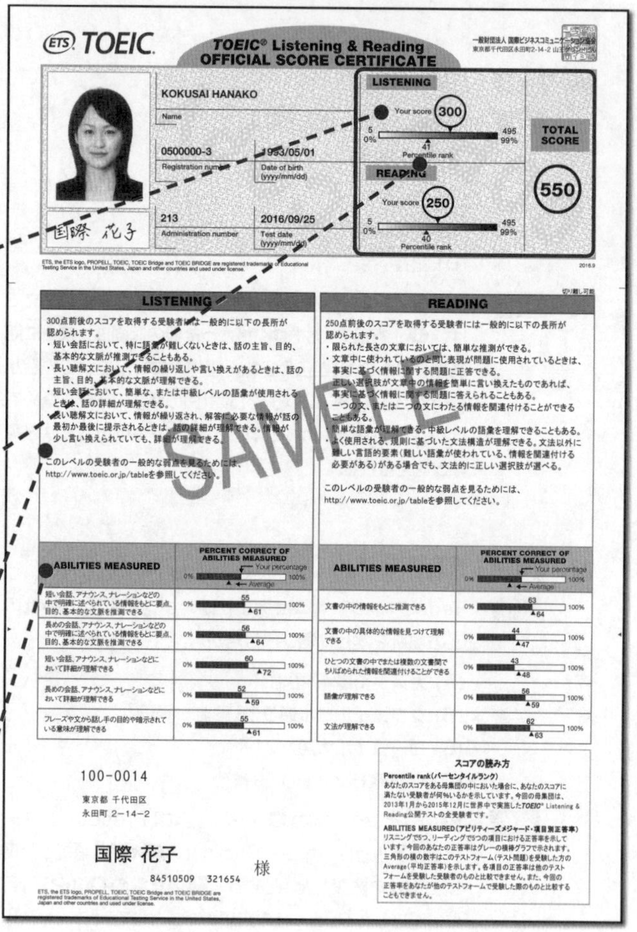

Your Score（スコア）：
今回取得したリスニング、リーディングの各セクションスコアです。右側にトータルスコアが記載されます。

Percentile Rank（パーセンタイルランク）：
あなたが取得したスコアに満たない受験者が全体でどのくらいを占めているかをパーセンテージで示しています。例えば、リスニングでスコア 300 点、パーセンタイルランクが 41%という場合には、リスニングスコア 300 点未満の受験者が全体の 41%いることを示します。つまり、リスニングスコア 300 点を取得した受験者は上位 59%に位置することになります。

Score Descriptors（スコアディスクリプターズ）：
レベル別評価です。今回取得したスコアをもとに、あなたの英語運用能力上の長所が書かれています。

Abilities Measured（アビリティーズメジャード）：
項目別正答率です。リスニング、リーディングの 5 つの項目における正答率を示しています。

TOEIC® Listening & Reading 公開テストのお申し込み

IIBC公式サイト **https://www.iibc-global.org** にてテスト日程、申込方法、注意事項をご確認の上、申込受付期間内にお申し込みください。試験の実施方法などに変更があった場合には IIBC 公式サイト等でご案内いたします。

お問い合わせ

一般財団法人 国際ビジネスコミュニケーション協会　IIBC 試験運営センター
〒 100-0014　東京都千代田区永田町 2-14-2　山王グランドビル
TEL：03-5521-6033（土・日・祝日・年末年始を除く 10:00 〜 17:00）

TEST 1

CD 1
11-92

＊解答用紙は本誌 p.112 の後ろに綴じ込まれています。

実際のテストでは問題用紙の裏側に、以下のようなテスト全体についての指示が印刷されています。
この指示を念頭においてテストに取り組みましょう。

General Directions

This test is designed to measure your English language ability. The test is divided into two sections: Listening and Reading.

You must mark all of your answers on the separate answer sheet. For each question, you should select the best answer from the answer choices given. Then, on your answer sheet, you should find the number of the question and fill in the space that corresponds to the letter of the answer that you have selected. If you decide to change an answer, completely erase your old answer and then mark your new answer.

訳

全体についての指示

このテストはあなたの英語言語能力を測定するよう設計されています。テストはリスニングとリーディングという2つのセクションに分けられています。

答えは全て別紙の解答用紙にマークしてください。それぞれの設問について、与えられた選択肢から最も適切な答えを選びます。そして解答用紙の該当する問題番号に、選択した答えを塗りつぶしてください。答えを修正する場合は、元の答えを完全に消してから新しい答えをマークしてください。

CD 1 12

LISTENING TEST

In the Listening test, you will be asked to demonstrate how well you understand spoken English. The entire Listening test will last approximately 45 minutes. There are four parts, and directions are given for each part. You must mark your answers on the separate answer sheet. Do not write your answers in your test book.

PART 1

Directions: For each question in this part, you will hear four statements about a picture in your test book. When you hear the statements, you must select the one statement that best describes what you see in the picture. Then find the number of the question on your answer sheet and mark your answer. The statements will not be printed in your test book and will be spoken only one time.

Statement (C), "They're sitting at a table," is the best description of the picture, so you should select answer (C) and mark it on your answer sheet.

1.

2.

GO ON TO THE NEXT PAGE

CD 1 15-16

3.

4.

5.

6.

GO ON TO THE NEXT PAGE

Directions CD 1 19 | Questions CD 1 20-44

PART 2

Directions: You will hear a question or statement and three responses spoken in English. They will not be printed in your test book and will be spoken only one time. Select the best response to the question or statement and mark the letter (A), (B), or (C) on your answer sheet.

7. Mark your answer on your answer sheet.

8. Mark your answer on your answer sheet.

9. Mark your answer on your answer sheet.

10. Mark your answer on your answer sheet.

11. Mark your answer on your answer sheet.

12. Mark your answer on your answer sheet.

13. Mark your answer on your answer sheet.

14. Mark your answer on your answer sheet.

15. Mark your answer on your answer sheet.

16. Mark your answer on your answer sheet.

17. Mark your answer on your answer sheet.

18. Mark your answer on your answer sheet.

19. Mark your answer on your answer sheet.

20. Mark your answer on your answer sheet.

21. Mark your answer on your answer sheet.

22. Mark your answer on your answer sheet.

23. Mark your answer on your answer sheet.

24. Mark your answer on your answer sheet.

25. Mark your answer on your answer sheet.

26. Mark your answer on your answer sheet.

27. Mark your answer on your answer sheet.

28. Mark your answer on your answer sheet.

29. Mark your answer on your answer sheet.

30. Mark your answer on your answer sheet.

31. Mark your answer on your answer sheet.

PART 3

Directions: You will hear some conversations between two or more people. You will be asked to answer three questions about what the speakers say in each conversation. Select the best response to each question and mark the letter (A), (B), (C), or (D) on your answer sheet. The conversations will not be printed in your test book and will be spoken only one time.

32. Where do the speakers most likely work?
(A) At an art gallery
(B) In a warehouse
(C) At a grocery store
(D) At a movie theater

33. According to the woman, what is the problem with the bags?
(A) They are too expensive.
(B) They are too small.
(C) The material is too thin.
(D) The design is too simple.

34. What does the man say he will do?
(A) Distribute some coupons
(B) Contact a factory
(C) Place an advertisement in the newspaper
(D) Research the competition

---

35. Why is the woman at the company?
(A) To inspect the property
(B) To serve as a consultant
(C) To apply for a position
(D) To sign a contract

36. What would the woman like to review?
(A) An employee handbook
(B) A list of potential clients
(C) Some recent sales data
(D) The map of the facilities

37. What is scheduled for next week?
(A) A focus group
(B) A renovation project
(C) A career fair
(D) A product launch

---

38. Where are the speakers?
(A) At an electronics shop
(B) At a sports stadium
(C) At a television studio
(D) At a fitness center

39. Why has the man arrived late?
(A) He wrote down the wrong time.
(B) He had several appointments.
(C) There was a lot of traffic.
(D) A location was hard to find.

40. Why has a satellite dish stopped working?
(A) It was damaged in a storm.
(B) It was not installed properly.
(C) A bill has not been paid.
(D) A password has been changed.

---

41. What does the man say Jim has decided to do?
(A) Hire some managers
(B) Get a business degree
(C) Request a budget increase
(D) Speak at a conference

42. What does the man ask the woman to do?
(A) Take over some accounts
(B) Lead a mentorship program
(C) Organize a training seminar
(D) Conduct some interviews

43. Where will the woman go next?
(A) To a cafeteria
(B) To a construction site
(C) To a colleague's office
(D) To a supply room

GO ON TO THE NEXT PAGE

CD 1 54-61

44. What did the man do in advance?
(A) He checked a bus map.
(B) He paid for a delivery.
(C) He completed some paperwork.
(D) He read some reviews online.

45. Where does the woman most likely work?
(A) At a pharmacy
(B) At a coffee shop
(C) At a medical office
(D) At a bookstore

46. What will the man probably do next?
(A) Reschedule his appointment
(B) Have some tea
(C) Call a friend
(D) Visit another location

---

47. What are the speakers preparing for?
(A) A safety inspection
(B) A sales presentation
(C) A training seminar
(D) A budget meeting

48. According to the man, why did the Smith Corporation call?
(A) To request an instruction manual
(B) To open an account
(C) To change a meeting time
(D) To complain about a service

49. What does the man mean when he says, "I helped Benjamin fix his webcam last week"?
(A) He is waiting for a payment.
(B) He can assist the woman.
(C) He was not able to attend an event.
(D) He does not have to purchase more equipment.

---

50. What are the speakers mainly discussing?
(A) A delayed shipment
(B) A construction project
(C) Some new technology
(D) Some software problems

51. Why does the man say, "There was a budget surplus at the end of last quarter"?
(A) To correct an error
(B) To offer congratulations
(C) To make a complaint about a policy
(D) To express interest in an idea

52. What does the woman offer to do?
(A) Contact a manufacturer
(B) Lead a tour
(C) Make a safety checklist
(D) Revise work assignments

---

53. What are the speakers doing?
(A) Conducting job interviews
(B) Visiting a property
(C) Ordering some supplies
(D) Applying for a loan

54. What type of business is the man opening?
(A) A bakery
(B) A restaurant
(C) A hardware store
(D) A furniture store

55. What does the man ask the woman about?
(A) A deadline
(B) A price
(C) A name
(D) A process

---

56. What does the company want to change?
(A) A database for storing customer information
(B) A policy for taking vacation time
(C) A process for evaluating employees
(D) A method for ordering office supplies

57. What does the man ask about?
(A) A vendor's address
(B) A room reservation
(C) A budget surplus
(D) A project deadline

58. What will the woman most likely suggest doing?
(A) Hiring an outside consultant
(B) Using a computer application
(C) Conducting a survey
(D) Promoting an employee

---

59. Where does the conversation most likely take place?
(A) At a university campus
(B) At a shipping company
(C) At a rental car agency
(D) At a moving company

60. What does Janet Chen inquire about?
(A) A discount
(B) A Web site
(C) A schedule change
(D) A new product

61. What does the man say is required?
(A) A password
(B) An employee ID
(C) A safety inspection
(D) An appointment

Graphite Designs—Directory

First floor	Lobby
Second floor	Suites 1–5
Third floor	Suites 6–8
Fourth floor	Suites 9–12

62. Why is the man visiting the building?
(A) To deliver a package
(B) To interview a job candidate
(C) To repair some equipment
(D) To discuss some catering details

63. What problem does the woman mention?
(A) Some mail has arrived late.
(B) Some supplies are not available.
(C) A staff member is not in the building.
(D) An elevator is not working.

64. Look at the graphic. Where will the man go next?
(A) To the first floor
(B) To the second floor
(C) To the third floor
(D) To the fourth floor

GO ON TO THE NEXT PAGE

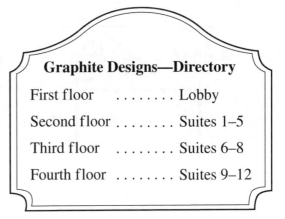

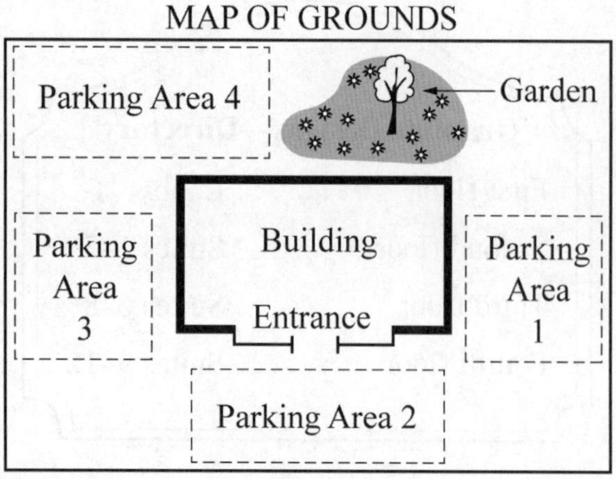

65. What most likely is the man's job?
(A) Fitness instructor
(B) Apartment manager
(C) Hotel clerk
(D) Interior decorator

66. What does the woman say she is excited about?
(A) Having more space
(B) Reducing an expense
(C) Taking a vacation
(D) Using a facility

67. Look at the graphic. Where should the woman park her car?
(A) In Parking Area 1
(B) In Parking Area 2
(C) In Parking Area 3
(D) In Parking Area 4

68. What problem does the man mention?
(A) He made a scheduling mistake.
(B) He forgot to buy some ingredients.
(C) A refrigerator was malfunctioning.
(D) A supply delivery was late.

69. Who most likely is the woman?
(A) A chef
(B) A waitress
(C) A dishwasher
(D) A cashier

70. Look at the graphic. How much does the new dessert cost?
(A) \$2.50
(B) \$4.00
(C) \$5.00
(D) \$3.50

PART 4

Directions: You will hear some talks given by a single speaker. You will be asked to answer three questions about what the speaker says in each talk. Select the best response to each question and mark the letter (A), (B), (C), or (D) on your answer sheet. The talks will not be printed in your test book and will be spoken only one time.

71. What is the advertisement mainly about?
(A) An art festival
(B) A concert series
(C) An architectural tour
(D) A museum exhibit opening

72. Who is Gregory Alvarez?
(A) A chef
(B) A scientist
(C) A photographer
(D) A university professor

73. What is included with the price of admission?
(A) On-site parking
(B) A movie ticket
(C) A food voucher
(D) A souvenir T-shirt

---

74. Where do the listeners work?
(A) At a hotel
(B) At a school
(C) At a news agency
(D) At a public library

75. What happened last January?
(A) A survey was distributed.
(B) A new employee was hired.
(C) A book was published.
(D) An award winner was announced.

76. Why does the speaker say, "The event's at the Stately Hotel at eight"?
(A) To explain why she cannot make an appointment
(B) To correct an event schedule
(C) To advise the listeners about a location change
(D) To encourage the listeners to attend an event

---

77. What did Tasty Treats do in July?
(A) It elected a board of directors.
(B) It acquired another business.
(C) It donated to a charity.
(D) It celebrated an anniversary.

78. According to the speaker, what is Tasty Treats hoping to do?
(A) Diversify its products
(B) Reduce its manufacturing waste
(C) Improve community relations
(D) Find qualified personnel

79. What does the speaker say about some packaging?
(A) It will be larger.
(B) It will be environmentally friendly.
(C) It will have a different logo.
(D) It will feature nutritional information.

---

80. Where is the announcement taking place?
(A) At a trade show
(B) At a grand opening
(C) At a press conference
(D) At a retirement dinner

81. What has caused the event to be relocated?
(A) Bad weather
(B) Technical difficulties
(C) Ongoing construction work
(D) A high number of participants

82. According to the speaker, what will happen in July?
(A) A holiday celebration will be held.
(B) A train line will be repaired.
(C) Seasonal staff will be added.
(D) Additional equipment will be delivered.

GO ON TO THE NEXT PAGE

83. What does the speaker mean when she says, "the new sweaters have all been sold"?
(A) She needs to order additional items.
(B) Customers will be disappointed.
(C) A goal has been met.
(D) A promotional sale has ended.

84. What new work assignment does the speaker mention?
(A) Organizing some files
(B) Cleaning a room
(C) Unloading a shipment
(D) Removing some labels

85. What does the speaker ask some listeners to do by the end of the week?
(A) Submit a form
(B) Read a manual
(C) Pick up a new uniform
(D) Sign up for a workshop

---

86. Where most likely are the listeners?
(A) At an airport
(B) At a sports arena
(C) At a bank
(D) At a supermarket

87. What new program feature does the speaker announce?
(A) A service can be used internationally.
(B) A group membership is available.
(C) A registration fee has been reduced.
(D) A shuttle service will run more often.

88. What will some customers receive?
(A) A coffee mug
(B) A coupon book
(C) A shopping bag
(D) A parking pass

---

89. What type of service is being advertised?
(A) Bottled water delivery
(B) Corporate catering
(C) Electronics repairs
(D) Automotive maintenance

90. What is unique about the business?
(A) It provides home visits.
(B) It employs industry experts.
(C) It is available 24 hours a day.
(D) It has locations around the world.

91. According to the speaker, what can the listeners do on a Web site?
(A) Request an appointment
(B) Read some reviews
(C) Watch informational videos
(D) Make a payment

---

92. What is the message mainly about?
(A) A sales report
(B) A travel itinerary
(C) A new computer
(D) A company vehicle

93. What does the speaker mean when he says, "I'm going to be training new employees next week"?
(A) He is not available for an assignment.
(B) He is inviting the listener to a training session.
(C) He is excited about a new responsibility.
(D) He would like to borrow some training materials.

94. What does the speaker ask the listener to do?
(A) Contact a manager
(B) Send an invoice
(C) Download a mobile application
(D) Make a reservation

Project Timeline

Project proposal due	August 10
Initial approval from client	August 20
Present first draft to client	September 25
Present second draft to client	October 27

95. Where do the listeners most likely work?
(A) At an advertising agency
(B) At an online newspaper
(C) At an art gallery
(D) At a supermarket

96. Look at the graphic. According to the speaker, on which date should the listeners be available?
(A) August 10
(B) August 20
(C) September 25
(D) October 27

97. What will the listeners most likely do next?
(A) Sign a contract
(B) Attend a workshop
(C) Set up a display
(D) Taste some samples

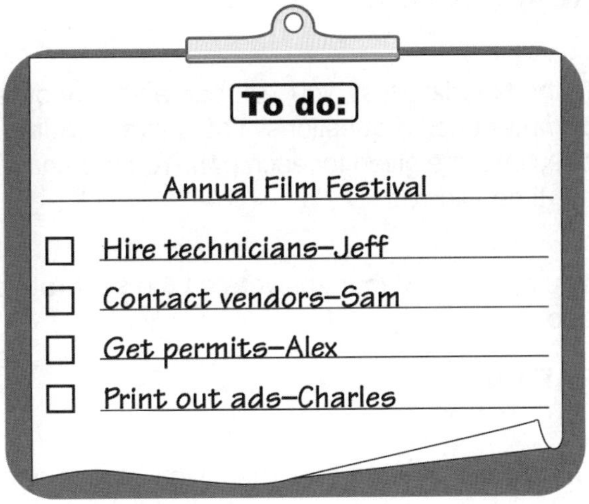

98. Look at the graphic. Who most likely is the speaker?
(A) Jeff
(B) Sam
(C) Alex
(D) Charles

99. Why is the speaker pleased?
(A) A review was positive.
(B) A Web site was completed.
(C) A promotion has been successful.
(D) A building has been renovated.

100. What will some festival attendees receive?
(A) A T-shirt
(B) A poster
(C) A key chain
(D) A book

This is the end of the Listening test. Turn to Part 5 in your test book.

GO ON TO THE NEXT PAGE

READING TEST

In the Reading test, you will read a variety of texts and answer several different types of reading comprehension questions. The entire Reading test will last 75 minutes. There are three parts, and directions are given for each part. You are encouraged to answer as many questions as possible within the time allowed.

You must mark your answers on the separate answer sheet. Do not write your answers in your test book.

PART 5

Directions: A word or phrase is missing in each of the sentences below. Four answer choices are given below each sentence. Select the best answer to complete the sentence. Then mark the letter (A), (B), (C), or (D) on your answer sheet.

101. In the article, Ms. Amanjit ------- her internship at a Chennai publishing company last year.

(A) describe
(B) described
(C) to describe
(D) describing

102. Please submit ------- travel-expense reports to Ms. Gresh in the finance department.

(A) your
(B) you
(C) yourself
(D) yours

103. Rent the perfect office space from one of Right Away Office's ------- locations.

(A) tolerant
(B) careful
(C) convenient
(D) uncertain

104. Ms. Lee reviews the ------- daily to prevent the banquet room from being double-booked.

(A) reservations
(B) reserves
(C) reserving
(D) reserve

105. The safety training session is scheduled to run ------- one hour.

(A) approximating
(B) approximately
(C) approximation
(D) approximate

106. Mr. Kwon will sign a lease ------- an apartment in the building at 624 Livingston Road.

(A) of
(B) by
(C) like
(D) for

107. To participate in the company charity run, employees must ------- a form certifying that they agree to certain rules.

(A) make
(B) see
(C) find
(D) sign

108. Innovation is key to success in ------- industries.

(A) none
(B) much
(C) many
(D) anything

109. Interns at the Kuan Mai law firm can ------- to help attorneys with paperwork and courtroom preparation.

(A) expect
(B) expected
(C) expectant
(D) expectantly

110. Drescher, Inc., is a ------- insurance company that has been serving Saskatchewan since it opened 50 years ago.

(A) respects
(B) respectability
(C) respected
(D) respect

111. The technician informed Mr. Becker that his laptop would ------- a repair covered under the warranty.

(A) require
(B) decide
(C) insist
(D) notify

112. Because several popular athletes endorsed them, Kantorele Skin Care products sold ------- well.

(A) amazing
(B) amazingly
(C) amaze
(D) amazement

113. The museum's newest acquisitions are usually exhibited in the Gorwin Gallery, ------- is located on the first floor.

(A) which
(B) where
(C) so
(D) as

114. Alicia's Grill ------- three changes in management in the last five years.

(A) is undergoing
(B) has undergone
(C) undergo
(D) to undergo

115. The marketing team from Tokyo is visiting this week and will ------- be using Conference Room A.

(A) occasions
(B) occasion
(C) occasionally
(D) occasional

116. ------- the fast-approaching deadline, the project manager is confident the team will have everything completed on time.

(A) Still
(B) However
(C) Despite
(D) Unlike

117. Customers ------- prepaid tickets are encouraged to use the express kiosk.

(A) picking up
(B) picked up
(C) pick up
(D) to pick up

118. ------- hiring someone to update her salon's decor, Jalissa Bryant interviewed several interior designers.

(A) Before
(B) Among
(C) Except
(D) Inside

119. ------- at the Pan-Pacifica Suites has increased since it began offering free breakfast.

(A) Occupancy
(B) Occupations
(C) Occupants
(D) Occupied

120. Barlox Motors claims its new all-electric truck goes ------- on one charge than any other electric truck on the market today.

(A) long
(B) farther
(C) again
(D) back

121. At the company's annual banquet, Mr. Karga received an award for his ------- record of community outreach projects.

(A) delicate
(B) distinguished
(C) periodic
(D) accurate

GO ON TO THE NEXT PAGE

122. The Ambrose Music Company markets its products only ------- its dedicated Web site.

(A) through
(B) while
(C) beside
(D) once

123. Given Rusdon Marketing's focus on ------- design, Mr. Ochoa's artistic background would be a great asset to the firm.

(A) create
(B) created
(C) creative
(D) creatively

124. The town council has ------- permission for the Autumn Festival to be held in Vista Park.

(A) responded
(B) exchanged
(C) performed
(D) granted

125. Eight ------- buyers inspected the property over the weekend, but only one seemed genuinely interested.

(A) certain
(B) descriptive
(C) conclusive
(D) potential

126. A majority of the residents have opposed the city's ------- to reroute traffic.

(A) trade
(B) plan
(C) supply
(D) total

127. When registering multiple people for the conference, enter the name that should appear on ------- of the badges.

(A) each
(B) other
(C) whose
(D) whichever

128. As part of a ------- to expand business abroad, Aneliya Innovations translated its Web site into multiple languages.

(A) push
(B) probe
(C) raise
(D) debate

129. Although a reduction in metal thickness would make the container ------- lighter, its strength would suffer as a result.

(A) repeatedly
(B) regardlessly
(C) decreasingly
(D) considerably

130. A research team at Halwell Agricultural Institute is studying the beneficial ------- of a newly developed fertilizer.

(A) charges
(B) effects
(C) replies
(D) senses

PART 6

Directions: Read the texts that follow. A word, phrase, or sentence is missing in parts of each text. Four answer choices for each question are given below the text. Select the best answer to complete the text. Then mark the letter (A), (B), (C), or (D) on your answer sheet.

Questions 131-134 refer to the following advertisement.

Half Off Your First Ride!

The Drive-Ride ride-sharing service is now available in your area! As a businessperson, you know that your time is valuable and that you ------- **131.** the best service when it comes to ground transportation. ------- **132.** driving yourself, experience the convenience of Drive-Ride. Going to the airport before sunrise? Drive-Ride can do that. Car trouble before a big presentation? Drive-Ride can help. Need to meet with a client without the hassle of driving a car yourself? Drive-Ride is here for you!

You can receive 50 percent off your first ride of 20 kilometers or less. ------- **133.**. Then type the promo code NEWSPEED at checkout to take advantage of this great ------- **134.**.

131. (A) deserves
(B) deserve
(C) deserving
(D) deserved

132. (A) Instead of
(B) While
(C) Even though
(D) Given that

133. (A) We also provide information about local auto mechanics.
(B) If you want to save money on frequent trips, this offer is for you.
(C) Simply download our app on your mobile device and enter your information.
(D) Thank you for serving as one of Drive-Ride's friendly drivers.

134. (A) dealing
(B) deals
(C) dealt
(D) deal

GO ON TO THE NEXT PAGE

Questions 135-138 refer to the following article.

SYDNEY (4 October) —Square Peg Pizzas, affectionately known to local residents as Peggie's, will open its first franchise in Malaysia in the new year. This ------- (135.) marks an important milestone for the Australia-based chain. Since its first restaurant opened five years ago in Melbourne, it has had great domestic success. ------- (136.).

This foray into the Southeast Asian market will be managed by one of the founders of the company, Mr. Ben Cummings. Mr. Cummings, who spent ------- (137.) childhood in Indonesia, has said that this new venture marks the realization of a lifelong ambition. He has always ------- (138.) to help run an international company.

135. (A) hire
(B) launch
(C) colleague
(D) award

136. (A) Peggie's is proud to use ingredients from these local areas.
(B) Last year Peggie's outperformed every other Australian pizza chain.
(C) Australians have shown a newfound love for food from this part of the world.
(D) Peggie's is excited to open its second Australian franchise soon.

137. (A) he
(B) him
(C) his
(D) himself

138. (A) supposed
(B) remembered
(C) concerned
(D) aspired

Questions 139-142 refer to the following letter.

September 28

Timothy Larkin
Camble Development, Inc.
284 Third Place
Chicago, IL 60610

Dear Mr. Larkin,

I enjoyed meeting you at the Factory Industrial Automation Expo in Madison. You expressed interest in how my company's products might benefit your ------- **139.** business. A member of our sales team will be in Chicago from October 23 to 27 to meet with entrepreneurs. She would be delighted to meet with you on any of those days between 1 P.M. and 3 P.M. ------- **140.**.

She can show you ways to streamline your inventory control and purchasing with our convenient software. ------- **141.**, if you decide to purchase the software, she can schedule a time to train your employees on how to use it.

Please let me know if any of those times work for ------- **142.**. My phone number is (225) 555-0193.

Sincerely,

Akshat Aranya
West Peak Solutions

139. (A) generous
(B) growing
(C) guaranteed
(D) gradual

140. (A) It will save your company time and expenses.
(B) She has a full schedule on those days.
(C) We have offices in twelve locations.
(D) The meeting would take a half hour.

141. (A) Although
(B) Instead
(C) Otherwise
(D) Also

142. (A) her
(B) me
(C) you
(D) them

GO ON TO THE NEXT PAGE

Questions 143-146 refer to the following information.

Policy Regarding Employee Workstations

Because clients visit our offices frequently, all office employees are required to keep their workstations in a ------- (143.) neat and organized state. Personal items such as coats, handbags, keys, and wallets must be stored out of sight in a closet or desk drawer. ------- (144.). Food items are permitted, but they must not be left out in workstations during nonworking hours. Files and other paperwork must also be ------- (145.) at the end of the workday. Employees should direct any questions about this policy to their ------- (146.).

143. (A) reasoning
(B) reasonability
(C) reasonably
(D) reasoned

144. (A) This also serves to keep personal items secure in the office environment.
(B) Lunch can also be purchased from food trucks near the office.
(C) All bags are screened by security staff as employees enter and leave.
(D) These rules will be posted online as well as in the employee lounge.

145. (A) dropped off
(B) set up
(C) taken apart
(D) put away

146. (A) supervise
(B) supervisor
(C) supervisory
(D) supervision

PART 7

Directions: In this part you will read a selection of texts, such as magazine and newspaper articles, e-mails, and instant messages. Each text or set of texts is followed by several questions. Select the best answer for each question and mark the letter (A), (B), (C), or (D) on your answer sheet.

Questions 147-148 refer to the following text message.

From Frida Sanchez **April 6, 7:54 P.M.**

Stacy, I see on the new schedule that you usually work in the afternoon, but could you possibly open the store for me tomorrow morning? I've been having problems with my car, and I need to take it to my mechanic. But the repair shop doesn't open until 10 tomorrow morning. I can do your usual Wednesday afternoon shift starting at 2, and because Wednesday nights have extended hours, I'll stay until 9. Let me know if this works for you.

147. Why did Ms. Sanchez send the text message?

(A) To apologize for missing work
(B) To recommend a car mechanic
(C) To ask about hiring another employee
(D) To propose a change to a work schedule

148. What is indicated in the text message?

(A) Stacy is currently on vacation.
(B) A car repair shop is no longer in business.
(C) Ms. Sanchez plans to buy a new car.
(D) The store is open late on Wednesdays.

GO ON TO THE NEXT PAGE

Questions 149-150 refer to the following form.

OZONO AIRLINE MISSING BAGGAGE FORM

Time and Date of Claim: 1:50 P.M., May 2 **Flight Number:** 1869

Passenger Name: Alessandra Spencer

Flight Departure City: Atlanta **Flight Arrival City:** Boston

Destination Address: Winthrop Street Hotel,
456 Quincy Street, Boston

Description of Contents:
Clothing, two pairs of shoes, toiletries, three books, hair dryer, gifts

Bag Description:
Kona Company hard-sided blue suitcase with wheels

Value of Contents: $200
(Amount to be reimbursed for bags that are not returned within two weeks.)

For Internal Use:
Bag is confirmed to be on later flight number 1921. Christoff Delivery will deliver item to the customer at the destination address within twenty-four hours of the time of claim.

Recorded by: Delonte Ahmad

149. What does the form indicate about Ms. Spencer?

(A) She is currently in Atlanta.
(B) Her home is in Boston.
(C) Her bag will be delivered to a hotel by May 3.
(D) She will receive $200 for her lost luggage.

150. Who most likely is Mr. Ahmad?

(A) A hotel manager
(B) A luggage company employee
(C) A delivery driver
(D) An airline representative

Questions 151-152 refer to the following memo.

To: All Brestwood Furnishing staff
From: Paul Ho, President
Date: Wednesday, 23 August
Subject: Ron Donowicz

Yesterday, I received notice that Ron Donowicz will retire at the end of October.

As many of you know, Ron has been our director of facilities for 30 years. Managing a facilities maintenance department is a challenge in any company, and Ron set the high standard by which his successors will be measured.

The Human Resources Division will be posting the facilities director position shortly. Our goal will be to fill the position internally. Ron will be using accrued vacation leave between now and his retirement date, but he will come in occasionally to train his replacement. He will also be here for a retirement luncheon on 20 October at noon in the cafeteria. All employees are welcome to attend.

151. What is the purpose of the memo?

(A) To introduce a new member of the maintenance staff
(B) To announce the promotion of the facilities director
(C) To inform staff that an employee will be leaving the company
(D) To explain a change in the company's hiring policy

152. What does the memo indicate about Brestwood Furnishing?

(A) It plans to fill an open position with a current employee.
(B) It is changing its vacation policy.
(C) It is starting a new training program.
(D) It will renovate its cafeteria.

GO ON TO THE NEXT PAGE

Questions 153-154 refer to the following text-message chain.

Fumio Komatsu (2:42 P.M.)
Hi, Nelly. By any chance, did someone from the Evergreen restaurant send you a list of the summer menu items? I wanted to start updating their site, but I don't have the latest list.

Nelly Artemyeva (2:43 P.M.)
The chef e-mailed it to me this morning, but I want to go over the changes with you first. Do you have time now?

Fumio Komatsu (2:44 P.M.)
I'm on my way back to the office. I just received the photographs for the aquarium's Web site. They're amazing!

Nelly Artemyeva (2:45 P.M.)
Excellent. Why don't I stop by your office around 4:30. Will you be available?

Fumio Komatsu (2:46 P.M.)
Most likely. I have to go to a training session at 3:30, but it shouldn't last long.

153. What is suggested about Mr. Komatsu and Ms. Artemyeva?

(A) They are studying photography.
(B) They work at an aquarium.
(C) They design Web sites.
(D) They own a restaurant.

154. At 2:44 P.M., what does Mr. Komatsu mean when he writes, "I'm on my way back to the office"?

(A) He is not able to review a document now.
(B) He agrees with Ms. Artemyeva's suggestions.
(C) He has been delayed by traffic.
(D) He did not check his e-mail this morning.

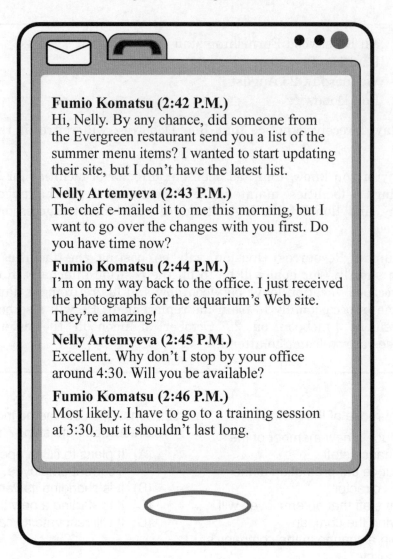

Questions 155-157 refer to the following letter.

Mr. Hugh Lander
86 Pascoe Road
Karori, Wellington 6012

Dear Mr. Lander,

It is time for your biannual checkup. Plantech Dental is honored to serve as your dental care provider. We understand that you have many options when it comes to finding a reliable and affordable dentist. To reward your loyalty, I am proud to offer you a complimentary teeth-whitening service! This special promotion is available only to clients who have completed at least six biannual checkups at Plantech Dental.

For you to qualify, I will need to examine your teeth to ensure they are healthy enough to undergo a professional whitening service. If your teeth are in good condition, you will receive four whitening-gel tubes, two trays custom-fit for your teeth, and one tube of whitening toothpaste.

Call Plantech Dental to schedule your next appointment and to take advantage of this special promotion.

Sincerely,

Marlys Martin

Dr. Marlys Martin, DMD

155. The word "complimentary" in paragraph 1, line 4, is closest in meaning to

(A) friendly
(B) discounted
(C) free
(D) admired

156. What is suggested about Mr. Lander?

(A) He is a longtime Plantech Dental client.
(B) He has visited several dentists in the area.
(C) He has never had a teeth-whitening procedure.
(D) He just returned from a dentist appointment.

157. What must clients do in order to qualify for the promotion?

(A) Refer five new clients to Dr. Martin
(B) Attend an informational meeting
(C) Purchase four whitening-gel tubes
(D) Have their teeth examined by Dr. Martin

GO ON TO THE NEXT PAGE

Questions 158-160 refer to the following article.

Wedding Planning Made Easy

TYNDALE (9 September)—Robert Marsh knows firsthand that planning a wedding can be a time-consuming and energy-draining endeavor. "My fiancée and I," he explains, "had to crisscross Tyndale to find vendors that suited our budget and style requirements. It occurred to me that there had to be a better way of making the necessary wedding preparations."

— [1] —. Barely a year into his marriage, he created Nuptials Paradise, a company that aims to simplify wedding planning. Located at 248 Palmchat Drive, site of the former Harrison Grocery Store, the company has partnered with 50 wedding industry professionals. — [2] —. "Our customers love the convenience of being able to book the services they need at one location," says Mr. Marsh. "Vendors, in turn, have easier access to a large number of clients." — [3] —.

Mr. Marsh says that he has received requests from various people interested in opening their own businesses under his brand name, which would make them distributors of his services. Evidently, he is open to that possibility. "Just months after having opened Nuptials Paradise," he says, "it became apparent to me that there was a great need for my services. I cannot be everywhere at once, so I certainly would welcome some help." — [4] —.

158. What is a purpose of the article?

(A) To broaden understanding of business partnerships
(B) To explore the growth of the wedding industry
(C) To describe the wedding planning process
(D) To explain the origins of a company

159. What is indicated about Nuptials Paradise?

(A) It has changed its business model.
(B) It has been in business for about a year.
(C) Its clients are pleased with its services.
(D) Its first contract was signed with a grocery store.

160. In which of the positions marked [1], [2], [3], and [4] does the following sentence best belong?

"Mr. Marsh came up with a way to act on that idea."

(A) [1]
(B) [2]
(C) [3]
(D) [4]

Questions 161-163 refer to the following information in a brochure.

Visit Finneran Tree Farm

Are you interested in old-growth forests, wildflowers, wildlife habitats, hiking, and being outdoors? If yes, Finneran Tree Farm is the perfect place for you!

Finneran Tree Farm was donated 25 years ago by the Finneran family to the Ladd Forestry Centre, which now operates the tree farm as an education site and park. It features 5 kilometres of hiking trails, as well as streams and a riverbank to explore. It is open to the public year-round for self-guided tours. Groups of ten or more must register at least two weeks before visiting.

From April to September, the hours are 7:00 A.M. to 9:00 P.M., and from October to March, the hours are 8:00 A.M. to 5:00 P.M.

Facilities include covered picnic areas and an indoor education centre, which can be reserved for a small fee. Visit www.finnerantreefarm.co.uk/reservations for more information.

Finneran Tree Farm
42 Maybury Rd, Edinburgh EH4 6BU
0131 496 1234

161. What is mentioned about Finneran Tree Farm?
(A) It is known around the world.
(B) It hosts community events in the summer.
(C) It is a family-run business.
(D) It is open all year.

162. What is indicated about large group visits?
(A) Hiking guides are available.
(B) Advance notice is required.
(C) Payment is due upon arrival.
(D) Groups over twenty are prohibited.

163. According to the brochure, how can someone learn more about facility reservations?
(A) By going to the forestry-center office
(B) By phoning the tree farm
(C) By visiting a Web site
(D) By sending in a request form

Questions 164-167 refer to the following article.

— [1] —. While the in-person interview is not going away, many human resources departments have come to rely on videoconferencing for candidate screening. Using video has reduced the amount of unproductive communication between job seekers and employers, and both parties appreciate the ability to more easily schedule an interview.

Finding a videoconferencing vendor can be a challenging process, especially for smaller companies. — [2] —. Phillipa Renwick, human resources director at Inama Clothing Manufacturers, recommends that all companies think broadly about their needs. For example, Ms. Renwick asks, "Are there on-site meetings happening now that might be conducted at least as effectively through a videoconference?" A further consideration, according to Ms. Renwick, is that businesses often use the same technology to engage in activities like employee training. — [3] —.

Ms. Renwick cautions that potential vendors should be asked how any proposed systems will be customized without creating unreasonable costs or straining information-technology staff. — [4] —. Some companies may only need basic video capabilities, while others may seek more advanced functions, such as built-in analytic software that allows managers to score and rank video interviewees in the moment.

164. What is the main topic of the article?

(A) Easier ways to set up a videoconference
(B) Factors to consider when choosing certain communication technology
(C) A video series offering advice to job seekers
(D) Improving processes in an information-technology department

165. Why is Ms. Renwick most likely quoted in the article?

(A) Her company regularly conducts videoconferences.
(B) Her company sells videoconferencing equipment.
(C) She performed well during a video interview.
(D) She developed a new type of video-editing software.

166. According to the article, what can interviewers do with advanced video functions?

(A) View instructional materials
(B) Post video files
(C) Monitor training programs
(D) Rate job candidates

167. In which of the positions marked [1], [2], [3], and [4] does the following sentence best belong?

"The cost savings in this situation could be significant for international companies."

(A) [1]
(B) [2]
(C) [3]
(D) [4]

Questions 168-171 refer to the following Web page.

http://www.talkfirsttechnologies.com

Talk First Technologies

News and Updates

You spoke. We listened.

Effective June 1, Talk First Technologies' customers will have the following options.

- **Month-to-month plans**—Talk First Technologies will cease offering one- and two-year service contracts. All services will be billed on a monthly basis.
- **New plans**—Our newly available options include a low-cost plan that provides unlimited calling and text messaging for just $45 a month. Purchase data by the gigabyte when you need it. Or, choose the Techfan plan, which allows you to try our state-of-the-art mobile devices before they are released for public sale.
- **Device upgrades**—You will be able to purchase any phone, at any time, at the full retail price. Our installment plan, which allows you to pay a little each month with no interest charge, is another option. Get the device you want now.
- **Simpler billing statements**—Your one-page monthly bill states just the essentials—what services you used, what you are charged, and when your payment is due. We hope you will try out the new Talk First app to view your statement and pay your balance using your phone.

168. What change will Talk First Technologies implement on June 1?

(A) Some mobile phone technology will not be supported.
(B) Long-term service contracts will not be required.
(C) Unlimited calling plans will no longer be offered.
(D) Some mobile phones will no longer be sold.

169. What does the Techfan plan feature?

(A) Early access to new mobile phones
(B) Discounts on large amounts of data
(C) Invitations to in-store special events
(D) Guaranteed buyback of older devices

170. According to the Web page, what can make getting a new phone more affordable?

(A) Purchasing a phone online
(B) Trading in an older device
(C) Disabling a text-messaging application
(D) Enrolling in a payment plan

171. What are Talk First Technologies' customers encouraged to do?

(A) Talk to a service representative
(B) Set up automatic payments
(C) Pay bills with a mobile app
(D) Submit an online review

GO ON TO THE NEXT PAGE

Questions 172-175 refer to the following online chat discussion.

Melvin Arocho (1:39 P.M.)
Hi, Brenda and Vince. Brenda, have you made flight arrangements for us yet?

Brenda Koster (1:40 P.M.)
Yes. We depart for Denmark on March 14 at 2:20 P.M. Any problems?

Melvin Arocho (1:42 P.M.)
Yes, actually. The meeting with our Danish partners has been moved up one week, to next Wednesday. That's because we just found out that Arrownetic will release its new laptop early next year. And that means we'll need to speed up the development of our own new model.

Vince Gayle (1:43 P.M.)
Really? I'm supposed to go camping with my family next week.

Brenda Koster (1:44 P.M.)
I signed up for a three-day amateur tennis tournament. My first match is on Wednesday.

Melvin Arocho (1:45 P.M.)
And I have tickets for a one-time-only performance by the Brandenburg Ballet Company that same day. It's out of our hands, I'm afraid. Brenda, please rebook us for March 7.

Brenda Koster (1:46 P.M.)
Sure. I'll check to see if there are flights available.

Brenda Koster (1:52 P.M.)
There's a flight at 11:35 P.M. Is that time OK with both of you?

Melvin Arocho (1:54 P.M.)
Sure. Incidentally, Ms. Mack said she realizes that this last-minute change is an imposition on us. She will make sure that we get compensated somehow.

Brenda Koster (1:55 P.M.)
That's very considerate of her.

Brenda Koster (1:59 P.M.)
There are only four seats left on that flight, Vince, so make your mind up fast.

Vince Gayle (2:01 P.M.)
Sorry, I had to step away from my desk. Yes, I suppose.

Melvin Arocho (2:02 P.M.)
Good. Brenda, please go ahead and make those arrangements now.

172. Why did Mr. Arocho contact his colleagues?

(A) To inform them of a change of plans
(B) To ask them about a recent meeting
(C) To go over a production schedule
(D) To discuss a merger the company is considering

173. What is suggested about the company the writers work for?

(A) It organizes sporting activities for its employees.
(B) It sponsors cultural events in its community.
(C) It operates in a competitive market.
(D) It has its headquarters in Denmark.

174. Who most likely is Ms. Mack?

(A) A tournament organizer
(B) A company manager
(C) A travel agent
(D) A ballet dancer

175. At 2:01 P.M., what does Mr. Gayle mean when he writes, "Yes, I suppose"?

(A) He will ask his family about the situation.
(B) He agrees to the suggested time.
(C) He believes four tickets are available.
(D) He thinks there are flights on Wednesday.

GO ON TO THE NEXT PAGE

Questions 176-180 refer to the following schedule and e-mail.

Conference & Location	Dates	Presenter(s)	Presentation
Adfinity Summit Sydney, NSW	1–4 June	Fergus Jones Martha Orr	Top Trends in Social Media Advertising Data Impact Revolution
Overdrive Marketing Melbourne, VIC	4–7 June	Martha Orr Victor Voss	Visuals That Tell Your Story Product Launch: Seven Pitfalls to Avoid
Pull Ahead Expo Brisbane, QLD	15–19 June	Fergus Jones Martha Orr	Effective Presentation Techniques Four Keys to Brand Loyalty
Diaspawn Perth, WA	20–24 June	Martha Orr Alexa Rojas	Let Your Success Do the Talking Navigating the Marketing Labyrinth

To:	All Rowin Consulting team members
From:	Tristan Fields, Manager
Re:	June conference schedule
Date:	15 April

Dear Rowin Consulting team members,

I need to bring several new developments regarding the conference schedule to your attention.

First, Mr. Voss has just been asked to be the closing keynote speaker on the last day of the Adfinity Summit. Since this conflicts with his current schedule, Ms. Rojas will take over for him at the annual Overdrive Marketing conference.

Secondly, Mr. Jones must go abroad in mid-June, so he cannot join Ms. Orr at the Pull Ahead Expo. We asked the conference organisers to drop his session from their schedule.

Finally, Ms. Orr has been requested by Diaspawn to change her presentation topic for their conference. They would like her to address the theme of her recent book, so she should deliver her "Data Impact Revolution" talk there instead of her planned topic.

Thank you,

Tristan Fields

176. At what conference will attendees learn about creating brand loyalty?

(A) Adfinity Summit
(B) Overdrive Marketing
(C) Pull Ahead Expo
(D) Diaspawn

177. Where will Mr. Voss give the closing presentation?

(A) In Sydney
(B) In Melbourne
(C) In Brisbane
(D) In Perth

178. Why will a presentation be canceled?

(A) The presenter will be out of the country.
(B) Not enough people will attend.
(C) The presenter will be speaking at another conference.
(D) Someone else is already addressing the same topic.

179. What is indicated about the Rowin Consulting team?

(A) Each member is from a different city.
(B) Each member delivers presentations remotely.
(C) One of its members is a published author.
(D) One of its members presents topics with a partner.

180. What presentation does Mr. Fields ask Ms. Orr to replace?

(A) Data Impact Revolution
(B) Visuals That Tell Your Story
(C) Four Keys to Brand Loyalty
(D) Let Your Success Do the Talking

GO ON TO THE NEXT PAGE

Questions 181-185 refer to the following letter and excerpt from a résumé.

January 15

Bernice J. Todd
Filvey Company
356 Main Street
Dearborn, MI 48124

Dear Ms. Todd,

I am writing to apply for the position of production-line worker at Filvey Company. I currently work for an electronics manufacturer, but I previously worked at the Collins Corporation, and I am excited at the prospect of working in that field again. I have been employed in manufacturing for fourteen years and have broad knowledge of assembly equipment in many industries, including furniture and textiles. Supervisors consistently praise my attention to detail and ability to learn new processes quickly.

As requested, I have enclosed my résumé and a list of references. I have also included my current supervisor's report from a course I led a few months ago. I had been asked to train new employees on our production-line assembly equipment, and my supervisor noted my effectiveness. In addition, I developed materials to teach about workplace cleanliness at my previous job, and I would be happy to discuss that experience with you.

Sincerely,

Andrew D. Chen

Andrew D. Chen

Enclosures

Andrew D. Chen • 2781 Moore Street • Ann Arbor, MI 48105

Overview:
Production-line worker employed for many years in manufacturing plants of various sizes. Experienced trainer of new employees on assembly equipment.

Work experience:
Kolpek, Inc., Ypsilanti, Michigan (current job, 5 years)
- Assemble electronic components for computers and communications equipment
- Assist in developing standards for safety and environmental compliance

Collins Corporation, Detroit, Michigan (4 years)
- Worked on various components of a new line of energy-efficient automobiles
- Received quality assurance ratings in the top 10% of all production-line workers

181. What does Filvey Company most likely manufacture?

(A) Automobiles
(B) Textiles
(C) Furniture
(D) Electronics

182. In the letter, the word "broad" in paragraph 1, line 4, is closest in meaning to

(A) open
(B) spacious
(C) extensive
(D) variable

183. In the letter, what does Mr. Chen mention as one of his qualifications for the job?

(A) He is good at repairing equipment.
(B) He learns new procedures easily.
(C) He writes very detailed reports.
(D) He has experience as a supervisor.

184. According to the letter, what did Mr. Chen NOT include with his application?

(A) A résumé
(B) A training evaluation
(C) Some references
(D) Some teaching materials

185. What is suggested about Kolpek, Inc.?

(A) It often invests in new assembly equipment.
(B) It had problems with workplace cleanliness.
(C) It specializes in producing safety equipment.
(D) It recently hired production-line workers.

GO ON TO THE NEXT PAGE

Questions 186-190 refer to the following flyer and e-mails.

This Month at Office Flash

Our Top Deals

- Multipurpose white copy paper—normally $34.95 per box, now only $27.50
- Pro-Forda printer ink (color or black)—normally $24.95 per cartridge, now only $19.95
- Boligraph ballpoint pens (all colors)—normally $8.95 per box of 24, now only $6.50

20% off All Antivirus Software

Save with an instant in-store rebate on all leading brands!

Free In-Store Workshops on Getting Yourself Organized

Sign up for our popular weekly workshops! Cut the clutter, both at home and in the office. Space is limited, and the workshop is filling up fast, so register soon at www.officeflash.net/classes.

May 4	2:00–4:00 P.M.
May 11	8:30–11:30 A.M.
May 18	7:00–9:00 P.M.
May 25	12:30–2:30 P.M.

E-mail

From: Deals <deals@officeflash.net>
To: Jae Choi <choi.j@bizmail.com>
Date: April 21
Subject: Correction

Dear Office Flash customer:

We regret to inform you that our latest flyer contained an error regarding an advertised item. The ballpoint pens are not available in all colors, only in black. To show our commitment to our customers, we are offering an e-coupon good for one box of blue or red pens at 50% off. The coupon can be used when our new shipment of colored pens arrives on April 28. Simply respond to this e-mail and request the coupon. Please note that this offer does not apply to the copy paper or printer ink because those items were in stock at the time the flyer was distributed. We thank you for your understanding and for being a loyal customer.

Sincerely,

The Office Flash Team

From:	Jae Choi <choi.j@bizmail.com>
To:	Deals <deals@officeflash.net>
Date:	April 22
Subject:	RE: Correction

Hi,

I would definitely like to be sent the coupon you offered in your e-mail. Also, I no longer have a copy of the flyer, but I remember reading that you are offering workshops on organizing a home or office space. I am very interested in attending one, but I am only available in the evenings. Do you offer any classes that would fit my schedule?

Thanks,

Jae Choi

186. What information is provided in the flyer?
(A) A list of discontinued items
(B) Changes to a class schedule
(C) Details about discounted products
(D) Instructions for downloading software

187. What is suggested about the classes?
(A) They are well attended.
(B) They are offered online.
(C) They require a small fee.
(D) They are held twice a week.

188. What is the purpose of the first e-mail?
(A) To apologize for a mistake
(B) To introduce a new service
(C) To ask for customer feedback
(D) To promote an upcoming sale

189. What workshop date would be best for Mr. Choi?
(A) May 4
(B) May 11
(C) May 18
(D) May 25

190. What product does Mr. Choi suggest that he wants to buy?
(A) Copy paper
(B) Printer ink
(C) Software
(D) Pens

GO ON TO THE NEXT PAGE

Questions 191-195 refer to the following cost estimate, notice, and e-mail.

Marlowe Movers ~ Your Choice for Ease and Security
Serving you from two convenient locations:
168 Roland Street, Brooklyn • 1422 Longway Avenue, Jersey City

Moving Job Cost Estimate

Prepared by	Date	Prices valid until
Denise Monteiro	March 15	April 30

Prepared for	Delivery from	Delivery to
Sri Lankan Imports, LLC	151 West 24th Street Suite 15 New York, NY 10011	240 Garrison Boulevard Floor 4, Suite 43 New York, NY 10013

Items to be moved

20 file-storage boxes, standard size
3 filing cabinets, 4-drawer vertical
1 desk, midsized
1 office chair, wheeled

Cost estimate

Labor: 2 crew members
Cost per hour per crew member: $30
Duration: 2 hours
Transport: Van rental, $35 flat fee
Estimated total: $155.00

Inclusions and Exclusions:

- Transport costs include fuel and tolls.
- Estimated labor fees *do not include* additional labor for pickups from or deliveries to buildings without elevator service. Where applicable, $3 per flight of stairs is added to the base hourly rate of each crew member.

Posted Tuesday, March 19

Notice to All Residential and Commercial Tenants

The elevator in this building will be out of service for routine maintenance on Wednesday, March 27.

Thank you,
Building Management
240 Garrison Blvd.

To:	Ram Jeyakumar
From:	Dinesha Gamage
Date:	March 20
Subject:	Move

Dear Mr. Jeyakumar,

I wanted to provide you with an update about the transition to our new office suite on Garrison Boulevard. I learned today that the elevator there will be out of service on your scheduled move date. We cannot move you early because the Garrison location is not yet properly set up. But we also do not want to postpone the move because of your role in the stakeholder meeting on Tuesday, April 2. I understand that you want to have time to settle in before then and prepare your remarks.

Rather than reschedule your move, I have informed the movers about this complication, and they are willing to work with it. I just wanted you to know so that you will not be caught by surprise on the day of the move. I am in the process of alerting other staff members who will be affected.

Best,

Dinesha Gamage
Office Manager

191. According to the cost estimate, why would a client pay an extra fee?

(A) To reschedule a moving date
(B) To have movers climb stairs
(C) To get additional moving supplies
(D) To have large furniture transported

192. What is the notice about?

(A) Scheduled maintenance
(B) Professional cleaning services
(C) A change in management
(D) A meeting of tenants

193. Where does Mr. Jeyakumar currently work?

(A) On Roland Street
(B) On Longway Avenue
(C) On West 24th Street
(D) On Garrison Boulevard

194. What does Ms. Gamage suggest Mr. Jeyakumar will do in April?

(A) Contact a moving company
(B) Begin a new job
(C) Visit a client's office
(D) Make a presentation

195. When will Mr. Jeyakumar's move take place?

(A) On March 19
(B) On March 20
(C) On March 27
(D) On April 2

GO ON TO THE NEXT PAGE

Questions 196-200 refer to the following editor's note, e-mail, and expense report.

Transport Quarterly

EDITOR'S NOTE:

The news often talks about the use of driverless passenger cars in the near future, but self-directed trucks (SDTs) will likely be transporting deliveries on the country's roadways even sooner, perhaps within the next several years. In our autumn issue, we check in with industry experts for analysis on issues related to SDTs. Kimiko Murayama of Myeong Solutions talks about the economic factors that are making SDTs a reality. Telotin Technology's Jane Tilly takes a look at the technology that is literally "driving" SDTs. Leo Radosh of The Tapton Engineering Group describes advances in global positioning system (GPS) technology and the role that it will play in the acceptance of SDTs.

E-mail

To:	kmurayama@msolutions.co.uk
From:	lgagnon@bunburyit.ac.uk
Subject:	Visiting BIT
Date:	14 January

Dear Ms. Murayama,

I teach an undergraduate course called Transportation and Distribution at the Bunbury Institute of Technology (BIT), which includes a unit on cost structures for freight carriers. I would like to invite you to visit my class as a guest speaker. I saw your article in *Transport Quarterly*, and I was going to assign it as required reading for my students. It then occurred to me that your company is only a 10-minute drive from our campus. My students would be very interested in your thoughts on self-driving fleets.

The class meets Tuesday and Thursday mornings from 9:00 to 11:15, and there are 74 students enrolled. I can fit your visit into the schedule at any point between now and our exams on 12 March. Although I do not have a budget to compensate you for your time and travel, I would be delighted to treat you to lunch after class. I do hope you will see your way to visiting us here at BIT in the near future.

Yours truly,

Dr. Loudon Gagnon
Department of Transportation Engineering
Bunbury Institute of Technology

Bunbury Institute of Technology

Employee Expense Report

Name: Dr. Loudon Gagnon
Department: Transportation Engineering
Date: 12 Feb
Amount: £40

Description of Purchase:
Lunch at the Faculty Club hosting guest lecturer for course 316 (Transportation and Distribution)

Attach original receipts in order to receive reimbursement.
All expenses above £200 must be preapproved by the dean of faculty.

Approved for payment by Frank Nadal on 19 February.

TEST 1

196. What is contained in the editor's note?
(A) A prediction about the future
(B) An analysis of GPS technology
(C) A summary of Ms. Tilly's career
(D) A description of driverless vehicles

197. What type of transportation is discussed in the fall issue of *Transport Quarterly*?
(A) Public mass transit
(B) Passenger railways
(C) Highway freight delivery
(D) Overseas cargo shipping

198. What company is a short distance from Bunbury Institute of Technology?
(A) Myeong Solutions
(B) Telotin Technology
(C) The Tapton Engineering Group
(D) *Transport Quarterly*'s publisher

199. What did Dr. Gagnon most likely do after reading the fall issue of *Transport Quarterly*?
(A) Write a letter to the editor
(B) Share it with his supervisor
(C) Encourage his students to submit articles to the publication
(D) Issue an invitation to a contributor

200. What did Dr. Gagnon do at the Faculty Club on February 12?
(A) He stopped by to pay an annual membership fee.
(B) He hosted Ms. Murayama for a meal.
(C) He welcomed a new department member.
(D) He requested approval for a payment from Mr. Nadal.

Stop! This is the end of the test. If you finish before time is called, you may go back to Parts 5, 6, and 7 and check your work.

NO TEST MATERIAL ON THIS PAGE

TEST 2

CD 2
01-82

＊解答用紙は本誌 p.112 の後ろに綴じ込まれています。

実際のテストでは問題用紙の裏側に、以下のようなテスト全体についての指示が印刷されています。
この指示を念頭においてテストに取り組みましょう。

General Directions

This test is designed to measure your English language ability. The test is divided into two sections: Listening and Reading.

You must mark all of your answers on the separate answer sheet. For each question, you should select the best answer from the answer choices given. Then, on your answer sheet, you should find the number of the question and fill in the space that corresponds to the letter of the answer that you have selected. If you decide to change an answer, completely erase your old answer and then mark your new answer.

訳

全体についての指示

このテストはあなたの英語言語能力を測定するよう設計されています。テストはリスニングとリーディングという2つのセクションに分けられています。

答えは全て別紙の解答用紙にマークしてください。それぞれの設問について、与えられた選択肢から最も適切な答えを選びます。そして解答用紙の該当する問題番号に、選択した答えを塗りつぶしてください。答えを修正する場合は、元の答えを完全に消してから新しい答えをマークしてください。

LISTENING TEST

In the Listening test, you will be asked to demonstrate how well you understand spoken English. The entire Listening test will last approximately 45 minutes. There are four parts, and directions are given for each part. You must mark your answers on the separate answer sheet. Do not write your answers in your test book.

PART 1

Directions: For each question in this part, you will hear four statements about a picture in your test book. When you hear the statements, you must select the one statement that best describes what you see in the picture. Then find the number of the question on your answer sheet and mark your answer. The statements will not be printed in your test book and will be spoken only one time.

Statement (C), "They're sitting at a table," is the best description of the picture, so you should select answer (C) and mark it on your answer sheet.

1.

2.

GO ON TO THE NEXT PAGE

CD 2 05-06

3.

4.

5.

6.

GO ON TO THE NEXT PAGE

Directions CD 2 09 | Questions CD 2 10-34

PART 2

Directions: You will hear a question or statement and three responses spoken in English. They will not be printed in your test book and will be spoken only one time. Select the best response to the question or statement and mark the letter (A), (B), or (C) on your answer sheet.

7. Mark your answer on your answer sheet.

8. Mark your answer on your answer sheet.

9. Mark your answer on your answer sheet.

10. Mark your answer on your answer sheet.

11. Mark your answer on your answer sheet.

12. Mark your answer on your answer sheet.

13. Mark your answer on your answer sheet.

14. Mark your answer on your answer sheet.

15. Mark your answer on your answer sheet.

16. Mark your answer on your answer sheet.

17. Mark your answer on your answer sheet.

18. Mark your answer on your answer sheet.

19. Mark your answer on your answer sheet.

20. Mark your answer on your answer sheet.

21. Mark your answer on your answer sheet.

22. Mark your answer on your answer sheet.

23. Mark your answer on your answer sheet.

24. Mark your answer on your answer sheet.

25. Mark your answer on your answer sheet.

26. Mark your answer on your answer sheet.

27. Mark your answer on your answer sheet.

28. Mark your answer on your answer sheet.

29. Mark your answer on your answer sheet.

30. Mark your answer on your answer sheet.

31. Mark your answer on your answer sheet.

PART 3

Directions: You will hear some conversations between two or more people. You will be asked to answer three questions about what the speakers say in each conversation. Select the best response to each question and mark the letter (A), (B), (C), or (D) on your answer sheet. The conversations will not be printed in your test book and will be spoken only one time.

32. Where does the conversation most likely take place?
(A) At a department store
(B) At a photography studio
(C) At a health clinic
(D) At a hair salon

33. What does the woman ask about?
(A) Receiving e-mail notifications
(B) Using a coupon
(C) Setting up an account
(D) Changing an appointment time

34. What does the woman say she will do?
(A) Look at some products
(B) Complete some paperwork
(C) Write a review
(D) Come back another day

---

35. What will Kinhex Corporation celebrate?
(A) The start of a holiday season
(B) The anniversary of its founding
(C) The opening of a new location
(D) The appointment of a company president

36. What does the man ask about?
(A) The cost of a service
(B) Operating hours
(C) Entertainment options
(D) The size of a space

37. What does the woman ask the man to do?
(A) Sample a menu item
(B) Look at a catalog
(C) Talk to a manager
(D) Make a payment

---

38. Where do the speakers most likely work?
(A) At a computer repair shop
(B) At a real estate firm
(C) At a restaurant
(D) At a home improvement store

39. What does the man offer to do?
(A) Wait on some customers
(B) Lead a workshop
(C) Take inventory
(D) Arrange a window display

40. What does the woman say she will do?
(A) Prepare some materials
(B) Call for transportation
(C) Return some merchandise
(D) Update a sign

---

41. Who most likely is the woman?
(A) A factory supervisor
(B) A Web site designer
(C) A financial planner
(D) A clothing manufacturer

42. What does the woman suggest?
(A) Changing a color
(B) Replacing a machine
(C) Hiring a consultant
(D) Lowering a price

43. What will happen at tomorrow's meeting?
(A) New team members will be introduced.
(B) A product demonstration will take place.
(C) The speakers will gather feedback.
(D) A budget will be revised.

GO ON TO THE NEXT PAGE

CD 2 44-51

44. What does the woman want the man to do?
(A) Process some paperwork
(B) Attend a presentation
(C) Draft a proposal
(D) Rearrange a conference room

45. Why does the woman say, "you're new here"?
(A) To express surprise
(B) To give a compliment
(C) To show understanding
(D) To disagree with a suggestion

46. What does the man ask about?
(A) Finding some supplies
(B) Delaying some training
(C) Submitting a time sheet
(D) Changing a password

47. Where most likely are the speakers?
(A) At a fitness center
(B) At a garden store
(C) At a clothing shop
(D) At a health food store

48. What does the woman want to purchase?
(A) Some running shoes
(B) Some organic tea
(C) A membership
(D) A jacket

49. What will Antonio probably do next?
(A) Check merchandise online
(B) Retrieve some items
(C) Call a different location
(D) Apply a discount

50. What will the new software allow patients to do?
(A) Schedule appointments
(B) Request a prescription refill
(C) Ask the doctor a question
(D) Write a review

51. Who will be visiting the office tomorrow?
(A) A sales representative
(B) A service technician
(C) A pharmacist
(D) A building inspector

52. What will the man include in an e-mail to patients?
(A) A list of specialists' phone numbers
(B) A reminder about required forms
(C) Directions to a new office
(D) Instructions on how to use a system

53. Why is the man at the post office?
(A) To mail a package
(B) To buy some stamps
(C) To apply for a job
(D) To pick up some documents

54. Why does the woman say, "regular mail takes three or four days"?
(A) To offer an apology
(B) To express disappointment
(C) To explain a refund policy
(D) To correct a misunderstanding

55. What will the man pay an additional fee for?
(A) Packaging materials
(B) Insurance
(C) A passport photo
(D) A confirmation notice

56. Who is the man?
(A) A journalist
(B) A taxi driver
(C) A laboratory assistant
(D) A parking garage attendant

57. What are the speakers mainly discussing?
(A) Updates to environmental regulations
(B) Effective magazine advertisements
(C) Self-parking technology for vehicles
(D) Cost estimates for a new project

58. What will the man most likely do next?
(A) Fill out an insurance form
(B) Read an instruction manual
(C) Complete a purchase
(D) Watch a demonstration

---

59. What is the man doing?
(A) Preparing an order form
(B) Putting labels on merchandise
(C) Checking employee time sheets
(D) Reading customer reviews

60. Why does the man say he is worried?
(A) Too many products have been returned.
(B) Too many plastic bags are being used.
(C) A competing business has recently opened.
(D) An entrance is blocked by construction.

61. What does the woman suggest doing?
(A) Changing business hours
(B) Starting a delivery service
(C) Hiring more staff
(D) Offering a discount

Mon 12	Brainstorming Meeting—2 P.M.
Tues 13	Client Consultation—10 A.M.
Wed 14	
Thurs 15	Singapore Conference
Fri 16	

62. What problem does the man point out?
(A) Some software needs to be updated.
(B) Some data were entered incorrectly.
(C) A conference room was not available.
(D) A project's due date needs to be extended.

63. Look at the graphic. What day will the woman most likely conduct the training?
(A) Monday
(B) Wednesday
(C) Thursday
(D) Friday

64. What does the woman ask the man to do?
(A) Contact a colleague
(B) Conduct an inspection
(C) E-mail some candidates
(D) Reserve some equipment

GO ON TO THE NEXT PAGE

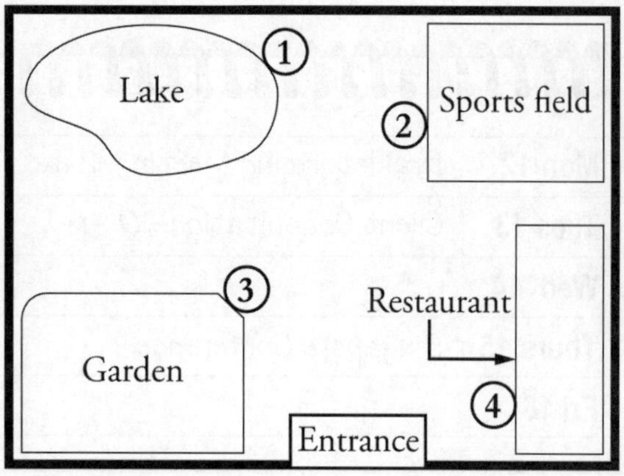

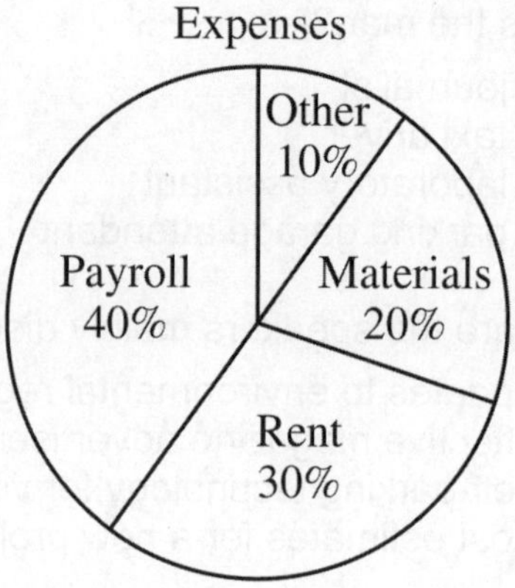

65. What are the speakers mainly discussing?
(A) Competing in a sports competition
(B) Planning a grand opening
(C) Attending an award ceremony
(D) Helping at a local festival

66. Look at the graphic. Where will the woman meet her coworker?
(A) By the lake
(B) By the sports field
(C) By the garden
(D) By the restaurant

67. According to the man, what should the woman pick up?
(A) Some brochures
(B) A training manual
(C) An identification badge
(D) Some refreshments

68. Look at the graphic. Which percentage do the speakers hope to reduce?
(A) 10%
(B) 20%
(C) 30%
(D) 40%

69. According to the man, what has changed at the company?
(A) Many employees now work from home.
(B) Several products are not selling well.
(C) The company is expanding into a new market.
(D) The company has updated its hiring policy.

70. What will the speakers do next?
(A) Update a presentation
(B) Speak with a consultant
(C) Check some inventory
(D) Make some travel reservations

PART 4

Directions: You will hear some talks given by a single speaker. You will be asked to answer three questions about what the speaker says in each talk. Select the best response to each question and mark the letter (A), (B), (C), or (D) on your answer sheet. The talks will not be printed in your test book and will be spoken only one time.

71. Where does Jessica Plank work?
(A) At a community center
(B) At a radio station
(C) At a park
(D) At a restaurant

72. What took place last month?
(A) A store opening
(B) A job fair
(C) A landscaping contest
(D) An awards ceremony

73. What did the Endo Company do?
(A) It started an internship program.
(B) It donated some tools.
(C) It created a new slogan.
(D) It opened a second location.

---

74. What does the speaker emphasize about the company's products?
(A) They are high quality.
(B) They are locally produced.
(C) Gift sets can be purchased online.
(D) A wide selection is available.

75. What does the speaker say all customers will receive?
(A) A gift card
(B) A teapot
(C) Product samples
(D) Overnight delivery

76. Why does the speaker say, "Registration takes five minutes"?
(A) To encourage participation in a program
(B) To apologize for a delay
(C) To volunteer to assist customers
(D) To invite customers to take a break

---

77. Where do the listeners most likely work?
(A) At a supermarket
(B) At a real estate agency
(C) At a bank
(D) At a print shop

78. What is the speaker's announcement mainly about?
(A) A business relocation
(B) A sales promotion
(C) A budget cut
(D) A change in ownership

79. What are the listeners asked to do?
(A) Adjust their work hours
(B) Participate in a staff training
(C) Renew an employment contract
(D) Pass out some informational flyers

---

80. Who is the message intended for?
(A) A farmworker
(B) A lawyer
(C) A journalist
(D) A supermarket owner

81. Why does the speaker say, "There's still some data in the report we're waiting to confirm"?
(A) To explain a delay
(B) To offer to help
(C) To show surprise about a conclusion
(D) To urge the listener to work quickly

82. Why does the speaker suggest communicating by e-mail?
(A) She will be out of town.
(B) She wants to keep a written record.
(C) She needs to send some pictures.
(D) She wants to include others in the discussion.

GO ON TO THE NEXT PAGE

83. What product is the speaker discussing?

(A) A car
(B) A refrigerator
(C) A computer
(D) An air conditioner

84. What does the speaker say is different about the product?

(A) Its size
(B) Its color
(C) Its material
(D) Its energy usage

85. What does the speaker want suggestions about?

(A) Lowering production costs
(B) Finding qualified staff
(C) Reorganizing a department
(D) Responding to customer complaints

---

86. What is the broadcast mainly about?

(A) An update about a building renovation project
(B) A plan to encourage recycling
(C) A request for community volunteers
(D) A proposal for a fee increase

87. According to the broadcast, what will take place in May?

(A) A local election
(B) A park expansion
(C) A sporting event
(D) A town festival

88. What will the listeners have an opportunity to do next month?

(A) Join a committee
(B) Provide some feedback
(C) Review a floor plan
(D) Purchase advance tickets

---

89. What does the company specialize in?

(A) Photography
(B) Interior decorating
(C) Accounting
(D) Publishing

90. What will the listeners be trained to do?

(A) Create a budget
(B) Write contracts
(C) Use a database
(D) Improve sales techniques

91. What will the listeners do next?

(A) Watch an instructional video
(B) Work with a colleague
(C) Get some refreshments
(D) Read a printed manual

---

92. Who is Alexis Morris?

(A) A nutrition expert
(B) A gardener
(C) A chef
(D) A supermarket owner

93. What does the speaker imply when he says, "I've tried a lot of other applications like this"?

(A) He wants to try other applications.
(B) He is offering to work with a colleague.
(C) The listeners can trust his opinion.
(D) The listeners should call the station.

94. According to the speaker, what will listeners hear next?

(A) A weather report
(B) A commercial break
(C) A traffic update
(D) A news bulletin

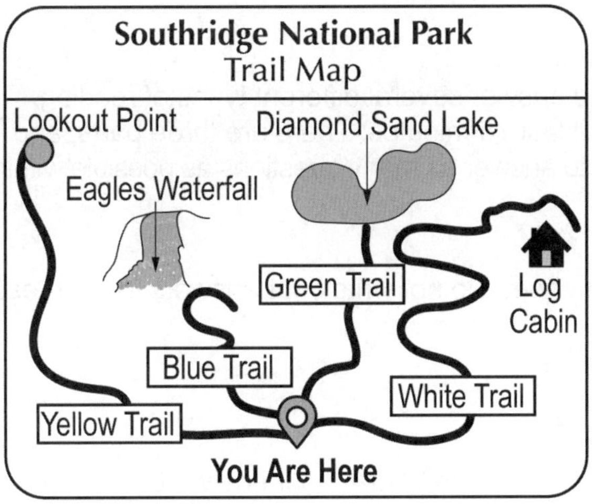

95. Look at the graphic. Which trail does the speaker plan on taking?

(A) Yellow Trail
(B) Blue Trail
(C) Green Trail
(D) White Trail

96. What does the speaker say the listeners are likely to see during the hike?

(A) Historic ruins
(B) Migrating birds
(C) Camping sites
(D) Wildflowers

97. What does the speaker suggest the listeners do?

(A) Pose for a photograph
(B) Bring healthy snacks
(C) Wear a raincoat
(D) Sign a visitors' book

Conference Room A Schedule

Wednesday, May 14

10:00 A.M.	Wang Sporting Goods
1:00 P.M.	Open
2:00 P.M.	Department Meeting
4:00 P.M.	Freeman Incorporated

98. What does the speaker say will be discussed at the meeting?

(A) An office renovation project
(B) A company merger
(C) A quarterly budget
(D) An advertising campaign

99. Look at the graphic. At what time will the meeting take place?

(A) 10:00 A.M.
(B) 1:00 P.M.
(C) 2:00 P.M.
(D) 4:00 P.M.

100. What does the speaker ask the listener to do?

(A) Take some measurements
(B) Bring a computer
(C) Prepare some slides
(D) Make a list of questions

This is the end of the Listening test. Turn to Part 5 in your test book.

GO ON TO THE NEXT PAGE

READING TEST

In the Reading test, you will read a variety of texts and answer several different types of reading comprehension questions. The entire Reading test will last 75 minutes. There are three parts, and directions are given for each part. You are encouraged to answer as many questions as possible within the time allowed.

You must mark your answers on the separate answer sheet. Do not write your answers in your test book.

PART 5

Directions: A word or phrase is missing in each of the sentences below. Four answer choices are given below each sentence. Select the best answer to complete the sentence. Then mark the letter (A), (B), (C), or (D) on your answer sheet.

101. Mr. Lang has been running ------- carpet store for more than twenty years.

(A) himself
(B) him
(C) his
(D) he

102. When designing the conference poster, be sure to ------- the company logo at the top.

(A) manage
(B) refer
(C) reach
(D) place

103. The hotel ballroom was ------- decorated for the wedding of the mayor's daughter.

(A) beauty
(B) beautiful
(C) beautifully
(D) beautify

104. The city completed its annual financial report ------- the state deadline.

(A) before
(B) between
(C) beside
(D) below

105. Guests at the Homer Hotel can expect ------- service from every member of our staff.

(A) attentive
(B) attention
(C) attentively
(D) attentiveness

106. YLT Supply Company offers its customers a 10 percent discount ------- they pay for their lumber order in cash.

(A) also
(B) if
(C) but
(D) and

107. Carolyn Fanner will speak about her new memoir at the next ------- at the Delville Public Library.

(A) lecture
(B) lecturer
(C) lecturing
(D) lectured

108. The number 17 bus is the quickest ------- to get from the rail station to the business district.

(A) style
(B) direction
(C) control
(D) way

109. Ms. Cho ------- the Busan office in the coming months in Ms. Kim's absence.

(A) to supervise
(B) supervised
(C) has been supervising
(D) will be supervising

110. A special ------- of porcelain sculptures by Riku Ohtani is being shown at the Vanport Art Museum.

(A) outlook
(B) function
(C) exhibit
(D) event

111. ------- who has not read the new information protection policy must do so today.

(A) Anyone
(B) Another
(C) Any
(D) Anything

112. Aapo Systems is ------- to be our distributor when we begin exporting to Finland.

(A) ahead
(B) likely
(C) over
(D) finely

113. The creation of the new park was only possible with the ------- of the town council.

(A) support
(B) supportive
(C) supported
(D) supportable

114. The pay increase for Lansuli Fishery employees is ------- from April 15.

(A) permissive
(B) effective
(C) collective
(D) objective

115. Patient reviews of Dunleavy Dental's staff and facility are ------- positive.

(A) consist
(B) consistent
(C) consisting
(D) consistently

116. The training program for new flight attendants ------- over the course of three weeks.

(A) insists
(B) protects
(C) allows
(D) extends

117. We would like to thank employees ------- ideas led to recent departmental improvements.

(A) whichever
(B) whom
(C) whose
(D) whatever

118. The Pimasoft four-person tent is light, strong, and ------- to tearing and ripping.

(A) resist
(B) resistant
(C) resisted
(D) resistance

119. ------- those at yesterday's meeting, Mr. Swartz has been with the company the longest.

(A) Around
(B) Despite
(C) Inside
(D) Among

120. The estate-planning position requires some ------- knowledge of finance or customer service.

(A) prompt
(B) constant
(C) equal
(D) prior

121. The CEO's opening remarks were rewritten to place more ------- on welcoming new employees.

(A) emphasis
(B) emphasize
(C) emphatic
(D) emphatically

122. Although concrete is one of the most durable construction materials, some form of maintenance work will ------- be needed.

(A) already
(B) eventually
(C) correctly
(D) further

GO ON TO THE NEXT PAGE

123. All shareholders of Techtraco Ltd. ------- to attend the upcoming annual meeting.

(A) are invited
(B) have been inviting
(C) had invited
(D) will be inviting

124. Of the new features at the Portview Gym, the rock-climbing wall is ------- members use most.

(A) close to
(B) other than
(C) the one
(D) one time

125. ------- the Sandmore Hotel is located in the city center, the Madrugada Inn is situated just outside of the city limits.

(A) Only if
(B) In case
(C) When
(D) While

126. Before the training, Mr. Bonnay was ------- unaware of recent developments in automated delivery systems.

(A) largely
(B) closely
(C) faintly
(D) finally

127. ------- weeks, it was clear that the long-term sponsorship deal with basketball star Joe Littleton would be successful.

(A) Within
(B) Several
(C) Just
(D) During

128. The ideal job candidate will quickly be able to become ------- with software packages that are designed in-house.

(A) compatible
(B) possible
(C) proficient
(D) fortunate

129. The retirement party surprised Mr. Rheims, who could not ------- his gratitude for his colleagues' thoughtfulness.

(A) be concealed
(B) conceal
(C) concealing
(D) to conceal

130. ------- on the age of the computer's operating system, the program may run more slowly than expected.

(A) Depending
(B) Focused
(C) Relying
(D) Centered

PART 6

Directions: Read the texts that follow. A word, phrase, or sentence is missing in parts of each text. Four answer choices for each question are given below the text. Select the best answer to complete the text. Then mark the letter (A), (B), (C), or (D) on your answer sheet.

Questions 131-134 refer to the following advertisement.

Corporate Team-Building Workshops

Strong teams with members that collaborate effectively are at the heart of any business organization. What better way to improve your employees' productivity and your company's profits than by strengthening team skills? -------. **131.** The result? Improved performance for your employees and increased ------- **132.** for your company!

We work with groups of all sizes to facilitate creative team activities that ------- **133.** to be fun and inspiring. However, there is a serious purpose ------- **134.** every activity—generating team spirit! Contact Plainfield Solutions at 512-555-0121 for a free consultation.

131. (A) Many employees are reluctant to participate in team-building activities.
(B) Most companies lack the time and resources for a team-building program.
(C) Our team-building workshops help build trust and improve communication.
(D) Team building is not just for established companies.

132. (A) property
(B) advertising
(C) competition
(D) revenue

133. (A) guarantees
(B) are guaranteed
(C) guaranteeing
(D) had been guaranteeing

134. (A) behind
(B) after
(C) above
(D) along

TEST 2

GO ON TO THE NEXT PAGE

Questions 135-138 refer to the following letter.

February 5

Dr. Jenna E. Delphin
671 South Prince Street
Missoula, MT 59804

Dear Dr. Delphin:

Thank you for ------- (135.) a proposal for the Atelic Chemical Association conference. I am delighted to confirm that your proposal has been approved. We have tentatively scheduled your presentation for the morning of July 25, which is the second full day of the conference. ------- (136.).

Dr. Henry Knecht ------- (137.) you with a list of guidelines for speakers, the preferred format for each presentation, and our logo and marketing materials. If you do not receive that e-mail by February 15, please feel free to reach out to him ------- (138.) at hknecht@atelicca.org.

I look forward to seeing you in July.

Best wishes,

Randall Antoun, Conference Manager

135. (A) studying
(B) changing
(C) submitting
(D) reviewing

136. (A) Please let me know if this is acceptable to you.
(B) Instead, a list of speakers is included with this letter.
(C) For this reason, the association's membership fees have increased.
(D) You should be prepared to join us here next week.

137. (A) provides
(B) provided
(C) used to provide
(D) will be providing

138. (A) directly
(B) directed
(C) directs
(D) director

Questions 139-142 refer to the following letter.

May 6

Fenella Hornstein
4099 Unison Street
Tampa, FL 33601

Dear Ms. Hornstein,

It has been brought to our attention that many of our customers ------- (139.) more options for paying their Tampa Bank credit card bill. ------- (140.), we are offering an option called Auto Pay starting on June 1.

With this new payment option, your credit card balance is automatically paid in full on the first day of each month with funds from your checking account. It's so ------- (141.)!

If you do not wish to use Auto Pay, there is no need to do anything. ------- (142.). If you would like to give Auto Pay a try, however, simply visit any Tampa Bank branch to get it set up.

Thank you for banking with Tampa Bank.

Ken Rhys
Customer Service Manager

139. (A) to like
(B) had liked
(C) are liking
(D) would like

140. (A) Instead
(B) Therefore
(C) Regretfully
(D) Nevertheless

141. (A) close
(B) familiar
(C) memorable
(D) convenient

142. (A) Our customer service department is available 24 hours a day.
(B) Many customers save 5 percent of their monthly income.
(C) You can continue making payments manually as usual.
(D) You can receive a $50 gift certificate for recommending our bank to a friend.

TEST 2

GO ON TO THE NEXT PAGE

Questions 143-146 refer to the following e-mail.

To: Laura Moreno <lm54@spotmail.ca>
From: Jack Chen <genmanager@qualityautosspringfield.ca>
Date: 3 March
Subject: Survey

Dear Ms. Moreno,

Thank you for ------- (143.) Quality Autos of Springfield for your recent car purchase. We would greatly appreciate feedback on your experience. Please follow the link below to answer a brief survey. Responses are anonymous. To show our appreciation, ------- (144.) who complete the survey will receive an exclusive offer. After you click "submit" at the end of the survey, a ------- (145.) will appear. This may be redeemed for three oil changes for $43.99 — or just under $15.00 per oil change. ------- (146.). If you find a better price for any maintenance service elsewhere, we will match it.

Survey link: www.qualityautosspringfield.ca/survey

Best regards,

Jack Chen, General Manager

143. (A) chose
(B) choose
(C) choosing
(D) chosen

144. (A) their
(B) those
(C) theirs
(D) that

145. (A) report
(B) coupon
(C) license
(D) preview

146. (A) We have just expanded our Springfield location.
(B) The terms of your purchase agreement are attached.
(C) You can pick up your purchase at the dealership.
(D) You will not find a better deal anywhere.

PART 7

Directions: In this part you will read a selection of texts, such as magazine and newspaper articles, e-mails, and instant messages. Each text or set of texts is followed by several questions. Select the best answer for each question and mark the letter (A), (B), (C), or (D) on your answer sheet.

Questions 147-148 refer to the following e-mail.

E-mail

To: All Staff
From: Enid Barton
Date: August 18
Subject: Invitation

My fellow Grand Investment Trust employees:

It has been 25 years since our company was founded. Please join us for a luncheon to mark the occasion.

The event will take place at L'Espoir Restaurant from noon until 2:30 p.m. on Friday, November 12. Attendees will receive commemorative desk clocks as gifts.

To ensure that we have an accurate count of attendees, please respond to llewis@grandit.com to confirm your attendance.

We hope to see you there.

Enid Barton

Social Events Coordinator

147. What is the purpose of the event?
(A) To celebrate a company's anniversary
(B) To observe the retirement of a company officer
(C) To honor a founder's birthday
(D) To announce important changes in a company

148. What are employees asked to do?
(A) Bring lunch
(B) Invite a friend
(C) Send an e-mail
(D) Buy a gift

TEST 2

GO ON TO THE NEXT PAGE

Questions 149-150 refer to the following notice.

Western Regional Rail—Changes to Train Schedule

Maintenance on the train lines begins mid-July. Repairs are expected to take six weeks, so please plan for the revised schedule to remain in force through August.

Tips for Passengers

- All trains will run on reduced frequency. Please consult the schedule posted in the station and on our Web site for specific times.
- Allow an extra 20 to 45 minutes per trip, depending on the route, day of the week, and time of day.
- Adjust your commute to avoid the peak times of 7 to 9 A.M. and 5 to 7 P.M., which will be more crowded than usual.
- Space for bicycles and baby strollers aboard trains will be more limited than usual.
- Use alternate transportation when possible.

149. What is indicated about the trains?

(A) They will not run as often as usual.
(B) They will be available earlier than usual.
(C) They will not have as many stops as usual.
(D) Their routes will be different than usual.

150. What is indicated in the notice that might concern passengers?

(A) The schedule has not yet been posted.
(B) There will be less room on the trains.
(C) The Web site is temporarily down.
(D) The ticket prices will increase.

Questions 151-152 refer to the following card.

Harper's Gym

Guest Membership

One of our valued members has invited you to Harper's Gym! As our guest, enjoy a complimentary membership for one month. Bring this card to Harper's Gym and an attendant at the front desk will activate your membership.

The guest membership entitles you to unlimited use of our facilities and equipment. You can also sign up for fitness classes and personal training sessions; extra charges may apply. This guest membership program is limited to first-time visitors.

For the member: complete the information below and give the card to your invitee. You will be entered into our drawing for fitness clothing.

Guest: Maria Zoranski

Member: Rick Armstrong

151. What is indicated about the offer?

(A) It is good for one year.
(B) Guests may use only certain equipment.
(C) Some activities may cost extra.
(D) A regular member must accompany the guest.

152. What is suggested about Ms. Zoranski?

(A) She is a personal trainer.
(B) She won some fitness clothing.
(C) She is Mr. Armstrong's supervisor.
(D) She has never been to Harper's Gym before.

TEST 2

GO ON TO THE NEXT PAGE

Questions 153-155 refer to the following article.

Burwell's Garage Celebrates Half-Century Mark

(May 11)—Many things have changed on Ridgeford's Main Street in recent years, but one thing has remained constant. Burwell's Garage, still in its original location at the north end of the street, continues to see a steady stream of customers.

When Roy Burwell first started his car repair shop, he worked on very few foreign cars and had never used a computer. Mr. Burwell, whose son Dean became chief mechanic at the shop two years ago, said, "Computers changed everything. We used to just look at the engine to see what the trouble was. Now we also need a lot of expensive equipment."

The full-service garage, which celebrates its fiftieth anniversary this month, offers services including oil changes, motor overhauls, and tire replacements. The younger Mr. Burwell will add towing services to the list next month.

When asked the secret to the continued success of the business, Roy Burwell's answer is straightforward. "We charge a fair price for honest work. We can fix any kind of car out there. And all our work is guaranteed."

153. What is suggested about Roy Burwell?
- (A) He specializes in repairing imported cars.
- (B) He had to gain experience using computers.
- (C) He no longer owns Burwell's Garage.
- (D) He recently moved his business.

154. The word "trouble" in paragraph 2, line 7, is closest in meaning to
- (A) drawback
- (B) effort
- (C) amount
- (D) problem

155. What service will Burwell's Garage soon offer?
- (A) Tire replacements
- (B) Vehicle towing
- (C) Oil changes
- (D) Vehicle loans

Questions 156-157 refer to the following text-message chain.

Amihan Mendoza [1:31 p.m.]
Can you meet me for coffee this afternoon?

Gavino Andrada [1:32 p.m.]
Sure. What's up?

Amihan Mendoza [1:32 p.m.]
I want to talk with you about the Dunhume account. I just heard I'll be taking it over.

Gavino Andrada [1:33 p.m.]
Good idea. They keep changing their minds about the number of software packages they want to purchase. But this is not unusual for them. You'll need to be careful in working with them.

Amihan Mendoza [1:34 p.m.]
How about 2:30 at Cha Cha Grill?

Gavino Andrada [1:35 p.m.]
Sounds good. If you haven't already, you should ask Thomas to give you any information he has on that account. He was the lead salesperson before you, and I'm sure he can fill you in on the challenges he faced.

Amihan Mendoza [1:36 p.m.]
OK. I'll see you there.

156. In what department does Ms. Mendoza most likely work?

(A) Personnel
(B) Sales
(C) Accounting
(D) Product Design

157. At 1:35 P.M., what does Mr. Andrada most likely mean when he writes, "Sounds good"?

(A) He likes a restaurant's chef.
(B) He agrees to represent his coworker Thomas at a luncheon.
(C) He thinks a client will like a restaurant.
(D) He agrees that he and Ms. Mendoza should meet.

TEST 2

GO ON TO THE NEXT PAGE

Questions 158-160 refer to the following e-mail.

E-Mail Message

To: Lila Mendham
From: Alcott Appliances Ltd.
Date: 10 May
Subject: Contract Number 09803

Dear Ms. Mendham,

This is a follow-up to our service call of 9 May at your restaurant located at 601 Elms Lane, Wembley, to confirm that you elected to have the ice maker repaired rather than replaced. To arrange a day and time for this service, the refrigeration technician assigned to your contract will be calling you in the next 1 to 3 business days. On the day of the service, please turn the device off and clear all ice and water from it before the technician arrives.

If you have any questions about the work, please telephone Alcott Appliances at 020-7946-9430 and make reference to the contract number given above. You may also visit our Web site, alcottappliances.co.uk, at any time for information regarding our prices and services.

158. What is the purpose of the e-mail?
(A) To recommend that Ms. Mendham purchase a new appliance
(B) To provide instructions for using a new ice maker
(C) To alert Ms. Mendham that a repair will be scheduled
(D) To explain why an ice maker should be repaired

159. What will most likely happen next?
(A) Ms. Mendham will visit Alcott Appliances.
(B) Ms. Mendham will have an ice maker delivered to her restaurant.
(C) A technician will remove ice and water from a faulty ice maker.
(D) A technician will telephone Ms. Mendham.

160. According to the e-mail, why would a customer visit Alcott Appliances' Web site?
(A) To find out how much products cost
(B) To review information about a contract
(C) To select a repair technician
(D) To schedule a service visit

Questions 161-164 refer to the following letter.

Opus 27 Ltd.
3241 Tupper Avenue
Vancouver BC Canada V5K 1A6
Telephone: 778-555-0134
www.opus27.ca

July 6

Julia Demers
Serano 455
C1026ABF CABA, Argentina

Dear Ms. Demers,

Thank you for booking a trip with Opus 27, the finest tour boat company in the North Island region. You will be traveling aboard the *Salty Mist*, our newest and most modern ship. Your reservation is for two adults and one child on a sight-seeing cruise leaving from Port McNeill, traveling to Sointula and Alert Bay, and returning to Port McNeill. Departure is on August 4 at 10 A.M. The duration of the trip is ten hours, including shore time at each destination.

Opus 27 has been in business for over twenty years, and we pride ourselves on creating an excellent passenger experience. The *Salty Mist* features comfortable seating, an outdoor deck, and a variety of dining options.

Please arrive at the Port McNeill terminal one hour before your departure time, and make sure you have identification for each passenger. Do not hesitate to contact me with any questions or concerns.

Sincerely,

Felix Li

Felix Li, Booking Agent
felix.li@opus27.ca

161. Why did Mr. Li send the letter?
(A) To request payment of a bill
(B) To confirm travel arrangements
(C) To ask for additional identification
(D) To describe sight-seeing attractions

162. What is suggested about Opus 27?
(A) It operates more than one ship.
(B) It recently changed management.
(C) It is the most popular way to visit the region.
(D) It is an inexpensive travel option.

163. How many seats have been reserved?
(A) One
(B) Two
(C) Three
(D) Four

164. What time should Ms. Demers arrive at the departure terminal?
(A) At 9:00 A.M.
(B) At 10:00 A.M.
(C) At 1:00 P.M.
(D) At 2:00 P.M.

TEST 2

GO ON TO THE NEXT PAGE

Questions 165-167 refer to the following article.

SACRAMENTO (August 1)—After receiving unwelcome attention in the press for its low levels of employee satisfaction, technology giant Sundale Systems is making changes. — [1] —. The company has hired Angela Lyons as its new chief culture officer, a position designed to address both human resources functions and employee morale.

Ms. Lyons is a renowned workplace wellness expert. — [2] —. As Hundrigen Health's Human Resources director, she reduced employee turnover by over 25 percent in just under three years. — [3] —.

"I look forward to addressing Sundale's challenges," said Ms. Lyons. "My team and I will do our best to meet staff expectations as quickly as possible."

Ms. Lyons has a stellar reputation in management circles. She authors the popular blog *Satisfy Your Staff* and teaches classes in human resource management at Sutter University. — [4] —.

165. What is the purpose of the article?

(A) To announce a corporate merger
(B) To report on a hiring decision
(C) To explain the origins of a company
(D) To advertise an upcoming event

166. What is indicated about Ms. Lyons?

(A) She is a university instructor.
(B) She is skilled at software programming.
(C) She has written several books.
(D) She runs her own business.

167. In which of the positions marked [1], [2], [3], and [4] does the following sentence best belong?

"She plans on doing the same thing at Sundale Systems."

(A) [1]
(B) [2]
(C) [3]
(D) [4]

Questions 168-171 refer to the following e-mail.

To:	rsetlur@okboxmail.com.au
From:	emontowski@montowskiandassociates.com.au
Date:	23 August
Subject:	Estimate

Dear Ms. Setlur,

Thank you for allowing me to examine the building you own in Perth. — [1] — . I would be happy to undertake the rehabilitation project. You were correct to assume that it will require extensive restoration work. — [2] —. Below is an approximate breakdown of costs, including all the major components of the work. — [3] —.

• Restoring the wood flooring, $3,000 to $5,000 (Labour cost depends on whether you would prefer laminate or wood flooring. Wood flooring would need to be polished and painted.)

• Replacing the plaster on the ceiling, $800

• Repainting the walls, $1,200

• Recreating the fireplace, $2,900 (Based on the photographs you provided, we could build it exactly to size in the spot where it was originally located.)

If you have any questions or prefer to talk over the phone, please call my office at (08) 5550 0177. Also, it is in your best interest to schedule as soon as possible. — [4] —. I look forward to hearing from you.

Sincerely,

Edward Montowski
Montowski & Associates

168. Why did Mr. Montowski write the e-mail?

(A) To schedule an inspection
(B) To inquire about the size of a project
(C) To offer renovation services
(D) To explain how payment should be made

169. According to the e-mail, what information will Ms. Setlur have to provide?

(A) Where the plaster should be replaced
(B) What flooring material she prefers
(C) What color she wants the walls painted
(D) Where she wants photographs to be taken

170. What is indicated about the fireplace?

(A) It is ready for use.
(B) It has been removed.
(C) It needs to be repainted.
(D) It will be expensive to maintain.

171. In which of the positions marked [1], [2], [3], and [4] does the following sentence best belong?

"My team is booked for the next four weeks, and we expect more requests soon."

(A) [1]
(B) [2]
(C) [3]
(D) [4]

TEST 2

GO ON TO THE NEXT PAGE

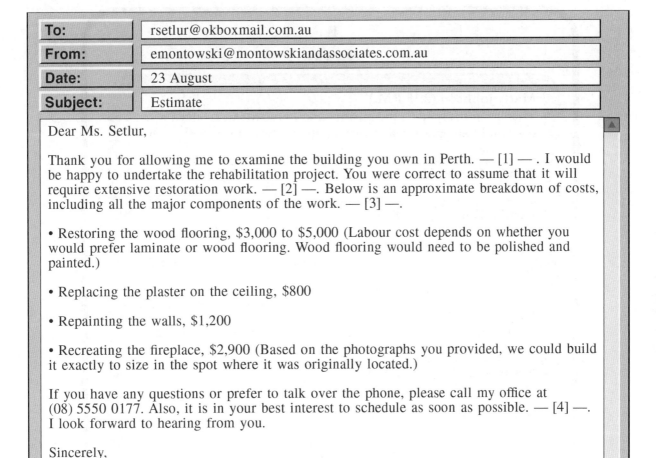

Questions 172-175 refer to the following text-message chain.

Marty Johnson (2:15 P.M.)
Thank you for sending the information to me today. I looked it over, and I am interested in viewing the property on Forest Avenue tomorrow.

Kendra Gomez (2:17 P.M.)
I could arrange a tour for tomorrow at 10 A.M. Would that work?

Kendra Gomez (2:18 P.M.)
Also, my colleague just mentioned that two other potential buyers are looking at it today.

Marty Johnson (2:18 P.M.)
I am available after 11:30 A.M. tomorrow or any time on Wednesday.

Kendra Gomez (2:20 P.M.)
Tomorrow at 11:30 is fine. Unless you would like to see it today, considering the interest it is generating.

Marty Johnson (2:22 P.M.)
Have you had any offers yet?

Kendra Gomez (2:24 P.M.)
Not yet.

Marty Johnson (2:25 P.M.)
OK. Then I'll be there tomorrow at 11:30 A.M.

172. Why did Mr. Johnson write to Ms. Gomez?

(A) To schedule an appointment
(B) To place an advertisement
(C) To arrange a sales call
(D) To make an offer

173. What most likely is Ms. Gomez' job?

(A) Interior designer
(B) Residential architect
(C) Building inspector
(D) Real estate agent

174. What does Ms. Gomez suggest about the property?

(A) It is not very old.
(B) It may sell quickly.
(C) It is in a good location.
(D) It is not well-known.

175. At 2:17 P.M., what does Ms. Gomez most likely mean when she writes, "Would that work"?

(A) She doubts that a plan will be successful.
(B) She is confirming the details of an assignment.
(C) She wants to know whether a time is convenient.
(D) She is unsure that there is enough time for a tour.

TEST 2

GO ON TO THE NEXT PAGE

Questions 176-180 refer to the following e-mail and Web page.

To:	Martine Depas <mdepas@imail.com>
From:	Anita Eckert <aeckert@fenogliotimes.com>
Date:	June 27
Subject:	Reader Campaign

Dear Ms. Depas:

Thank you for being a loyal reader of *Fenoglio Times.* As one of the few remaining news outlets that does not require a subscription fee for access to our content, we proudly provide news that is accessible to all.

To support our valuable investigative journalism, we have depended almost entirely on a single revenue source, the sale of advertising. However, we have added three new features over the past year in response to reader feedback, and our primary source of revenue is no longer enough. It takes a lot of money to conduct interviews, compile reports, and produce well-researched stories that interest our readers around the globe.

Please consider making a contribution before our fiscal year ends on June 30. A contribution of $250 or more will put your name on our Silver Sponsors list, which will appear prominently on our Web site. But even a gift of $25 would go a long way toward meeting our goal of $10,000. If every reader pitches in, we can ensure the continued high-quality content that you have come to expect from us over the past decade.

Starting in January, watch for our special weekly news summaries geared toward school-age children.

Sincerely,

Anita Eckert, Managing Editor

Donor Name: Martine Depas

Donation Amount: $300

Comments:

After receiving an e-mail from the managing editor of *Fenoglio Times* yesterday, I went online first thing this morning to make my donation. *Fenoglio Times* produces some of the best journalism out there. Your articles are lengthy and thorough—I can tell how much effort has gone into each story. This news source is worth supporting.

176. What is indicated in the e-mail about *Fenoglio Times*?

(A) It specializes in financial journalism.
(B) It has been in operation for 20 years.
(C) It does not charge a fee to its readers.
(D) It has increased its readership by 30 percent.

177. Why does Ms. Eckert mention advertising?

(A) To identify a source of funding
(B) To attract new businesses
(C) To announce the launch of a marketing campaign
(D) To urge readers to buy promoted products

178. According to the e-mail, what does *Fenoglio Times* plan to do in the future?

(A) Conduct more interviews
(B) Attract younger readers
(C) Expand its reporting staff
(D) Merge with another publication

179. When did Ms. Depas post her comment?

(A) On June 27
(B) On June 28
(C) On June 29
(D) On June 30

180. What can Ms. Depas expect to receive from *Fenoglio Times*?

(A) A gift in the mail
(B) A tour of the newsroom
(C) Access to the archives
(D) Public recognition

TEST 2

GO ON TO THE NEXT PAGE

Questions 181-185 refer to the following information and e-mail.

http://www.wheelsaway.com

Thank you! Your payment has been successfully processed, and your booking at www.wheelsaway.com is now complete. Your confirmation number is #SEA52411.

Notes about this reservation: The reservation holder is the only authorized driver on this reservation. You may authorize a second driver with one of our representatives at no cost when you pick up your vehicle. Your reservation is for our Seattle-Tacoma branch, conveniently located at 17203 Pacific Highway, just minutes from the airport. Our complimentary airport shuttle stops at each terminal.

Changes and cancellations: If you need to make a change to your vehicle type, reservation date, or pickup or drop-off location, please fill out a change request form at www.wheelsaway.com/changes. A $20 change fee will be assessed for changes requested less than 24 hours in advance. If you reduce the length of your reservation or change to a lower-cost vehicle, you will be refunded the difference immediately upon returning the vehicle. If you need to cancel your reservation, you must do so at least 48 hours in advance, or you will incur a $30 cancellation fee.

To:	Jun Hong <junhong@tomail.com>
From:	Madison Hurley <customercare@wheelsaway.com>
Subject:	Reservation change for booking #SEA52411
Date:	May 12

Dear Mr. Hong,

We have received and processed your reservation change request. The details are as follows:

Booking change request:
Product: 1 midsize sedan — **Dates:** May 16–May 19
Pickup location: 17203 Pacific Hwy, SeaTac — **Drop-off location:** 17203 Pacific Hwy, SeaTac

If you owe an additional fee because of this change, we will charge your credit card within the next 24 hours.

The details of your original booking are below for your records.

Original booking:
Product: 1 midsize sedan — **Dates:** May 16–May 20
Pickup location: 17203 Pacific Hwy, SeaTac — **Drop-off location**: 17203 Pacific Hwy, SeaTac

Please do not hesitate to contact us if you have any questions.

181. What type of business is Wheelsaway.com?

(A) A hotel
(B) An airline
(C) A holiday resort
(D) A car-rental company

182. According to the information, how can a customer add a person to a reservation?

(A) By visiting a Web site
(B) By paying an administrative fee
(C) By speaking with a representative
(D) By e-mailing a change request form

183. In the information, the word "assessed" in paragraph 3, line 3, is closest in meaning to

(A) graded
(B) charged
(C) evaluated
(D) discounted

184. What did Mr. Hong ask to have changed?

(A) The address of his destination
(B) The length of his reservation
(C) His payment method
(D) His arrival date

185. When will Mr. Hong probably receive his refund?

(A) On May 12
(B) On May 16
(C) On May 19
(D) On May 20

GO ON TO THE NEXT PAGE

Questions 186-190 refer to the following Web page, order form, and e-mail.

www.faonebakery.com/wholesale

Desserts to Delight

Faone Bakery's wholesale division creates delicious cakes, pies, cookies, and specialty products that are sure to leave your customers smiling and coming back for more. Our bakery in Baltimore allows us to service the greater mid-Atlantic region of the United States and we hope to expand nationwide soon. (Check back in March of next year!)

In order to set up a wholesale account with us, create a username and password. Once your registration is confirmed (within two days of your initial account sign-up), simply log in to the Web-based ordering system and begin making your selections!

http://www.faonebakery.com/cust_howsercoff231

Faone Bakery Online Wholesale Order Form

Wholesale order number: AS2145768 **Contact person:** Mr. George Howser

Business name: Howser Coffees and Cakes

Delivery: Tuesdays or Fridays between 8 A.M. and 1 P.M.

Order date: Monday, June 13 **Desired delivery date:** Friday, June 17

ITEM	QUANTITY	PRICE PER UNIT	TOTAL
Chocolate Dream Cake	5	$18	$90
Apple Crumb Cake	4	$15	$60
Lemon Pie	6	$12	$72
		Subtotal	$222
		Delivery Charge	$11
			$233

For questions or changes to your order after it is placed, please contact *mreynolds@faonebakery.com*.

To:	mreynolds@faonebakery.com
From:	management@howsercoffee.com
Date:	Tuesday, June 14
Re:	Re: Order

Dear Ms. Reynolds,

We have been very pleased with our customers' responses to your desserts and are considering increasing our selections. We are interested in offering the carrot cake but are concerned about how long it will stay moist. We would like to test it out—would you be able to send a couple of slices with Friday's delivery?

We would also like to add an additional pie to our June 13 order to accommodate a special request from one of our customers.

Thanks for your help.

George Howser, Owner
Howser Coffees and Cakes

186. Where does Faone Bakery deliver?

(A) Within the mid-Atlantic region only
(B) Within Baltimore only
(C) Throughout the United States
(D) Throughout various countries

187. What is indicated about Faone Bakery?

(A) It has opened another retail store.
(B) It offers a full breakfast menu.
(C) It opened in March.
(D) It is planning to grow.

188. What did Mr. Howser most likely do before June 13?

(A) He created an online account.
(B) He added sandwiches to his menu.
(C) He visited Faone Bakery to taste a product.
(D) He sent a promotional link to customers.

189. What is one reason why Mr. Howser sent the e-mail?

(A) To cancel a delivery
(B) To complain about a cake
(C) To invite Ms. Reynolds to his business
(D) To request samples from Faone Bakery

190. How many pies will Mr. Howser most likely receive on June 17?

(A) Five
(B) Six
(C) Seven
(D) Nine

GO ON TO THE NEXT PAGE

Questions 191-195 refer to the following e-mail, job summaries, and Web page.

To:	Regional managers
From:	Mie Ichikawa <m.ichikawa@kiraku.co.jp>
Subject:	Western Canada
Date:	July 10

Regional Managers,

As you know, Kiraku is planning an expansion to Western Canada. A top priority this quarter is to fill several staff positions in this region, including a new midlevel position being created to strengthen communication with sales teams. Please send an e-mail to Maya Janit, our National Director (Canada), if you are interested in being on the hiring team for this expansion.

Warm regards,
Mie Ichikawa

Kiraku Japanese Furniture

Western Canada Region—Available Positions

Regional Manager (Winnipeg; reports to the National Director)

- researches and recruits new corporate clients and retailers; maintains client relationships
- coordinates with the logistics team to make sure merchandise is available
- travels regularly to all locations within the region

District Supervisor (Saskatoon and Vancouver; reports to the Regional Manager)

- assists Regional Manager in maintaining client relationships
- attends conferences and trade shows to stay up-to-date on industry trends
- builds and maintains ongoing communication with sales teams

Sales Associate (Calgary, Saskatoon, Vancouver, and Winnipeg; reports to the District Supervisor)

- delivers presentations to clients
- attends conferences and trade shows to maintain design skills
- works evenings and weekends as necessary
- must have background in interior design

Delivery Associate (Calgary, Saskatoon, Vancouver, and Winnipeg; reports to the District Supervisor)

- provides customer service
- must have commercial driver's license and be able to carry 25 kilograms

http://www.kiraku.co.jp/aboutus

Home	Products	Contact	**About Us**

Xiang Chen

Western Canada Region

Mr. Chen is responsible for recruiting businesses and retail stores in Western Canada. He helps ensure merchandise availability. Mr. Chen, who has a degree in business management, worked in textile sales with major Canadian clients before joining the Kiraku team. He has worked extensively with top Canadian designers and has previous experience in southeastern China.

191. What is the purpose of the e-mail?

(A) To report on quarterly sales
(B) To share regional data
(C) To thank salespeople
(D) To provide plans for staffing

192. What position was recently created?

(A) Regional manager
(B) District supervisor
(C) Sales associate
(D) Delivery associate

193. What is required of a Kiraku sales associate?

(A) Providing training in interior design
(B) Working outside of regular business hours
(C) Organizing trade shows
(D) Delivering furniture to client work sites

194. In what city is Mr. Chen most likely based?

(A) Calgary
(B) Saskatoon
(C) Vancouver
(D) Winnipeg

195. According to the Web page, what is true about Mr. Chen?

(A) He studied business.
(B) He designs furniture.
(C) He owns textile companies in China.
(D) He works in human resources.

GO ON TO THE NEXT PAGE

Questions 196-200 refer to the following Web site, form, and e-mail.

https://www.humstellhotel.com

About | Rooms | Dining | **Meeting Spaces** | Contact

Humstell Hotel is a great place to host events, conferences, or meetings. Spaces can be arranged in rows of individual chairs or with tables seating groups of 4 to 8 persons. Please refer to the chart below for pricing and room capacities.

Room Specifications

Room	Price per day	Capacity (If seated in rows)	Capacity (If seated in groups)
Blue Room	$800	200 persons	160 persons
Green Room	$650	100 persons	72 persons
Yellow Room	$500	50 persons	32 persons
Purple Room	$350	25 persons	16 persons

All rooms with the exception of the Purple Room are equipped with audio capabilities and a computer. Additional equipment is available on-site at the prices listed below.

Equipment Rental Costs (NOT included in room prices):
Microphone: $25 Screen: $45
LCD Projector: $100 Projector and screen package: $130

To reserve equipment or a meeting space at Humstell Hotel, fill out our Event Space Request Form at https://www.humstellhotel.com/event.

Humstell Hotel–Event Space Request Form

A member of our staff will contact you within 24 business hours to confirm availability.

Name:	Samuel Ma
Job title:	Manager
Phone:	541-555-0157
Email:	samma@corgetinsurance.com
Company name:	Corget Insurance
Event type:	Meetings
Event date(s):	September 19
Equipment needed:	1 LCD Projector and screen
Room(s) requested:	Purple Room, Green Room
Set-up request:	Rows

Please note that we offer on-site catering. If you are interested in offering meal or beverage services for your event, please contact our Kitchen Manager, Cooper Blackley, directly at cblackley@humstellhotel.com.

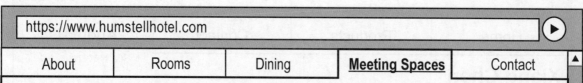

E-mail

To:	Carissa Stanley
From:	Samuel Ma
Subject:	Change of rooms
Date:	June 12

Hello, Ms. Stanley:

I submitted an Event Space Request Form yesterday, but I am hoping to make a change. We will be running a number of small meetings and presentations in our two rooms throughout the day, but we now expect over 120 employees to attend our all-staff meeting. So while the Purple Room should be suitable for the small meetings, I don't think the Green Room will be adequate. Could you please let me know if the larger room is still available for September 19?

I apologize for the confusion and thank you in advance for your help.

Samuel Ma, Corget Insurance

TEST 2

196. What is indicated about the meeting rooms?

(A) All are on the same hotel floor.
(B) All can seat more than 50 people.
(C) All can be set up for groups.
(D) All are equipped with a computer.

197. How much will Mr. Ma pay for equipment?

(A) $25
(B) $45
(C) $100
(D) $130

198. According to the form, why should a customer contact Mr. Blackley?

(A) To change a booking
(B) To make a payment
(C) To order food for an event
(D) To schedule an equipment pickup

199. Who most likely is Ms. Stanley?

(A) A presenter
(B) A friend of Mr. Ma
(C) A Humstell Hotel employee
(D) A manager at Corget Insurance

200. Where will Corget Insurance most likely hold its all-staff meeting?

(A) In the Blue Room
(B) In the Green Room
(C) In the Yellow Room
(D) In the Purple Room

Stop! This is the end of the test. If you finish before time is called, you may go back to Parts 5, 6, and 7 and check your work.

公式 TOEIC® Listening & Reading 問題集 6（音声 CD 2 枚付）

2020 年 2 月 25 日　第 1 版 第 1 刷発行
2024 年 2 月　5 日　第 1 版 第 6 刷発行

著者　Educational Testing Service

発行元　一般財団法人 国際ビジネスコミュニケーション協会
〒 100-0014
東京都千代田区永田町 2-14-2
山王グランドビル
電話 (03) 5521-5935

印刷　TOPPAN株式会社

Printed in Japan
ISBN 978-4-906033-58-4

TEST 1

解答用紙

REGISTRATION No. 受験番号								

フリガナ	
NAME 氏名	

LISTENING SECTION

Part 1		Part 2						Part 3						Part 4					
No.	ANSWER A B C D	No.	ANSWER A B C	No.	ANSWER A B C	No.	ANSWER A B C D	No.	ANSWER A B C D	No.	ANSWER A B C D	No.	ANSWER A B C D	No.	ANSWER A B C D	No.	ANSWER A B C D	No.	ANSWER A B C D
1	Ⓐ Ⓑ Ⓒ Ⓓ	11	Ⓐ Ⓑ Ⓒ	21	Ⓐ Ⓑ Ⓒ	31	Ⓐ Ⓑ Ⓒ	41	Ⓐ Ⓑ Ⓒ Ⓓ	51	Ⓐ Ⓑ Ⓒ Ⓓ	61	Ⓐ Ⓑ Ⓒ Ⓓ	71	Ⓐ Ⓑ Ⓒ Ⓓ	81	Ⓐ Ⓑ Ⓒ Ⓓ	91	Ⓐ Ⓑ Ⓒ Ⓓ
2	Ⓐ Ⓑ Ⓒ Ⓓ	12	Ⓐ Ⓑ Ⓒ	22	Ⓐ Ⓑ Ⓒ	32	Ⓐ Ⓑ Ⓒ Ⓓ	42	Ⓐ Ⓑ Ⓒ Ⓓ	52	Ⓐ Ⓑ Ⓒ Ⓓ	62	Ⓐ Ⓑ Ⓒ Ⓓ	72	Ⓐ Ⓑ Ⓒ Ⓓ	82	Ⓐ Ⓑ Ⓒ Ⓓ	92	Ⓐ Ⓑ Ⓒ Ⓓ
3	Ⓐ Ⓑ Ⓒ Ⓓ	13	Ⓐ Ⓑ Ⓒ	23	Ⓐ Ⓑ Ⓒ	33	Ⓐ Ⓑ Ⓒ Ⓓ	43	Ⓐ Ⓑ Ⓒ Ⓓ	53	Ⓐ Ⓑ Ⓒ Ⓓ	63	Ⓐ Ⓑ Ⓒ Ⓓ	73	Ⓐ Ⓑ Ⓒ Ⓓ	83	Ⓐ Ⓑ Ⓒ Ⓓ	93	Ⓐ Ⓑ Ⓒ Ⓓ
4	Ⓐ Ⓑ Ⓒ Ⓓ	14	Ⓐ Ⓑ Ⓒ	24	Ⓐ Ⓑ Ⓒ	34	Ⓐ Ⓑ Ⓒ Ⓓ	44	Ⓐ Ⓑ Ⓒ Ⓓ	54	Ⓐ Ⓑ Ⓒ Ⓓ	64	Ⓐ Ⓑ Ⓒ Ⓓ	74	Ⓐ Ⓑ Ⓒ Ⓓ	84	Ⓐ Ⓑ Ⓒ Ⓓ	94	Ⓐ Ⓑ Ⓒ Ⓓ
5	Ⓐ Ⓑ Ⓒ Ⓓ	15	Ⓐ Ⓑ Ⓒ	25	Ⓐ Ⓑ Ⓒ	35	Ⓐ Ⓑ Ⓒ Ⓓ	45	Ⓐ Ⓑ Ⓒ Ⓓ	55	Ⓐ Ⓑ Ⓒ Ⓓ	65	Ⓐ Ⓑ Ⓒ Ⓓ	75	Ⓐ Ⓑ Ⓒ Ⓓ	85	Ⓐ Ⓑ Ⓒ Ⓓ	95	Ⓐ Ⓑ Ⓒ Ⓓ
6	Ⓐ Ⓑ Ⓒ Ⓓ	16	Ⓐ Ⓑ Ⓒ	26	Ⓐ Ⓑ Ⓒ	36	Ⓐ Ⓑ Ⓒ Ⓓ	46	Ⓐ Ⓑ Ⓒ Ⓓ	56	Ⓐ Ⓑ Ⓒ Ⓓ	66	Ⓐ Ⓑ Ⓒ Ⓓ	76	Ⓐ Ⓑ Ⓒ Ⓓ	86	Ⓐ Ⓑ Ⓒ Ⓓ	96	Ⓐ Ⓑ Ⓒ Ⓓ
7	Ⓐ Ⓑ Ⓒ	17	Ⓐ Ⓑ Ⓒ	27	Ⓐ Ⓑ Ⓒ	37	Ⓐ Ⓑ Ⓒ Ⓓ	47	Ⓐ Ⓑ Ⓒ Ⓓ	57	Ⓐ Ⓑ Ⓒ Ⓓ	67	Ⓐ Ⓑ Ⓒ Ⓓ	77	Ⓐ Ⓑ Ⓒ Ⓓ	87	Ⓐ Ⓑ Ⓒ Ⓓ	97	Ⓐ Ⓑ Ⓒ Ⓓ
8	Ⓐ Ⓑ Ⓒ	18	Ⓐ Ⓑ Ⓒ	28	Ⓐ Ⓑ Ⓒ	38	Ⓐ Ⓑ Ⓒ Ⓓ	48	Ⓐ Ⓑ Ⓒ Ⓓ	58	Ⓐ Ⓑ Ⓒ Ⓓ	68	Ⓐ Ⓑ Ⓒ Ⓓ	78	Ⓐ Ⓑ Ⓒ Ⓓ	88	Ⓐ Ⓑ Ⓒ Ⓓ	98	Ⓐ Ⓑ Ⓒ Ⓓ
9	Ⓐ Ⓑ Ⓒ	19	Ⓐ Ⓑ Ⓒ	29	Ⓐ Ⓑ Ⓒ	39	Ⓐ Ⓑ Ⓒ Ⓓ	49	Ⓐ Ⓑ Ⓒ Ⓓ	59	Ⓐ Ⓑ Ⓒ Ⓓ	69	Ⓐ Ⓑ Ⓒ Ⓓ	79	Ⓐ Ⓑ Ⓒ Ⓓ	89	Ⓐ Ⓑ Ⓒ Ⓓ	99	Ⓐ Ⓑ Ⓒ Ⓓ
10	Ⓐ Ⓑ Ⓒ	20	Ⓐ Ⓑ Ⓒ	30	Ⓐ Ⓑ Ⓒ	40	Ⓐ Ⓑ Ⓒ Ⓓ	50	Ⓐ Ⓑ Ⓒ Ⓓ	60	Ⓐ Ⓑ Ⓒ Ⓓ	70	Ⓐ Ⓑ Ⓒ Ⓓ	80	Ⓐ Ⓑ Ⓒ Ⓓ	90	Ⓐ Ⓑ Ⓒ Ⓓ	100	Ⓐ Ⓑ Ⓒ Ⓓ

READING SECTION

Part 5						Part 6				Part 7									
No.	ANSWER A B C D	No.	ANSWER A B C D	No.	ANSWER A B C D	No.	ANSWER A B C D	No.	ANSWER A B C D	No.	ANSWER A B C D	No.	ANSWER A B C D	No.	ANSWER A B C D	No.	ANSWER A B C D	No.	ANSWER A B C D
101	Ⓐ Ⓑ Ⓒ Ⓓ	111	Ⓐ Ⓑ Ⓒ Ⓓ	121	Ⓐ Ⓑ Ⓒ Ⓓ	131	Ⓐ Ⓑ Ⓒ Ⓓ	141	Ⓐ Ⓑ Ⓒ Ⓓ	151	Ⓐ Ⓑ Ⓒ Ⓓ	161	Ⓐ Ⓑ Ⓒ Ⓓ	171	Ⓐ Ⓑ Ⓒ Ⓓ	181	Ⓐ Ⓑ Ⓒ Ⓓ	191	Ⓐ Ⓑ Ⓒ Ⓓ
102	Ⓐ Ⓑ Ⓒ Ⓓ	112	Ⓐ Ⓑ Ⓒ Ⓓ	122	Ⓐ Ⓑ Ⓒ Ⓓ	132	Ⓐ Ⓑ Ⓒ Ⓓ	142	Ⓐ Ⓑ Ⓒ Ⓓ	152	Ⓐ Ⓑ Ⓒ Ⓓ	162	Ⓐ Ⓑ Ⓒ Ⓓ	172	Ⓐ Ⓑ Ⓒ Ⓓ	182	Ⓐ Ⓑ Ⓒ Ⓓ	192	Ⓐ Ⓑ Ⓒ Ⓓ
103	Ⓐ Ⓑ Ⓒ Ⓓ	113	Ⓐ Ⓑ Ⓒ Ⓓ	123	Ⓐ Ⓑ Ⓒ Ⓓ	133	Ⓐ Ⓑ Ⓒ Ⓓ	143	Ⓐ Ⓑ Ⓒ Ⓓ	153	Ⓐ Ⓑ Ⓒ Ⓓ	163	Ⓐ Ⓑ Ⓒ Ⓓ	173	Ⓐ Ⓑ Ⓒ Ⓓ	183	Ⓐ Ⓑ Ⓒ Ⓓ	193	Ⓐ Ⓑ Ⓒ Ⓓ
104	Ⓐ Ⓑ Ⓒ Ⓓ	114	Ⓐ Ⓑ Ⓒ Ⓓ	124	Ⓐ Ⓑ Ⓒ Ⓓ	134	Ⓐ Ⓑ Ⓒ Ⓓ	144	Ⓐ Ⓑ Ⓒ Ⓓ	154	Ⓐ Ⓑ Ⓒ Ⓓ	164	Ⓐ Ⓑ Ⓒ Ⓓ	174	Ⓐ Ⓑ Ⓒ Ⓓ	184	Ⓐ Ⓑ Ⓒ Ⓓ	194	Ⓐ Ⓑ Ⓒ Ⓓ
105	Ⓐ Ⓑ Ⓒ Ⓓ	115	Ⓐ Ⓑ Ⓒ Ⓓ	125	Ⓐ Ⓑ Ⓒ Ⓓ	135	Ⓐ Ⓑ Ⓒ Ⓓ	145	Ⓐ Ⓑ Ⓒ Ⓓ	155	Ⓐ Ⓑ Ⓒ Ⓓ	165	Ⓐ Ⓑ Ⓒ Ⓓ	175	Ⓐ Ⓑ Ⓒ Ⓓ	185	Ⓐ Ⓑ Ⓒ Ⓓ	195	Ⓐ Ⓑ Ⓒ Ⓓ
106	Ⓐ Ⓑ Ⓒ Ⓓ	116	Ⓐ Ⓑ Ⓒ Ⓓ	126	Ⓐ Ⓑ Ⓒ Ⓓ	136	Ⓐ Ⓑ Ⓒ Ⓓ	146	Ⓐ Ⓑ Ⓒ Ⓓ	156	Ⓐ Ⓑ Ⓒ Ⓓ	166	Ⓐ Ⓑ Ⓒ Ⓓ	176	Ⓐ Ⓑ Ⓒ Ⓓ	186	Ⓐ Ⓑ Ⓒ Ⓓ	196	Ⓐ Ⓑ Ⓒ Ⓓ
107	Ⓐ Ⓑ Ⓒ Ⓓ	117	Ⓐ Ⓑ Ⓒ Ⓓ	127	Ⓐ Ⓑ Ⓒ Ⓓ	137	Ⓐ Ⓑ Ⓒ Ⓓ	147	Ⓐ Ⓑ Ⓒ Ⓓ	157	Ⓐ Ⓑ Ⓒ Ⓓ	167	Ⓐ Ⓑ Ⓒ Ⓓ	177	Ⓐ Ⓑ Ⓒ Ⓓ	187	Ⓐ Ⓑ Ⓒ Ⓓ	197	Ⓐ Ⓑ Ⓒ Ⓓ
108	Ⓐ Ⓑ Ⓒ Ⓓ	118	Ⓐ Ⓑ Ⓒ Ⓓ	128	Ⓐ Ⓑ Ⓒ Ⓓ	138	Ⓐ Ⓑ Ⓒ Ⓓ	148	Ⓐ Ⓑ Ⓒ Ⓓ	158	Ⓐ Ⓑ Ⓒ Ⓓ	168	Ⓐ Ⓑ Ⓒ Ⓓ	178	Ⓐ Ⓑ Ⓒ Ⓓ	188	Ⓐ Ⓑ Ⓒ Ⓓ	198	Ⓐ Ⓑ Ⓒ Ⓓ
109	Ⓐ Ⓑ Ⓒ Ⓓ	119	Ⓐ Ⓑ Ⓒ Ⓓ	129	Ⓐ Ⓑ Ⓒ Ⓓ	139	Ⓐ Ⓑ Ⓒ Ⓓ	149	Ⓐ Ⓑ Ⓒ Ⓓ	159	Ⓐ Ⓑ Ⓒ Ⓓ	169	Ⓐ Ⓑ Ⓒ Ⓓ	179	Ⓐ Ⓑ Ⓒ Ⓓ	189	Ⓐ Ⓑ Ⓒ Ⓓ	199	Ⓐ Ⓑ Ⓒ Ⓓ
110	Ⓐ Ⓑ Ⓒ Ⓓ	120	Ⓐ Ⓑ Ⓒ Ⓓ	130	Ⓐ Ⓑ Ⓒ Ⓓ	140	Ⓐ Ⓑ Ⓒ Ⓓ	150	Ⓐ Ⓑ Ⓒ Ⓓ	160	Ⓐ Ⓑ Ⓒ Ⓓ	170	Ⓐ Ⓑ Ⓒ Ⓓ	180	Ⓐ Ⓑ Ⓒ Ⓓ	190	Ⓐ Ⓑ Ⓒ Ⓓ	200	Ⓐ Ⓑ Ⓒ Ⓓ

TEST 2

解答用紙

REGISTRATION No. 受験番号								

フリガナ	
NAME 氏名	

LISTENING SECTION

Part 1		Part 2						Part 3						Part 4					
No.	ANSWER A B C D	No.	ANSWER A B C	No.	ANSWER A B C	No.	ANSWER A B C D	No.	ANSWER A B C D	No.	ANSWER A B C D	No.	ANSWER A B C D	No.	ANSWER A B C D	No.	ANSWER A B C D	No.	ANSWER A B C D
1	Ⓐ Ⓑ Ⓒ Ⓓ	11	Ⓐ Ⓑ Ⓒ	21	Ⓐ Ⓑ Ⓒ	31	Ⓐ Ⓑ Ⓒ	41	Ⓐ Ⓑ Ⓒ Ⓓ	51	Ⓐ Ⓑ Ⓒ Ⓓ	61	Ⓐ Ⓑ Ⓒ Ⓓ	71	Ⓐ Ⓑ Ⓒ Ⓓ	81	Ⓐ Ⓑ Ⓒ Ⓓ	91	Ⓐ Ⓑ Ⓒ Ⓓ
2	Ⓐ Ⓑ Ⓒ Ⓓ	12	Ⓐ Ⓑ Ⓒ	22	Ⓐ Ⓑ Ⓒ	32	Ⓐ Ⓑ Ⓒ Ⓓ	42	Ⓐ Ⓑ Ⓒ Ⓓ	52	Ⓐ Ⓑ Ⓒ Ⓓ	62	Ⓐ Ⓑ Ⓒ Ⓓ	72	Ⓐ Ⓑ Ⓒ Ⓓ	82	Ⓐ Ⓑ Ⓒ Ⓓ	92	Ⓐ Ⓑ Ⓒ Ⓓ
3	Ⓐ Ⓑ Ⓒ Ⓓ	13	Ⓐ Ⓑ Ⓒ	23	Ⓐ Ⓑ Ⓒ	33	Ⓐ Ⓑ Ⓒ Ⓓ	43	Ⓐ Ⓑ Ⓒ Ⓓ	53	Ⓐ Ⓑ Ⓒ Ⓓ	63	Ⓐ Ⓑ Ⓒ Ⓓ	73	Ⓐ Ⓑ Ⓒ Ⓓ	83	Ⓐ Ⓑ Ⓒ Ⓓ	93	Ⓐ Ⓑ Ⓒ Ⓓ
4	Ⓐ Ⓑ Ⓒ Ⓓ	14	Ⓐ Ⓑ Ⓒ	24	Ⓐ Ⓑ Ⓒ	34	Ⓐ Ⓑ Ⓒ Ⓓ	44	Ⓐ Ⓑ Ⓒ Ⓓ	54	Ⓐ Ⓑ Ⓒ Ⓓ	64	Ⓐ Ⓑ Ⓒ Ⓓ	74	Ⓐ Ⓑ Ⓒ Ⓓ	84	Ⓐ Ⓑ Ⓒ Ⓓ	94	Ⓐ Ⓑ Ⓒ Ⓓ
5	Ⓐ Ⓑ Ⓒ Ⓓ	15	Ⓐ Ⓑ Ⓒ	25	Ⓐ Ⓑ Ⓒ	35	Ⓐ Ⓑ Ⓒ Ⓓ	45	Ⓐ Ⓑ Ⓒ Ⓓ	55	Ⓐ Ⓑ Ⓒ Ⓓ	65	Ⓐ Ⓑ Ⓒ Ⓓ	75	Ⓐ Ⓑ Ⓒ Ⓓ	85	Ⓐ Ⓑ Ⓒ Ⓓ	95	Ⓐ Ⓑ Ⓒ Ⓓ
6	Ⓐ Ⓑ Ⓒ Ⓓ	16	Ⓐ Ⓑ Ⓒ	26	Ⓐ Ⓑ Ⓒ	36	Ⓐ Ⓑ Ⓒ Ⓓ	46	Ⓐ Ⓑ Ⓒ Ⓓ	56	Ⓐ Ⓑ Ⓒ Ⓓ	66	Ⓐ Ⓑ Ⓒ Ⓓ	76	Ⓐ Ⓑ Ⓒ Ⓓ	86	Ⓐ Ⓑ Ⓒ Ⓓ	96	Ⓐ Ⓑ Ⓒ Ⓓ
7	Ⓐ Ⓑ Ⓒ	17	Ⓐ Ⓑ Ⓒ	27	Ⓐ Ⓑ Ⓒ	37	Ⓐ Ⓑ Ⓒ Ⓓ	47	Ⓐ Ⓑ Ⓒ Ⓓ	57	Ⓐ Ⓑ Ⓒ Ⓓ	67	Ⓐ Ⓑ Ⓒ Ⓓ	77	Ⓐ Ⓑ Ⓒ Ⓓ	87	Ⓐ Ⓑ Ⓒ Ⓓ	97	Ⓐ Ⓑ Ⓒ Ⓓ
8	Ⓐ Ⓑ Ⓒ	18	Ⓐ Ⓑ Ⓒ	28	Ⓐ Ⓑ Ⓒ	38	Ⓐ Ⓑ Ⓒ Ⓓ	48	Ⓐ Ⓑ Ⓒ Ⓓ	58	Ⓐ Ⓑ Ⓒ Ⓓ	68	Ⓐ Ⓑ Ⓒ Ⓓ	78	Ⓐ Ⓑ Ⓒ Ⓓ	88	Ⓐ Ⓑ Ⓒ Ⓓ	98	Ⓐ Ⓑ Ⓒ Ⓓ
9	Ⓐ Ⓑ Ⓒ	19	Ⓐ Ⓑ Ⓒ	29	Ⓐ Ⓑ Ⓒ	39	Ⓐ Ⓑ Ⓒ Ⓓ	49	Ⓐ Ⓑ Ⓒ Ⓓ	59	Ⓐ Ⓑ Ⓒ Ⓓ	69	Ⓐ Ⓑ Ⓒ Ⓓ	79	Ⓐ Ⓑ Ⓒ Ⓓ	89	Ⓐ Ⓑ Ⓒ Ⓓ	99	Ⓐ Ⓑ Ⓒ Ⓓ
10	Ⓐ Ⓑ Ⓒ	20	Ⓐ Ⓑ Ⓒ	30	Ⓐ Ⓑ Ⓒ	40	Ⓐ Ⓑ Ⓒ Ⓓ	50	Ⓐ Ⓑ Ⓒ Ⓓ	60	Ⓐ Ⓑ Ⓒ Ⓓ	70	Ⓐ Ⓑ Ⓒ Ⓓ	80	Ⓐ Ⓑ Ⓒ Ⓓ	90	Ⓐ Ⓑ Ⓒ Ⓓ	100	Ⓐ Ⓑ Ⓒ Ⓓ

READING SECTION

Part 5						Part 6				Part 7									
No.	ANSWER A B C D	No.	ANSWER A B C D	No.	ANSWER A B C D	No.	ANSWER A B C D	No.	ANSWER A B C D	No.	ANSWER A B C D	No.	ANSWER A B C D	No.	ANSWER A B C D	No.	ANSWER A B C D	No.	ANSWER A B C D
101	Ⓐ Ⓑ Ⓒ Ⓓ	111	Ⓐ Ⓑ Ⓒ Ⓓ	121	Ⓐ Ⓑ Ⓒ Ⓓ	131	Ⓐ Ⓑ Ⓒ Ⓓ	141	Ⓐ Ⓑ Ⓒ Ⓓ	151	Ⓐ Ⓑ Ⓒ Ⓓ	161	Ⓐ Ⓑ Ⓒ Ⓓ	171	Ⓐ Ⓑ Ⓒ Ⓓ	181	Ⓐ Ⓑ Ⓒ Ⓓ	191	Ⓐ Ⓑ Ⓒ Ⓓ
102	Ⓐ Ⓑ Ⓒ Ⓓ	112	Ⓐ Ⓑ Ⓒ Ⓓ	122	Ⓐ Ⓑ Ⓒ Ⓓ	132	Ⓐ Ⓑ Ⓒ Ⓓ	142	Ⓐ Ⓑ Ⓒ Ⓓ	152	Ⓐ Ⓑ Ⓒ Ⓓ	162	Ⓐ Ⓑ Ⓒ Ⓓ	172	Ⓐ Ⓑ Ⓒ Ⓓ	182	Ⓐ Ⓑ Ⓒ Ⓓ	192	Ⓐ Ⓑ Ⓒ Ⓓ
103	Ⓐ Ⓑ Ⓒ Ⓓ	113	Ⓐ Ⓑ Ⓒ Ⓓ	123	Ⓐ Ⓑ Ⓒ Ⓓ	133	Ⓐ Ⓑ Ⓒ Ⓓ	143	Ⓐ Ⓑ Ⓒ Ⓓ	153	Ⓐ Ⓑ Ⓒ Ⓓ	163	Ⓐ Ⓑ Ⓒ Ⓓ	173	Ⓐ Ⓑ Ⓒ Ⓓ	183	Ⓐ Ⓑ Ⓒ Ⓓ	193	Ⓐ Ⓑ Ⓒ Ⓓ
104	Ⓐ Ⓑ Ⓒ Ⓓ	114	Ⓐ Ⓑ Ⓒ Ⓓ	124	Ⓐ Ⓑ Ⓒ Ⓓ	134	Ⓐ Ⓑ Ⓒ Ⓓ	144	Ⓐ Ⓑ Ⓒ Ⓓ	154	Ⓐ Ⓑ Ⓒ Ⓓ	164	Ⓐ Ⓑ Ⓒ Ⓓ	174	Ⓐ Ⓑ Ⓒ Ⓓ	184	Ⓐ Ⓑ Ⓒ Ⓓ	194	Ⓐ Ⓑ Ⓒ Ⓓ
105	Ⓐ Ⓑ Ⓒ Ⓓ	115	Ⓐ Ⓑ Ⓒ Ⓓ	125	Ⓐ Ⓑ Ⓒ Ⓓ	135	Ⓐ Ⓑ Ⓒ Ⓓ	145	Ⓐ Ⓑ Ⓒ Ⓓ	155	Ⓐ Ⓑ Ⓒ Ⓓ	165	Ⓐ Ⓑ Ⓒ Ⓓ	175	Ⓐ Ⓑ Ⓒ Ⓓ	185	Ⓐ Ⓑ Ⓒ Ⓓ	195	Ⓐ Ⓑ Ⓒ Ⓓ
106	Ⓐ Ⓑ Ⓒ Ⓓ	116	Ⓐ Ⓑ Ⓒ Ⓓ	126	Ⓐ Ⓑ Ⓒ Ⓓ	136	Ⓐ Ⓑ Ⓒ Ⓓ	146	Ⓐ Ⓑ Ⓒ Ⓓ	156	Ⓐ Ⓑ Ⓒ Ⓓ	166	Ⓐ Ⓑ Ⓒ Ⓓ	176	Ⓐ Ⓑ Ⓒ Ⓓ	186	Ⓐ Ⓑ Ⓒ Ⓓ	196	Ⓐ Ⓑ Ⓒ Ⓓ
107	Ⓐ Ⓑ Ⓒ Ⓓ	117	Ⓐ Ⓑ Ⓒ Ⓓ	127	Ⓐ Ⓑ Ⓒ Ⓓ	137	Ⓐ Ⓑ Ⓒ Ⓓ	147	Ⓐ Ⓑ Ⓒ Ⓓ	157	Ⓐ Ⓑ Ⓒ Ⓓ	167	Ⓐ Ⓑ Ⓒ Ⓓ	177	Ⓐ Ⓑ Ⓒ Ⓓ	187	Ⓐ Ⓑ Ⓒ Ⓓ	197	Ⓐ Ⓑ Ⓒ Ⓓ
108	Ⓐ Ⓑ Ⓒ Ⓓ	118	Ⓐ Ⓑ Ⓒ Ⓓ	128	Ⓐ Ⓑ Ⓒ Ⓓ	138	Ⓐ Ⓑ Ⓒ Ⓓ	148	Ⓐ Ⓑ Ⓒ Ⓓ	158	Ⓐ Ⓑ Ⓒ Ⓓ	168	Ⓐ Ⓑ Ⓒ Ⓓ	178	Ⓐ Ⓑ Ⓒ Ⓓ	188	Ⓐ Ⓑ Ⓒ Ⓓ	198	Ⓐ Ⓑ Ⓒ Ⓓ
109	Ⓐ Ⓑ Ⓒ Ⓓ	119	Ⓐ Ⓑ Ⓒ Ⓓ	129	Ⓐ Ⓑ Ⓒ Ⓓ	139	Ⓐ Ⓑ Ⓒ Ⓓ	149	Ⓐ Ⓑ Ⓒ Ⓓ	159	Ⓐ Ⓑ Ⓒ Ⓓ	169	Ⓐ Ⓑ Ⓒ Ⓓ	179	Ⓐ Ⓑ Ⓒ Ⓓ	189	Ⓐ Ⓑ Ⓒ Ⓓ	199	Ⓐ Ⓑ Ⓒ Ⓓ
110	Ⓐ Ⓑ Ⓒ Ⓓ	120	Ⓐ Ⓑ Ⓒ Ⓓ	130	Ⓐ Ⓑ Ⓒ Ⓓ	140	Ⓐ Ⓑ Ⓒ Ⓓ	150	Ⓐ Ⓑ Ⓒ Ⓓ	160	Ⓐ Ⓑ Ⓒ Ⓓ	170	Ⓐ Ⓑ Ⓒ Ⓓ	180	Ⓐ Ⓑ Ⓒ Ⓓ	190	Ⓐ Ⓑ Ⓒ Ⓓ	200	Ⓐ Ⓑ Ⓒ Ⓓ

ETS® TOEIC®

公式 TOEIC® Listening & Reading 問題集 6

別冊『解答・解説』

IIBC
一般財団法人 国際ビジネスコミュニケーション協会

ETS TOEIC®
OFFICIAL TEST PREPARATION AND LEARNING

目 次

解答・解説で使われている表記の説明

●CD のトラック番号（Part 1 ～ 4）

会話の音声が CD 2 のトラック番号 48 に、
問題の音声が CD 2 のトラック番号 49 に入っていることを示しています。

●スクリプトの前の記号（Part 1 ～ 4）

= 米国の発音
= 英国の発音
= カナダの発音
= オーストラリアの発音

M = 男性（Man）
W = 女性（Woman）

●スクリプト中の ❶❷ 等の番号（Part 3、4）

解説の中で説明している箇所を示しています。

会話 CD 2 48　問題 CD 2 49

Questions 50 through 52 refer to the following conversation.

M Hi, Dr. Garcia. ❶That software program you ordered for our medical office just arrived—❷the one that will allow patients to schedule appointments online. Would you like me to install it today?

W Oh, good. Actually, ❸a service technician will be stopping by tomorrow to install it for us. But could you please let our patients know about this new option for making appointments?

M OK. ❹Once the program is ready tomorrow, I'll send an e-mail to our patients that will instruct them on how to use the scheduling system.

問題50-52は次の会話に関するものです。

こんにちは、Garcia医師。ちょうど、当診療所用にあなたが注文したあのソフトウエアプログラムが届きました――患者さんがオンラインで予約を入れるのを可能にするものです。私が今日、それをインストールしましょうか。

ああ、良かった。実は、サービス技術者が明日、当診療所のためにそれをインストールしに立ち寄ることになっています。でも、予約を行うこの新しい手段について、あなたから患者さんに知らせてくれますか。

分かりました。明日、プログラムの準備ができましたら、スケジュールシステムの使用方法について説明するEメールを私が患者さんに送ります。

50 What will the new software allow patients to do?

(A) Schedule appointments
(B) Request a prescription refill
(C) Ask the doctor a question
(D) Write a review

新しいソフトウエアは、患者が何をすることを可能にしますか。

(A) 予約を入れる。
(B) 処方薬の再調剤を依頼する。
(C) 医師に質問する。
(D) レビューを書く。

正解 A　男性は❶で、診療所用に注文したソフトウエアが届いたことを女性に知らせ、続けて❷で、そのソフトウエアについて「患者がオンラインで予約を入れるのを可能にするものだ」と説明している。
(B) prescription「処方（薬）」、refill「再調剤」。
(C) ソフトウエアは医師の女性が注文したとあるが、患者がそのソフトウエアを使って医師に質問できるとは述べられていない。

51 Who will be visiting the office tomorrow?

正解 B　ソフトウエアが届いたという報告を受け

●色の区別

青字：正答に関する解説
黒字：誤答に関する解説や語句の意味

●特典音声ファイルの番号（Part 5～7）

「104-105」は特典音声のファイル番号を示しています。ダウンロード音声ファイルのタイトル名に、「特典104」、「特典105」と表示されています。

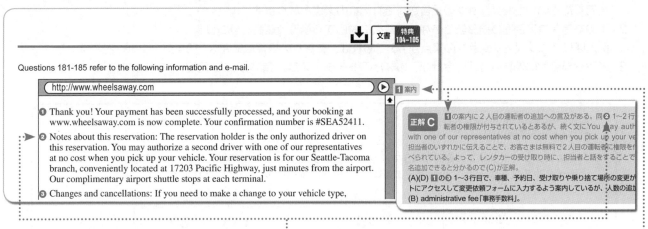

文書 特典 104-105

Questions 181-185 refer to the following information and e-mail.

http://www.wheelsaway.com

1 案内

❶ Thank you! Your payment has been successfully processed, and your booking at www.wheelsaway.com is now complete. Your confirmation number is #SEA52411.

❷ Notes about this reservation: The reservation holder is the only authorized driver on this reservation. You may authorize a second driver with one of our representatives at no cost when you pick up your vehicle. Your reservation is for our Seattle-Tacoma branch, conveniently located at 17203 Pacific Highway, just minutes from the airport. Our complimentary airport shuttle stops at each terminal.

❸ Changes and cancellations: If you need to make a change to your vehicle type,

正解 C 1の案内に2人目の運転者の追加への言及がある。同❷ 1～2行 転者の権限が付与されているとあるが、続く文にYou may auth with one of our representatives at no cost when you pick up your ve 担当者のいずれかに伝えることで、お客さまは無料で2人目の運転者に権限を べられている。よって、レンタカーの受け取り時に、担当者と話をすることで 名追加できると分かるので(C)が正解。
(A)(D) 1の❸ 1～3行目で、車種、予約日、受け取りや乗り捨て場所の変更が トにアクセスして変更依頼フォームに入力するよう案内しているが、人数の追加
(B) administrative fee「事務手数料」。

●文書中の ❶ ❷ 等の番号（Part 6、7）

解説の中で説明している文書中の段落番号等を示しています。解説文中の段落番号に続く行数は、英文中の各段落の何行目かを表しています。

●文書を示す 1 2 等の番号（Part 7）

解説の中で説明している文書を示しています。

●Words & Phrases（Part 3、4、6、7）

会話やトーク、文書などに含まれる重要な語句と意味を紹介しています。Part 6、7では、上記に示した 1 2 や ❶ ❷ の番号により、本文で使われている場所が参照できます。

Words & Phrases

1 案内 ❶ successfully うまく　process ～を処理する　booking 予約　confirmation 確認　❷ note 注記　holder 所有者　authorize ～に権限を与える、～を許可する　representative 担当者　at no cost 無料で　pick up ～ ～を受け取る　vehicle 車　branch 支店　conveniently 便利に　complimentary 無料の　shuttle シャトルバス　❸ cancellation キャンセル　make a change 変更する　pickup 受け取り　drop-off 乗り捨て、降車　fill out ～ ～に記入する　in advance 前もって　reduce ～を減らす　length 期間、長さ　refund ～ … ～に…を払い戻す　difference 差額　immediately すぐに　upon ～ ～のすぐあとで　incur ～を負担する

2 Eメール ❶ details 詳細　as follows 次の通りで　❷ midsize 中型の　sedan セダン車　❸ owe ～を支払う義務がある　❹ original 元の　record 記録

●Expressions（Part 6、7）

文書の中から、知っておくと便利な表現を例文とともに紹介しています。覚えて使えるようになると、大変便利です。

Expressions

Please do not hesitate to *do*　「ご遠慮なく～してください」(2の❻ 1行目)

If you have any questions about our photocopiers, please do not hesitate to call our office.
当社のコピー機に関するご質問がございましたら、どうぞご遠慮なく当営業所にお電話ください。

＊『公式 *TOEIC*® Listening & Reading 問題集 6』の特典として、ダウンロード音声の中には、TEST 1、2のリーディングセクションの以下の音声が入っています。音声ダウンロードの手順は本誌 p. 3 をご参照ください。

- 正解が入った問題音声（Part 5、6）
- 文書の音声（Part 7）

参考スコア範囲の算出方法 ※ TEST 1、2 共通

1. 正解一覧（p.5、p.102）を参照し、リスニングセクションとリーディングセクションそれぞれの正答数を数えてください。各セクションの正答数がそれぞれの素点となります。
2. 下の参考スコア範囲の換算表であなたの素点に対応する換算点範囲を見つけます。
   例えばリスニングセクションの素点が 45 であれば、あなたの換算点範囲は「155 点～ 230 点」です。
3. 各セクションの換算点範囲の合計が、あなたのトータルスコア（参考スコア範囲）となります。

参考スコア範囲の算出例

リスニングセクションの素点が 45 で、リーディングセクションの素点が 64 だった場合、トータルスコアは①と②の合計である③ 405―565 の間ということになります。

	素点	換算点範囲	
リスニングセクション	45	155―230	①
リーディングセクション	64	250―335	②
トータルスコア（参考スコア範囲）		405―565	③（①+②）

参考スコア範囲の換算表

リスニングセクション	
素点	換算点範囲
96 －100	475－495
91 － 95	435－495
86 － 90	405－475
81 － 85	370－450
76 － 80	345－420
71 － 75	320－390
66 － 70	290－360
61 － 65	265－335
56 － 60	235－310
51 － 55	210－280
46 － 50	180－255
41 － 45 (算出例①)	155－230
36 － 40	125－205
31 － 35	105－175
26 － 30	85 －145
21 － 25	60 －115
16 － 20	30 － 90
11 － 15	5 － 70
6 － 10	5 － 60
1 － 5	5 － 50
0	5 － 35

リーディングセクション	
素点	換算点範囲
96 －100	460－495
91 － 95	425－490
86 － 90	395－465
81 － 85	370－440
76 － 80	335－415
71 － 75	310－390
66 － 70	280－365
61 － 65 (算出例②)	250－335
56 － 60	220－305
51 － 55	195－270
46 － 50	165－240
41 － 45	140－215
36 － 40	115－180
31 － 35	95 －145
26 － 30	75 －120
21 － 25	60 － 95
16 － 20	45 － 75
11 － 15	30 － 55
6 － 10	10 － 40
1 － 5	5 － 30
0	5 － 15

TEST 1の正解一覧

リスニングセクション

問題番号	正解
Part 1	
1	B
2	D
3	A
4	C
5	D
6	C
Part 2	
7	A
8	B
9	A
10	B
11	B
12	A
13	B
14	A
15	B
16	C
17	B
18	B
19	A
20	B
21	B
22	A
23	A
24	C
25	B
26	A
27	A
28	A
29	C
30	C
31	A
Part 3	
32	C
33	D
34	C
35	B
36	C
37	A
38	D
39	B
40	A
41	B
42	A
43	C
44	C
45	C
46	B
47	B
48	C
49	B
50	C

問題番号	正解
51	D
52	A
53	B
54	A
55	B
56	C
57	D
58	B
59	C
60	A
61	B
62	A
63	D
64	C
65	B
66	D
67	D
68	A
69	B
70	D
Part 4	
71	D
72	C
73	B
74	B
75	C
76	D
77	B
78	A
79	C
80	C
81	A
82	B
83	C
84	B
85	A
86	D
87	B
88	A
89	C
90	A
91	B
92	C
93	A
94	D
95	A
96	C
97	D
98	B
99	D
100	B

リーディングセクション

問題番号	正解
Part 5	
101	B
102	A
103	C
104	A
105	B
106	D
107	D
108	C
109	A
110	C
111	A
112	B
113	A
114	B
115	C
116	C
117	A
118	A
119	A
120	B
121	B
122	A
123	C
124	D
125	D
126	B
127	A
128	A
129	D
130	B
Part 6	
131	B
132	A
133	C
134	D
135	B
136	B
137	C
138	D
139	B
140	D
141	D
142	C
143	C
144	A
145	D
146	B
Part 7	
147	D
148	D
149	C
150	D

問題番号	正解
151	C
152	A
153	C
154	A
155	C
156	A
157	D
158	D
159	C
160	A
161	D
162	B
163	C
164	B
165	A
166	D
167	C
168	B
169	A
170	D
171	C
172	A
173	C
174	B
175	B
176	C
177	A
178	A
179	C
180	D
181	A
182	C
183	B
184	D
185	D
186	C
187	A
188	A
189	C
190	D
191	B
192	A
193	C
194	D
195	C
196	A
197	C
198	A
199	D
200	B

1

2

3

1 M

(A) Some dishes are in a sink.
(B) Some food is on a plate.
(C) A cook is wearing gloves.
(D) A waiter is standing in a doorway.

(A) 数枚の皿が流しにある。
(B) 食べ物が皿に載っている。
(C) 料理人は手袋を着用している。
(D) 給仕人は出入り口に立っている。

正解 B 男性の左手側にある平皿に食べ物が載っている。plate「平皿」。
(A) dish「盛り皿、料理」があるのは男性の前であり、sink「流し」は写っていない。
(C) cook「料理人」やglove「手袋」は写っていない。wear「～を着用している」。
(D) 男性はwaiter「給仕人」のようだが、doorway「出入り口」に立ってはいない。

2 W

(A) She's hanging up her coat.
(B) She's installing some shelves.
(C) She's carrying some boxes.
(D) She's reaching for an item.

(A) 彼女は自分のコートを掛けている。
(B) 彼女は幾つかの棚を取り付けている。
(C) 彼女は幾つかの箱を運んでいる。
(D) 彼女は品物を取ろうと手を伸ばしている。

正解 D 女性は棚の上部にある物を取ろうと右手を伸ばしている。reach for ～「～を取ろうと手を伸ばす」、item「品物」。
(A) 女性の手元にコートは写っていない。hang up ～「～を掛ける」。
(B) 棚は写っているが、女性がそれを取り付けているところではない。install「～を取り付ける」。shelvesはshelf「棚」の複数形。
(C) carry「～を運ぶ」。

3 W

(A) Some people are waiting to get into a vehicle.
(B) Some people are taking luggage into a house.
(C) Some people are removing leaves from a street.
(D) Some people are cutting branches from a tree.

(A) 何人かの人々が車に乗り込むために待っている。
(B) 何人かの人々が旅行用かばんを家の中に入れている。
(C) 何人かの人々が通りから葉を取り除いている。
(D) 何人かの人々が木から枝を切っている。

正解 A 複数の人々が車に乗り込むために並んで待っている。get into ～「〈車など〉に乗り込む」、vehicle「車、乗り物」。
(B) luggageは「旅行用かばん類」を表す集合名詞。
(C) 動詞leave「～を出発する」と似た音の名詞leaves（leaf「葉」の複数形）に注意。remove「～を取り除く」。
(D) branch「枝」。

4

5

6

4 M

(A) The man's adjusting his glasses.
(B) The man's putting on running shoes.
(C) The man's using an exercise machine.
(D) The man's turning on a television.

(A) 男性は眼鏡を調節している。
(B) 男性はランニングシューズを履いているところである。
(C) 男性は運動機器を使用している。
(D) 男性はテレビをつけているところである。

正解 C 男性はランニング用の機器を使って運動している。exercise「運動」、machine「機械」。
(A) 男性は眼鏡をかけているが、調節してはいない。adjust「～を調節する」。
(B) 男性はランニングシューズを着用しているが、それを履いているところではない。put on ～は「～を身に着ける、～を着る」という動作を表す。
(D) turn on ～「〈電源・明かりなど〉をつける」。

5 W

(A) Some papers have been left on a windowsill.
(B) A sofa is being pushed up a ramp.
(C) A woman is dusting a piano.
(D) A woman is playing an instrument.

(A) 書類が窓敷居に置かれたままになっている。
(B) ソファが傾斜を押し上げられているところである。
(C) 女性がピアノのほこりを払っている。
(D) 女性が楽器を演奏している。

正解 D 女性がピアノを弾いている。ピアノを(D)ではan instrument「楽器」と表している。
(A) 楽譜は写っているが、それはwindowsill「窓敷居」に置かれてはいない。
(B) push up ～「～を押し上げる」、ramp「傾斜」。
(C) ピアノは写っているが、女性はそれを掃除しているところではない。dust「～のほこりを払う」。

6 M

(A) Some building materials are blocking a walkway.
(B) Some bicycles have been left in a parking area.
(C) There are some benches along a path.
(D) There are some water fountains in a garden.

(A) 幾つかの建築資材が歩道をふさいでいる。
(B) 数台の自転車が駐車場に置かれたままである。
(C) 小道沿いに幾つかのベンチがある。
(D) 庭に幾つかの噴水がある。

正解 C 小道に沿って手前と奥にベンチがある。path「小道」。
(A) building material「建築資材」、block「～をふさぐ」、walkway「歩道」。
(B) 自転車や駐車場は写っていない。parking area「駐車場」。
(D) water fountain「噴水」。

7 W Did you add cleaning products to the shopping list?
M (A) Yes, I did.
(B) A new television commercial.
(C) The kitchen floor.

あなたは掃除用製品を買い物リストに追加しましたか。
(A) はい、しました。
(B) 新しいテレビコマーシャルです。
(C) キッチンの床です。

正解 A 掃除用製品を買い物リストに追加したかを尋ねているのに対し、Yes, I did.と答えて、追加したことを伝えている(A)が正解。add「～を追加する」、cleaning「掃除」、product「製品」、shopping list「買い物リスト」。
(B) commercial「コマーシャル」。
(C) 掃除をする箇所は尋ねられていない。floor「床」。

8 M Who supplies the vegetables for your restaurant?
M (A) In the refrigerator.
(B) Some local farmers.
(C) A loading dock.

誰があなたのレストランに野菜を供給していますか。
(A) 冷蔵庫の中です。
(B) 地元の農業経営者です。
(C) 搬入口です。

正解 B Who ～?でレストランに野菜を供給する取引先を尋ねているのに対し、地元の農業経営者と答えている(B)が正解。supply「～を供給する」。local「地元の」、farmer「農業経営者、農家」。
(A) 保管場所は尋ねられていない。
(C) loading dock「搬入口、荷物の積み降ろし場」。

9 M How many people will be in the group interview?
W (A) There will be six applicants.
(B) He's in my group.
(C) Not at the moment.

グループ面接には何名参加しますか。
(A) 6名の応募者になるでしょう。
(B) 彼は私のグループにいます。
(C) 今のところは違います。

正解 A How many ～?でグループ面接への参加予定人数を尋ねているのに対し、「6名の応募者になるだろう」と、予定人数を伝えている(A)が正解。interview「面接」。applicant「応募者」。
(B) 質問にあるgroupが含まれるが、Heが誰を指すのか不明。
(C) at the moment「今のところ」。

10 W Can you review my conference presentation for me?
M (A) Not far from Detroit.
(B) Sure, send it to me.
(C) The conference room.

私のために会議のプレゼンテーションを精査してもらえますか。
(A) デトロイトから遠くありません。
(B) いいですよ、それを私に送ってください。
(C) 会議室です。

正解 B Can you ～?で会議のプレゼンテーションの精査を依頼しているのに対し、Sureと承諾して、それを自分に送るよう伝えている(B)が正解。itは質問にあるconference presentationを指す。review「～を精査する、～を見直す」、conference「会議」。
(A) 距離は尋ねられていない。
(C) 質問にあるconferenceが含まれるが、応答になっていない。

11 M What were you doing before you started working here?
W (A) Yes, I plan to start soon.
(B) I was a real estate agent.
(C) Nine o'clock every morning.

あなたはここで働き始める前には何をしていましたか。
(A) はい、私はすぐに始める予定です。
(B) 私は不動産業者でした。
(C) 毎朝9時です。

正解 B ここで働き始める前の職業を尋ねているのに対し、「私は不動産業者だった」と、具体的な職種を答えている(B)が正解。do「〈職業として〉する」、start *doing*「～し始める」。real estate agent「不動産業者」。
(A) 質問にあるstartが含まれるが、前職を尋ねられているのに対し、応答になっていない。
(C) 時刻は尋ねられていない。

12 M Hasn't anyone purchased that painting yet?
W (A) No, business has been slow recently.
(B) We accept all credit cards.
(C) Three cans of light blue, please.

まだ誰もあの絵画を購入していないのですか。
(A) 購入していません、商売は最近不調になっています。
(B) 当店は全てのクレジットカードを受け付けています。
(C) 薄い青色の缶を3つお願いします。

正解 A 否定疑問文で、「まだ誰もあの絵画を購入していないのか」と確認しているのに対し、Noと購入者がいないことを伝えた上で、「商売は最近不調だ」と事業全体の低迷に言及している(A)が正解。purchase「～を購入する」、painting「絵画」。business「商売、景気」、recently「最近」。
(B) 質問にあるpurchasedと関連するcredit cards「クレジットカード」が含まれるが、応答になっていない。accept「～を受け付ける、～を受け入れる」。

---

13 W You offer a senior discount, don't you?
W (A) A new calculator.
(B) Yes, I just need to see some identification.
(C) I'll count up the days I missed.

そちらではシニア割引を提供していますよね？
(A) 新しい計算機です。
(B) はい、ただ私が身元証明書を拝見する必要があります。
(C) 私は自分が欠席した日を合計します。

正解 B 肯定文の文末に ～, don't you?を付けて「～していますよね」とシニア割引の提供があるかを確認している。これに対し、Yesと肯定し、「ただ私が身元証明書を見る必要がある」と手順を伝えている(B)が正解。senior「シニア、高齢者」、discount「割引」。identification「身元証明書」。
(A) calculator「計算機」。
(C) 質問にあるdiscountと似た音の動詞countに注意。count up ～「～を合計する」、miss「～を欠席する、～を逃す」。

---

14 W Where can I find a charger for this laptop?
M (A) There's one in the cabinet.
(B) About four hours.
(C) I don't mind.

このノートパソコンの充電器をどこで見つけることができますか。
(A) 戸棚の中に1つあります。
(B) 約4時間です。
(C) 構いません。

正解 A Where ～?でノートパソコンの充電器がどこにあるかを尋ねているのに対し、「戸棚の中に1つある」と、具体的な場所を伝えている(A)が正解。oneは質問にあるa chargerを指す。charger「充電器」、laptop「ノートパソコン」。cabinet「戸棚」。
(B) 所要時間は尋ねられていない。
(C) 場所を尋ねられているのに対し、応答になっていない。

---

15 M When should we hold the company picnic?
W (A) Around 50 people.
(B) Mr. Han is arranging that.
(C) Hold the handle carefully.

私たちはいつ会社のピクニックを開催したらいいですか。
(A) およそ50名です。
(B) Hanさんがそれを準備しています。
(C) 取っ手を注意深く握ってください。

正解 B When ～?で会社のピクニックを開催するとよい時期を尋ねているのに対し、それを準備する担当者の名を伝えて、その人物に尋ねるよう示唆している(B)が正解。thatは質問にあるthe company picnicを指す。hold「〈会など〉を開催する」。arrange「～を準備する」。
(A) 人数は尋ねられていない。
(C) 質問にあるholdが含まれるが、ここでは「～を握る」という意味で、応答になっていない。handle「取っ手」。

16 W Are the new packaging machines fully operational?

M (A) A box or two.

(B) I'm glad to hear that.

(C) Not yet, but they will be soon.

新しい包装機は完全に稼働中ですか。

(A) 1、2箱です。
(B) 私はそれを聞いてうれしく思います。
(C) まだです、しかし間もなくそうなるでしょう。

正解 C 「新しい包装機は完全に稼働中なのか」と状況を尋ねているのに対し、「まだだ」と答えて、「間もなくそうなるだろう」と補足している(C)が正解。theyは質問にあるthe new packaging machinesを指す。packaging machine「包装機」、fully「完全に」、operational「運転中の」。
(A) 質問にあるpackagingと関連する名詞box「箱」が含まれるが、応答になっていない。

---

17 W I need to purchase a ticket for my flight to Dublin.

M (A) Did you have a good time?

(B) You can do that online.

(C) Seven hours long.

私はダブリン行きの航空券を購入する必要があります。

(A) あなたは楽しみましたか。
(B) あなたはオンラインでそれをすることができます。
(C) 7時間の長さです。

正解 B 「ダブリン行きの航空券を購入する必要がある」という発言に対し、「オンラインでそれができる」とチケット購入方法の一つを伝えている(B)が正解。thatは質問にある、航空券を購入することを指す。online「オンラインで」。
(A) have a good time「楽しむ」。
(C) 時間の長さは尋ねられていない。

---

18 W I'd like to renew this library book.

M (A) The library does host wonderful events.

(B) OK, I can help you with that.

(C) No, not that I can remember.

この図書館の本の貸し出しを延長したいのです。

(A) その図書館は確かに、素晴らしいイベントを開催します。
(B) 分かりました、私がそれについてお手伝いできますよ。
(C) いいえ、私の覚えている限りではそうではありません。

正解 B 「本の貸し出しを延長したい」という要望を受けて、OKと了承した上で、「私がそれについて手伝える」と申し出ている(B)が正解。thatは質問にある、図書館の本の貸し出しを延長することを指す。renew「〈図書館の本など〉の貸し出しを延長する、～を更新する」。
(A) 質問にあるlibraryが含まれるが、応答になっていない。ここでのdoesは文の内容の強調を表す。

---

19 M You'd prefer an office on the third floor, right?

W (A) No, I like the second floor better.

(B) Take the elevator on the right.

(C) It was a discussion about contracts.

あなたは3階のオフィスの方を希望しているのですよね？

(A) いいえ、私は2階の方が気に入っています。
(B) 右手のエレベーターに乗ってください。
(C) それは契約についての議論でした。

正解 A 肯定文の文末に ～, right?を付けて「～ですよね」と、3階のオフィスの方を希望しているのか確認している。これに対しNoと否定して、「2階の方が気に入っている」と希望の階を伝えている(A)が正解。prefer「～の方を好む」。
(B) 質問にある the third floor と関連する名詞elevator「エレベーター」が含まれるが、応答になっていない。
(C) Itが何を指すのか不明。contract「契約」。

20 M Why is there food in the conference room?

W (A) After the press release is finished.
(B) For the client luncheon.
(C) Yes, the phone is working.

会議室になぜ食べ物があるのですか。
(A) プレスリリースが終了した後です。
(B) 顧客の昼食用です。
(C) はい、電話は機能しています。

正解 B Why ～?で会議室に食べ物がある理由を尋ねているのに対し、「顧客の昼食用だ」と用途を伝えている(B)が正解。client「顧客」、luncheon「昼食(会)」。
(A) 時期は尋ねられていない。press release「プレスリリース、報道発表」。
(C) 理由を尋ねられているので、Yes、Noでは応答にならない。work「〈正常に〉機能する」。

---

21 M These bowls are all hand-painted.

W (A) An interior decorator.
(B) They're very beautiful.
(C) No, it's quite convenient.

これらの深鉢は全て手描きです。
(A) 室内装飾家です。
(B) それらは非常に美しいですね。
(C) いいえ、それはかなり便利です。

正解 B 「これらの深鉢は全て手描きだ」という説明に対し、「それらは非常に美しい」と肯定的な感想で応じている(B)が正解。Theyは質問にあるThese bowlsを指す。bowl「深鉢、ボウル」、hand-painted「手描きの」。
(A) interior decorator「室内装飾家」。
(C) itが何を指すのか不明で、相手の説明とかみ合わない。convenient「便利な」。

---

22 M What's the address for the music festival?

M (A) It's on the Web site.
(B) That's a good song.
(C) In about a week.

その音楽祭の開催場所の住所はどこですか。
(A) それはウェブサイトにあります。
(B) それは良い曲です。
(C) 約1週間後です。

正解 A 音楽祭の開催場所の住所を尋ねているのに対し、「それはウェブサイトにある」と答え、その住所がウェブ上で確認できることを伝えている(A)が正解。Itは質問にある、音楽祭の開催場所の住所を指す。
(B) 質問にあるmusicと関連する名詞song「曲」が含まれるが、Thatが何を指すのか不明で、応答になっていない。
(C) 時期は尋ねられていない。

---

23 M Didn't you take notes during the meeting?

W (A) Steven usually does that.
(B) Notebooks are in aisle five.
(C) Conference room B.

あなたは会議中にメモを取らなかったのですか。
(A) Stevenがいつもそれをしています。
(B) ノートは5番通路にあります。
(C) 会議室Bです。

正解 A 否定疑問文で、「あなたは会議中にメモを取らなかったのか」と確認しているのに対し、「Stevenがいつもそれをしている」と答えて、メモを取ったと思われる人物の名を伝えている(A)が正解。does thatは質問にある、会議中にメモを取ることを指す。take notes「メモを取る」。
(B) 質問にあるnotesと似た音の名詞notebooksに注意。aisle「通路」。
(C) 場所は尋ねられていない。

24 W Would you like me to update the bookstore's Web site?

M (A) That's my favorite book.
(B) I haven't met him yet.
(C) Thanks, that'd be really helpful.

私が書店のウェブサイトを更新しましょうか。

(A) それは私のお気に入りの本です。
(B) 私は彼にまだ会ったことがありません。
(C) ありがとう、そうしてくれると大変助かります。

正解 C Would you like me to *do* ～?「私が～しましょうか」で、ウェブサイトを更新することを申し出ているのに対し、お礼を述べて、「そうしてくれると助かる」と伝えている(C)が正解。thatは質問にある、書店のウェブサイトを更新することを指す。update「～を更新する」。that'dはthat wouldの略。

(A) 質問にあるbookstoreと関連する名詞book「本」が含まれるが、Thatが何を指すのか不明。

(B) himが誰を指すのか不明。

---

25 M Would you rather go shopping or go to the movies tonight?

W (A) Do you have the receipt?
(B) I have to work until eight.
(C) A shipment of new shoes.

あなたは今夜、買い物に行きたいですか、それとも映画を見に行きたいですか。

(A) あなたは領収書を持っていますか。
(B) 私は8時まで働かなければなりません。
(C) 新しい靴の積み荷です。

正解 B *A* or *B*?の形で、今夜、買い物と映画鑑賞のどちらの方がしたいか相手の意向を尋ねているのに対し、「私は8時まで働かなければならない」と今夜は都合がつかないことを伝えている(B)が正解。

(A) 質問にあるshoppingと関連する名詞receipt「領収書」が含まれるが、応答になっていない。

(C) shipment「積み荷、発送品」。

---

26 W The machines are being repaired tomorrow, aren't they?

W (A) The technician came yesterday.
(B) I have another pair of sunglasses.
(C) On the way to the airport.

その機械は明日、修理されるのですよね?

(A) 技術者は昨日来ました。
(B) 私はもう1本サングラスを持っています。
(C) 空港に行く途中に。

正解 A 肯定文の文末に ～, aren't they?を付けて、「～ですよね」と機械の修理が明日行われる予定か確認している。これに対し、「技術者は昨日来た」と答え、機械がすでに修理済みであることを示唆している(A)が正解。repair「～を修理する」。technician「技術者」。

(B) 質問にあるrepairedと似た音のpairに注意。

(C) on the way to ～「～に行く途中に」。

---

27 M When will you be finished reading that training manual?

M (A) There's another copy on the shelf.
(B) Linda from Human Resources.
(C) Downstairs and to the left.

あなたはその研修マニュアルをいつ読み終わりますか。

(A) 棚にもう1部ありますよ。
(B) 人事部のLindaです。
(C) 階下へ降りて、左側に進んでください。

正解 A When ～?で研修マニュアルを読み終える時期を尋ねているのに対し、「棚にもう1部ある」と答え、利用できる研修マニュアルが他にあることを伝えている(A)が正解。training「研修、訓練」。

(B) Human Resources「人事(部)」。

(C) 場所は尋ねられていない。downstairs「階下へ」、to the left「左側に」。

28 W Isn't our delivery supposed to be here by now?

M (A) I'll call the supplier.
(B) Three new assistants.
(C) That's on page ten.

今頃はもう、ここに納品が来ているはずではないのですか。

(A) 私が納入業者に電話します。
(B) 3名の新しい助手です。
(C) それは10ページにあります。

正解 A 否定疑問文で、「今頃はもう、ここに納品が来ているはずではないのか」と確認しているのに対し、「納入業者に電話する」と配達状況を調べることを伝えている(A)が正解。delivery「納品、荷渡し」、be supposed to *do*「～するはずである、～することになっている」。supplier「納入業者、供給会社」。
(B) assistant「助手」。

---

29 W Have you seen the contemporary art exhibit?

M (A) I'm sorry to hear that.
(B) Jane's a temporary employee.
(C) The museum is pretty far from my house.

あなたはその現代美術展覧会を見ましたか。

(A) 私はそれを聞いて残念に思います。
(B) Janeは臨時職員です。
(C) その美術館は私の家からはかなり遠いのです。

正解 C 現代美術展覧会を見たかと尋ねているのに対し、「その美術館は私の家からはかなり遠い」と答え、その展覧会を見ていないことを示唆している(C)が正解。contemporary「現代の」、exhibit「展覧会」。pretty「かなり」。
(B) 質問にあるcontemporaryと似た音のtemporary「臨時の」に注意。employee「職員、従業員」。

---

30 W Should I e-mail the tax forms or send hard copies?

M (A) I didn't order any new desk chairs.
(B) He's at the car mechanic.
(C) How did you do it last year?

私は納税申告書をEメールで送るべきですか、それとも紙に印刷したものを送付するべきですか。

(A) 私は新しいデスクチェアを一つも注文しませんでした。
(B) 彼は自動車整備工のところにいます。
(C) あなたは昨年は、どのようにそれをしたのですか。

正解 C *A* or *B*?の形で、Eメールまたは印刷文書送付のどちらの方法で申告書を送るべきかを尋ねている。これに対し、「あなたは昨年は、どのようにそれをしたのか」と聞き返している(C)が正解。do itは、納税申告書を送ることを指す。e-mail「～をEメールで送る」、tax form「納税申告書」、hard copy「紙に印刷したもの」。
(A) order「～を注文する」。
(B) mechanic「整備工」。

---

31 M Would you be able to come to work early on Tuesday?

W (A) Maybe Sam can.
(B) About ten months ago.
(C) That table's made out of cedarwood.

あなたは火曜日に早く出勤することができますか。

(A) Samならできるかもしれません。
(B) 約10カ月前です。
(C) そのテーブルはスギ材でできています。

正解 A 「あなたは火曜日に早く出勤できるか」と尋ねているのに対し、「Samならできるかもしれない」と、早く出勤できそうな他の人物を伝えている(A)が正解。come to work「出勤する」。
(B) 時期は尋ねられていない。
(C) 材料については尋ねられていない。cedarwood「スギ材」。

Questions 32 through 34 refer to the following conversation.

問題32-34は次の会話に関するものです。

M Tanya, ❶when did we start selling these reusable grocery bags? Has it been two weeks? ❷I want to see our customers using them to carry their groceries home from our store, but nobody's buying them…

Tanya、当店ではこの再利用できる買い物バッグをいつ売り始めたのでしたっけ？２週間経ちますか。お客さまがこれらを利用して当店から家に食料品を持ち帰るのを見たいのですが、誰も購入していません…。

W Well, ❸they are rather simple. They're in plain colors and only have the store's name on them.

そうですね、それらはちょっと地味です。無地で、店名が付いているだけですから。

M Hmm… What could we do to make them more interesting?

ええと…もっと興味をそそるようなものにするには何ができるでしょうか。

W Well, the store's name is on one side of the bag. What if we asked some local artists to design images to put on the other side?

そうですね、店名がバッグの片側にあります。地元のアーティストたちに、反対側に載せる画像をデザインするよう頼んだらどうでしょうか。

M I like that. ❹I'll get an ad in the local newspaper about this, asking any interested artists to contact us.

それはいいですね。この件について地元紙に広告を載せ、関心を持ってくれるアーティストに当店に連絡するよう呼びかけましょう。

32 Where do the speakers most likely work?

(A) At an art gallery
(B) In a warehouse
(C) At a grocery store
(D) At a movie theater

話し手たちはどこで働いていると考えられますか。

(A) 画廊
(B) 倉庫
(C) 食料雑貨店
(D) 映画館

正解 C 男性は❶で、自分たちが買い物バッグを売り始めた時期について女性に確認し、続けて❷「客がこれらを利用して当店から家に食料品を持ち帰るのを見たいが、誰も購入していない」と述べている。よって、話し手たちは食料品を扱う店で働いていると考えられる。grocery store「食料雑貨店」。
(A) art gallery「画廊、美術館」。
(B) warehouse「倉庫」。

33 According to the woman, what is the problem with the bags?

(A) They are too expensive.
(B) They are too small.
(C) The material is too thin.
(D) The design is too simple.

女性によると、それらのバッグに関して何が問題ですか。

(A) それらは高価過ぎる。
(B) それらは小さ過ぎる。
(C) 素材が薄過ぎる。
(D) デザインが地味過ぎる。

正解 D ❷で、誰も買い物バッグを購入していないと言う男性に対し、女性は❸「それらはちょっと地味だ」と買い物バッグのデザインについて意見を述べ、さらに「無地で、店名が付いているだけだ」とその問題点を具体的に説明している。according to ～「～によると」。
(A) expensive「高価な」。
(C) material「素材」、thin「薄い」。

34 What does the man say he will do?

(A) Distribute some coupons
(B) Contact a factory
(C) Place an advertisement in the newspaper
(D) Research the competition

男性は何をするつもりだと言っていますか。

(A) クーポンを配布する。
(B) 工場に連絡する。
(C) 新聞に広告を出す。
(D) その競合会社を調査する。

正解 C 買い物バッグの改善のために、地元のアーティストにデザインを依頼するという女性の提案に対し、男性は賛同して、❹「この件について地元紙に広告を載せ、関心を持ってくれるアーティストに当店に連絡するよう呼びかけよう」と述べている。place an advertisement「広告を出す」。
(A) distribute「～を配布する」、coupon「クーポン」。
(D) research「～を調査する」、competition「競合会社、競争相手」。

Words & Phrases

reusable 再利用できる　grocery bag 買い物バッグ　groceries 食料雑貨類　rather ちょっと
simple 地味な、単純な　plain 無地の　interesting 興味を起こさせる　What if ～? ～したらどうですか
ask ～ to *do* ～に…するよう頼む　local 地元の　image 画像　ad 〈advertisementの略で〉広告
interested 関心を持っている　contact ～に連絡する

Questions 35 through 37 refer to the following conversation.

M ❶Welcome to Hersch Automotives, Linda. We appreciate your coming in as a marketing consultant for the next few months.

W Glad to be here. I've worked with many companies to improve their marketing strategies. I'm sure I'll be able to help you increase your sales as well.

M Wonderful! ❷If you need access to any of our data, just let me know.

W Well, ❸it would be useful to look at your sales figures for the past six months.

M OK—I'll get those to you shortly. Also, ❹we had already scheduled a focus group for next week on Monday. You're welcome to attend.

W Thanks. I'll put it on my calendar.

問題35-37は次の会話に関するものです。

Hersch自動車関連社へようこそ、Linda。これからの数カ月間、あなたがマーケティングコンサルタントとしていらしてくださることに感謝しています。

ここに来られてうれしく思います。私は多数の企業と仕事をし、マーケティング戦略を改善してきました。同様に私は、御社の売り上げを伸ばすお手伝いもできると確信しています。

素晴らしい！ 当社のデータへアクセスする必要がある場合は、私に知らせてください。

そうですね、御社の過去6カ月間の売上高を見られれば役に立つでしょう。

分かりました——すぐにそれらをお渡しします。またわれわれは、来週の月曜日にフォーカスグループを1件すでに予定に入れておりました。あなたもどうぞご出席ください。

ありがとうございます。それを私の予定表に入れておきます。

35 Why is the woman at the company?

(A) To inspect the property
(B) To serve as a consultant
(C) To apply for a position
(D) To sign a contract

女性はなぜその会社にいるのですか。

(A) 不動産を検査するため。
(B) コンサルタントとして勤めるため。
(C) 職に応募するため。
(D) 契約書に署名するため。

正解 B 男性は女性を、❶「Hersch自動車関連社へようこそ」と会社に迎え入れ、続けて「これからの数カ月間、あなたがマーケティングコンサルタントとして来てくれることに感謝している」と言っている。serve as ～「～として勤める」。
(A) inspect「～を検査する」、property「不動産」。
(C) apply for ～「～に応募する」、position「職」。
(D) sign「～に署名する」、contract「契約書」。

36 What would the woman like to review?

(A) An employee handbook
(B) A list of potential clients
(C) Some recent sales data
(D) The map of the facilities

女性は何を調査したいと思っていますか。

(A) 従業員ハンドブック
(B) 潜在顧客のリスト
(C) 最近の売り上げデータ
(D) 施設の地図

正解 C 男性から❷で、会社のデータへのアクセスが必要な場合は知らせるように言われたコンサルタントの女性は、❸「御社の過去6カ月間の売上高を見られれば役に立つだろう」と伝えている。よって、女性は男性の会社の最近の売り上げデータを調査したいと思っていると分かる。review「～を調査する、～を見直す」。
(B) potential「潜在的な」、client「顧客」。
(D) facility「施設」。

37 What is scheduled for next week?

(A) A focus group
(B) A renovation project
(C) A career fair
(D) A product launch

来週に何が予定されていますか。

(A) フォーカスグループ
(B) 改修プロジェクト
(C) 就職フェア
(D) 製品の発売

正解 A 男性は❹「われわれは、来週の月曜日にフォーカスグループを1件すでに予定に入れていた」と言い、女性にもそれに出席するよう誘っている。
(B) renovation「改修」。
(C) career「職業」。
(D) launch「発売、開始」。

Words & Phrases

automotive 自動車関連業　appreciate ～に感謝する　improve ～を改善する
strategy 戦略　increase ～を増やす　as well 同様に　useful 役に立つ　sales figures 売上高　past 過去の
shortly すぐに、間もなく　schedule ～の予定を組む　focus group フォーカスグループ（市場調査のために抽出された集団）
attend 出席する　calendar 予定表、日程表

Questions 38 through 40 refer to the following conversation with three speakers.

問題38-40は3人の話し手による次の会話に関するものです。

W ❶Welcome to Carly's Fitness. Can I help you?

Carly'sフィットネスへようこそ。ご用件は何でしょうか。

M Yes, hi. I'm here to fix your satellite dish.

はい、こんにちは。衛星放送受信アンテナを修理するためにこちらに伺いました。

W Oh, wonderful! ❷We haven't been able to get any signal on the TV in our workout room. Hey, Marsha! This gentleman's here to repair the satellite dish.

まあ、素晴らしい！ トレーニングルームのテレビで、まったく信号を受信できていないんです。ねえ、Marsha! こちらの男性は、衛星放送受信アンテナを修理するために、ここにいらしたのよ。

W Great! We had several unhappy club members here this morning. They're used to watching TV while they use the exercise machines.

良かった！ 今朝は不満を抱いたクラブ会員が数名いたんですよ。彼らは運動器具を使用する間、テレビを見るのに慣れているんです。

M ❸Sorry I'm late. ❹I've had lots of appointments for repairs today.

遅れて申し訳ありません。私は本日、修理のための予約が多数あったのです。

W I bet. ❺Last night's stormy weather must've knocked out quite a few satellite dishes. ❻That's what happened to ours.

そうでしょうね。昨夜の荒天が、かなりたくさんの衛星放送受信アンテナを使用不能にしたに違いありません。まさにそれが、私たちのものに起こったことです。

38 Where are the speakers?

(A) At an electronics shop
(B) At a sports stadium
(C) At a television studio
(D) At a fitness center

話し手たちはどこにいますか。

(A) 家電製品店
(B) スポーツスタジアム
(C) テレビ関連のスタジオ
(D) フィットネスセンター

正解 D 1人目の女性は❶「Carly'sフィットネスへようこそ」と男性を迎えている。その後も❷「トレーニングルームのテレビで、まったく信号を受信できていない」と述べているので、話し手たちはフィットネスセンターにいると分かる。
(A) 衛星放送受信アンテナについて話しているが、男性はその修理が目的でこの場にいると言っている。electronics shop「家電製品店」。

39 Why has the man arrived late?

(A) He wrote down the wrong time.
(B) He had several appointments.
(C) There was a lot of traffic.
(D) A location was hard to find.

男性はなぜ遅れて到着したのですか。

(A) 彼は間違った時間を書き留めたから。
(B) 彼は幾つもの予約があったから。
(C) 交通量が多かったから。
(D) 場所が見つけにくかったから。

正解 B アンテナの修理に来た男性は❸「遅れて申し訳ない」と謝罪した後、❹で「私は本日、修理の予約が多数あった」と遅れて到着した理由を説明している。
(A) write down ～「～を書き留める」。
(C) a lot of ～「たくさんの～」、traffic「交通量」。
(D) location「場所」。

40 Why has a satellite dish stopped working?

(A) It was damaged in a storm.
(B) It was not installed properly.
(C) A bill has not been paid.
(D) A password has been changed.

衛星放送受信アンテナはなぜ作動しなくなったのですか。

(A) それは荒天で損傷したから。
(B) それは適切に設置されていなかったから。
(C) 料金が支払われていないから。
(D) パスワードが変更されているから。

正解 A 2人目の女性は❺で、昨夜の荒天のせいで多くの衛星放送受信アンテナが使用不能になったに違いないと述べ、続けて❻「まさにそれが、私たちのものに起こったことだ」と説明している。oursは、女性たちの所のアンテナを指すので、荒天が原因でそのアンテナが使用不能になったと判断できる。damage「～を損傷させる」。
(B) install「～を設置する」、properly「適切に」。
(C) bill「料金、請求書」。

Words & Phrases

fix ～を修理する　satellite dish 衛星放送受信アンテナ　signal 信号
workout トレーニング、運動　repair 〈動詞で〉～を修理する、〈名詞で〉修理　several 幾つかの、〈多い感じで〉幾つもの
unhappy 不満を抱いた　be used to *doing* ～することに慣れている　appointment 予約　I bet. そうでしょうね。
stormy 荒天の　knock out ～ ～を使用不能にする　quite a few ～ かなりたくさんの～　happen to ～ ～に起こる

Questions 41 through 43 refer to the following conversation.

問題41-43は次の会話に関するものです。

M Hi, Claire. As I'm sure you know, Jim's last day at the company is this Friday. ❶He's decided to pursue an advanced business degree. He's going back to university full-time next month.

こんにちは、Claire。きっと知っていると思いますが、Jimの出社最終日は今度の金曜日なんです。彼は、経営学の上級学位を進み続けることに決めました。来月、彼はフルタイムで大学に戻ります。

W He mentioned that to me. That's exciting for him! So, what will happen to everything he's been working on?

彼はそのことを私に話してくれました。彼にとって、心を躍らせることですね！それで、彼が取り組んできたこと全てについては、どうなるんですか。

M Actually, that's what I wanted to talk to you about. ❷The management team would like you to take over some of his accounts. ❸Jim can bring you up to date on the details of all his work.

実は、それがまさにあなたと話したかったことです。経営陣は、彼の得意先の幾つかをあなたに引き継いでもらいたいと考えています。Jimは、自分の仕事全ての詳細に関する最新情報をあなたに伝えてくれます。

W OK. ❹I just saw him go into his office. I'll go there to talk to him now.

分かりました。ちょうど彼が自身の執務室に入っていくのが見えました。すぐにそこへ行って彼と話してみます。

41 What does the man say Jim has decided to do?

(A) Hire some managers
(B) Get a business degree
(C) Request a budget increase
(D) Speak at a conference

男性は、Jimが何をすることに決めたと言っていますか。

(A) 管理者を雇う。
(B) 経営学の学位を取得する。
(C) 予算の増額を依頼する。
(D) 協議会で話す。

正解 B 男性は、今度の金曜日はJimの出社最終日であると伝えた後、❶「彼は、経営学の上級学位を進み続けることに決めた」と言っている。上級学位を続けることをget a business degreeと表している(B)が正解。
(A) hire「～を雇う」、manager「管理者」。
(C) request「～を依頼する」、budget「予算」、increase「増加」。
(D) conference「協議会」。

42 What does the man ask the woman to do?

(A) Take over some accounts
(B) Lead a mentorship program
(C) Organize a training seminar
(D) Conduct some interviews

男性は女性に何をするよう求めていますか。

(A) 幾つかの得意先を引き継ぐ。
(B) 指導プログラムを主導する。
(C) 研修セミナーを企画する。
(D) 面接を実施する。

正解 A Jimが取り組んできた仕事はどうなるのかと尋ねる女性に対し、男性は❷「経営陣は、彼の得意先の幾つかをあなたに引き継いでもらいたいと考えている」と説明している。続けて❸で、Jimが仕事の詳細に関する最新情報を女性に伝えてくれると引き継ぎについて述べている。
(B) lead「～を主導する」、mentorship「指導」。
(C) organize「～を企画する」、training「研修」。
(D) conduct「～を実施する、～を行う」。

43 Where will the woman go next?

(A) To a cafeteria
(B) To a construction site
(C) To a colleague's office
(D) To a supply room

女性は次にどこへ行きますか。

(A) カフェテリア
(B) 建設現場
(C) 同僚の執務室
(D) 備品室

正解 C ❷・❸で、自分がJimの得意先を引き継ぐことと、Jimから仕事の詳細を伝えてもらえると聞いた女性は、❹「ちょうど彼が自身の執務室に入っていくのが見えた。すぐにそこへ行って彼と話してみる」と述べている。Jimのことをcolleague「同僚」と表している(C)が正解。
(B) construction「建設」、site「現場、場所」。
(D) supply「備品」。

Words & Phrases

decide to *do* ～することに決める　pursue 〈進路など〉を進み続ける、～を追い求める　advanced degree 〈学士号より上の修士号や博士号を指して〉上級学位　full-time フルタイムで　mention ～について述べる　work on ～ ～に取り組む　actually 実は　management team 経営陣　take over ～ ～を引き継ぐ　account 〈会社の〉得意先　bring ～ up to date on … …に関する最新の情報を～に伝える　details 詳細

Questions 44 through 46 refer to the following conversation.

M Hi, my name is Joseph Kent. I have an appointment at three o'clock today—❶I brought the new patient forms that you asked me to fill out at home.

W Great, thanks. That will save us some time. Um… unfortunately, ❷the doctor is running about 30 minutes behind. Please take a seat. We have some magazines, and ❸there's coffee and tea.

M Oh, ❹tea sounds nice, especially since it's such a cold day.

問題44-46は次の会話に関するものです。

こんにちは、Joseph Kentと申します。今日の3時に予約しています――家で記入するように頼まれた、初診患者向けの用紙を持ってきました。

良かった、ありがとうございます。これで時間を節約できます。ええと…あいにく、医師は30分ほど予定より遅れています。どうぞお座りください。当院では、雑誌をご用意しており、またコーヒーと紅茶もございます。

ああ、紅茶はいいですね、特にこんな寒い日ですから。

44 What did the man do in advance?

(A) He checked a bus map.
(B) He paid for a delivery.
(C) He completed some paperwork.
(D) He read some reviews online.

男性は前もって何をしましたか。

(A) 彼はバスの路線図を確認した。
(B) 彼は配送の代金を払った。
(C) 彼は書類に全て記入した。
(D) 彼はオンラインでレビューを読んだ。

正解 C 3時に予約を入れていると言う男性は❶「家で記入するように頼まれた、初診患者向けの用紙を持ってきた」と述べている。用紙に記入することをcomplete paperworkと表している(C)が正解。in advance「前もって」。complete「～に全て記入する」、paperwork「書類」。
(B) pay for ～「～の代金を払う」、delivery「配送」。
(D) review「レビュー、評価」、online「オンラインで」。

45 Where does the woman most likely work?

(A) At a pharmacy
(B) At a coffee shop
(C) At a medical office
(D) At a bookstore

女性はどこで働いていると考えられますか。

(A) 薬局
(B) コーヒーショップ
(C) 診療所
(D) 書店

正解 C 男性は女性に、❶「家で記入するように頼まれた、初診患者向けの用紙を持ってきた」と伝えている。また、女性は❷「医師は30分ほど予定より遅れている」と述べている。よって、女性は患者や医師のいる、medical office「診療所」で働いていると考えられる。
(A) pharmacy「薬局」。
(B) コーヒーの用意があると伝えているが、販売しているとは述べていない。

46 What will the man probably do next?

(A) Reschedule his appointment
(B) Have some tea
(C) Call a friend
(D) Visit another location

男性はおそらく次に何をしますか。

(A) 自分の予約の日時を変更する。
(B) 紅茶を飲む。
(C) 友人に電話する。
(D) 別の場所を訪問する。

正解 B 男性は、医師が予定より遅れていると伝えられた後、診療所には❸「コーヒーと紅茶もある」と説明を受けたのに対し、❹「紅茶はいいね、特にこんな寒い日だから」と応じている。よって男性は、これから紅茶を飲むと考えられる。
(A) reschedule「～の日時を変更する」。
(D) location「場所」。

Words & Phrases

appointment 予約　patient 患者　form 用紙　fill out ～ ～に記入する
save ～ … ～の…を節約する　unfortunately あいにく、残念ながら　run behind 予定より遅れる　take a seat 座る
sound ～のように思われる　especially 特に

Questions 47 through 49 refer to the following conversation.

問題47-49は次の会話に関するものです。

M Hi, Beverly. ❶How's the sales presentation for the Smith Corporation going? It would be great to pick up such a large company as a new client for our accounting software.

こんにちは、Beverly。Smith社への販売プレゼンテーションの進み具合はどうですか。当社の会計ソフトウエアの新規顧客としてあんな大企業を獲得できたら素晴らしいですね。

W ❷I just finished updating the slides for that presentation.

私はちょうど、そのプレゼンテーション用のスライドを更新し終えました。

M ❸That's good to hear, because they called to ask if we could move the video chat meeting to this afternoon instead of tomorrow. Will that work for you?

それは良かったです。というのも、彼らが電話をしてきて、ビデオチャット会議を明日ではなく今日の午後に変えられるかどうか尋ねてきたので。それはあなたの都合に合いますか。

W Hmm, ❹the webcam on my laptop stopped working this morning.

ええと、今朝、私のノートパソコンのウェブカメラが作動しなくなったのです。

M Well, I helped Benjamin fix his webcam last week.

なるほど、僕は先週、Benjaminが自身のウェブカメラを直すのを手助けしましたよ。

W Oh, perfect!

あら、完璧ですね！

47 What are the speakers preparing for?

(A) A safety inspection
(B) A sales presentation
(C) A training seminar
(D) A budget meeting

話し手たちは何の準備をしていますか。

(A) 安全検査
(B) 販売プレゼンテーション
(C) 研修セミナー
(D) 予算会議

正解 B 男性は女性に❶で、Smith社への販売プレゼンテーションの進み具合を尋ねている。さらに❸で、そのプレゼンテーションを行うビデオチャット会議の日程変更について述べている。prepare for ～「～の準備をする」。
(A) safety「安全」、inspection「検査」。
(C) training「研修」。
(D) Smith社とのビデオチャット会議に言及はあるが、予算会議については述べられていない。

48 According to the man, why did the Smith Corporation call?

(A) To request an instruction manual
(B) To open an account
(C) To change a meeting time
(D) To complain about a service

男性によると、Smith社はなぜ電話をしてきたのですか。

(A) 取扱説明書を求めるため。
(B) 口座を開設するため。
(C) 会議の時間を変更するため。
(D) サービスについて苦情を言うため。

正解 C ❷で、Smith社へのプレゼンテーション用のスライドの更新作業を終えたと聞いた男性は、❸「それは良かった。というのも、彼らが電話をしてきて、ビデオチャット会議を明日ではなく今日の午後に変えられるかどうか尋ねてきたので」と伝えている。
(A) request「～を求める」、instruction manual「取扱説明書」。
(B) account「口座」。
(D) complain about ～「～について苦情を言う」。

49 What does the man mean when he says, "I helped Benjamin fix his webcam last week"?

(A) He is waiting for a payment.
(B) He can assist the woman.
(C) He was not able to attend an event.
(D) He does not have to purchase more equipment.

男性は"I helped Benjamin fix his webcam last week"という発言で、何を意味していますか。

(A) 彼は支払いを待っている。
(B) 彼は女性を手伝うことができる。
(C) 彼はイベントに参加することができなかった。
(D) 彼は機器をさらに購入する必要がない。

正解 B ❹「今朝、私のノートパソコンのウェブカメラが作動しなくなった」と述べる女性に対し、男性は下線部で「僕は先週、Benjaminが自身のウェブカメラを直すのを手助けした」と伝えている。よって、そのときと同様に男性は女性のウェブカメラを直す手伝いができることを示唆していると判断できる。assist「～を手伝う」。
(A) payment「支払い」。
(C) attend「～に参加する」。
(D) purchase「～を購入する」、equipment「機器」。

Words & Phrases

corporation 企業　pick up ～ ～を獲得する　accounting 会計　chat チャット、談話
instead of ～ ～ではなくて　work for ～ ～の都合に合う　webcam ウェブカメラ　fix ～を直す

Questions 50 through 52 refer to the following conversation.

問題50-52は次の会話に関するものです。

W Yoshi, ❶at last week's manufacturing trade show I saw some new technology that could really help improve productivity here at the factory—by up to ten percent.

Yoshi、私は先週の製造業見本市で、うちの工場の生産性を向上させるのにまさに役立ちそうな新しい機器を目にしました。——最大で10パーセントもです。

M Really? What is it?

本当ですか。それは何ですか。

W ❷A smart helmet—a helmet with a screen attached that managers can pull down to access information and communicate with the control room. Managers can wear the technology instead of carrying it around so their hands will be free.

ハイテクのヘルメットで——スクリーンが付属していて、管理者がそれを引き下ろして情報にアクセスし、制御室とやりとりできるヘルメットです。管理者は持ち歩く代わりに機器を着用できるので、両手が自由になるんです。

M There was a budget surplus at the end of last quarter.

前四半期末には予算の余剰がありましたよ。

W Great. ❸I could talk to the helmet's makers about a possible demonstration for everyone.

素晴らしい。皆のために実演可能か、私がそのヘルメット製造業者に相談してみてもいいですよ。

M That'd be good. Thanks.

そうしてもらえるといいですね。ありがとう。

50 What are the speakers mainly discussing?

(A) A delayed shipment
(B) A construction project
(C) Some new technology
(D) Some software problems

話し手たちは主に何について話し合っていますか。

(A) 遅延している発送品
(B) 建設プロジェクト
(C) 新しい機器
(D) ソフトウエアの問題

正解 C 女性は❶「私は先週の製造業見本市で、うちの工場の生産性を向上させるのにまさに役立ちそうな新しい機器を目にした」と述べている。その後も、話し手たちはその新しい機器の詳細や実演について会話を続けている。
(A) delay「～を遅延させる」、shipment「発送品」。
(B) construction「建設」。

51 Why does the man say, "There was a budget surplus at the end of last quarter"?

(A) To correct an error
(B) To offer congratulations
(C) To make a complaint about a policy
(D) To express interest in an idea

男性はなぜ "There was a budget surplus at the end of last quarter"と言っていますか。

(A) 誤りを訂正するため。
(B) 祝辞を述べるため。
(C) 方針について苦情を言うため。
(D) アイデアに関心を示すため。

正解 D 女性から❷で、新しい機器の説明を聞いた男性は、下線部で「前四半期末には予算の余剰があった」と伝えている。これは、余った予算をその機器の購入に充てられる可能性があることを意味すると考えられるので、男性は機器への関心を示すためにこの発言をしていると判断できる。新しい機器を導入することをan ideaと表している(D)が正解。express interest in ～「～に興味を示す」。
(A) correct「～を訂正する」、error「誤り」。
(C) make a complaint about ～「～について苦情を言う」、policy「方針」。

52 What does the woman offer to do?

(A) Contact a manufacturer
(B) Lead a tour
(C) Make a safety checklist
(D) Revise work assignments

女性は何をすることを申し出ていますか。

(A) 製造会社に連絡する。
(B) ツアーを主導する。
(C) 安全チェックリストを作成する。
(D) 業務の割り当てを見直す。

正解 A 女性は工場の生産性の向上に役立ちそうなハイテクのヘルメットについて、❸「皆のために実演可能か、私がそのヘルメット製造業者に相談してみてもいい」と申し出ているので、(A)が正解。manufacturer「製造会社、製作者」。
(C) safety checklist「安全チェックリスト」。
(D) revise「～を見直す、～を修正する」、assignment「割り当てられた仕事」。

Words & Phrases

manufacturing 製造業　trade show 見本市　technology 〈科学技術を用いた〉機器
improve ～を向上させる　productivity 生産性　up to ～ 最大で～まで　smart ハイテクの　attach ～を付属させる
pull down ～ ～を引き下ろす　communicate with ～ ～とやりとりする　carry around ～ ～を持ち歩く
budget 予算(額)　surplus 余剰　quarter 四半期　possible 可能な　demonstration 実演、デモ

Questions 53 through 55 refer to the following conversation.

問題53-55は次の会話に関するものです。

W OK, ❶this is the last commercial property I'll be showing you today. What do you think? ❷This kitchen will work for your business, won't it?

さて、こちらが本日私がお見せする最後の商業用物件です。どう思われますか。このキッチンはお客さまのお店の役に立つのではないでしょうか。

M Yes! ❸I can definitely bake a lot of bread here. Plus, I like that the building's on a main street—that'll be good for attracting customers to my new business.

はい。ここなら間違いなくたくさんのパンを焼けます。それに、建物が大通りにあるのが気に入っています――顧客を私の新しい店に引き付けるのに良いでしょう。

W And, ❹there isn't much competition in the area. There are some restaurants, but no bakeries for a couple of miles.

また、この地域にはあまり競争がありません。レストランは何軒かありますが、2～3マイル内にパン屋はありません。

M Interesting. And ❺what about the rent? Does it fall within my budget?

いいですね。それから、家賃はどうでしょうか。私の予算の範囲内に収まりますか。

W Well, the price is a little higher than you wanted, but we can negotiate with the landlord.

ええと、価格はご希望されたものより若干高いですが、私たちは家主と交渉することができます。

53 What are the speakers doing?

(A) Conducting job interviews
(B) Visiting a property
(C) Ordering some supplies
(D) Applying for a loan

話し手たちは何をしていますか。

(A) 就職面接を行っている。
(B) 物件を訪問している。
(C) 供給品を注文している。
(D) 融資を申し込んでいる。

正解 B 女性は❶「これが本日私が見せる最後の商業用物件だ」と伝えた後、男性に物件の感想を求め、続けて❷で、キッチンが男性の店に適しているのではないかと確認している。よって、女性は不動産業者で、男性は顧客であり、物件を訪問していると判断できる。
(A) conduct「～を行う」、job interview「就職面接」。
(C) order「～を注文する」、supply「供給（品）」。
(D) apply for ～「～を申し込む」、loan「融資」。

54 What type of business is the man opening?

(A) A bakery
(B) A restaurant
(C) A hardware store
(D) A furniture store

男性はどのような店を始めますか。

(A) パン屋
(B) レストラン
(C) 金物店
(D) 家具店

正解 A 男性は❸「ここなら間違いなくたくさんのパンを焼ける」と述べている。また、女性は❹「この地域にはあまり競争がない。レストランは何軒かあるが、2～3マイル内にパン屋はない」と説明している。
(B) 候補物件の立地について、女性は競争はないと述べた後、レストランはあると述べているので、男性が始める店はレストランではない。
(C) hardware store「金物店」。

55 What does the man ask the woman about?

(A) A deadline
(B) A price
(C) A name
(D) A process

男性は女性に何について尋ねていますか。

(A) 期限
(B) 価格
(C) 名前
(D) 手続き

正解 B 物件についての説明を聞いた男性は、❺「家賃はどうか。私の予算の範囲内に収まるか」と女性に尋ねている。rentをprice「価格」と表している(B)が正解。
(D) process「手続き」。

Words & Phrases

commercial 商業用の　property 不動産物件　work 役に立つ、うまくいく
business 店、事業　definitely 間違いなく　bake 〈パンなど〉を焼く　plus それに、加えて　attract ～を引き付ける
competition 競争　rent 家賃　fall within ～ ～の範囲内に収まる　negotiate with ～ ～と交渉する　landlord 家主

Questions 56 through 58 refer to the following conversation.

問題56-58は次の会話に関するものです。

W David, ❶the company wants to update the way we conduct performance reviews for employees. ❷Would you like to be on the committee to choose the new evaluation process?

David、会社では従業員の勤務評定を実施するやり方を新しくしたいと考えています。新しい評価プロセスを選定する委員会に入りたいですか。

M I'm interested, but I'm pretty busy with other work now. ❸What's the deadline for finalizing the new process?

興味はありますが、私は現在、他の仕事でかなり忙しいのです。新しいプロセスを最終決定する期限はいつですか。

W We'd have to be finished by the end of March. But I already have some ideas. For example, ❹I read about a computer application that lets employees set short-term goals and provides more immediate feedback. ❺An application like that could work well for our company.

3月末までに終えなければならないでしょう。でも、私にはすでに幾つかアイデアがあります。例えば、従業員に短期的目標を設定させて、より迅速なフィードバックを提供するコンピューターアプリケーションについて読みました。そのようなアプリケーションは、当社にとても役立つでしょう。

56 What does the company want to change?

(A) A database for storing customer information
(B) A policy for taking vacation time
(C) A process for evaluating employees
(D) A method for ordering office supplies

会社は何を変更したいと考えていますか。

(A) 顧客情報保存用データベース
(B) 休暇取得の方針
(C) 従業員評価のプロセス
(D) 事務用品の注文方法

正解 C 女性は❶「会社では従業員の勤務評定を実施するやり方を新しくしたいと考えている」と述べてから、❷「新しい評価プロセスを選定する委員会に入りたいか」と男性に尋ねている。evaluate「～を評価する」。
(A) store「～を保存する、～を保管する」。
(D) method「方法」、office supply「事務用品」。

57 What does the man ask about?

(A) A vendor's address
(B) A room reservation
(C) A budget surplus
(D) A project deadline

男性は何について尋ねていますか。

(A) 販売業者の住所
(B) 部屋の予約
(C) 予算の余剰
(D) プロジェクトの最終期限

正解 D ❷で、新しい評価プロセスを選定する委員会に入る意向を問われた男性は、興味はあるが忙しいと述べてから、❸「新しいプロセスを最終決定する期限はいつか」と女性に尋ねている。新しい評価のプロセスを選定することをproject「プロジェクト」と表している(D)が正解。
(A) vendor「販売業者」。
(B) reservation「予約」。
(C) surplus「余剰」。

58 What will the woman most likely suggest doing?

(A) Hiring an outside consultant
(B) Using a computer application
(C) Conducting a survey
(D) Promoting an employee

女性は何をすることを提案すると考えられますか。

(A) 社外コンサルタントを雇用すること。
(B) コンピューターアプリケーションを使用すること。
(C) 調査を実施すること。
(D) ある従業員を昇進させること。

正解 B 新しい評価プロセスについて、すでに幾つかアイデアがあると言う女性は、❹「従業員に短期的目標を設定させて、より迅速なフィードバックを提供するコンピューターアプリケーションについて読んだ」と具体例を説明し、続けて❺で、そのようなアプリケーションが会社に役立つ可能性を伝えているので(B)が正解。
(A) hire「～を雇用する」。
(C) survey「調査」。
(D) promote「～を昇進させる」。

Words & Phrases

conduct ～を実施する　performance review 勤務評定　employee 従業員
committee 委員会　evaluation 評価　process プロセス、過程　pretty かなり　deadline 最終期限
finalize ～を最終決定する　application アプリケーション　short-term 短期的な　goal 目標
provide ～を提供する　immediate 迅速な、即座の　feedback フィードバック、意見

Questions 59 through 61 refer to the following conversation with three speakers.

問題59-61は3人の話し手による次の会話に関するものです。

W ❶I'm here to pick up my rental car. My name's Janet Chen. Here's my confirmation number.

こちらにレンタカーを受け取りに来ました。Janet Chenと申します。こちらが私の確認番号です。

W One moment... ❷OK, I found your reservation, Ms. Chen—a midsize sedan. The total for your rental will be 226 dollars.

少々お待ちください…はい、ご予約を見つけました、Chenさん——中型のセダン車ですね。レンタル料金の合計は226ドルになります。

W ❸I read online that your company offers a discount to teachers?

こちらの会社は教師に割引を提供していると、オンラインで読んだのですが。

W Hmm, not that I'm aware of. ❹Let me ask my supervisor. Hey, Ernesto? Do we give a discount to teachers?

ええと、私の知る限りはありません。上司に尋ねさせてください。あの、Ernesto。当店は教師の方々に割引を提供していますか。

M Yeah, ❺teachers get ten percent off if they show their employee identification card.

はい、教師の方々はご自身の従業員用の身元証明書を提示すれば、10パーセント引きが得られます。

59 Where does the conversation most likely take place?

(A) At a university campus
(B) At a shipping company
(C) At a rental car agency
(D) At a moving company

会話はどこで行われていると考えられますか。

(A) 大学のキャンパス
(B) 運送会社
(C) レンタカーの代理店
(D) 引越会社

正解 C 1人目の女性が❶で、レンタカーを受け取りに来たと言っているのに対し、2人目の女性は、❷で予約の確認が取れたと述べ、車種とレンタル料金を伝えている。よって、会話はレンタカーの代理店で行われていると考えられる。take place「行われる」。
(A) campus「〈大学などの〉キャンパス、構内」。
(B) shipping company「運送会社」。

60 What does Janet Chen inquire about?

(A) A discount
(B) A Web site
(C) A schedule change
(D) A new product

Janet Chenは何について尋ねていますか。

(A) 割引
(B) ウェブサイト
(C) 予定変更
(D) 新製品

正解 A ❶で、レンタカーを受け取りに来たと述べた女性は、Janet Chenと名乗っている。さらにこの女性は❸で、「こちらの会社は教師に割引を提供していると、オンラインで読んだのだが」と割引について尋ねている。inquire about ～「～について尋ねる」。
(B) Chenさんはオンラインに割引情報が載っていたと述べているだけで、ウェブサイトについて尋ねてはいない。

61 What does the man say is required?

(A) A password
(B) An employee ID
(C) A safety inspection
(D) An appointment

男性は何が必要であると言っていますか。

(A) パスワード
(B) 従業員用の身元証明書
(C) 安全検査
(D) 面会の予約

正解 B 教師への割引について尋ねられた2人目の女性が、❹でそれを上司の男性に確認している。男性は❺で、「教師は自身の従業員用の身元証明書を提示すれば、10パーセント引きが得られる」と述べている。require「～を必要とする」。IDはidentification (card)の略。
(C) safety「安全」、inspection「検査」。
(D) appointment「面会の予約」。

Words & Phrases

pick up ～ ～を受け取る　rental car レンタカー　confirmation 確認　reservation 予約
midsize 中型の　sedan セダン車　total 合計　rental レンタル料金、賃貸料　discount 割引
be aware of ～ ～を知っている、～に気付いている　supervisor 上司　identification card 身元証明書

Questions 62 through 64 refer to the following conversation and sign.

問題62-64は次の会話と掲示板に関するものです。

W Hello. Welcome to Graphite Designs. How can I help you?

こんにちは。Graphiteデザイン社へようこそ。どのようなご用件でしょうか。

M Hi. ❶I have a package delivery here for… uh… Ava Hashimoto.

こんにちは。こちらへの小包の配達物があるのですが…ええと…Ava Hashimoto様宛てです。

W Certainly. But ❷our elevator's out of service right now, so if you'd like, I can just sign for it. Then you won't have to take the stairs.

承知しました。ですが、こちらのエレベーターがちょうど今運転休止中なので、よろしければ、私がそれに署名だけできますよ。そうすれば、あなたは階段を使う必要がないでしょう。

M Oh, thanks. But ❸this delivery requires her signature. So I'll need to bring the signed slip back to the post office with me.

ああ、ありがとうございます。ですが、この配達物は本人の署名が不可欠なんです。それで私は、署名済みの伝票を郵便局まで持ち帰らなくてはいけないのです。

W OK, no problem. ❹Her office is located in Suite Eight. Our directory's right next to the stairwell. I'll let her know you're coming.

なるほど、問題ありません。彼女の執務室はスイート8にあります。当館の案内板は、階段の吹き抜けのちょうど隣です。あなたが来ることを彼女に知らせますね。

Graphite Designs—Directory

First floor	.... Lobby
Second floor	.... Suites 1–5
Third floor	.... Suites 6–8
Fourth floor	.... Suites 9–12

Graphiteデザイン社——案内板

1階	.... ロビー
2階	.... スイート1〜5
3階	.... スイート6〜8
4階	.... スイート9〜12

62 Why is the man visiting the building?

(A) To deliver a package
(B) To interview a job candidate
(C) To repair some equipment
(D) To discuss some catering details

男性はなぜ建物を訪れているのですか。

(A) 小包を配達するため。
(B) 仕事の候補者と面接するため。
(C) 設備を修理するため。
(D) ケータリングの詳細を話し合うため。

正解 A 来訪の用件を尋ねられた男性は、❶「ここへの小包の配達物がある」と答えている。a package deliveryをdeliver a packageと表している(A)が正解。deliver「～を配達する」。
(B) interview「～と面接する」、candidate「候補者」。
(C) エレベーターが運転休止中だと述べられているが、男性はその修理に来たとは言っていない。repair「～を修理する」、equipment「設備、機器」。
(D) catering「ケータリング」。

---

63 What problem does the woman mention?

(A) Some mail has arrived late.
(B) Some supplies are not available.
(C) A staff member is not in the building.
(D) An elevator is not working.

女性はどんな問題について述べていますか。

(A) 郵便物が遅れて届いた。
(B) 備品が手に入らない。
(C) ある職員が建物内にいない。
(D) エレベーターが作動していない。

正解 D 女性は❷「こちらのエレベーターがちょうど今運転休止中だ」と小包の配達に訪れた男性に伝えている。out of serviceをnot workingと表している(D)が正解。
(A) mail「郵便物」。
(B) supply「備品」、available「手に入る、利用できる」。

---

64 Look at the graphic. Where will the man go next?

(A) To the first floor
(B) To the second floor
(C) To the third floor
(D) To the fourth floor

図を見てください。男性は次にどこへ行きますか。

(A) 1階
(B) 2階
(C) 3階
(D) 4階

正解 C ❶で小包の配達に来たと述べた男性は❸で、配達の完了には宛名の本人による署名が必要だと説明している。それに対して女性は、❹「彼女の執務室はスイート8にある」とその人物の居所を伝えている。図を見ると、スイート8があるのは3階。よって、男性は次に3階へ行くと分かる。(C)が正解。

Words & Phrases

sign 掲示板、看板　package 小包　delivery 配達(物)　out of service 運転中止になって、使われていない
right now ちょうど今　sign for ～ ～に署名をする　stairs 階段　require ～を不可欠とする　signature 署名
slip 伝票　be located in ～ ～にある、～に位置する　suite スイート(オフィスやホテルなどの一続きの部屋)
directory 〈ビルなどの〉案内板　next to ～ ～の隣に　stairwell 〈階段を含む〉吹き抜け
掲示板 lobby ロビー

Questions 65 through 67 refer to the following conversation and map.

M ❶I'm very glad you've decided to rent an apartment in our complex, Ms. Kendall. I'm sure you're going to love living here.

W Thank you! ❷I'm excited that the complex has a gym. I'll definitely use that!

M Absolutely. Just don't forget that you'll need a key to get in. The gym key's included on the ring with the keys to your new apartment.

W OK! Oh... do I have an assigned parking spot?

M I'm glad you asked. ❸Let me give you a map of the grounds. ❹Each tenant is assigned one parking spot. Yours is in the lot next to the garden, behind the building.

問題65-67は次の会話と地図に関するものです。

Kendallさん、当総合住宅のアパートの１室を借りることに決めてくださり、とてもうれしいです。あなたはきっと、ここでの生活を好きになるでしょう。

ありがとうございます。総合住宅にジムがあることに、私は心を躍らせています。必ずそれを利用しますよ！

もちろんです。ただ、中に入るには鍵が必要だということを忘れないでください。ジムの鍵は、あなたの新しいアパートの鍵と一緒にキーリングに含まれています。

分かりました！あ…私には割り当ての駐車場所がありますか。

聞いてくださって良かったです。敷地の地図を差し上げましょう。各借家人に１つの駐車場所が割り当てられています。あなたのものは建物の裏側、庭の隣の区画にあります。

MAP OF GROUNDS

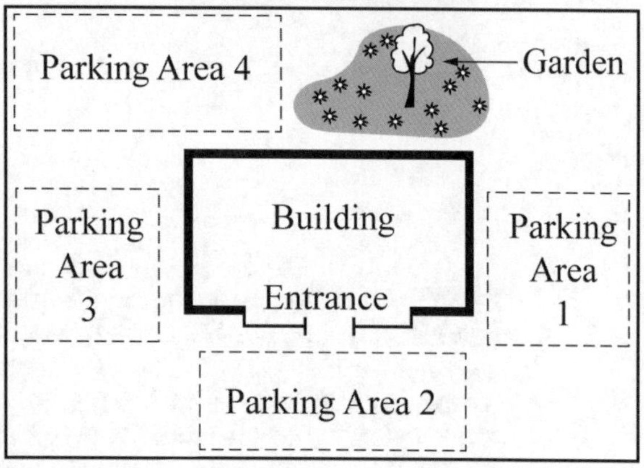

敷地地図

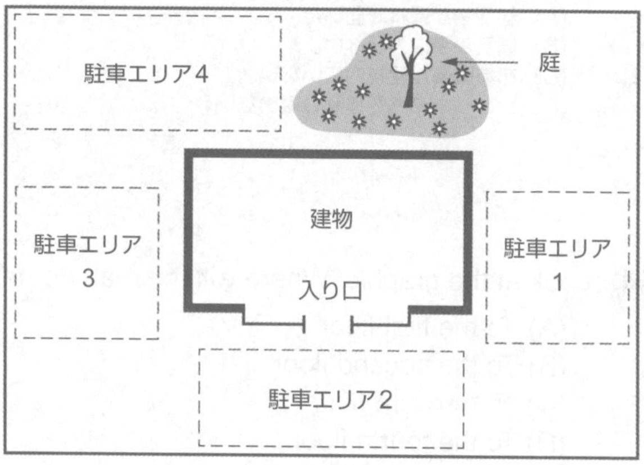

65 What most likely is the man's job?

(A) Fitness instructor
(B) Apartment manager
(C) Hotel clerk
(D) Interior decorator

男性の職業は何だと考えられますか。

(A) フィットネスインストラクター
(B) アパートの管理人
(C) ホテルのフロント係
(D) 室内装飾家

正解 B 男性は女性に、❶「当総合住宅のアパートの１室を借りることに決めてくれて、とてもうれしい」と言っている。その後も、総合住宅のジムを利用するための鍵の所在と駐車場について説明していることから、男性はアパートの管理人だと考えられる。manager「管理人」。
(A) instructor「インストラクター、講師」。
(C) clerk「フロント係、事務職員」。
(D) interior「室内、インテリア」、decorator「装飾家」。

---

66 What does the woman say she is excited about?

(A) Having more space
(B) Reducing an expense
(C) Taking a vacation
(D) Using a facility

女性は何について心を躍らせていると言っていますか。

(A) より広いスペースを持つこと。
(B) 費用を削減すること。
(C) 休暇を取ること。
(D) 施設を利用すること。

正解 D 女性は❷「総合住宅にジムがあることに、私は心を躍らせている。必ずそれを利用するつもりだ」と伝えている。gymをfacility「施設」と言い換えている(D)が正解。❷の２文目のuse thatのthatはgymを指す。
(A) アパートや駐車場について述べられているが、広さに言及はない。
(B) reduce「～を削減する」、expense「費用」。

---

67 Look at the graphic. Where should the woman park her car?

(A) In Parking Area 1
(B) In Parking Area 2
(C) In Parking Area 3
(D) In Parking Area 4

図を見てください。女性はどこに自分の車を駐車すべきですか。

(A) 駐車エリア1
(B) 駐車エリア2
(C) 駐車エリア3
(D) 駐車エリア4

正解 D 割り当ての駐車場所について尋ねられた男性は、❸で女性に敷地内の地図を渡している。続けて❹「各借家人に１つの駐車場所が割り当てられている。あなたのものは建物の裏側、庭の隣の区画にある」と説明している。図を見ると、建物の裏側に位置し、かつ庭の隣にある区画は駐車エリア4。よって、女性が自分の車を駐車すべき場所は(D)。

Words & Phrases

decide to *do* ～することに決める　rent ～を借りる、～を賃借する　apartment アパート(の１室)
complex 複合施設、団地　gym ジム　definitely 必ず　absolutely もちろん　include ～を含む
ring リング、輪　assign ～を割り当てる　parking spot 駐車場所　grounds 敷地、地面　tenant 借家人、賃借人
assign ～ … ～に…を割り当てる　lot 区画、場所
地図 entrance 入り口

Questions 68 through 70 refer to the following conversation and menu.

問題68-70は次の会話とメニューに関するものです。

M Hi, Marissa. Thanks for coming in to work on your day off.

やあ、Marissa。あなたの休みの日に出勤してくれてありがとう。

W Oh, it's no problem. I could use the extra money.

ああ、それは問題ありません。余分なお金をいただけるのはありがたいです。

M Well, I really appreciate it. ❶I completely forgot about Jon's vacation and didn't schedule enough waitstaff... The restaurant's really busy tonight.

ええと、本当に感謝しています。私はJonの休暇のことをすっかり忘れていて、十分な給仕スタッフを予定に入れなかったんですよ…。今夜、レストランは本当に忙しいのです。

W ❷Which tables would you like me to cover?

私はどのテーブルを担当しましょうか。

M ❸I'd like you to wait on tables two, three, and four. Oh, and don't forget to remind the customers about our new dessert: pumpkin pie. It's on special right now, so I've added it to the menu with the special price. We're hoping to sell a lot of it.

あなたには、2番、3番、4番テーブルの給仕をしてもらいたいのです。ああ、それからお客さまに当店の新しいデザートである、カボチャパイについてお知らせするのを忘れないでください。現在は特価になっているので、特別価格でメニューに加えました。それをたくさん販売したいと思っています。

68 What problem does the man mention?

(A) He made a scheduling mistake.
(B) He forgot to buy some ingredients.
(C) A refrigerator was malfunctioning.
(D) A supply delivery was late.

男性はどんな問題について述べていますか。

(A) 彼はスケジュール作成の間違いを犯した。
(B) 彼は幾つかの材料を買い忘れた。
(C) 冷蔵庫が故障していた。
(D) 供給品の配達が遅れた。

正解 A 男性は女性に、休みの日だったにもかかわらず出勤してもらったことについてお礼を述べてから、❶「私はJonの休暇のことをすっかり忘れていて、十分な給仕スタッフを予定に入れなかった」と言っている。scheduling「スケジュール作成、日程計画」、mistake「間違い、ミス」。
(B) ingredient「材料」。
(C) refrigerator「冷蔵庫」、malfunction「〈機械などが〉故障する」。
(D) supply「供給(品)」。

69 Who most likely is the woman?

(A) A chef
(B) A waitress
(C) A dishwasher
(D) A cashier

女性は誰だと考えられますか。

(A) シェフ
(B) ウエートレス
(C) 洗い場担当
(D) レジ係

正解 B ❶で十分な給仕スタッフを予定に入れなかったと述べた男性に対し、女性は❷「私はどのテーブルを担当しましょうか」と指示を仰いでいる。それに対し男性は❸で、女性に担当してほしいテーブル番号を伝え、接客時の注意点を説明している。よって、女性は給仕スタッフだと考えられる。waitstaffを(B)ではa waitressと表している。
(C) dishwasher「洗い場担当、食器洗い機」。
(D) cashier「レジ係」。

70 Look at the graphic. How much does the new dessert cost?

(A) $2.50
(B) $4.00
(C) $5.00
(D) $3.50

図を見てください。新しいデザートは幾らの値段ですか。

(A) 2.50ドル
(B) 4.00ドル
(C) 5.00ドル
(D) 3.50ドル

正解 D 男性は❸で、「客に当店の新しいデザートである、カボチャパイについて知らせるのを忘れないでください」と言っている。図を見ると、カボチャパイの価格は1切れ3.50ドルなので、(D)が正解。cost「〜の値段である」。

Words & Phrases

day off 休みの日　I could use 〜 〜が欲しい　extra 余分な　completely すっかり、完璧に　waitstaff 給仕スタッフ
would like 〜 to *do* 〜に…してもらいたい　cover 〜を担当する　wait on 〜 〜の給仕をする
remind 〜 about … 〜に…について気付かせる　dessert デザート　pumpkin カボチャ　pie パイ
on special 特価で　add 〜 to … 〜を…に加える

メニュー per 〜当たり、〜につき　scoop 〈アイスクリームの〉スクープ、1すくい　assortment 盛り合わせ
dozen 1ダース　slice 1切れ

TEST1 PART 3

Questions 71 through 73 refer to the following advertisement.

問題71-73は次の広告に関するものです。

M

Looking for something to do this week? ❶The exhibit "Our Galaxy" opens on September third at the Ashton Science Museum. Learn about the planets in our galaxy and step into a real spacecraft. ❷On opening night, Gregory Alvarez, the world-famous photographer, will be talking about his experience photographing the stars. ❸Tickets for the exhibit include admission to the movie *Nature's Wonders*. This award-winning movie is entertaining for people of all ages. So be sure to purchase your museum tickets online now!

今週何かすることをお探しですか。9月3日にAshton科学博物館で、展覧会「私たちの銀河」が開幕します。私たちの銀河系内の惑星について学び、本物の宇宙船の中に足を踏み入れてください。初日の夜には、世界的に有名な写真家であるGregory Alvarezが、星を撮影した自身の経験について話します。展覧会のチケットは、映画『自然の驚異』の入場料も含んでいます。賞を獲得したこの映画は、あらゆる年齢の人々にお楽しみいただけます。ですから、必ず今すぐオンラインで博物館のチケットをご購入ください!

71 What is the advertisement mainly about?

(A) An art festival
(B) A concert series
(C) An architectural tour
(D) A museum exhibit opening

広告は主に何についてですか。

(A) 芸術祭
(B) 一連のコンサート
(C) 建築ツアー
(D) 博物館の展覧会の開幕

正解 D 話し手は❶「9月3日にAshton科学博物館で、展覧会『私たちの銀河』が開幕する」と述べ、その展覧会の説明を続けている。その後も、❷で展覧会初日の夜に開催されるトークイベントについて述べている。
(A) art「芸術」。
(C) architectural「建築の」。

72 Who is Gregory Alvarez?

(A) A chef
(B) A scientist
(C) A photographer
(D) A university professor

Gregory Alvarezとは誰ですか。

(A) シェフ
(B) 科学者
(C) 写真家
(D) 大学教授

正解 C 話し手は❷「初日の夜には、世界的に有名な写真家であるGregory Alvarezが、星を撮影した自身の経験について話す」と述べている。
(B) 科学博物館での展覧会を知らせる広告だが、scientist「科学者」については言及がない。
(D) professor「教授」。

73 What is included with the price of admission?

(A) On-site parking
(B) A movie ticket
(C) A food voucher
(D) A souvenir T-shirt

入場料の価格には何が含まれていますか。

(A) 敷地内の駐車許可
(B) 映画の鑑賞券
(C) 食べ物の引換券
(D) 記念品のTシャツ

正解 B 話し手は❸「展覧会のチケットは、映画『自然の驚異』の入場料も含む」と述べている。よって、展覧会の入場料には、映画の鑑賞券も含まれていると分かる。
(A) on-site「敷地内の」、parking「駐車許可」。
(C) voucher「引換券」。
(D) souvenir「記念品、土産」。

Words & Phrases

advertisement 広告　look for ～ ～を探す　exhibit 展覧会　galaxy 銀河(系)　planet 惑星　step into ～ ～に踏み込む　real 本物の　spacecraft 宇宙船　photographer 写真家　experience 経験　photograph ～を撮影する、～の写真を撮る　include ～を含む　admission 入場料　wonder 驚異　award-winning 受賞した　entertaining 楽しませる、面白い　be sure to *do* 必ず～する　purchase ～を購入する　online オンラインで

Questions 74 through 76 refer to the following announcement.

問題74-76は次のお知らせに関するものです。

W

❶There's one last thing I want to mention at this school staff meeting. ❷It's about our colleague, Paulo Gardenal, who couldn't be here today. As many of you already know, ❸Paulo's not just a history teacher—he's also an author! ❹His first novel was published last January, and ❺he'll be reading a chapter from it at a community fund-raiser tomorrow night. The event's at the Stately Hotel at eight.

今回の学校職員会議で話しておきたいことが最後にもう1つあります。本日ここに来られなかった、私たちの同僚であるPaulo Gardenalについてです。皆さんの多くがすでにご存じの通り、Pauloは歴史の教師であるだけではないのです——彼は作家でもあります。彼の初の小説が去る1月に出版され、彼は明日の夜、地域の資金集めのイベントで、その中の1章を朗読することになっています。イベントは8時にStatelyホテルで行われます。

74 Where do the listeners work?

(A) At a hotel
(B) At a school
(C) At a news agency
(D) At a public library

聞き手はどこで働いていますか。

(A) ホテル
(B) 学校
(C) 通信社
(D) 公共図書館

正解 B 話し手は❶「今回の学校職員会議で話しておきたいことが最後にもう1つある」と述べ、❷でこの会議を欠席した自分たちの同僚のPaulo Gardenalに言及し、続けて❸で、彼は教師であるだけでなく作家でもあると述べている。よって、聞き手はPauloと話し手と共に学校で働いていると判断できる。
(C) news agency「通信社」。
(D) public「公共の」。

75 What happened last January?

(A) A survey was distributed.
(B) A new employee was hired.
(C) A book was published.
(D) An award winner was announced.

この前の1月に何が起こりましたか。

(A) アンケート調査票が配布された。
(B) 新しい従業員が雇用された。
(C) 本が出版された。
(D) 受賞者が発表された。

正解 C 話し手は同僚のPauloについて❸で、彼は教師であるだけでなく作家でもあると述べてから、❹で「彼の初の小説が去る1月に出版された」と言っている。His first novelをa bookと表している(C)が正解。
(A) survey「アンケート調査、調査表」、distribute「～を配布する」。
(B) employee「従業員」。
(D) award「賞」、winner「受賞者」、announce「～を発表する」。

76 Why does the speaker say, "The event's at the Stately Hotel at eight"?

(A) To explain why she cannot make an appointment
(B) To correct an event schedule
(C) To advise the listeners about a location change
(D) To encourage the listeners to attend an event

話し手はなぜ"The event's at the Stately Hotel at eight"と言っていますか。

(A) 自分がなぜ予約を取れないのか説明するため。
(B) イベントのスケジュールを訂正するため。
(C) 聞き手に場所の変更について忠告するため。
(D) 聞き手にイベントに参加するよう勧めるため。

正解 D 話し手は、❹で同僚のPauloの初の小説が出版されたことを伝え、❺で明日の夜、地域のイベントでPauloがその本の朗読をすると案内している。続けて下線部で「イベントは8時にStatelyホテルで行われる」と述べていることから、話し手は場所と時間を伝えて、聞き手にイベントに参加するよう勧めていると考えられる。
encourage ～ to *do*「～に…するよう勧める」。
(A) make an appointment「予約を取る」。
(C) advise ～ about …「～に…について忠告する」。

Words & Phrases

mention ～を話に出す、～に言及する　school staff 学校職員　colleague 同僚
history 歴史　author 作家　novel 小説　publish ～を出版する　read ～を朗読する　chapter 章
community 地域社会、コミュニティー　fund-raiser 資金集めのイベント

Questions 77 through 79 refer to the following broadcast.

問題77-79は次の放送に関するものです。

W

This is Christine Li with the business news. ❶In July, Tasty Treats, an Australian candy manufacturer, officially purchased Hilltorn Enterprises. Hilltorn sells a wide variety of healthy snacks. Since sales of sugary products are declining worldwide, ❷Tasty Treats hopes to diversify its products by expanding into this rapidly growing market. Look for their rebranded packaging on store shelves near you. ❸The packages carry a new logo that features the initials of both companies.

Christine Liがビジネスニュースをお届けします。7月に、オーストラリアの菓子製造会社であるTasty Treats社はHilltorn社を正式に買収しました。Hilltorn社は幅広い種類の健康的なスナック菓子を販売しています。糖分を多く含む製品の売り上げは世界的に減少中であるため、Tasty Treats社は、急成長中のこの市場に進出して自社製品を多様化することを望んでいます。イメージが一新された同社の商品パッケージを、お近くの店頭の棚で探してみてください。パッケージには両方の会社のイニシャルを備えた新しいロゴが掲載されています。

77 What did Tasty Treats do in July?

(A) It elected a board of directors.
(B) It acquired another business.
(C) It donated to a charity.
(D) It celebrated an anniversary.

Tasty Treats社は7月に何をしましたか。

(A) 同社は取締役会を選任した。
(B) 同社は他の企業を買収した。
(C) 同社は慈善団体に寄付をした。
(D) 同社は記念日を祝った。

正解 B 話し手は❶「7月に、オーストラリアの菓子製造会社であるTasty Treats社はHilltorn社を正式に買収した」と述べている。acquire「～を買収する、～を獲得する」、business「企業」。
(A) elect「～を選出する」、board of directors「取締役会」。
(C) donate to ～「～に寄付をする」、charity「慈善団体」。
(D) celebrate「～を祝う」、anniversary「記念日」。

78 According to the speaker, what is Tasty Treats hoping to do?

(A) Diversify its products
(B) Reduce its manufacturing waste
(C) Improve community relations
(D) Find qualified personnel

話し手によると、Tasty Treats社は何をすることを望んでいますか。

(A) 自社製品を多様化する。
(B) 自社の製造廃棄物を削減する。
(C) 地域社会との関係を改善する。
(D) 有能な人員を見つける。

正解 A 話し手は、Tasty Treats社が健康スナック菓子会社のHilltorn社を買収したと伝えた後、❷「Tasty Treats社は、急成長中のこの市場に進出して自社製品を多様化することを望んでいる」と述べている。
(B) manufacturing waste「製造廃棄物」。
(C) improve「～を改善する」、relation「関係」。
(D) qualified「有能な、資格のある」、personnel「人員」。

79 What does the speaker say about some packaging?

(A) It will be larger.
(B) It will be environmentally friendly.
(C) It will have a different logo.
(D) It will feature nutritional information.

話し手は、商品パッケージについて何と言っていますか。

(A) それは大きくなる。
(B) それは環境に優しくなる。
(C) それには異なるロゴが付く。
(D) それは栄養成分情報を表示する。

正解 C 話し手は、イメージが一新されたTasty Treats社の商品パッケージについて言及してから、❸「パッケージには両方の会社のイニシャルを備えた新しいロゴが掲載されている」と説明している。carry a new logoをhave a different logoと表している(C)が正解。
(B) environmentally friendly「環境に優しい」。
(D) nutritional「栄養の」。

Words & Phrases

broadcast 放送　candy 〈あめ、チョコレートを含む〉砂糖菓子
manufacturer 製造会社、メーカー　officially 正式に　purchase ～を買収する、～を購入する　enterprise 会社、企業
a wide variety of ～ 幅広い種類の～　healthy 健康的な　snack スナック菓子、軽食　sugary 糖分を多く含む
decline 減少する　worldwide 世界的に　diversify ～を多様化する　expand into ～ ～に進出する　rapidly 急速に
market 市場　rebrand ～のイメージを一新する、～のブランドイメージを変える　packaging 商品パッケージ、包装
shelf 棚　carry 〈ラベルなどに〉～を載せている　logo ロゴ　feature ～を特徴として備える、～を特筆する
initial イニシャル、頭文字

Questions 80 through 82 refer to the following announcement.

問題80-82は次のお知らせに関するものです。

M

On behalf of the Transportation Department of Alton City, ❶thank you for joining us at today's press conference. ❷I'm sorry for the last-minute location change. ❸The weather reports are predicting heavy rain this afternoon, so we decided to move the conference indoors. Now, ❹I called this press conference to announce that we will be temporarily closing the Green Line from July first to July tenth. ❺The closing will allow us to make necessary repairs to the train tracks. We understand that this may cause an inconvenience for some riders, but there are many alternate routes available.

オールトン市運輸局を代表して、本日の記者会見にご参加くださったことを感謝いたします。土壇場での場所変更につきましておわび申し上げます。天気予報で本日午後に大雨が予測されているので、会見を屋内に移す決定をいたしました。さて、この記者会見を開いたのは、7月1日から7月10日までGreen線を一時的に閉鎖することになっているとお知らせするためです。この閉鎖により、線路に必要な補修作業を行うことが可能になります。一部の乗客の方々にご不便をお掛けする可能性があることは承知しておりますが、多くの代替路線が利用可能です。

80 Where is the announcement taking place?

(A) At a trade show
(B) At a grand opening
(C) At a press conference
(D) At a retirement dinner

お知らせはどこで行われていますか。

(A) 見本市
(B) 開設記念イベント
(C) 記者会見
(D) 退職記念の夕食会

正解 C 話し手は❶で、「本日の記者会見への参加に感謝する」と聞き手にお礼を述べている。その後も❹で記者会見を開いた理由を説明しているので、このお知らせは記者会見で行われていると分かる。
(A) trade show「見本市」。
(B) grand opening「開設記念、グランドオープン」。
(D) retirement「退職」。

81 What has caused the event to be relocated?

(A) Bad weather
(B) Technical difficulties
(C) Ongoing construction work
(D) A high number of participants

催しが新しい場所に移された原因は何ですか。

(A) 悪天候
(B) 技術的障害
(C) 進行中の建設作業
(D) 多数の参加者

正解 A 設問文のeventはpress conferenceを指す。話し手は、❷で記者会見場所の急な変更をわびた後、❸で「天気予報で本日午後に大雨が予測されているので、会見を屋内に移す決定をした」と変更理由を説明している。cause ～ to *do*「～に…させる」、relocate「～を新しい場所に置く」。
(B) technical「技術的な」、difficulty「障害、困難」。
(C) ongoing「進行中の」。
(D) participant「参加者」。

82 According to the speaker, what will happen in July?

(A) A holiday celebration will be held.
(B) A train line will be repaired.
(C) Seasonal staff will be added.
(D) Additional equipment will be delivered.

話し手によると、7月に何が起こりますか。

(A) 祭日の祝典が催される。
(B) 電車の線路が補修される。
(C) 季節限定のスタッフが加わる。
(D) 追加の機器が配達される。

正解 B 話し手は❹で、7月1日～10日までGreen線を一時閉鎖する予定を知らせた後、❺「この閉鎖により、線路に必要な補修作業を行うことが可能になる」と述べている。よって、この7月の一時閉鎖中に線路が補修されると考えられる。(B)が正解。repair「～を補修する、～を修繕する」。
(A) celebration「祝典」、hold「～を催す」。
(C) seasonal「季節的な」、add「～を加える」。
(D) additional「追加の」

Words & Phrases

on behalf of ～ ～を代表して　transportation 運輸　department 局　join ～に参加する　press conference 記者会見　last-minute 土壇場の　location 場所　weather report 天気予報　predict ～を予測する　heavy rain 大雨　indoors 屋内に　call 〈会議など〉を招集する　announce ～を知らせる　temporarily 一時的に　allow ～ to *do* ～が…するのを可能にする　repairs 修繕作業　track 鉄道線路　cause ～を引き起こす　inconvenience 不便　rider 乗客　alternate 代替の　route 路線、ルート　available 利用可能な

Questions 83 through 85 refer to the following excerpt from a meeting.

問題83-85は次の会議の抜粋に関するものです。

W

Good morning, everyone. ❶Remember how we had been concerned about meeting our monthly sales goal? Well, the new sweaters have all been sold. However, ❷now the storage room is a mess and needs to be cleaned up—we have a lot of empty boxes and packaging in there. ❸I've updated the duty roster with this assignment. And speaking of the roster, I know some of you are planning on being away soon for vacation. ❹Please make sure I have your time-off request forms by the end of the week.

おはようございます、皆さん。私たちが月間売り上げ目標の達成についてどんなに懸念していたか覚えていますか。ええと、新しいセーターは完売しました。しかし現在、収納室はめちゃくちゃで片付ける必要があります——あの中には大量の空き箱や梱包材があります。この割り当てに関して業務当番表を更新しました。また、当番表と言えば、何名かの方は間もなく休暇のため不在にするつもりであることは承知しています。必ず今週末までに、私が皆さんの休暇申請書を受け取っているようにしてください。

83 What does the speaker mean when she says, "the new sweaters have all been sold"?

(A) She needs to order additional items.
(B) Customers will be disappointed.
(C) A goal has been met.
(D) A promotional sale has ended.

話し手は"the new sweaters have all been sold"という発言で、何を意味していますか。

(A) 彼女は追加の品を注文する必要がある。
(B) 顧客は落胆するだろう。
(C) 目標が達成された。
(D) 販売促進セールが終了した。

正解 C 話し手は会議の話の始めに❶で、皆が月間売り上げ目標の達成を非常に懸念していたことを聞き手に思い出させた後、下線部で「新しいセーターは完売した」と報告している。よって、話し手は皆の懸念にも関わらず、売り上げ目標が達成できたことを伝えていると考えられる。
(B) disappointed「落胆した」。
(D) 売り上げ目標の達成について言及しているが、販売促進セールについては述べられていない。promotional「販売促進の」。

84 What new work assignment does the speaker mention?

(A) Organizing some files
(B) Cleaning a room
(C) Unloading a shipment
(D) Removing some labels

話し手は、どんな新たな業務割り当てについて述べていますか。

(A) ファイルを整理すること。
(B) 部屋をきれいにすること。
(C) 積み荷を降ろすこと。
(D) ラベルをはがすこと。

正解 B 話し手は❷「現在、収納室はめちゃくちゃで片付ける必要がある——あの中には大量の空き箱や梱包材がある」と述べ、❸でその片付けの割り当ての業務当番表を更新したと聞き手に知らせている。収納室を片付けることをcleaning a roomと表している(B)が正解。
(A) organize「～を整理する」。
(C) unload「〈荷物など〉を降ろす」。
(D) remove「～を取り除く」。

85 What does the speaker ask some listeners to do by the end of the week?

(A) Submit a form
(B) Read a manual
(C) Pick up a new uniform
(D) Sign up for a workshop

話し手は一部の聞き手に、週末までに何をするよう求めていますか。

(A) 用紙を提出する。
(B) マニュアルを読む。
(C) 新しい制服を受け取る。
(D) 研修会の参加登録をする。

正解 A 話し手は、近々休暇のため不在にする予定の人たちがいると承知していると述べてから、❹「必ず今週末までに、私が皆の休暇申請書を受け取っているようにしてほしい」と休暇取得予定の人たちに対して、用紙の提出を求めている。submit「～を提出する」。
(C) pick up ～「～を受け取る」、uniform「制服」。
(D) sign up for ～「〈講座などの〉参加登録をする」。

Words & Phrases

excerpt 抜粋　be concerned about ～ ～を懸念する　meet ～を達成する
monthly 月間の　sales goal 売上目標　sweater セーター　storage room 収納室　mess めちゃくちゃな状態
clean up ～ ～を片付ける　empty 空の　packaging 梱包材　duty 業務　roster 当番表、勤務表
assignment 割り当て、割り当てられた仕事　speaking of ～ ～と言えば　plan on *doing* ～するつもりである
away 不在で　make sure (that) ～ 必ず～する　time-off 休暇　request form 申請書

Questions 86 through 88 refer to the following announcement.

問題86-88は次のお知らせに関するものです。

M

❶Attention, Lenner's Supermarket shoppers! ❷Are you a member of our loyal-shopper rewards program? Then you know that this program allows you to earn reward points on every purchase you make. ❸We're now offering a group membership that you and your family can share. With this group membership, anyone in your family can earn points and use them for discounts on future purchases at Lenner's. ❹The first 100 customers to register will receive a free coffee mug. So sign up and receive your mug at our customer service desk today!

Lenner'sスーパーマーケットのお買い物客の皆さまにお知らせいたします。皆さまは、当店のお得意さま向けの謝礼プログラムの会員でいらっしゃいますか。でしたら、このプログラムでお客さまはお買い上げごとに謝礼ポイントを獲得できることはご存じでしょう。当店では現在、お客さまとご家族が共有できるグループ会員資格をご提供しています。このグループ会員資格があれば、ご家族のどなたでもポイントを獲得でき、Lenner'sでの今後のお買い上げに対し、そのポイントを割引に利用することができます。登録くださる先着100名のお客さまは、無料のコーヒーマグカップを受け取れます。ですから、本日お客さまサービスカウンターでご登録の上、マグカップをお受け取りください。

86 Where most likely are the listeners?

(A) At an airport
(B) At a sports arena
(C) At a bank
(D) At a supermarket

聞き手はどこにいると考えられますか。

(A) 空港
(B) 競技場
(C) 銀行
(D) スーパーマーケット

正解 D 話し手は❶で、Lenner'sスーパーマーケットで買い物中の客に対してお知らせすると呼びかけ、続けて❷で、同店の上顧客向けの謝礼プログラムの会員になっているかと尋ねている。その後もこのプログラムのグループ会員特典の詳細を述べていることから、聞き手がいる場所はスーパーマーケットと考えられる。
(B) sports arena「競技場」。

87 What new program feature does the speaker announce?

(A) A service can be used internationally.
(B) A group membership is available.
(C) A registration fee has been reduced.
(D) A shuttle service will run more often.

話し手は、プログラムのどんな新しい特徴を知らせていますか。

(A) サービスが国際的に利用できる。
(B) グループ会員資格が利用できる。
(C) 登録料が引き下げられた。
(D) シャトルバスのサービスがもっと頻繁に提供される。

正解 B 話し手は上顧客向けの謝礼プログラムに言及し、❸「当店では現在、お客さまと家族が共有できるグループ会員資格を提供している」と述べ、続けてそのプログラムに新たに加わった、グループ会員資格について説明している。available「利用できる」。
(A) internationally「国際的に」。
(C) registration「登録」、fee「料金」、reduce「～を引き下げる、～を減少させる」。

88 What will some customers receive?

(A) A coffee mug
(B) A coupon book
(C) A shopping bag
(D) A parking pass

一部の客は何を受け取りますか。

(A) コーヒーマグカップ
(B) クーポン冊子
(C) 買い物バッグ
(D) 無料駐車証

正解 A グループ会員資格の説明に続いて話し手は❹で、登録する先着100名は無料のコーヒーマグカップを受け取れるので、本日登録してマグカップを受け取るよう聞き手を促している。
(B) coupon「クーポン」、book「〈切符などの〉つづり」。
(D) pass「無料入場券、通行証」。

Words & Phrases

Attention, ～ 〈アナウンスで〉～にお知らせいたします　shopper 買い物客　loyal 忠実な　reward 謝礼、報酬　allow ～ to *do* ～が…するのを可能にする　earn ～を獲得する　make a purchase 購入する　offer ～を提供する　membership 会員資格　share ～を共有する　discount 割引　future 今後の、将来の　purchase 購入　register 登録する　receive ～を受け取る　mug マグカップ　sign up 登録する

Questions 89 through 91 refer to the following advertisement.

問題89-91は次の広告に関するものです。

W

❶Why buy a new mobile device when you can repair your current one? ❷Cranfield Electronics Repair can replace batteries, fix broken screens, and repair water damage. ❸We are the only store in the area that will come to your home so you don't need to come to our store. And most repairs can be finished in less than an hour. ❹To read reviews from our many satisfied customers, just go to cranfieldrepair.com.

なぜ新しい携帯機器を買うのですか、現在お使いのものを修理できるのに? Cranfield電子機器修理店は、電池を交換し、破損した画面を直し、水による損傷を修理することができます。当店は、地域で唯一のご自宅まで伺うタイプの店なので、お客さまは店舗にお越しいただく必要がありません。また、大多数の修理作業は1時間未満で終了可能です。当店にご満足いただいている多くのお客さまからのレビューをご覧いただくには、cranfieldrepair.comにアクセスしてください。

89 What type of service is being advertised?

(A) Bottled water delivery
(B) Corporate catering
(C) Electronics repairs
(D) Automotive maintenance

どのような種類のサービスが宣伝されていますか。

(A) ボトル入り飲料水の配達
(B) 企業向けケータリング
(C) 電子機器の修理
(D) 自動車の整備

正解 C 話し手は❶で、使用中のものを修理できるのに、なぜ新しい携帯機器を買うのか、と問いかけた後、❷「Cranfield電子機器修理店は、電池を交換し、破損した画面を直し、水による損傷を修理することができる」と言っている。❶のoneはa mobile deviceを指す。advertise「~を宣伝する」。
(A) bottled「ボトル入りの」。
(B) corporate「企業の」、catering「ケータリング」。
(D) automotive「自動車の」、maintenance「整備、保守」。

90 What is unique about the business?

(A) It provides home visits.
(B) It employs industry experts.
(C) It is available 24 hours a day.
(D) It has locations around the world.

この店について何が独特ですか。

(A) それは自宅訪問を行っている。
(B) それは業界の専門家を雇用している。
(C) それは24時間対応可能である。
(D) それは世界中に店舗を持つ。

正解 A ❷でCranfield電子機器修理店のサービス内容を述べた後、話し手は❸で「当店は、地域で唯一の自宅まで伺うタイプの店なので、顧客は店舗に来る必要がない」と伝えている。provide「~を提供する」、visit「訪問」。
(B) employ「~を雇用する」、industry「業界」、expert「専門家」。
(C) 修理作業の所要時間についての言及はあるが、24時間対応可能とは述べられていない。
(D) location「店舗、所在地」。

91 According to the speaker, what can the listeners do on a Web site?

(A) Request an appointment
(B) Read some reviews
(C) Watch informational videos
(D) Make a payment

話し手によると、聞き手はウェブサイトで何をすることができますか。

(A) 予約を頼む。
(B) レビューを読む。
(C) 情報に関する動画を見る。
(D) 支払いをする。

正解 B 話し手は聞き手に対し、❹「当店に満足している多くの顧客からのレビューを見るには、cranfieldrepair.comにアクセスしてください」とウェブサイト上のレビューを読むよう促している。
(C) informational「情報を提供する、情報の」。

Words & Phrases

mobile device 携帯機器　repair 〈動詞で〉~を修理する、〈名詞で〉修理　current 現在の　electronics 電子機器　replace ~を交換する　battery 電池　fix ~を直す、~を修理する　screen 画面　damage 損傷　less than ~ ~未満　review レビュー、評価　satisfied 満足した

Questions 92 through 94 refer to the following telephone message.

問題92-94は次の電話のメッセージに関するものです。

M

Hi, Magda. ❶Just calling to say I reviewed your product development report. ❷I'm glad the focus groups are responding so well to the prototype of our tablet computer. I think it's going to be our next best-selling product. Now, ❸I'm in charge of market testing, which should start on Monday, but umm... I'm going to be training new employees next week. ❹Let's meet this afternoon to discuss a solution. By the way, ❺can you reserve a space for us at the technology expo in Berlin next month? It'd be a great place to show the tablet computer to major international buyers. Thanks.

こんにちは、Magda。私が、あなたの製品開発報告書を精査したと伝えるために、ちょっと電話しています。フォーカスグループが、当社のタブレットコンピューターの試作品に対してとても良い反応をしていて良かったです。あれは当社の次のベストセラー製品になると思います。さて、私は市場テストの担当で、テストは月曜に開始しなければならないのですが、うーん…私は来週、新入社員を教育することになっているのです。今日の午後、解決策を話し合うために会いましょう。ところで、来月のベルリンのテクノロジー博覧会でのスペースを当社用に予約してもらえませんか。主要な海外のバイヤーにあのタブレットコンピューターを見せるのに絶好の場となるでしょう。よろしくお願いします。

92 What is the message mainly about?

(A) A sales report
(B) A travel itinerary
(C) A new computer
(D) A company vehicle

メッセージは主に何についてですか。

(A) 営業報告
(B) 旅行日程
(C) 新しいコンピューター
(D) 社用車

正解 C 話し手は、❶「私が、あなたの製品開発報告書を精査したと伝えるために、ちょっと電話している」と用件を述べた後、❷「フォーカスグループが、当社のタブレットコンピューターの試作品に対してとても良い反応をしていて良かった」と言っている。その後も、その新たに売り出す予定のコンピューターについて話を続けている。
(B) itinerary「日程、旅程表」。
(D) vehicle「車、乗り物」。

93 What does the speaker mean when he says, "I'm going to be training new employees next week"?

(A) He is not available for an assignment.
(B) He is inviting the listener to a training session.
(C) He is excited about a new responsibility.
(D) He would like to borrow some training materials.

話し手は "I'm going to be training new employees next week" という発言で、何を意味していますか。

(A) 彼は割り当てられた業務に対応できない。
(B) 彼は聞き手を研修会に招待している。
(C) 彼は新しい職責に心を躍らせている。
(D) 彼は研修資料を借りたいと思っている。

正解 A 話し手は❸「私は市場テストの担当で、テストは月曜に開始しなければならない」と自身の割り当て業務について述べ、言葉を詰まらせた後、下線部で「私は来週、新入社員を教育することになっている」と伝えている。続けて❹で、解決策を話し合うために会おうと提案しているので、話し手は業務が重なり、自分が市場テストに対応できないことを示唆していると考えられる。
(B) 新入社員の教育に言及しているが、研修会に聞き手を招待してはいない。invite「～を招待する」。
(C) responsibility「職責、責任」。

94 What does the speaker ask the listener to do?

(A) Contact a manager
(B) Send an invoice
(C) Download a mobile application
(D) Make a reservation

話し手は聞き手に何をするよう求めていますか。

(A) 管理者に連絡を取る。
(B) 請求書を送付する。
(C) 携帯端末用アプリをダウンロードする。
(D) 予約をする。

正解 D 話し手は❺「来月のベルリンのテクノロジー博覧会でのスペースを当社用に予約してもらえないか」と聞き手に頼んでいる。reserveをmake a reservationと表している(D)が正解。
(A) manager「管理者」。
(B) invoice「請求書」。
(C) application「アプリ」。

Words & Phrases

review ～を精査する　development 開発　report 報告書
focus group フォーカスグループ(市場調査のために抽出された集団)　respond to ～ ～に反応する　prototype 試作品
tablet computer タブレットコンピューター　best-selling ベストセラーの　in charge of ～ ～を担当して
testing テスト、検査　train ～を教育する　solution 解決策　reserve ～を予約する、～を確保する
technology テクノロジー、科学技術　expo 博覧会　major 主要な　international 国際的な　buyer バイヤー、買い手

Questions 95 through 97 refer to the following talk and timeline.

問題95-97は次の話と日程表に関するものです。

W

OK, team. ❶Here's the timeline for our next big project. ❷It's a print ad campaign for ThirstQuench Beverages. They want us to create a campaign for their new line of all-natural organic soft drinks. **Our proposal's due to ThirstQuench in early August. Once they approve it, we should have plenty of time to create our first draft of the ads.** ❸The client would like us to present our first draft at their offices, so please keep your schedules clear that day. **So,** ❹in order to help us develop the campaign, the client sent over some samples of the new beverages. ❺I'll pass some around for everyone to try.

では、チームの皆さん。こちらが次のわれわれの大型プロジェクトの日程表です。ThirstQuench飲料社用の印刷広告キャンペーンです。先方は、全て天然のオーガニック清涼飲料の新商品ラインのキャンペーンを当社に制作してほしいと望んでいます。当社からの提案書は8月初旬にThirstQuench社に提出することになっています。先方がそれを承認したら、当社には広告の初案を制作するためにたっぷり時間があるはずです。クライアントは、当社が初案を先方のオフィスでプレゼンすることを望んでいるので、その日は予定のないようにしておいてください。それから、当社がキャンペーンを練り上げるのに役立つようにと、クライアントは新しい飲料のサンプルを幾つか送ってくれました。皆さんに試してもらうために順々に回します。

Project Timeline

Project proposal due	August 10
Initial approval from client	August 20
Present first draft to client	September 25
Present second draft to client	October 27

プロジェクトの日程表

プロジェクトの提案書の締め切り	8月10日
クライアントからの一次承認	8月20日
クライアントへの初案プレゼン	9月25日
クライアントへの再考案プレゼン	10月27日

95 Where do the listeners most likely work?

(A) At an advertising agency
(B) At an online newspaper
(C) At an art gallery
(D) At a supermarket

聞き手はどこで働いていると考えられますか。

(A) 広告代理店
(B) オンライン新聞社
(C) 画廊
(D) スーパーマーケット

正解 A 話し手は聞き手であるチームの皆に対して、❶で次のプロジェクトの日程表を示し、❷「ThirstQuench飲料社用の印刷広告キャンペーンだ。先方は、全て天然のオーガニック清涼飲料の新商品ラインのキャンペーンを当社に制作してほしいと望んでいる」とプロジェクトの内容を説明している。その後も広告キャンペーンの制作進行について説明しているので、話し手と聞き手は共に広告代理店に勤めていると考えられる。advertising「広告」、agency「代理店」。
(B) online「オンラインの」。

---

96 Look at the graphic. According to the speaker, on which date should the listeners be available?

(A) August 10
(B) August 20
(C) September 25
(D) October 27

図を見てください。話し手によると、聞き手は何日に都合がつくようにしておくべきですか。

(A) 8月10日
(B) 8月20日
(C) 9月25日
(D) 10月27日

正解 C 話し手は❸「クライアントは、当社が初案を先方のオフィスでプレゼンすることを望んでいるので、その日は予定のないようにしてください」と聞き手に指示している。図を見ると、3行目に「クライアントへの初案プレゼン」とあり、日付は9月25日となっている。よって、初案をプレゼンするために、9月25日を空けておく必要があると分かるので、(C)が正解。available「都合がつく」。
(A) 話し手は8月初旬に提案書を提出すると述べているが、これに関して都合をつけるよう聞き手に指示はしていない。

---

97 What will the listeners most likely do next?

(A) Sign a contract
(B) Attend a workshop
(C) Set up a display
(D) Taste some samples

聞き手は次に何をすると考えられますか。

(A) 契約書に署名する。
(B) 研修会に参加する。
(C) 展示品を設置する。
(D) サンプルを試飲する。

正解 D 話し手は聞き手であるチームの皆に対し❹で、キャンペーン制作に役立てるよう、クライアントから新しい飲料のサンプルが送られてきたと知らせ、❺で「皆に試してもらうために順々に回す」と伝えている。❺のsomeの後にはsamplesが省略されているので、(D)が正解。taste「～を試飲する」。
(A) sign a contract「契約書に署名する」。
(C) set up ～「～を設置する」、display「展示品」。

Words & Phrases

timeline 日程表　print ad 印刷広告　campaign キャンペーン　beverage 飲料　create ～を制作する
line 商品ライン　all-natural 全て天然の　organic オーガニックの、有機栽培の　soft drink 清涼飲料
proposal 提案書　due to ～ ～に当然与えられるべきで　once いったん～すると　approve ～を承認する
plenty of ～ たっぷりの～　draft 草案、ドラフト　ad 〈advertisementの略で〉広告　client クライアント、顧客
present ～を発表する　clear 〈予定などが〉ふさがっていない　in order to *do* ～するために　develop ～を練り上げる
pass ～ around ～を順々に回す
日程表 due 提出期限　initial 初期の、最初の　approval 承認

トーク CD 1 91 問題 CD 1 92

Questions 98 through 100 refer to the following excerpt from a meeting and assignment list.

問題 98-100 は次の会議の抜粋と割り当てのリストに関するものです。

M

Time to start planning the city's annual film festival. ❶Here's a list of tasks I've assigned to everyone. ❷I'll get in touch with vendors about concessions like food and souvenirs. Jeff couldn't be here today, but I'll let him know what he'll be doing. ❸I'm also happy to say that the Reynold Movie Theater just finished its building renovations. ❹This is exciting because it now has more seats—which means we can have many more festival attendees this year. So, ❺this year the first 200 attendees will get a free poster of one of the movies we'll be showing.

市の毎年恒例の映画祭を計画し始める時期になりました。こちらが、私が皆さんに割り当てた任務のリストです。食べ物や記念品といった場内売店で販売される品物に関しては、私が販売業者と連絡を取ります。Jeffは今日、ここに来られませんでしたが、彼がやることになるものは私が知らせておきます。また私は、Reynold映画館が建物の改装をちょうど終えたとお伝えできてうれしく思っています。同館には今やより多くの座席があるので、これは心が躍ることです。──つまり、今年はさらに多くの映画祭の参加者をお迎えできるということですから。そういうことで、今年は先着200名の参加者が、上映予定映画のうちの1つの無料ポスターを1枚もらえます。

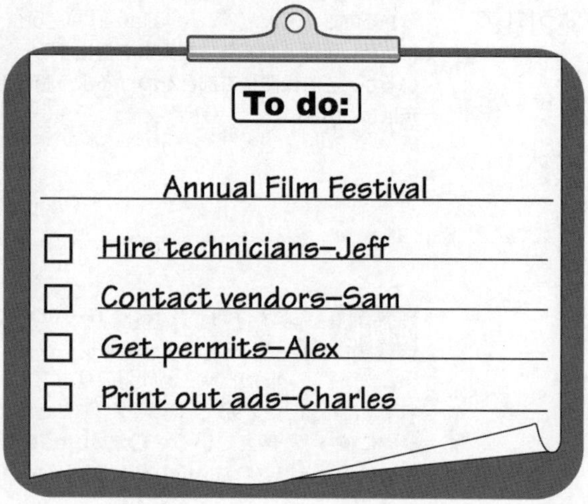
To do:
Annual Film Festival
Hire technicians–Jeff
Contact vendors–Sam
Get permits–Alex
Print out ads–Charles

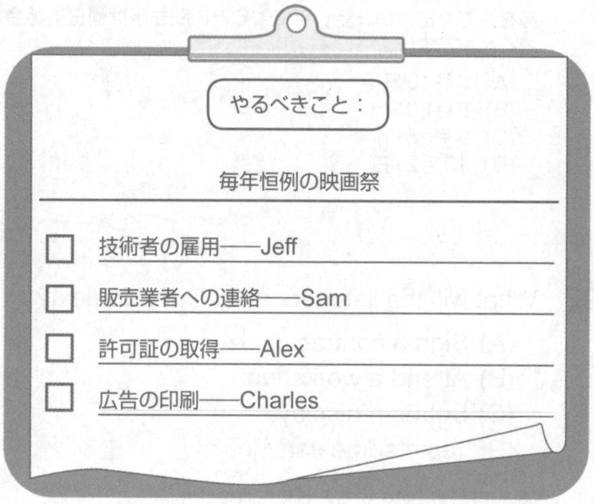
やるべきこと：
毎年恒例の映画祭
技術者の雇用──Jeff
販売業者への連絡──Sam
許可証の取得──Alex
広告の印刷──Charles

98 Look at the graphic. Who most likely is the speaker?

(A) Jeff
(B) Sam
(C) Alex
(D) Charles

図を見てください。話し手は誰だと考えられますか。

(A) Jeff
(B) Sam
(C) Alex
(D) Charles

正解 B 話し手は❶で、割り当てた任務のリストを示し、❷「食べ物や記念品といった場内売店で販売される品物に関しては、私が販売業者と連絡を取る」と述べている。よって、話し手の任務は販売業者に連絡を取ることだと分かる。図を見ると、リストの２項目目に「販売業者への連絡」とあり、その担当者名はSamなので(B)が正解。
(A) Jeffはこの会議を欠席していると述べられており、話し手とは考えられない。

---

99 Why is the speaker pleased?

(A) A review was positive.
(B) A Web site was completed.
(C) A promotion has been successful.
(D) A building has been renovated.

話し手はなぜ喜んでいますか。

(A) レビューが肯定的だったから。
(B) ウェブサイトが完成したから。
(C) 販売促進が成功したから。
(D) 建物が改装されたから。

正解 D 話し手は❸で、「また私は、Reynold映画館が建物の改装をちょうど終えたと伝えることができてうれしく思う」と述べている。さらに❹でも、改装の結果、座席数が増えてより多くの参加者を映画祭に迎えられるのは、心が躍ることだと述べているので、(D)が正解と判断できる。
renovate「～を改装する」。
(A) positive「肯定的な」。
(B) complete「～を完成させる」。
(C) promotion「販売促進」、successful「成功した」。

---

100 What will some festival attendees receive?

(A) A T-shirt
(B) A poster
(C) A key chain
(D) A book

一部の映画祭参加者は何を受け取りますか。

(A) Tシャツ１枚
(B) ポスター１枚
(C) キーホルダー１個
(D) 本１冊

正解 B 映画祭の計画について説明している話し手は、❺「今年は先着200名の参加者が、上映予定映画のうちの１つの無料ポスターを１枚もらえる」と述べている。
(C) key chain「キーホルダー」。

Words & Phrases

assignment　(特別な任務などの)割り当て　plan　～を計画する　annual　毎年恒例の　task　任務、仕事
assign ～ to …　～を…に割り当てる　get in touch with ～　～と連絡を取る　vendor　販売業者
concessions　場内売店で販売される品物　souvenir　記念品、土産　renovation　改装　seat　座席　attendee　参加者
free　無料の　show　～を上映する
リスト　hire　～を雇う　technician　技術者　contact　～に連絡する　permit　許可証　print out ～　～を印刷する
ad　〈advertisementの略で〉広告

101 In the article, Ms. Amanjit ------- her internship at a Chennai publishing company last year.

(A) describe
(B) described
(C) to describe
(D) describing

記事の中で、Amanjitさんはチェンナイにある出版社での昨年の自身のインターンシップについて述べました。

＊選択肢の訳は省略

正解 B 動詞describe「～について述べる」の適切な形を選ぶ。この文には述語動詞がないため、空所に必要。主語はMs. Amanjitで三人称単数なので、適切なのは過去形の(B) describedのみ。article「記事」、internship「インターンシップ」、publishing「出版」。
(A) 動詞の原形。主語が三人称単数なので不適切。
(C) to不定詞。
(D) 現在分詞。現在分詞は単独では述語動詞にならない。

---

102 Please submit ------- travel-expense reports to Ms. Gresh in the finance department.

(A) your
(B) you
(C) yourself
(D) yours

あなたの出張経費報告書を、財務部のGreshさんに提出してください。

(A) あなたの
(B) あなたを
(C) あなた自身
(D) あなたのもの

正解 A Please ～で始まる命令文。空所の前に述語動詞submit「～を提出する」、後ろに名詞句travel-expense reports「出張経費報告書」がある。名詞を修飾してsubmitの目的語を作る所有格の(A) yourが適切。finance department「財務部」。
(B) 二人称代名詞の目的格、または主格。
(C) 再帰代名詞。
(D) 所有代名詞。

---

103 Rent the perfect office space from one of Right Away Office's ------- locations.

(A) tolerant
(B) careful
(C) convenient
(D) uncertain

Right Away Office社のお近くの店舗の一つから、理想的なオフィススペースを賃貸してください。

(A) 寛大な
(B) 注意深い
(C) 近くて便利な
(D) 不確かな

正解 C 選択肢は全て形容詞。オフィス賃貸の宣伝文で、空所の後ろのlocationsを修飾する形容詞として文意に合うのは、(C) convenient「近くて便利な、手近な」。rent「～を賃貸する、～を賃借する」、perfect「理想的な、完璧な」、space「スペース」、location「立地、所在」。

104 Ms. Lee reviews the ------- daily to prevent the banquet room from being double-booked.

(A) reservations
(B) reserves
(C) reserving
(D) reserve

Leeさんは、宴会場が二重に予約されることを防ぐため、予約を毎日見直します。

(A) 予約
(B) 予備品
(C) 予約すること
(D) ～を予約する

正解 A 空所の前に冠詞theがあり、後ろに副詞daily「毎日」とto不定詞が続くので、空所には述語動詞reviewsの目的語となる名詞が入る。文意に合うのは、名詞reservation「予約」の複数形の(A)。prevent ～ from *doing*「～が…するのを防ぐ」、banquet room「宴会場」、double-book「～に二重に予約を受ける」。
(B) 名詞reserve「予備品」の複数形。文意に合わない。
(C) 動名詞。
(D) 動詞reserve「～を予約する」の原形。

---

105 The safety training session is scheduled to run ------- one hour.

(A) approximating
(B) approximately
(C) approximation
(D) approximate

安全講習会は、おおよそ1時間にわたって行われる予定です。

(A) ～を概算している
(B) おおよそ
(C) 概算
(D) おおよその

正解 B 空所に何も入れなくても文が成立するので、空所には副詞が入る。後ろの数詞oneを修飾する副詞の(B) approximately「おおよそ」が適切。safety「安全」、training session「講習会」、be scheduled to *do*「～する予定である」。
(A) 動詞approximate「～を概算する」の現在分詞。
(C) 名詞。
(D) 形容詞、または動詞の原形。

---

106 Mr. Kwon will sign a lease ------- an apartment in the building at 624 Livingston Road.

(A) of
(B) by
(C) like
(D) for

Kwonさんは、リビングストン通り624番地にある建物内の1室の賃貸契約をするつもりです。

(A) ～の
(B) ～による
(C) ～のような
(D) ～のための

正解 D 選択肢は全て前置詞の働きを持つ語。空所の後ろにあるan apartmentを続けて文意に合う前置詞は、目的や意図を表す(D) for「～のための」。sign a lease for ～で「～の賃貸契約をする」という意味になる。apartment「アパート(の1室)」。

107 To participate in the company charity run, employees must ------- a form certifying that they agree to certain rules.

(A) make
(B) see
(C) find
(D) sign

会社のチャリティーランに参加するためには、従業員は自身が所定のルールに同意することを証明する用紙に署名しなければなりません。

(A) ～を作る
(B) ～を見る
(C) ～を見つける
(D) ～に署名する

正解 D 選択肢は全て動詞の働きを持つ語。文頭からカンマまではto不定詞句で、目的を表している。カンマの後ろの節の主語はemployeesで、述語動詞は助動詞mustと空所の動詞。後ろのa formを目的語として続けて文意に合うのは、(D) sign「～に署名する」。現在分詞certifying以降は、a formを後ろから修飾して用紙の役割を説明している。participate in ～「～に参加する」、charity run「チャリティーラン（慈善目的の競走）」、form「用紙」、certify「～を証明する」、agree to ～「～に同意する」、certain「特定の」。

---

108 Innovation is key to success in ------- industries.

(A) none
(B) much
(C) many
(D) anything

技術革新は、多数の産業において成功への鍵です。

(A) 何も～ない
(B) 多くの
(C) 多数の
(D) 何か

正解 C 空所の前に前置詞inがあり、後ろに名詞industry「産業」の複数形industriesがあるので、空所にはindustriesを修飾する語が入る。形容詞で、数えられる名詞を修飾できる(C) many「多数の」が適切。innovation「技術革新」、success「成功」。
(A) 代名詞。
(B) 形容詞だが、数えられる名詞は修飾できないので不適切。
(D) 代名詞。

---

109 Interns at the Kuan Mai law firm can ------- to help attorneys with paperwork and courtroom preparation.

(A) expect
(B) expected
(C) expectant
(D) expectantly

Kuan Mai法律事務所のインターン生は、弁護士の事務手続きや法廷準備を手伝うことを期待できます。

(A) ～を期待する
(B) ～を期待した
(C) 期待している
(D) 期待して

正解 A 空所の前に助動詞canがあり、後ろにto不定詞句が続いているので、空所には動詞の原形が入る。よって、(A) expect「～を期待する」が適切。expect to *do*「～することを期待する」。intern「インターン生、研修生」、law firm「法律事務所」、attorney「弁護士」、paperwork「事務手続き」、courtroom「法廷」。
(B) 動詞の過去形、または過去分詞。
(C) 形容詞。
(D) 副詞。

110 Drescher, Inc., is a ------- insurance company that has been serving Saskatchewan since it opened 50 years ago.

(A) respects
(B) respectability
(C) respected
(D) respect

Drescher社は50年前に創業して以来、サスカチュワン州の用命に応え続けている評判の高い保険会社です。

(A) ～を尊敬する
(B) 尊敬に値すること
(C) 評判の高い
(D) 点

正解 C 空所の前に冠詞aがあり、後ろに名詞句 insurance company「保険会社」が続いているので、空所には名詞句を修飾する語が入る。形容詞の(C) respected「評判の高い」が適切。serve「〈地域〉の役に立つ、～に商品を提供する」。it はDrescher, Inc.を指している。Inc.はincorporatedの略で「～社」を表す。
(A) 動詞respectの三人称単数現在形。
(B) 名詞。
(D) 名詞。

---

111 The technician informed Mr. Becker that his laptop would ------- a repair covered under the warranty.

(A) require
(B) decide
(C) insist
(D) notify

その技術者はBeckerさんに、彼のノートパソコンは保証で賄われる修理が必要であると告げました。

(A) ～を必要とする
(B) ～を決める
(C) ～と主張する
(D) ～に知らせる

正解 A 選択肢は全て動詞の原形。thatに続く節において、his laptop「彼のノートパソコン」を主語とし、空所の後ろに続く名詞句a repair covered under the warranty「保証で賄われる修理」を目的語に取り、文意に合うのは(A) require「～を必要とする」。technician「技術者」、inform ～ that … 「～に…と告げる」、laptop「ノートパソコン」、cover「〈費用など〉を賄う」、warranty「保証」。

---

112 Because several popular athletes endorsed them, Kantorele Skin Care products sold ------- well.

(A) amazing
(B) amazingly
(C) amaze
(D) amazement

何人かの人気のあるスポーツ選手が推薦したため、Kantoreleスキンケアの製品は驚くほどよく売れました。

(A) 驚くべき
(B) 驚くほど
(C) ～を驚かせる
(D) 驚き

正解 B 空所に何も入れなくても「スポーツ選手が推薦したため、Kantoreleスキンケアの製品はよく売れた」という主旨の文が成立しているので、空所には副詞が入る。well「よく」を修飾する(B) amazingly「驚くほど」が適切。athlete「スポーツ選手」、endorse「〈広告文などで〉～を推薦する、～を支持する」。
(A) 形容詞。
(C) 動詞amazeの原形。
(D) 名詞。

113 The museum's newest acquisitions are usually exhibited in the Gorwin Gallery, ------- is located on the first floor.

(A) which
(B) where
(C) so
(D) as

美術館の最新の入手作品は通常、Gorwin展示室に陳列され、それは1階にあります。

(A) そしてそれは
(B) そしてそこで
(C) ～するように
(D) ～ように

正解 A カンマの前には〈主語＋動詞〉の形があるが、カンマの後ろには主語がなく文が不完全なので、Gorwin Galleryを先行詞として受けて2つの文をつなぐことのできる主格の関係代名詞の(A) whichが適切。acquisition「入手作品」、exhibit「～を陳列する、～を展示する」、be located「位置する」。
(B) 関係副詞。場所を表す語句を先行詞として受けるが、空所の後ろに〈主語＋動詞〉の形がないので不適切。
(C)(D) 接続詞。空所の後ろに〈主語＋動詞〉の形がないので不適切。

---

114 Alicia's Grill ------- three changes in management in the last five years.

(A) is undergoing
(B) has undergone
(C) undergo
(D) to undergo

Alicia's Grill社は、この5年間に経営陣の交代を3回経験しました。

＊選択肢の訳は省略

正解 B 動詞undergo「～を経験する」の適切な形を選ぶ。空所の後ろの部分でin the last five years「この5年間に」と期間を示しているので、完了していることと現在の状況を関連付ける現在完了形の(B) has undergoneが適切。management「経営陣」。
(A) 現在進行形。過去の動作に関する文なので、現在形は不適切。
(C) 動詞の原形。主語が三人称単数なので原形は不適切。
(D) to不定詞。

---

115 The marketing team from Tokyo is visiting this week and will ------- be using Conference Room A.

(A) occasions
(B) occasion
(C) occasionally
(D) occasional

今週は東京のマーケティングチームが来訪しており、時折、会議室Aを使用するでしょう。

(A) 機会
(B) 機会
(C) 時折
(D) 時折の

正解 C andの前まではThe marketing team from Tokyoを主語、is visitingを述語動詞とする文で、andの後ろは同じ主語について述語動詞will ------- be usingを並べて説明を加えている。空所に何も入れなくても文が成立するので、空所前後のwill be usingを修飾する副詞の(C) occasionally「時折」が適切。conference room「会議室」。
(A) 名詞の複数形。
(B) 名詞の単数形。(D) 形容詞。

116 ------- the fast-approaching deadline, the project manager is confident the team will have everything completed on time.

(A) Still
(B) However
(C) Despite
(D) Unlike

刻々と近づく締め切り期限にもかかわらず、プロジェクトマネージャーは、チームが予定通りに全てを完了させるだろうと確信しています。

(A) それでもやはり
(B) しかしながら
(C) ～にもかかわらず
(D) ～と異なり

正解 C カンマの前までは、空所と名詞句the fast-approaching deadlineだけなので、空所には前置詞が入る。カンマの前の「刻々と近づく締め切り期限」という不安要素に対し、後ろに「予定通りに完了させる」という肯定的な内容が続くので、逆接を表す(C) Despite「～にもかかわらず」を入れると文意が通る。fast-approaching「刻々と近づいている」、deadline「締め切り期限」、confident「確信して」、complete「～を完了する」、on time「予定通りに」。
(A)(B) 副詞。(D) 前置詞。

---

117 Customers ------- prepaid tickets are encouraged to use the express kiosk.

(A) picking up
(B) picked up
(C) pick up
(D) to pick up

前払いチケットを受け取られるお客さまは、自動発券端末機をご利用になることをお勧めします。

＊選択肢の訳は省略

正解 A 句動詞 pick up ～「～を受け取る」の適切な形を選ぶ。Customers ------- prepaid ticketsが主部で、述語動詞はare encouraged。prepaid ticketsを続けて、名詞Customers「客」を後ろから修飾でき、文意に合うのは「～する」という能動の意味を表す現在分詞の(A) picking up。prepaid「前払いの」、encourage ～ to *do*「～に…するよう勧める」、express kiosk「自動発券端末機」。
(B) 過去分詞。受動の意味を表すので、不適切。(C) 原形。
(D) to不定詞。「チケットを受け取るための」では、文意が通らない。

---

118 ------- hiring someone to update her salon's decor, Jalissa Bryant interviewed several interior designers.

(A) Before
(B) Among
(C) Except
(D) Inside

店内の装飾を新しくするために誰かを雇う前に、Jalissa Bryantは数名のインテリアデザイナーと面接しました。

(A) ～より前に
(B) ～の間に
(C) ～を除いて
(D) ～の中に

正解 A 選択肢は全て前置詞の働きを持つ語。カンマの前の「店内の装飾を新しくするために誰かを雇う」と、カンマの後ろの「数名のインテリアデザイナーと面接した」という2つの内容をつないで文意が通るのは、順序・優先を表す(A) Before「～より前［先］に」。hire「～を雇う」、update「～を新しくする」、salon「〈服飾・美容などの高級な〉店」、decor「室内装飾」、interview「～と面接する、～と会見する」。

119 ------- at the Pan-Pacifica Suites has increased since it began offering free breakfast.

(A) Occupancy
(B) Occupations
(C) Occupants
(D) Occupied

Pan-Pacifica Suitesホテルの稼働率は、無料の朝食を提供し始めて以来、増しています。

(A) 稼働率
(B) 占有期間
(C) 占有者
(D) 占有された

正解 A 選択肢は全て動詞occupy「～を占める」の変化した形と派生語。文の主語に当たる名詞がないので、空所に必要。述語動詞は三人称単数形のhas increasedなので、主語は名詞の単数形の(A) Occupancy。occupancy「〈ホテルなどの〉稼働率、占有」。suite「スイート、ホテルなどの一続きの部屋」、increase「増す」。
(B)(C) 名詞の複数形。三人称単数形の主語に続く述語動詞 has increasedと合わない。(D) 過去分詞。

---

120 Barlox Motors claims its new all-electric truck goes ------- on one charge than any other electric truck on the market today.

(A) long
(B) farther
(C) again
(D) back

Barloxモーターズ社は、同社の新しい完全電動式トラックは１回の充電で、現在市場に出ている他のどの電動式トラックよりも遠くまで走ると主張しています。

(A) 長く
(B) より遠くへ
(C) 再び
(D) 戻って

正解 B 空所の前は動詞goesで後ろは前置詞onなので、空所には動詞goesを修飾する副詞が入ると考えられる。選択肢は全て副詞の働きを持つ語。文の主語はBarlox Motors、述語動詞はclaimsで、その後ろはthatが省略された節になっている。空所の後ろにthanとあり、Barloxモーターズ社のトラックを他社のものと比較しているので、farの比較級の(B) farther「より遠くへ」が適切。claim「～と主張する」、all-electric「完全電動式の」、on the market「市場に出て」。

---

121 At the company's annual banquet, Mr. Karga received an award for his ------- record of community outreach projects.

(A) delicate
(B) distinguished
(C) periodic
(D) accurate

会社の年次夕食会でKargaさんは、地域社会への奉仕活動プロジェクトの際立った業績によって賞を受けました。

(A) 繊細な
(B) 際立った
(C) 周期的な
(D) 正確な

正解 B 選択肢は全て形容詞の働きを持つ語。受賞について述べる文において、for以降で受賞理由を示している。record of community outreach projects「地域社会への奉仕活動プロジェクトの業績」を修飾する形容詞として文意に合うのは(B) distinguished「際立った」。annual「年次の」、banquet「夕食会」、receive an award「受賞する」、record「業績、経歴」、outreach「奉仕活動の」。

122 The Ambrose Music Company markets its products only ------- its dedicated Web site.

(A) through
(B) while
(C) beside
(D) once

Ambroseミュージック社は、同社の専用ウェブサイトを通じてのみ自社製品を販売しています。

(A) ～を通じて
(B) ～している間に
(C) ～のそばに
(D) いったん～すると

正解 A 空所の後ろは、名詞句 its dedicated Web site「同社の専用ウェブサイト」だけなので、空所には前置詞が入る。自社製品の販売について述べている文で、手段を表す(A) through「～を通じて」を入れると文意が通る。market「～を販売する」、dedicated「〈ある目的で〉専用の」。
(B)(D) 接続詞。空所の後ろには〈主語＋動詞〉の形がないので不適切。
(C) 前置詞だが、文意に合わない。

123 Given Rusdon Marketing's focus on ------- design, Mr. Ochoa's artistic background would be a great asset to the firm.

(A) create
(B) created
(C) creative
(D) creatively

Rusdonマーケティング社の創造的なデザインへの注力を考えると、Ochoaさんの芸術面の経歴は同社にとって素晴らしい財産となるでしょう。

(A) ～を創造する
(B) 創造された
(C) 創造的な
(D) 創造的に

正解 C 空所の前は前置詞onで、後ろに名詞designが続いているので、空所には名詞を修飾する語が入る。文意から、形容詞の(C) creative「創造的な」が適切。given「～を考えると」、focus「重視、焦点」、artistic「芸術に関する」、background「経歴、素養」、asset「財産」、firm「会社」。
(A) 動詞create「～を創造する」の原形。
(B) 過去分詞。過去分詞は名詞を修飾できるが、文意に合わない。
(D) 副詞。

124 The town council has ------- permission for the Autumn Festival to be held in Vista Park.

(A) responded
(B) exchanged
(C) performed
(D) granted

町議会は、秋祭りがVista公園で開催されることに対して許可を与えました。

(A) ～と答えた
(B) ～を交換した
(C) ～を行った
(D) ～を与えた

正解 D 選択肢は全て動詞の過去分詞。hasと共に文の述語動詞となり、文意に合うものを選ぶ。空所の後ろはpermission for ～「～に対する許可」なので、grant「〈許可など〉を与える、～を認める」の過去分詞(D) grantedを入れると、「町議会が秋祭りに対して許可を与えた」となり、文意が通る。town council「町議会」、hold「～を開催する」。
(A) respond「～と答える」の過去分詞。
(B) exchange「～を交換する」の過去分詞。
(C) perform「～を行う、～を果たす」の過去分詞。

125 Eight ------- buyers inspected the property over the weekend, but only one seemed genuinely interested.

(A) certain
(B) descriptive
(C) conclusive
(D) potential

買い主となる可能性がある8名が週末にかけてその物件を視察しましたが、1名だけが心から興味を持ったようでした。

(A) 確かな
(B) 記述的な
(C) 決定的な
(D) 可能性がある

正解 D 選択肢は全て形容詞の働きを持つ語。物件の内覧について述べている文なので、空所の後ろの名詞buyersを修飾して文意に合うのは(D) potential「可能性がある、潜在的な」。only oneの直後にはbuyerが省略されている。buyer「買い主、買い手」、inspect「～を視察する、～を詳しく調べる」、property「物件、不動産」、genuinely「心から、真に」。

---

126 A majority of the residents have opposed the city's ------- to reroute traffic.

(A) trade
(B) plan
(C) supply
(D) total

住民の大多数が、交通を迂回させるという市の計画に反対してきました。

(A) 貿易
(B) 計画
(C) 供給
(D) 合計

正解 B 選択肢は全て名詞の働きを持つ語。文頭から空所までは、「住民の大多数が市の-------に反対してきた」と述べており、その反対している対象はthe city's ------- to reroute traffic「交通を迂回させる市の-------」なので、文意から(B) plan「計画」が適切。majority「大多数」、resident「住民」、oppose「～に反対する」、reroute「～を迂回させる」、traffic「交通」。

---

127 When registering multiple people for the conference, enter the name that should appear on ------- of the badges.

(A) each
(B) other
(C) whose
(D) whichever

会議に複数の人々を登録する際には、各々の名札に載るべき名前を入力してください。

(A) 各々
(B) 他のもの
(C) その人の～が…する
(D) ～するどれでも

正解 A 選択肢は全て代名詞の働きを持つ語。空所に(A) each「各々」を入れると、「各々の名札に載るべき名前」を入力するよう求める内容となり、文意が通る。register「～を登録する」、multiple「複数の」、conference「会議」、enter「～を入力する」、appear「〈名前などが〉載る」。
(C) 所有格の関係代名詞、(D) 複合関係代名詞。どちらも後ろに〈主語＋動詞〉の形を続けるので、ここでは不適切。

128 As part of a ------- to expand business abroad, Aneliya Innovations translated its Web site into multiple languages.

(A) push
(B) probe
(C) raise
(D) debate

海外に事業を拡大する攻勢の一環として、Aneliya Innovations社は自社のウェブサイトを複数言語に翻訳しました。

(A) 攻勢
(B) 厳密な調査
(C) 上げること
(D) 討論

正解 A 選択肢は全て名詞の働きを持つ語。カンマの後ろに「自社のウェブサイトを複数言語に翻訳した」とあるので、(A) push「〈市場への〉攻勢、売り込み」を入れると、カンマまでは「海外に事業を拡大する攻勢の一環として」という内容になり文意が通る。as part of ～「～の一部として」、expand「～を拡大する」、translate ～ into …「～を…に翻訳する」。

---

129 Although a reduction in metal thickness would make the container ------- lighter, its strength would suffer as a result.

(A) repeatedly
(B) regardlessly
(C) decreasingly
(D) considerably

金属の厚さの削減は容器を著しく軽くしますが、結果としてその強度は損なわれるでしょう。

(A) 繰り返して
(B) 無関心に
(C) 徐々に減少して
(D) 著しく

正解 D 選択肢は全て副詞。カンマの前は譲歩を表すAlthoughで始まる節で、「金属の厚さの削減は容器を-------軽くするが」という意味。空所の後ろに形容詞の比較級のlighter「より軽く」があるので、比較級を修飾して「著しく」を意味する(D) considerablyが適切。カンマの後ろの「結果としてその強度は損なわれるだろう」という文意にもつながる。itsはthe container'sを指す。reduction「削減」、metal「金属」、thickness「厚さ」、container「容器」、strength「強度」、suffer「損なわれる」、as a result「結果として」。

---

130 A research team at Halwell Agricultural Institute is studying the beneficial ------- of a newly developed fertilizer.

(A) charges
(B) effects
(C) replies
(D) senses

Halwell農業研究所の調査チームは、新たに開発された肥料の有益な効果を調べています。

(A) 費用
(B) 効果
(C) 返事
(D) 感覚

正解 B 選択肢は全て名詞の複数形。空所の前のbeneficial「有益な」に修飾され、後ろにof a newly developed fertilizer「新たに開発された肥料の」を続けて文意に合うのは、(B) effects。research「調査、研究」、institute「研究所」、newly「新たに」、fertilizer「肥料」。

Questions 131-134 refer to the following advertisement.

Half Off Your First Ride!

❶ The Drive-Ride ride-sharing service is now available in your area! As a businessperson, you know that your time is valuable and that you ------- (131.) the best service when it comes to ground transportation. ------- (132.) driving yourself, experience the convenience of Drive-Ride. Going to the airport before sunrise? Drive-Ride can do that. Car trouble before a big presentation? Drive-Ride can help. Need to meet with a client without the hassle of driving a car yourself? Drive-Ride is here for you!

❷ You can receive 50 percent off your first ride of 20 kilometers or less. ------- (133.). Then type the promo code NEWSPEED at checkout to take advantage of this great ------- (134.).

問題131-134は次の広告に関するものです。

初回のご乗車から5割引き！

Drive-Ride自動車相乗りサービスが現在、お住まいの地域でご利用いただけます。皆さまはビジネスパーソンとして、ご自分の時間が貴重であること、そしてご自分が陸上交通手段に関して最高のサービスを受ける価値があることをご承知でしょう。ご自分で運転する代わりに、Drive-Rideの便利さを体験してください。日の出前に空港に向かう？Drive-Rideならそれができます。大事なプレゼンテーションの前に車の故障？Drive-Rideがお役に立ちます。ご自分で車を運転する煩わしさなしに顧客に会う必要がある？Drive-Rideがあなたのご用命にお応えします。

初回で20キロメートル以下のご乗車には50パーセント引きが受けられます。*ただお手持ちの携帯機器に当社のアプリをダウンロードし、ご自身の情報を入力するだけです。それから、この大変お得な待遇を利用するために、精算時にプロモーションコードNEWSPEEDを入力してください。

*問題133の挿入文の訳

Words & Phrases

half　半分　off　～から割り引いて　ride　乗車　❶ ride-sharing　自動車の相乗りの　available　利用できる
area　地域　businessperson　ビジネスパーソン、実業家　valuable　貴重な　ground　地上の、地面の
transportation　交通手段、輸送機関　experience　～を体験する　convenience　便利さ　sunrise　日の出
trouble　〈機械などの〉故障　big　大事な　client　顧客　hassle　煩わしさ、面倒　❷ receive　～を受ける
type　〈キーボードなどで〉～を入力する　promo　〈promotionalの略で〉販促用の　checkout　精算
take advantage of ～　～を利用する

Expressions

when it comes to ～　「～に関して言えば、～のことになると」（❶ 2行目）

When it comes to high-tech gadgets, Fred knows more than anyone in the office.
ハイテク機器のことになると、Fredはオフィスの誰よりもよく知っています。

131 (A) deserves
(B) deserve
(C) deserving
(D) deserved

＊選択肢の訳は省略

正解 B 動詞deserve「～を受ける価値がある」の適切な形を選ぶ。空所を含む文は、you knowに続いて、その目的語になる2つのthat節がandを用いて並べられている。空所の後ろではwhen it comes to ground transportation「陸上交通手段に関して」と現在形が使われているので、空所も同様に時制は現在形。空所を含む後ろのthat節における主語はyouなので、(B) deserveが適切。
(A) 三人称単数現在形。
(C) 動名詞、または現在分詞。
(D) 過去形。

---

132 (A) Instead of
(B) While
(C) Even though
(D) Given that

(A) ～の代わりに
(B) ～する間に
(C) ～にもかかわらず
(D) ～と仮定すると

正解 A ❶1行目より、この広告は車の相乗りサービスに関するものだと分かる。空所を含む文は「自分で運転する-------、Drive-Rideの便利さを体験してください」という意味。続けて同3～5行目で、具体的にその利便性が列挙されており、その中で同5行目にwithout the hassle of driving a car yourself「自分で車を運転する煩わしさなしに」という例が挙げられている。よって(A) Instead ofを入れると、「自分で運転する代わりに」となり文意が通る。instead of *doing*「～する代わりに、～しないで」。
(B) 接続詞。While節の主語とbe動詞を省略して現在分詞を直接続けることもできるが、文意に合わない。
(C)(D) 群接続詞。後ろに〈主語＋動詞〉の形を続けるが、ここでは後ろが名詞句なので不適切。

---

133 (A) We also provide information about local auto mechanics.
(B) If you want to save money on frequent trips, this offer is for you.
(C) Simply download our app on your mobile device and enter your information.
(D) Thank you for serving as one of Drive-Ride's friendly drivers.

(A) 当社は、地元の自動車整備工に関する情報も提供しています。
(B) 頻繁な移動にかかる費用を節約したいのなら、この値引きはあなた向きです。
(C) ただお手持ちの携帯機器に当社のアプリをダウンロードし、ご自身の情報を入力するだけです。
(D) Drive-Rideの親切な運転手の一人として務めていただき、ありがとうございます。

正解 C 空所の前の文に、初回乗車が20キロメートル以下の場合に割引が適用されるとある。空所の後ろの文では、「これを利用するために、精算時にプロモーションコードNEWSPEEDを入力してください」と、割引の利用方法が述べられている。よって、空所にはプロモーションコードを入力する前に行う手順を説明している(C)を入れると、割引の利用手順を示す流れになる。simply「ただ～のみ」、app「〈applicationの略で〉アプリ」、device「機器」、enter「～を入力する」。
(A) local「地元の」、auto「自動車の」、mechanic「整備工」。
(B) 言及されているのは初回の乗車の割引のみなので、頻繁な乗車に関する記述は文脈に合わない。save「～を節約する」、frequent「頻繁な」、offer「値引き、提示額」。
(D) serve as ～「〈ある職〉を務める」、friendly「親切な」。

---

134 (A) dealing
(B) deals
(C) dealt
(D) deal

(A) 売買
(B) お買得品
(C) 分配された
(D) 待遇

正解 D 空所の前にto take advantage ofとあるので、この目的語となり、直前のthis greatによって修飾される名詞が入ると考えられる。thisに修飾されているので名詞は単数形。❷では、割引を利用できる対象やそれを利用するための方法が述べられているので、(D) deal「待遇、(有利な)取り決め」を入れると、「この大変お得な待遇を利用するために」となり文意が通る。
(A) 名詞または動名詞。文意に合わない。
(B) 名詞の複数形。空所の前にthisとあるので、複数形は不適切。
(C) 過去分詞。

Questions 135-138 refer to the following article.

❶ SYDNEY (4 October)—Square Peg Pizzas, affectionately known to local residents as Peggie's, will open its first franchise in Malaysia in the new year. This ------- (135.) marks an important milestone for the Australia-based chain. Since its first restaurant opened five years ago in Melbourne, it has had great domestic success. ------- (136.).

❷ This foray into the Southeast Asian market will be managed by one of the founders of the company, Mr. Ben Cummings. Mr. Cummings, who spent ------- (137.) childhood in Indonesia, has said that this new venture marks the realization of a lifelong ambition. He has always ------- (138.) to help run an international company.

問題135-138は次の記事に関するものです。

シドニー(10月4日)――Peggie'sの愛称で地元住民に親しまれているSquare Pegピザ社は、新年にマレーシアでのフランチャイズ第1号店をオープンする予定だ。この開業は、オーストラリアに拠点を置く同チェーンにとって重要な出来事となる。同社の第1号レストランが5年前にメルボルンにオープンして以来、同社は国内で大成功を収めている。*昨年Peggie'sは、オーストラリアの他のどのピザチェーンよりも利益を上げた。

この東南アジア市場への進出は、同社の創業者の一人であるBen Cummings氏によって取り仕切られることになる。インドネシアで幼年時代を過ごしたCummings氏は、この新事業は生涯にわたる野望を実現したものだと語っている。彼は常に、国際的企業の経営を助けることを熱望してきた。

*問題136の挿入文の訳

Words & Phrases

❶ affectionately 親しみを込めて　(be) known to ～ ～に知られている　resident 住民、居住者
franchise フランチャイズ店　mark ～を示す　milestone 画期的な出来事　-based 〈地名の後に付けて〉～に拠点を置く
chain チェーン(店)　domestic 国内の　❷ foray 進出　manage ～を運営する　founder 創業者
childhood 幼年時代　venture 冒険的事業、ベンチャー事業　realization 実現(したもの)　lifelong 生涯にわたる
ambition 野望　run ～を経営する　international 国際的な

Expressions

help (to) *do* 「～するのを助ける、～するのを手伝う」(❷ 3～4行目)

Many organizations helped improve the water quality of the lake.
多くの組織体が、その湖の水質を改善するのを助けました。

135 (A) hire
(B) launch
(C) colleague
(D) award

(A) 雇用
(B) 開業
(C) 同僚
(D) 賞

正解 B 選択肢は全て名詞の働きを持つ語。空所を含む文は「この-------は、オーストラリアに拠点を置く同チェーンにとって重要な出来事となる」という意味。直前の文ではSquare Pegピザ社がマレーシアでのフランチャイズ第1号店をオープンすると述べられているので、空所にはThisに続けてこの内容を受ける名詞が入ると考えられる。文意に合うのは、(B) launch「開業、〈活動などの〉開始」。
(A)(C)(D) いずれも、フランチャイズ店のオープンを伝える前文の内容を受ける語として文意に合わない。

---

136 (A) Peggie's is proud to use ingredients from these local areas.
(B) Last year Peggie's outperformed every other Australian pizza chain.
(C) Australians have shown a newfound love for food from this part of the world.
(D) Peggie's is excited to open its second Australian franchise soon.

(A) Peggie'sは、これらの地元産の材料を使用することを誇りに思っている。
(B) 昨年Peggie'sは、オーストラリアの他のどのピザチェーンよりも利益を上げた。
(C) オーストラリア人は、世界のこの地域の食べ物に対して新たな愛着を示している。
(D) Peggie'sは、オーストラリアのフランチャイズ第2号店を間もなくオープンすることに非常に心を躍らせている。

正解 B 空所の直前の文に、「同社の第1号レストランが5年前にメルボルンにオープンして以来、同社は国内で大成功を収めている」とある。ここでのitとは、冒頭のSquare Pegピザ社を指す。空所に(B)を入れると、同社のオーストラリア国内での5年間の成功への言及に続いて、昨年の具体的な実績を述べる文が続くこととなり、流れとして自然。outperform「～より利益を上げる、～をしのぐ」。
(A) be proud to *do*「～することを誇りに思う」、ingredient「材料」。
(C) newfound「新たに得た、新発見の」。
(D) 空所の前にある❶2行目でマレーシアの新店舗への言及があり、空所の後ろの❷でもマレーシアでの店舗オープンに関する内容が述べられているので、オーストラリア国内での店舗オープンの話は流れに合わない。excited to *do*「～することに興奮して」。

---

137 (A) he
(B) him
(C) his
(D) himself

(A) 彼は
(B) 彼を
(C) 彼の
(D) 彼自身

正解 C 空所の前のwhoは、直前のMr. Cummingsを先行詞とした主格の関係代名詞。空所の前に動詞の過去形spentがあり、後ろに名詞childhoodがあるので、空所には名詞を修飾し、共に動詞の目的語を作ることができる所有格の(C) hisが適切。
(A) 人称代名詞の主格。
(B) 人称代名詞の目的格。
(D) 再帰代名詞。

---

138 (A) supposed
(B) remembered
(C) concerned
(D) aspired

(A) ～だと思った
(B) ～を覚えていた
(C) ～に関係した
(D) 熱望した

正解 D ❷では、Square Pegピザ社の東南アジア市場進出を取り仕切るCummingsさんについて紹介がされている。空所の直前の文では、「この新事業は生涯にわたる野望を実現したものだ」とCummingsさんの発言を引用しているので、この海外進出は彼が長年夢見てきたことだと分かる。文意に合うのは、aspire to *do*で「～することを熱望する」という意味になるaspireの過去分詞の(D) aspired。
(A)(B)(C) いずれも文意に合わない。
(A) 動詞suppose「～だと思う」の過去分詞。
(B) remember to *do*「忘れずに～する」。
(C) 動詞concern「～に関係する」の過去分詞。

Questions 139-142 refer to the following letter.

September 28

Timothy Larkin
Camble Development, Inc.
284 Third Place
Chicago, IL 60610

Dear Mr. Larkin,

❶ I enjoyed meeting you at the Factory Industrial Automation Expo in Madison. You expressed interest in how my company's products might benefit your ------- (139.) business. A member of our sales team will be in Chicago from October 23 to 27 to meet with entrepreneurs. She would be delighted to meet with you on any of those days between 1 P.M. and 3 P.M. ------- (140.).

❷ She can show you ways to streamline your inventory control and purchasing with our convenient software. ------- (141.), if you decide to purchase the software, she can schedule a time to train your employees on how to use it.

❸ Please let me know if any of those times work for ------- (142.). My phone number is (225) 555-0193.

Sincerely,

Akshat Aranya
West Peak Solutions

問題139-142は次の手紙に関するものです。

9月28日

Timothy Larkin様
Camble Development社
サードプレイス284番地
シカゴ、IL 60610

Larkin様

マディソンでの工場用産業オートメーション博覧会にて、あなたにお目にかかれて光栄でした。あなたは、当社製品がいかにあなたの成長中の事業に利益をもたらす可能性があるかに関心を示していらっしゃいました。当社営業チームの一人が、起業家の方々とお会いするために、10月23日から27日までシカゴに滞在することになっています。彼女は、この日程のいずれかの日の午後1時から午後3時の間にあなたと喜んでお会いしたいとのことです。*会合は30分ほどかかるでしょう。

当社の便利なソフトウエアを用いて貴社の在庫管理と仕入れを合理化する方法を、彼女がご案内できます。また、貴社が当ソフトウエアのご購入を決定されましたら、彼女はその使い方に関して貴社従業員の方々にお教えする時間を予定に組み込むこともできます。

これらのいずれかの日時があなたにとってご都合が良いかどうか、お知らせください。私の電話番号は、(225)555-0193です。

敬具

Akshat Aranya
West Peak Solutions社

*問題140の挿入文の訳

139 (A) generous
(B) growing
(C) guaranteed
(D) gradual

(A) 寛大な
(B) 成長している
(C) 保証された
(D) 徐々の

正解 B 選択肢は全て形容詞の働きを持つ語。空所を含む文は「あなたは、当社製品がいかにあなたの-------事業に利益をもたらす可能性があるかに関心を示した」という意味で、空所に入る語は直前のyourと共に後ろの名詞business「事業、企業」を修飾している。❶・❷より、この手紙の受取人のLarkinさんは、自分の会社のオートメーション化・合理化を検討中であると考えられる。このLarkinさんの会社の現状を表し、businessを修飾するのに適切なのは(B) growing「成長している」。
(A)(C)(D) いずれも文意に合わない。

---

140 (A) It will save your company time and expenses.
(B) She has a full schedule on those days.
(C) We have offices in twelve locations.
(D) The meeting would take a half hour.

(A) それは貴社の時間と経費を節約するでしょう。
(B) 彼女は、それらの日程に予定がぎっしり詰まっています。
(C) 当社は12カ所に営業所があります。
(D) 会合は30分ほどかかるでしょう。

正解 D ❶ 2〜3行目に、手紙の差出人のAranyaさんの会社の営業担当者がシカゴに滞在する期間が書かれており、空所直前の同3〜4行目に、「彼女(=営業担当者)は、この日程のいずれかの日の午後1時から午後3時の間にあなたと喜んで会う」とある。一方、空所の後ろの❷ 1〜2行目では、営業担当者がLarkinさんにソフトウエアを用いた在庫管理と仕入れの合理化方法を案内する、と具体的な会合の内容が述べられているので、総じて会合にかかる時間を述べている(D)を入れると流れとして自然。
(A) Itは営業担当者が会いに来ることを表せるが、文脈から(D)がより自然。expense「経費」。
(B) 直前の文で営業担当者の空いている時間帯が提示されているので、不適切。full「ぎっしり詰まった」。

---

141 (A) Although
(B) Instead
(C) Otherwise
(D) Also

(A) 〜だけれども
(B) その代わりに
(C) そうでなければ
(D) また

正解 D 直前の文では、営業担当者が自社のソフトウエアを使った業務の合理化方法についてLarkinさんに説明できる旨が述べられている。空所を含む文では「貴社が当ソフトウエアの購入を決定したら、彼女はその使い方に関して貴社従業員に教える時間を予定に組み込むことができる」と、この営業担当者がさらに追加で提供できることが述べられている。よって、追加を表す(D) Also「また」を入れると、前後の流れがつながる。
(A)(B)(C) 前後の話の内容が論理的につながらない。

---

142 (A) her
(B) me
(C) you
(D) them

(A) 彼女に
(B) 私に
(C) あなたに
(D) 彼らに

正解 C 空所を含む文は「これらのいずれかの日時が-------にとって都合が良いかどうか、知らせてください」という意味。ここでのthose timesは、❶ 2〜4行目で営業担当者が会える日時として、手紙の受取人であるLarkinさんに提示しているもの。空所の前の❷では、営業担当者がLarkinさんと会う際に話す内容などが述べられているので、空所を含む文ではLarkinさんの都合を尋ねていると判断できる。よって、手紙の受取人を指す(C) you「あなたに」が適切。

Words & Phrases

❶ industrial 産業の　automation オートメーション、自動化　expo 〈expositionの略で〉博覧会　express 〜を表す　interest 関心　product 製品　benefit 〜に利益をもたらす　sales 営業　entrepreneur 起業家
❷ streamline 〜を合理化する　inventory 在庫　control 管理　purchasing 仕入れ、購買　convenient 便利な　schedule 〜を予定に組み込む　train 〜を教育する　employee 従業員　❸ work for 〜 〜にとって都合が良い

Expressions

be delighted to *do* 「喜んで〜する」(❶ 3〜4行目)
I would be delighted to attend the opening of your new office.
喜んで、貴社新事務所の開設式に出席いたします。

Questions 143-146 refer to the following information.

Policy Regarding Employee Workstations

❶ Because clients visit our offices frequently, all office employees are required to keep their workstations in a ------- (143.) neat and organized state. Personal items such as coats, handbags, keys, and wallets must be stored out of sight in a closet or desk drawer. ------- (144.). Food items are permitted, but they must not be left out in workstations during nonworking hours. Files and other paperwork must also be ------- (145.) at the end of the workday. Employees should direct any questions about this policy to their ------- (146.).

問題143-146は次の案内に関するものです。

従業員の個人作業スペースに関する方針

当社のオフィスには顧客が頻繁に訪れるため、全従業員は自身の作業スペースを適度にきれいで整った状態に保つ必要があります。コート、ハンドバッグ、鍵、財布のような私物は、戸棚や机の引き出しなど見えない所に保管されていなければなりません。*これは、オフィス環境で私物を安全に保管された状態にしておくためにも役立ちます。食べ物類は容認されていますが、それらは非就業時間中は作業スペースに出したままにしないでください。ファイルやその他の事務書類も、勤務時間の終わりに片付けられていなければなりません。従業員は、この方針に関する質問は自身の上司にするものとします。

*問題144の挿入文の訳

Words & Phrases

policy 方針　regarding ～に関して　workstation 〈個人の〉作業スペース、机　❶ frequently 頻繁に
neat きれいな、きちんとした　organized 整った　state 状態　personal 私的な　item 品物、品目
such as ～ ～のような　store ～を保管する　out of sight 見えない所に　closet 戸棚　drawer 引き出し
permit ～を容認する、～を許可する　leave out ～ ～を(外に)出したままにしておく　nonworking hours 非就業時間
paperwork 事務書類　workday 〈1日の〉勤務時間、就業日　direct ～ to … 〈言葉など〉を…に向ける

Expressions

be required to *do* 「～する必要がある、～しなければならない」(❶ 1行目)

Applicants are required to submit all the application materials by the end of March.
応募者は、3月末までに全ての応募資料を提出しなければなりません。

143 (A) reasoning
(B) reasonability
(C) reasonably
(D) reasoned

(A) 推論
(B) 妥当なこと
(C) 適度に
(D) 筋の通った

正解 C 空所の前は冠詞のa、後ろは名詞stateを修飾する2つの形容詞neatとorganizedがあるので、この2つの形容詞を修飾できる副詞の(C) reasonably「適度に」が適切。
(A)(B) 名詞。(D) 形容詞。いずれも後ろに形容詞を続けることができないので不適切。

---

144 (A) This also serves to keep personal items secure in the office environment.
(B) Lunch can also be purchased from food trucks near the office.
(C) All bags are screened by security staff as employees enter and leave.
(D) These rules will be posted online as well as in the employee lounge.

(A) これは、オフィス環境で私物を安全に保管された状態にしておくためにも役立ちます。
(B) 昼食は、事務所近くの食べ物の移動販売車から購入することもできます。
(C) 従業員が出入りする際、全ての手荷物は警備員によって検査されます。
(D) これらの規則は、オンラインでも従業員用ラウンジでも掲示されます。

正解 A 見出しより、この案内は従業員の作業スペースに関する方針と分かる。空所の直前では、私物を見えない所に保管しておくという決まりが述べられている。空所に(A)を入れると、追加効果を述べる自然な流れとなり、またThisが前文の「私物を見えない所に保管すること」を受け、そのことが私物を安全に保管された状態に保つためにも役立つという内容につながる。serve to *do*「～するのに役立つ」、secure「〈物が〉安全に保管されて」、environment「環境」。
(B) 空所の後ろに食べ物への言及があるが、前文とつながらない。
(C) screen「～を検査する」、security「警備」。
(D) post「～を掲示する」、*A* as well as *B*「*A*も*B*も」。

---

145 (A) dropped off
(B) set up
(C) taken apart
(D) put away

(A) 降ろされて
(B) 設置されて
(C) 分解されて
(D) 片付けられて

正解 D 個人作業スペースの方針として義務のmustを用いて、❶2～3行目で、私物はしまう、同3～4行目で、食べ物は放置しない、という整頓のための順守事項が述べられている。続く空所を含む文では、Files and other paperwork must also be ------- at the end of the workday.と、同様にmustを用いてalso「また」を伴っているので、追加の順守事項が述べられていると考えられる。put away ～「～を片付ける」の過去分詞の(D)を入れると「ファイルやその他の事務書類も、勤務時間の終わりに片付けられていなければならない」となり、文意が通る。
(A) drop off ～「〈車などから〉～を降ろす」の過去分詞。
(B) set up ～「～を設置する」の過去分詞。
(C) take apart ～「～を分解する」の過去分詞。

---

146 (A) supervise
(B) supervisor
(C) supervisory
(D) supervision

(A) ～を管理する
(B) 管理者
(C) 管理の
(D) 管理

正解 B 空所の直前には、この文の主語Employeesを受けている代名詞の所有格theirがあるので、空所には名詞が入る。この文は、「従業員は、この方針に関する質問は自身の-------に向けるものとする」という意味なので、(B) supervisor「上司、管理者」が適切。
(A) 動詞supervise「～を管理する」の原形。
(C) 形容詞。
(D) 名詞。文意に合わない。

TEST1 PART 6

文書 特典 35

Questions 147-148 refer to the following text message.

From Frida Sanchez **April 6, 7:54 P.M.**

❶ Stacy, I see on the new schedule that you usually work in the afternoon, but could you possibly open the store for me tomorrow morning? I've been having problems with my car, and I need to take it to my mechanic. But the repair shop doesn't open until 10 tomorrow morning. I can do your usual Wednesday afternoon shift starting at 2, and because Wednesday nights have extended hours, I'll stay until 9. Let me know if this works for you.

問題147-148は次のテキストメッセージに関するものです。

送信者 Frida Sanchez 4月6日、午後7時54分

Stacy、新しいスケジュール表で、あなたが通常は午後に勤務だと分かっていますが、できれば明日の朝、私の代わりに店を開けていただけませんか。私の車に問題があって、修理工の所へ持って行く必要があるのです。でも、修理店は明日の朝10時まで開きません。私は2時に始まるあなたの通常の水曜午後のシフトに入ることができますし、水曜日の夜は延長営業があるので、9時まで残るつもりです。これがあなたに都合が良いかどうか教えてください。

Words & Phrases

❶ usually 通常は　take ～ to … ～を…へ持って行く　mechanic 修理工　repair shop 修理店
shift 〈仕事の〉シフト　extended hours 延長営業（通常より遅くまで店を営業すること）　work for ～ ～に都合が良い

147 Why did Ms. Sanchez send the text message?

(A) To apologize for missing work
(B) To recommend a car mechanic
(C) To ask about hiring another employee
(D) To propose a change to a work schedule

Sanchezさんはなぜテキストメッセージを送信したのですか。

(A) 仕事を休んだことを謝罪するため。
(B) 自動車修理工を推薦するため。
(C) 別の従業員を雇うことについて尋ねるため。
(D) 勤務スケジュールの交替を提案するため。

正解 D ❶ 1～3行目でSanchezさんは、通常は午後の勤務予定のStacyに、「明日の朝、私の代わりに店を開けてくれないか」と頼んでいる。同3～5行目でその理由を説明した後、同5～7行目で水曜午後のStacyのシフトに自分が代わりに入ることを提案している。propose「～を提案する」。
(A) apologize for ～「～を謝罪する」、miss「～を休む」。
(B) 自動車修理工に言及はあるが、推薦してはいない。recommend「～を推薦する」。
(C) hire「～を雇う」。

148 What is indicated in the text message?

(A) Stacy is currently on vacation.
(B) A car repair shop is no longer in business.
(C) Ms. Sanchez plans to buy a new car.
(D) The store is open late on Wednesdays.

テキストメッセージで何が示されていますか。

(A) Stacyは現在、休暇中である。
(B) 自動車修理店はもはや事業を行っていない。
(C) Sanchezさんは新しい車を買う予定である。
(D) その店は、水曜日は遅くまで営業している。

正解 D ❶ 5～6行目に、水曜午後のシフトに代わりに入ることが可能だとあり、続けてbecause Wednesday nights have extended hours, I'll stay until 9「水曜日の夜は延長営業があるので、9時まで残るつもりだ」と述べられている。late「〈通常より〉遅くまで」。
(A) currently「現在」、on vacation「休暇中で」。
(B) ❶ 4～5行目に、自動車修理店は明朝10時まで開かないとあるので、事業は行っている。be in business「事業を行っている」、no longer ～「もはや～ない」。
(C) ❶ 3～4行目で、車を修理に出す予定が伝えられているが、新しく買うとは述べられていない。

Expressions

Could you possibly *do* ～? 「できたら～していただけませんか」（❶ 2行目）
Could you possibly call me before five today?
できましたら、今日の5時前に私にお電話いただけませんか。

Questions 149-150 refer to the following form.

OZONO AIRLINE MISSING BAGGAGE FORM

1 **Time and Date of Claim:** 1:50 P.M., May 2 **Flight Number:** 1869

Passenger Name: Alessandra Spencer

Flight Departure City: Atlanta **Flight Arrival City:** Boston

Destination Address: Winthrop Street Hotel,
456 Quincy Street, Boston

2 **Description of Contents:**
Clothing, two pairs of shoes, toiletries, three books, hair dryer, gifts

Bag Description:
Kona Company hard-sided blue suitcase with wheels

3 **Value of Contents:** $200
(Amount to be reimbursed for bags that are not returned within two weeks.)

4 **For Internal Use:**
Bag is confirmed to be on later flight number 1921. Christoff Delivery will deliver item to the customer at the destination address within twenty-four hours of the time of claim.

5 **Recorded by:** Delonte Ahmad

問題149-150は次の用紙に関するものです。

OZONO航空　紛失手荷物の用紙

申請日時：　5月2日午後1時50分　　便名：　1869

乗客名：　Alessandra Spencer

便の出発都市：アトランタ　　便の到着都市：　ボストン

届け先住所：　Winthrop市街ホテル
クインシー通り456番地、ボストン

内容物の説明：
衣類、靴2足、洗面用品、本3冊、ヘアドライヤー、土産物

かばんの説明：
Kona社製ハードタイプの青色スーツケース車輪付き

内容物の価値：　200ドル
（2週間以内に返却されなかったかばんに対して賠償される金額）

内部用記入欄：
かばんは、後発の1921便に積載されていることが確認されている。Christoff配送社が、申請時刻から24時間以内に届け先住所にいる顧客に品物を配達する。

記録者：　Delonte Ahmad

149 What does the form indicate about Ms. Spencer?

(A) She is currently in Atlanta.
(B) Her home is in Boston.
(C) Her bag will be delivered to a hotel by May 3.
(D) She will receive $200 for her lost luggage.

用紙はSpencerさんについて何を示していますか。

(A) 彼女は現在、アトランタにいる。
(B) 彼女の自宅はボストンにある。
(C) 彼女のかばんは5月3日までにホテルに配達される。
(D) 彼女は、紛失手荷物の賠償として200ドルを受け取る。

正解 C 「OZONO航空　紛失手荷物の用紙」の❶の乗客名欄にSpencerさんの名前があるので、Spencerさんは手荷物を紛失した人物。❹の内部用記入欄に「Christoff配送社が、申請時刻から24時間以内に届け先住所にいる顧客に品物を配達する」とあり、❶の申請日時の欄に「5月2日午後1時50分」とあるので、手荷物はその翌日の5月3日午後1時50分までにSpencerさんの元に配達されると分かる。❶の届け先住所欄にWinthrop市街ホテルとあるので、(C)が正解。
(A) ❶の「便の出発都市」はアトランタだが、Spencerさんが現在そこにいるとは述べられていない。
(B) ❶の「便の到着都市」はボストンだが、「届け先住所」はホテルで、自宅があるとは述べられていない。
(D) ❸より、賠償は2週間以内に手荷物が返却されなかった場合のみ発生すると分かる。luggage「旅行かばん」。

---

150 Who most likely is Mr. Ahmad?

(A) A hotel manager
(B) A luggage company employee
(C) A delivery driver
(D) An airline representative

Ahmadさんとは誰だと考えられますか。

(A) ホテルの支配人
(B) 旅行かばん会社の従業員
(C) 配送の運転手
(D) 航空会社の担当者

正解 D Ahmadという名前は❺の記録者欄にあるので、Ahmadさんとは内部用記入欄を記入した人物だと分かる。また、用紙の表題のOZONO AIRLINE MISSING BAGGAGE FORM「OZONO航空　紛失手荷物の用紙」より、AhmadさんはOZONO航空会社の関係者だと考えられる。よって、(D)が正解。representative「担当者」。

Words & Phrases

airline 航空会社　missing 紛失している、行方不明の　baggage 旅行用手荷物　❶ claim 請求
flight 〈航空機の〉便、フライト　passenger 乗客　departure 出発　arrival 到着　destination 届け先、目的地
❷ description 説明　contents 中身　clothing 衣類　toiletry 洗面用品　hard 硬質の、硬い
-sided ～の面を持つ　wheel 車輪　❸ value 価値　amount 金額　reimburse ～を賠償する
❹ internal 内部の　confirm ～を確認する　delivery 配送　deliver ～を配達する　item 品物
❺ record ～を記録する

Expressions

within ～ of … 「〈時間または距離が〉…から～以内に」(❹ 3～4行目)

Lillie's Hotel is located within a mile of Central Station.
Lillie'sホテルはセントラル駅から1マイル以内に位置しています。

Questions 151-152 refer to the following memo.

To: All Brestwood Furnishing staff
From: Paul Ho, President
Date: Wednesday, 23 August
Subject: Ron Donowicz

❶ Yesterday, I received notice that Ron Donowicz will retire at the end of October.

❷ As many of you know, Ron has been our director of facilities for 30 years. Managing a facilities maintenance department is a challenge in any company, and Ron set the high standard by which his successors will be measured.

❸ The Human Resources Division will be posting the facilities director position shortly. Our goal will be to fill the position internally. Ron will be using accrued vacation leave between now and his retirement date, but he will come in occasionally to train his replacement. He will also be here for a retirement luncheon on 20 October at noon in the cafeteria. All employees are welcome to attend.

問題151-152は次のメモに関するものです。

宛先：Brestwood家具社従業員各位
差出人：Paul Ho、社長
日付：8月23日水曜日
件名：Ron Donowicz

昨日、私はRon Donowiczが10月末で退職するという通知を受け取りました。

皆さんの多くがご存じの通り、Ronは30年間にわたり当社の設備管理部長を務めてきました。設備管理部を監督することはどんな会社でも難題ですが、Ronの存在がその基準を高めました。そして彼の後任者たちはそれにより、評価されることになるでしょう。

人事部は間もなく、設備管理部長の職を掲示します。われわれの目標は、その職を社内で補充することです。Ronは今から退職日までの間、未取得の休暇を使用しますが、自分の後任者を指導するために時折出社することになっています。彼はまた、10月20日正午カフェテリアにおける退職記念昼食会のためにここに来ます。全従業員の出席を歓迎します。

Words & Phrases

furnishing 家具調度品　❶ notice 通知　retire 〈定年などで〉退職する　❷ director 部長　facility 設備、施設
manage ～を監督する　maintenance 維持管理　challenge 難題　successor 後任者　measure ～を評価する
❸ Human Resources Division 人事部　post ～を掲示する　position 職　shortly 間もなく　fill 〈空位〉を補充する
internally 社内で、内部で　accrue ～を蓄積する　vacation 休暇　leave 休暇期間　retirement 退職
come in 〈職場に〉来る　occasionally 時折　train ～を指導する　replacement 後任者　luncheon 昼食会
welcome to *do* ～するのは大歓迎で　attend 出席する

151 What is the purpose of the memo?

(A) To introduce a new member of the maintenance staff
(B) To announce the promotion of the facilities director
(C) To inform staff that an employee will be leaving the company
(D) To explain a change in the company's hiring policy

メモの目的は何ですか。

(A) 管理部従業員の新しい一員を紹介すること。
(B) 設備管理部長の昇進を知らせること。
(C) ある従業員が会社を去ると職員に知らせること。
(D) 会社の雇用方針の変更を説明すること。

正解 C ❶に、I received notice that Ron Donowicz will retire at the end of October「私はRon Donowiczが10月末で退職するという通知を受け取った」とある。❷ではDonowiczさんによる会社への貢献が、❸ではその後任募集と退職記念昼食会についてが述べられている。inform「～に知らせる」。

(A) ❶・❷にfacilities maintenance departmentの従業員1名が退職するとあるが、❸ 1～2行目で後任についてはこれから募集すると述べられている。introduce「～を紹介する」。
(B) ❶・❷より、メモに記載されているのは設備管理部長の退職であり、昇進ではない。promotion「昇進」。
(D) hire「～を雇用する」、policy「方針」。

152 What does the memo indicate about Brestwood Furnishing?

(A) It plans to fill an open position with a current employee.
(B) It is changing its vacation policy.
(C) It is starting a new training program.
(D) It will renovate its cafeteria.

メモは、Brestwood家具社について何を示していますか。

(A) 同社は空いた職を現在の従業員で補充する計画である。
(B) 同社は休暇方針を変更する予定である。
(C) 同社は新しい研修プログラムを開始する予定である。
(D) 同社はカフェテリアを改装するつもりである。

正解 A メモでは、❶で設備管理部長のDonowiczさんの退職を知らせた後、❸ 1～2行目で「人事部は間もなく、設備管理部長の職を掲示する」と続け、さらにOur goal will be to fill the position internally.「われわれの目標は、その職を社内で補充することだ」と述べている。よって、Brestwood家具社は外部の人材ではなく、社内公募でその空職を満たす計画であると判断できるので、(A)が正解。open「〈仕事などに〉空きのある」、current「現在の」。

(C) ❸ 3～4行目で、後任の指導に言及しているが、研修プログラムについては述べられていない。
(D) renovate「～を改装する」。

Expressions

set a standard 「基準を設ける」(❷ 3行目)

We set a high standard for our products.
当社では、製品に高い基準を設けております。

Questions 153-154 refer to the following text-message chain.

❶ **Fumio Komatsu (2:42 P.M.)**
Hi, Nelly. By any chance, did someone from the Evergreen restaurant send you a list of the summer menu items? I wanted to start updating their site, but I don't have the latest list.

❷ **Nelly Artemyeva (2:43 P.M.)**
The chef e-mailed it to me this morning, but I want to go over the changes with you first. Do you have time now?

❸ **Fumio Komatsu (2:44 P.M.)**
I'm on my way back to the office. I just received the photographs for the aquarium's Web site. They're amazing!

❹ **Nelly Artemyeva (2:45 P.M.)**
Excellent. Why don't I stop by your office around 4:30. Will you be available?

❺ **Fumio Komatsu (2:46 P.M.)**
Most likely. I have to go to a training session at 3:30, but it shouldn't last long.

問題153-154は次のテキストメッセージのやりとりに関するものです。

Fumio Komatsu（午後2時42分）
こんにちは、Nelly。ひょっとして、Evergreenレストランの誰かが夏のメニュー品目のリストをあなたに送ってきましたか。彼らのサイトの更新を始めたかったのですが、僕は最新のリストを持っていないのです。

Nelly Artemyeva（午後2時43分）
シェフが今朝、それを私にEメールで送ってきましたが、まずはあなたと一緒に変更点を詳しく調べたいと思っています。今、時間はありますか。

Fumio Komatsu（午後2時44分）
僕は会社に戻る途中です。ちょうど水族館のウェブサイト用の写真を受け取ったところです。それらは素晴らしいですよ！

Nelly Artemyeva（午後2時45分）
良かったですね。私が4時30分ごろにあなたの執務室に立ち寄りましょうか。あなたは都合がつきますか。

Fumio Komatsu（午後2時46分）
おそらく。3時30分に研修会に行かなければなりませんが、それは長くはかからないはずです。

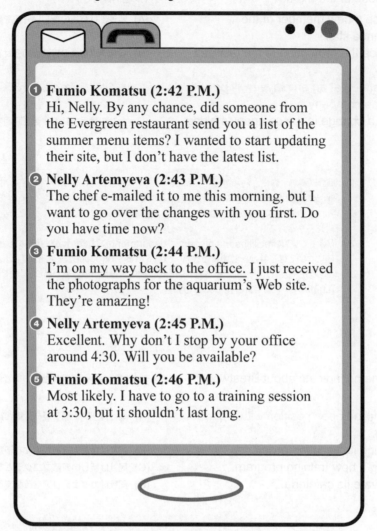

153 What is suggested about Mr. Komatsu and Ms. Artemyeva?

(A) They are studying photography.
(B) They work at an aquarium.
(C) They design Web sites.
(D) They own a restaurant.

KomatsuさんとArtemyevaさんについて何が分かりますか。

(A) 彼らは写真撮影術を勉強している。
(B) 彼らは水族館で働いている。
(C) 彼らはウェブサイトを制作している。
(D) 彼らはレストランを所有している。

正解 C Komatsuさんはレストランの夏メニューに関して❶で、I wanted to start updating their site, but I don't have the latest list.「彼らのサイトの更新を始めたかったが、僕は最新のリストを持っていない」と述べ、それに対しArtemyevaさんは❷で、リストをEメールで受け取ったことを伝えて、まずはKomatsuさんと変更点を詳しく調べたいと述べている。さらに❸で、Komatsuさんが「ちょうど水族館のウェブサイト用の写真を受け取ったところだ」と述べている。2人はさまざまな業種のウェブサイトを手がけているので、ウェブサイトを制作する仕事をしていると判断できる。

(A) photography「写真撮影術」。
(D) own「~を所有している」。

---

154 At 2:44 P.M., what does Mr. Komatsu mean when he writes, "I'm on my way back to the office"?

(A) He is not able to review a document now.
(B) He agrees with Ms. Artemyeva's suggestions.
(C) He has been delayed by traffic.
(D) He did not check his e-mail this morning.

午後2時44分に、Komatsuさんは "I'm on my way back to the office"という発言で、何を意味していますか。

(A) 彼は今、文書を精査することができない。
(B) 彼はArtemyevaさんの提案に同意する。
(C) 彼は交通渋滞によって遅れている。
(D) 彼は今朝、Eメールを確認しなかった。

正解 A Artemyevaさんは❷で、Eメールで受信したメニューの最新リストをKomatsuさんと一緒に詳しく調べたいと思っていると述べた後に、「今、時間はあるか」と尋ねている。それに対しKomatsuさんは下線部で「僕は会社に戻る途中だ」と外出先から会社に移動している最中だと伝えている。よってKomatsuさんは、自分が今リストを精査できないことを示すため、下線部の発言をしたと判断できるので(A)が正解。❶のa list of the summer menu itemsを(A)ではa documentと表している。review「~を精査する」。

(B) agree with ~「~に同意する」、suggestion「提案」。
(C) delay「~を遅らせる」、traffic「交通(量)」。

Words & Phrases

❶ item 品目　update ~を更新する　latest 最新の　❷ e-mail ~をEメールで送る
go over ~ ~を詳しく調べる、~に目を通す　❸ on *one's* way back to ~ ~に戻る途中で　aquarium 水族館
amazing 素晴らしい　❹ Why don't I ~ ~しましょうか　stop by ~ ~に立ち寄る　available 都合がつく
❺ most likely おそらく　training session 研修会　last 続く

Expressions

by any chance 「ひょっとして」(❶)

Were you looking for me, by any chance?
ひょっとして、あなたは私を探していましたか。

Questions 155-157 refer to the following letter.

Mr. Hugh Lander
86 Pascoe Road
Karori, Wellington 6012

Dear Mr. Lander,

❶ It is time for your biannual checkup. Plantech Dental is honored to serve as your dental care provider. We understand that you have many options when it comes to finding a reliable and affordable dentist. To reward your loyalty, I am proud to offer you a complimentary teeth-whitening service! This special promotion is available only to clients who have completed at least six biannual checkups at Plantech Dental.

❷ For you to qualify, I will need to examine your teeth to ensure they are healthy enough to undergo a professional whitening service. If your teeth are in good condition, you will receive four whitening-gel tubes, two trays custom-fit for your teeth, and one tube of whitening toothpaste.

❸ Call Plantech Dental to schedule your next appointment and to take advantage of this special promotion.

Sincerely,

Marlys Martin

Dr. Marlys Martin, DMD

問題155-157は次の手紙に関するものです。

Hugh Lander様
パスコー通り86番地
カロリ、ウェリントン 6012

Lander様

あなたの半年ごとの検診の時期となりました。Plantech歯科医院は、あなたの歯の治療を担当させていただき光栄に存じます。信頼できて、かつご予算に合う歯科医を見つけることに関して、多くの選択肢があることを承知しております。お引き立てのお礼に、当院は歯の無料のホワイトニングサービスを誇りを持ってご提供いたします。この特別プロモーションは、Plantech歯科医院で半年ごとの検診を少なくとも6回終えられた患者さまだけがご利用いただけます。

あなたがその資格を得るには、私があなたの歯を検査して、それらが専門的なホワイトニングサービスを受けるのに十分健康であることを確かめる必要があります。あなたの歯が良好な状態であれば、ホワイトニングジェルのチューブを4本、あなたの歯にぴったり合わせたホワイトニング用トレーを2つ、またホワイトニング歯磨きのチューブ1本をお受け取りになれます。

Plantech歯科医院までお電話いただき、次回の予約を入れてこの特別プロモーションをご利用ください。

敬具

Marlys Martin（署名）
Marlys Martin医師、歯学博士

Words & Phrases

❶ biannual 半年ごとの　checkup 検診　dental 歯科の、歯の　be honored to *do* ～することを光栄に思う
serve as ～ ～を務める　care 〈治療などの〉ケア、手入れ　provider 提供者　option 選択肢　reliable 信頼できる
affordable 手頃な価格の　dentist 歯科医　reward ～にお返しをする　loyalty 忠誠心、愛顧
be proud to *do* ～することを誇りに思う　promotion プロモーション、販売促進　available 利用できる
complete ～を終える　at least 少なくとも　❷ qualify 資格を得る　examine ～を検査する　ensure ～を確かめる
undergo ～を受ける　professional 専門的な　in good condition 良好な状態で　gel ジェル　tube チューブ
tray トレー（歯のホワイトニングのために前歯にはめるもの）　custom-fit ぴったり合うようにあつらえた
toothpaste 練り歯磨き　❸ schedule ～を予定する　appointment 予約
DMD 歯学博士（Doctor of Dental Medicineを表す）

155 The word "complimentary" in paragraph 1, line 4, is closest in meaning to

(A) friendly
(B) discounted
(C) free
(D) admired

第1段落・4行目にある"complimentary"に最も意味が近いのは

(A) 親切な
(B) 値引きされた
(C) 無料の
(D) 称賛された

正解 C ❶1～2行目より、手紙の受取人のLanderさんはPlantech歯科医院に定期的に通院する患者。同3～4行目に「お引き立てのお礼に、当院は歯の-------ホワイトニングサービスを誇りを持って提供する」とあるので、同院がLanderさんに定期的な通院のお礼に歯のホワイトニングサービスの提供を申し出ていると分かる。❷1～2行目で、このサービスの条件として、検診で歯が専門的なホワイトニングを受けるのに十分健康な状態だと確認することを挙げている。よって、歯の健康状態に問題がなければ手紙を受け取った誰もがこのサービスを受けられると判断できるので、料金は不要と考えられる。(C) free「無料の」が正解。

---

156 What is suggested about Mr. Lander?

(A) He is a longtime Plantech Dental client.
(B) He has visited several dentists in the area.
(C) He has never had a teeth-whitening procedure.
(D) He just returned from a dentist appointment.

Landerさんについて何が分かりますか。

(A) 彼は、Plantech歯科医院の長期にわたる患者である。
(B) 彼はその地域のさまざまな歯科医を受診したことがある。
(C) 彼は歯のホワイトニングの処置を受けたことがない。
(D) 彼は歯医者の予約からちょうど帰ってきた。

正解 A Landerさんに宛てた手紙の❶3～4行目に歯のホワイトニングサービスについて言及があり、続けてThis special promotion is available only to clients who have completed at least six biannual checkups at Plantech Dental.「この特別プロモーションは、Plantech歯科医院で半年ごとの検診を少なくとも6回終えた患者だけが利用できる」とある。よって、Landerさんは少なくとも数年間は同院に通っていると分かる。longtime「長期にわたる」。
(C) procedure「処置」。

---

157 What must clients do in order to qualify for the promotion?

(A) Refer five new clients to Dr. Martin
(B) Attend an informational meeting
(C) Purchase four whitening-gel tubes
(D) Have their teeth examined by Dr. Martin

患者は、プロモーションを受ける資格を得るために何をしなければなりませんか。

(A) Martin医師に新規患者を5名紹介する。
(B) 情報提供の会合に出席する。
(C) ホワイトニングジェルのチューブを4本購入する。
(D) Martin医師に歯の検査をしてもらう。

正解 D ❶3～6行目に歯のホワイトニングの特別プロモーションの提示があり、続けて❷でFor you to qualify, I will need to examine your teeth to ensure they are healthy enough to undergo a professional whitening service.「あなたがその資格を得るには、私があなたの歯を検査して、それらが専門的なホワイトニングサービスを受けるのに十分健康であることを確かめる必要がある」と述べている。末尾の署名より「私」とは、この手紙の差出人のMartin医師と分かるので、(D)が正解。
(A) refer ～ to …「～を…に紹介する」。(B) informational「情報を提供する」。
(C) ❷の2～3行目にジェル4本への言及があるが、これは特別プロモーションで受け取れるもの。

Expressions

take advantage of ～ 「～を利用する、～を活用する」(❸1～2行目)
I took advantage of every opportunity to expand my career network.
私は、職業上の人脈を広げるためにあらゆる機会を利用しました。

Questions 158-160 refer to the following article.

Wedding Planning Made Easy

❶ TYNDALE (9 September)—Robert Marsh knows firsthand that planning a wedding can be a time-consuming and energy-draining endeavor. "My fiancée and I," he explains, "had to crisscross Tyndale to find vendors that suited our budget and style requirements. It occurred to me that there had to be a better way of making the necessary wedding preparations."

❷ — [1] —. Barely a year into his marriage, he created Nuptials Paradise, a company that aims to simplify wedding planning. Located at 248 Palmchat Drive, site of the former Harrison Grocery Store, the company has partnered with 50 wedding industry professionals. — [2] —. "Our customers love the convenience of being able to book the services they need at one location," says Mr. Marsh. "Vendors, in turn, have easier access to a large number of clients." — [3] —.

❸ Mr. Marsh says that he has received requests from various people interested in opening their own businesses under his brand name, which would make them distributors of his services. Evidently, he is open to that possibility. "Just months after having opened Nuptials Paradise," he says, "it became apparent to me that there was a great need for my services. I cannot be everywhere at once, so I certainly would welcome some help." — [4] —.

問題158-160は次の記事に関するものです。

結婚式の計画立案が簡単に

ティンダル（9月9日）──Robert Marshは、結婚式の計画の立案は時間がかかり、かつエネルギーを消耗させる試みになることがあると自らの体験から知っている。「婚約者と私は、自分たちの予算とやり方の条件に合う業者を探すためにティンダル中を行ったり来たりしなければなりませんでした。結婚式の必要な準備をするのにもっと良い方法があるはずだ、という考えが私の頭に浮かびました」と彼は説明する。

*Marsh氏は、その考えを実行する方法を思い付いた。結婚生活がやっと1年に入ろうとする頃、彼は結婚式の計画立案を簡素化することを目指す会社、Nuptials Paradise社を創立した。かつてのHarrison食料雑貨店の跡地、パームチャット大通り248番地に位置する同社は、ブライダル業界の専門家50名と提携している。「当社の顧客は、必要なサービス業務を1カ所で予約できる利便性をとても気に入っています」とMarsh氏は語る。「同様に、業者も多数の顧客に、より容易に接触できます」。

Marsh氏は、彼のブランド名の下で自身の事業を始めたいと思っているさまざまな人々から要請を受けていると話しており、それはつまりそれらの人々が彼のサービス業の代理店になるということだ。明らかに、彼はその可能性を快く受け入れている。「Nuptials Paradise社を開業してわずか数カ月で、私のサービス業には高い需要があることが自分にははっきり分かりました。私が同時にどこにでもいることは不可能なので、お力添えをもちろん歓迎いたします」と彼は語る。

*問題160の挿入文の訳

Words & Phrases

❶ firsthand 直接体験によって　time-consuming 時間のかかる　drain ～を失わせる　endeavor 試み、努力　fiancée 婚約中の女性　crisscross ～を縦横に動く　vendor 供給業者　suit ～に合う　budget 予算　requirement 条件、要求　preparation 準備　❷ barely やっと、わずかに　marriage 結婚生活　aim to *do* ～することを目指す　simplify ～を簡素化する　be located 位置する　site 跡地　former かつての　grocery store 食料雑貨店　partner with ～ ～と提携する　industry 業界　professional 専門家　convenience 利便性　book ～を予約する　location 場所　in turn 同様に　access 接触　❸ request 要請　various さまざまな　distributor 代理店　evidently 明らかに　be open to ～ ～を快く受け入れる　possibility 可能性　apparent はっきり分かる　at once 同時に　certainly もちろん、間違いなく

158 What is a purpose of the article?

(A) To broaden understanding of business partnerships
(B) To explore the growth of the wedding industry
(C) To describe the wedding planning process
(D) To explain the origins of a company

記事の目的の1つは何ですか。

(A) 事業提携に対する理解を広げること。
(B) ブライダル業界の成長を探ること。
(C) 結婚式の計画立案の過程を説明すること。
(D) 会社の起源を説明すること。

正解 D ❶ 7～9行目に「結婚式の必要な準備をするのにもっと良い方法があるはずだ、という考えが私の頭に浮かんだ」というMarshさんの発言があり、❷ 1～4行目で、Marshさんが結婚式の計画の立案を簡素化することを目指す会社を創立した経緯が述べられている。
(A) ❷ 4～7行目に、Marshさんの会社の事業提携に関する記述はあるが、会社の現状の説明として述べられているだけ。broaden「～を広げる」、partnership「提携」。
(B) explore「～を探る」、growth「成長」。

159 What is indicated about Nuptials Paradise?

(A) It has changed its business model.
(B) It has been in business for about a year.
(C) Its clients are pleased with its services.
(D) Its first contract was signed with a grocery store.

Nuptials Paradise社について何が示されていますか。

(A) 同社はそのビジネスモデルを変えた。
(B) 同社は創業して約1年である。
(C) 同社の顧客はそのサービス業務に満足している。
(D) 同社の最初の契約は食料雑貨店と交わされた。

正解 C ❷ 2行目より、Nuptials Paradise社とはMarshさんが創立した会社だと分かる。同7～10行目に「当社の顧客は、必要なサービス業務を1カ所で予約できる利便性をとても気に入っている」というMarshさんの発言がある。
(B) ❷ 1～2行目に、Marshさんが結婚1年後に会社を創立したとあるが、創業年数の記載はない。
(D) ❷ 4～7行目に、同社の所在地はかつての食料雑貨店の跡地とあるが、契約に関する言及はない。

160 In which of the positions marked [1], [2], [3], and [4] does the following sentence best belong?

"Mr. Marsh came up with a way to act on that idea."

(A) [1]
(B) [2]
(C) [3]
(D) [4]

[1]、[2]、[3]、[4]と記載された箇所のうち、次の文が入るのに最もふさわしいのはどれですか。

「Marsh氏は、その考えを実行する方法を思い付いた」

正解 A ❶ 7～9行目のMarshさんの発言に、「結婚式の必要な準備をするのにもっと良い方法があるはずだ、という考えが私の頭に浮かんだ」とあり、この直後の(A) [1]に挿入文を入れると、前文の「もっと良い方法がある」という考えを挿入文中のthat idea「その考え」で受けることができ、適切。また、直後の文で「結婚式の計画立案を簡素化することを目指す会社を創立した」と、その考えに基づいて実行したことを具体的に述べており、流れとして自然。act on ～「～を実行する」。

Expressions

It occurs to ～ that … 「…という考えが～の頭に浮かぶ」(❶ 7行目)

It occurred to me that my new business proposal might be rejected.
自分の新しい事業の提案は却下されるかもしれない、という考えが私の頭に浮かびました。

Questions 161-163 refer to the following information in a brochure.

Visit Finneran Tree Farm

❶ Are you interested in old-growth forests, wildflowers, wildlife habitats, hiking, and being outdoors? If yes, Finneran Tree Farm is the perfect place for you!

❷ Finneran Tree Farm was donated 25 years ago by the Finneran family to the Ladd Forestry Centre, which now operates the tree farm as an education site and park. It features 5 kilometres of hiking trails, as well as streams and a riverbank to explore. It is open to the public year-round for self-guided tours. Groups of ten or more must register at least two weeks before visiting.

❸ From April to September, the hours are 7:00 A.M. to 9:00 P.M., and from October to March, the hours are 8:00 A.M. to 5:00 P.M.

❹ Facilities include covered picnic areas and an indoor education centre, which can be reserved for a small fee. Visit www.finnerantreefarm.co.uk/reservations for more information.

Finneran Tree Farm
42 Maybury Rd, Edinburgh EH4 6BU
0131 496 1234

問題161-163は次のパンフレットの情報に関するものです。

Finneran樹木園にお越しください

原生林や野生の草花、野生生物の生息地、ハイキング、屋外で過ごすことに興味がありますか。もし「イエス」ならば、Finneran樹木園はあなたにぴったりの場所です!

Finneran樹木園は、25年前にFinneran家からLadd森林管理センターに寄贈され、現在、同センターがこの樹木園を教育の場および公園として運営しています。当園は5キロメートルのハイキングコースおよび、探索できる小川と川岸を特色としています。自分で見て回る形で一年中、一般に公開されています。10名以上のグループは、ご来園の少なくとも2週間前に登録する必要があります。

4月から9月までは、開園時間は午前7時から午後9時まで、そして10月から3月までは、開園時間は午前8時から午後5時までです。

施設として、屋根付きのピクニック場と屋内の教育センターもあり、低料金で予約可能です。より詳しい情報につきましては、www.finnerantreefarm.co.uk/reservationsにアクセスしてください。

Finneran樹木園
メイブリー通り42番地、エディンバラ EH4 6BU
0131 496 1234

Words & Phrases

brochure パンフレット ❶ old-growth 原生の wildflower 野生の草花 wildlife 野生生物 habitat 生息地 outdoors 屋外で ❷ donate ～を寄贈する forestry 森林管理 operate ～を運営する site 場所 feature ～を特色とする、～を目玉とする trail コース、道 stream 小川 riverbank 川岸 explore ～を探索する the public 一般の人々 year-round 一年中 self-guided 〈案内人なしで〉自ら行う register 登録する ❸ hours 営業時間 ❹ facility 施設 include ～を含む covered 屋根付きの indoor 屋内の fee 料金

161 What is mentioned about Finneran Tree Farm?

(A) It is known around the world.
(B) It hosts community events in the summer.
(C) It is a family-run business.
(D) It is open all year.

Finneran樹木園について何が述べられていますか。

(A) 同園は世界中で知られている。
(B) 同園は夏に地域行事を主催する。
(C) 同園は家族経営の会社である。
(D) 同園は一年中開いている。

正解 D Finneran樹木園について、❷4〜5行目にIt is open to the public year-round for self-guided tours.「自分で見て回る形で一年中、一般に公開されている」とあるので、(D)が正解。

(C) ❷1〜3行目に、Finneran樹木園は以前Finneran家から寄贈されたとあるが、現在はLadd森林管理センターが運営していると分かるので、家族経営ではない。

---

162 What is indicated about large group visits?

(A) Hiking guides are available.
(B) Advance notice is required.
(C) Payment is due upon arrival.
(D) Groups over twenty are prohibited.

大人数のグループ来園について何が示されていますか。

(A) ハイキングの案内をしてもらえる。
(B) 事前の通知が必要である。
(C) 到着時に支払いをしなければならない。
(D) 20名を超えるグループの来園は禁止されている。

正解 B 大人数のグループに関しては、❷5行目にGroups of ten or more must register at least two weeks before visiting.「10名以上のグループは、来園の少なくとも2週間前に登録する必要がある」と同園を大人数のグループで訪問する際は事前登録が必要だと説明している。事前登録することをadvance noticeと表している(B)が正解。advance「事前の」、notice「通知」。

(C) due「支払われるべき」、upon arrival「到着時に」。

(D) 人数制限については述べられていない。prohibit「〜を禁止する」。

---

163 According to the brochure, how can someone learn more about facility reservations?

(A) By going to the forestry-center office
(B) By phoning the tree farm
(C) By visiting a Web site
(D) By sending in a request form

パンフレットによると、どのようにして施設の予約についてさらに知ることができますか。

(A) 森林管理センターの事務所に行くことによって。
(B) 樹木園に電話をすることによって。
(C) あるウェブサイトにアクセスすることによって。
(D) 要望書を送付することによって。

正解 C ❹1〜2行目で、ピクニック場や教育センターなどの施設が低料金で予約可能であると述べられている。続く同2〜3行目に、「より詳しい情報につきましては、www.finnerantreefarm.co.uk/reservationsにアクセスしてほしい」とあるので、施設の予約に関する詳細情報がウェブサイトに掲載されていると考えられる。(C)が正解。

(B) phone「〜に電話をかける」。

(D) send in 〜「〜を送付する」。

Expressions

A **as well as** *B* 「*A*も*B*も」(❷3〜4行目)

Moderate exercise is helpful in relieving your stress as well as keeping you healthy.
適度な運動は、ストレス軽減にも健康維持にも役立ちます。

Questions 164-167 refer to the following article.

❶ — [1] —. While the in-person interview is not going away, many human resources departments have come to rely on videoconferencing for candidate screening. Using video has reduced the amount of unproductive communication between job seekers and employers, and both parties appreciate the ability to more easily schedule an interview.

❷ Finding a videoconferencing vendor can be a challenging process, especially for smaller companies. — [2] —. Phillipa Renwick, human resources director at Inama Clothing Manufacturers, recommends that all companies think broadly about their needs. For example, Ms. Renwick asks, "Are there on-site meetings happening now that might be conducted at least as effectively through a videoconference?" A further consideration, according to Ms. Renwick, is that businesses often use the same technology to engage in activities like employee training. — [3] —.

❸ Ms. Renwick cautions that potential vendors should be asked how any proposed systems will be customized without creating unreasonable costs or straining information-technology staff. — [4] —. Some companies may only need basic video capabilities, while others may seek more advanced functions, such as built-in analytic software that allows managers to score and rank video interviewees in the moment.

問題164-167は次の記事に関するものです。

対面での面接がなくなることはないだろうが、多くの人事部が候補者の選考をテレビ会議に頼るようになってきている。テレビ映像の使用は、求職者と雇用主との間の非生産的なやりとりの量を減らし、両当事者とも、より簡単に面接の予定を組むことができることを高く評価している。

テレビ会議の業者を探すことは、とりわけ小規模企業にとっては困難な過程になることがある。Inama衣料品製造会社の人事部長Phillipa Renwickは、全ての企業が自社のニーズについて広く考えるべきと助言している。例えば、Renwickさんは「現在行われている実地の会合で、テレビ会議方式ででも、少なくとも同じくらい効果的に行える可能性のあるものはありませんか」と問いかける。Renwickさんによると、さらに考慮すべきは、企業はしばしば従業員研修のような活動を行う際に同一の技術を使用するということだ。*このような状況での経費節減は、国際的企業にとって重要かもしれない。

Renwickさんは、候補業者には、どうすれば提案されたシステムを法外な経費を発生させたり情報技術スタッフに過度の負担をかけたりすることなしに、カスタマイズできるかを尋ねるべきだ、と警告する。基本的な動画性能のみを必要とする企業もある一方で、テレビ面接を受けている人を管理者が瞬時に採点して順位を付けることが可能な内蔵型分析ソフトウエアのような、より高度な機能を求める企業もある。

*問題167の挿入文の訳

Words & Phrases

❶ while　〜だけれども　in-person　直接の　go away　なくなる　human resources　人事
come to *do*　〜するようになる　videoconferencing　テレビ会議　candidate　候補者　screening　選考
reduce　〜を減らす　unproductive　非生産的な　job seeker　求職者　employer　雇用主　party　当事者
appreciate　〜を高く評価する　ability to *do*　〜することができること　❷ vendor　供給業者
challenging　骨の折れる、大変な　process　過程　clothing　衣料品　manufacturer　製造会社　broadly　(幅)広く
on-site　現地での　conduct　〜を行う　at least　少なくとも　effectively　効果的に　further　さらに付け加えられた
consideration　考慮すべきこと　engage in 〜　〜に従事する　❸ caution　〜と警告する　potential　潜在的な
proposed　提案された　customize　〜をカスタマイズする　unreasonable　法外な　strain　〜に過度の負担をかける
capability　性能　seek　〜を求める　advanced　高度な　function　機能　built-in　内蔵の　analytic　分析の
score　〜を採点する　rank　〜に順位を付ける　interviewee　面接を受ける人

Expressions

rely on 〜 for …　「…を〜に頼る」(❶3〜4行目)

Some say that we should avoid relying on smartphones for everything.
全てをスマートフォンに頼るのは避けるべきだと言う人もいます。

164 What is the main topic of the article?

(A) Easier ways to set up a videoconference
(B) Factors to consider when choosing certain communication technology
(C) A video series offering advice to job seekers
(D) Improving processes in an information-technology department

記事の主題は何ですか。

(A) テレビ会議を設定するためのより簡単な方法
(B) 特定の通信技術を選択する際に考慮すべき要素
(C) 求職者に助言を提供する動画のシリーズ
(D) 情報技術部門における工程の改善

正解 B ❶ 2～4 行目で人事部が候補者選考をテレビ会議に頼る傾向の高まりが紹介され、❷ 1～7行目で、テレビ会議の業者探しの現状と助言が、また、同 7～14 行目では、テレビ会議システム導入の際に考慮すべきことが提示されている。さらに、❸ 1～5 行目では、テレビ会議の業者を選ぶ際に尋ねるべき点が述べられている。よって、(B)が正解。
(A) set up ～「～を設定する」。
(D) improve「～を改善する」。

165 Why is Ms. Renwick most likely quoted in the article?

(A) Her company regularly conducts videoconferences.
(B) Her company sells videoconferencing equipment.
(C) She performed well during a video interview.
(D) She developed a new type of video-editing software.

Renwickさんの言葉はなぜ、記事で引用されていると考えられますか。

(A) 彼女の会社は定期的にテレビ会議を行っているから。
(B) 彼女の会社はテレビ会議の設備を販売しているから。
(C) 彼女はテレビ面接の間、うまくやってのけたから。
(D) 彼女は新型の動画編集ソフトウエアを開発したから。

正解 A ❶では、多くの企業の人事部が採用面接にテレビ会議を利用している現状が紹介され、❷ 1～3行目でテレビ会議の業者選びは、特に小規模企業にとって困難だと述べられている。続けて、同 3～7 行目でテレビ会議の業者選びの際には自社のニーズについて広く考えるべきという、衣料品製造会社人事部長のRenwickさんの助言が引用されている。よって、Renwickさんの会社ではテレビ会議を行っていると考えられるので、(A)が正解。quote「～の言葉を引用する」。regularly「定期的に」。
(B) equipment「設備」。(D) editing「編集」。

166 According to the article, what can interviewers do with advanced video functions?

(A) View instructional materials
(B) Post video files
(C) Monitor training programs
(D) Rate job candidates

記事によると、面接者は高度な動画機能を用いて何をすることができますか。

(A) 教材を見る。
(B) 動画ファイルを投稿する。
(C) 研修プログラムを監視する。
(D) 職の候補者を評価する。

正解 D ❸ 7～10 行目に「テレビ面接を受けている人を管理者が瞬時に採点して順位を付けることが可能な内蔵型分析ソフトウエアのような、より高度な機能を求める企業もある」とあるので(D)が正解。rate「～を評価する」。
(A) instructional「教育の」。
(C) monitor「～を監視する」。

167 In which of the positions marked [1], [2], [3], and [4] does the following sentence best belong?

"The cost savings in this situation could be significant for international companies."

(A) [1]
(B) [2]
(C) [3]
(D) [4]

[1]、[2]、[3]、[4]と記載された箇所のうち、次の文が入るのに最もふさわしいのはどれですか。

「このような状況での経費節減は、国際的企業にとって重要かもしれない」

正解 C ❷ 12～14 行目に、企業はしばしば従業員研修などの活動にテレビ会議の技術を使用するとあり、企業において面接以外の目的にテレビ会議を利用できる状況があることが述べられている。(C) [3]に挿入文を入れると、挿入文の the cost savings in this situation「このような状況での経費節減」が前文の「企業が従業員研修のような活動にテレビ会議の技術を使用する」という、面接の他にテレビ会議技術を併用できる状況を示す。そしてそのような複数の活動目的でのテレビ会議利用は経費節減につながり、国際的企業では重要だ、とまとめる流れとなるので適切。saving「節約」、significant「重要な」。

Questions 168-171 refer to the following Web page.

http://www.talkfirsttechnologies.com

Talk First Technologies
News and Updates

❶ **You spoke. We listened.**
Effective June 1, Talk First Technologies' customers will have the following options.

❷ • **Month-to-month plans**—Talk First Technologies will cease offering one- and two-year service contracts. All services will be billed on a monthly basis.

❸ • **New plans**—Our newly available options include a low-cost plan that provides unlimited calling and text messaging for just $45 a month. Purchase data by the gigabyte when you need it. Or, choose the Techfan plan, which allows you to try our state-of-the-art mobile devices before they are released for public sale.

❹ • **Device upgrades**—You will be able to purchase any phone, at any time, at the full retail price. Our installment plan, which allows you to pay a little each month with no interest charge, is another option. Get the device you want now.

❺ • **Simpler billing statements**—Your one-page monthly bill states just the essentials—what services you used, what you are charged, and when your payment is due. We hope you will try out the new Talk First app to view your statement and pay your balance using your phone.

問題168-171は次のウェブページに関するものです。

http://www.talkfirsttechnologies.com

Talk Firstテクノロジー社
お知らせと最新情報

皆さまがご要望を述べ、当社はそれを取り入れました。
6月1日より、Talk Firstテクノロジー社のお客さまは次の選択肢をご利用いただけます。

- **月決めプラン**——Talk Firstテクノロジー社は、1年および2年のサービス契約の提供を終了いたします。全てのサービスは月単位で請求されます。
- **新プラン**——新たに利用可能となった選択肢には、無制限の通話とテキストメッセージの送受信を1カ月当たりわずか45ドルでご提供する低価格プランも含まれています。必要なときにギガバイト単位でデータをご購入ください。もしくは、一般発売前に当社の最新型携帯機器のお試しができるTechfanプランをお選びください。
- **機器のアップグレード**——どの電話機も、いつでも定価でご購入いただけるようになります。当社の分割払いプランは、無利子で月々少額ずつのお支払いが可能で、もう一つの選択肢です。今すぐご希望の機器を手に入れてください。
- **より簡潔な請求明細書**——1ページの月々の請求書は要点だけを記載——お客さまがご利用されたサービス、請求金額、お支払期限です。お持ちの電話機を利用して明細を閲覧し残高を支払うために、新しいTalk Firstのアプリをぜひお試しください。

Words & Phrases

update 最新情報　❶ effective 有効な　option 選択肢　❷ month-to-month 月決めの
cease *doing* ～することをやめる　bill ～に請求書を送る　❸ unlimited 無制限の
text messaging テキストメッセージの送受信　gigabyte ギガバイト　state-of-the-art 最新式の　device 機器
public 一般の　❹ upgrade アップグレード　full 正式の、完全な　retail price 小売り価格　installment 分割払いの
allow ～ to *do* ～が…できるようにする　interest 利子　charge 請求金額　❺ billing statement 請求明細書
essential 要点　due 支払うべき　try out ～ ～を試してみる　balance 残高

Expressions

on a ～ basis 「～単位で、～の方式で」(❷2行目)

In our Vietnam factory, the managers' meeting is held on a monthly basis.
当社のベトナム工場では、管理職会議は月1回の頻度で開かれています。

168 What change will Talk First Technologies implement on June 1?

(A) Some mobile phone technology will not be supported.
(B) Long-term service contracts will not be required.
(C) Unlimited calling plans will no longer be offered.
(D) Some mobile phones will no longer be sold.

Talk Firstテクノロジー社は、6月1日にどんな変更を実施しますか。

(A) 携帯電話の技術の一部がサポートされなくなる。
(B) 長期のサービス契約が必要でなくなる。
(C) 無制限通話プランがもはや提供されなくなる。
(D) 一部の携帯電話がもはや販売されなくなる。

正解 B ❶ 2行目の「6月1日より、Talk Firstテクノロジー社のお客さまは次の選択肢を利用できる」という前置きに続けて、❷ 1～2行目に、cease offering one- and two-year service contracts「1年および2年のサービス契約の提供を終了する」とあり、さらにAll services will be billed on a monthly basis.「全てのサービスは月単位で請求される」と述べられている。よって、同社では6月1日から、サービスの年単位の長期契約を廃止し、月単位の短期契約のみにすると分かるので、(B)が正解。implement「～を実施する」。long-term「長期の」、required「必要な」。

169 What does the Techfan plan feature?

(A) Early access to new mobile phones
(B) Discounts on large amounts of data
(C) Invitations to in-store special events
(D) Guaranteed buyback of older devices

Techfanプランは何を目玉にしていますか。

(A) 新しい携帯電話を早期に利用できる機会
(B) 大容量データの割引
(C) 店内での特別イベントへの招待
(D) 古い機器の買い取り保証

正解 A ❸ 3～4行目に、the Techfan plan, which allows you to try our state-of-the-art mobile devices before they are released for public sale「一般発売前に当社の最新型携帯機器のお試しができるTechfanプラン」とある。state-of-the-art mobile devicesをnew mobile phonesと表している(A)が正解。access to ～「～を利用する機会」。
(D) guaranteed「保証付きの」、buyback「買い取り」。

170 According to the Web page, what can make getting a new phone more affordable?

(A) Purchasing a phone online
(B) Trading in an older device
(C) Disabling a text-messaging application
(D) Enrolling in a payment plan

ウェブページによると、何が新しい電話機の入手をより手頃にしますか。

(A) オンラインでの電話機の購入
(B) 古い機器の下取り
(C) テキストメッセージのアプリの無効化
(D) 支払いプランへの加入

正解 D ❹ 1行目に、「どの電話機も、定価で購入できるようになる」とあり、続けてOur installment plan, which allows you to pay a little each month with no interest charge, is another option.「当社の分割払いプランは、無利子で月々少額ずつの支払いが可能で、もう一つの選択肢だ」と述べられている。よって、分割払いプランを利用することで、新しい電話機を無利子で手軽に購入できるようになると分かるので(D)が正解。affordable「手頃な」。enroll in ～「～に加入する」。
(B) trade in ～「～を下取りに出す」。
(C) disable「～の機能を無効にする」。

171 What are Talk First Technologies' customers encouraged to do?

(A) Talk to a service representative
(B) Set up automatic payments
(C) Pay bills with a mobile app
(D) Submit an online review

Talk Firstテクノロジー社の顧客は、何をすることを勧められていますか。

(A) サービス担当者と話す。
(B) 自動支払いを設定する。
(C) 携帯用アプリで請求金額を支払う。
(D) オンラインのレビューを投稿する。

正解 C ❺ 2～3行目に、We hope you will try out the new Talk First app to view your statement and pay your balance using your phone.「お持ちの電話機を利用して明細を閲覧し残高を支払うために、新しいTalk Firstのアプリを試してほしい」とあるので(C)が正解。encourage ～ to *do*「～に…するよう勧める」。bill「請求金額」。
(A) representative「担当者」。
(B) set up ～「～を設定する」、automatic「自動の」。
(D) submit「～を投稿する」。

Questions 172-175 refer to the following online chat discussion.

❶ **Melvin Arocho (1:39 P.M.)**
Hi, Brenda and Vince. Brenda, have you made flight arrangements for us yet?

❷ **Brenda Koster (1:40 P.M.)**
Yes. We depart for Denmark on March 14 at 2:20 P.M. Any problems?

❸ **Melvin Arocho (1:42 P.M.)**
Yes, actually. The meeting with our Danish partners has been moved up one week, to next Wednesday. That's because we just found out that Arrownetic will release its new laptop early next year. And that means we'll need to speed up the development of our own new model.

❹ **Vince Gayle (1:43 P.M.)**
Really? I'm supposed to go camping with my family next week.

❺ **Brenda Koster (1:44 P.M.)**
I signed up for a three-day amateur tennis tournament. My first match is on Wednesday.

❻ **Melvin Arocho (1:45 P.M.)**
And I have tickets for a one-time-only performance by the Brandenburg Ballet Company that same day. It's out of our hands, I'm afraid. Brenda, please rebook us for March 7.

❼ **Brenda Koster (1:46 P.M.)**
Sure. I'll check to see if there are flights available.

❽ **Brenda Koster (1:52 P.M.)**
There's a flight at 11:35 P.M. Is that time OK with both of you?

❾ **Melvin Arocho (1:54 P.M.)**
Sure. Incidentally, Ms. Mack said she realizes that this last-minute change is an imposition on us. She will make sure that we get compensated somehow.

❿ **Brenda Koster (1:55 P.M.)**
That's very considerate of her.

⓫ **Brenda Koster (1:59 P.M.)**
There are only four seats left on that flight, Vince, so make your mind up fast.

⓬ **Vince Gayle (2:01 P.M.)**
Sorry, I had to step away from my desk. Yes, I suppose.

⓭ **Melvin Arocho (2:02 P.M.)**
Good. Brenda, please go ahead and make those arrangements now.

問題172-175は次のオンラインチャットの話し合いに関するものです。

Melvin Arocho（午後1時39分）
こんにちは、BrendaとVince。Brenda、私たちの飛行機の手配はもうしましたか。

Brenda Koster（午後1時40分）
はい。私たちは3月14日午後2時20分にデンマークに向けて出発します。何か問題がありますか。

Melvin Arocho（午後1時42分）
実は、あるんです。デンマークの提携先との会議が1週間早まって、今度の水曜日になりました。Arrownetic社が来年早々に新しいノートパソコンを発売すると今しがた分かったためです。そして、それはつまり、当社はうちの新モデルの開発のスピードを上げなければならないということです。

Vince Gayle（午後1時43分）
本当ですか。私は来週、家族とキャンプに行くことになっているんです。

Brenda Koster（午後1時44分）
私は、3日間のアマチュアのテニストーナメントへの参加登録をしました。私の最初の試合が水曜日にあるのです。

Melvin Arocho（午後1時45分）
そして私は、その同日のブランデンブルク・バレエ団による1回限りの公演のチケットを買ってあるんです。これは私たちにはどうにもできませんね、残念ですが。Brenda、私たちを3月7日で再予約してください。

Brenda Koster（午後1時46分）
分かりました。予約可能な便があるかどうか確認してみます。

Brenda Koster（午後1時52分）
午後11時35分の便があります。その時間でお2人とも大丈夫ですか。

Melvin Arocho（午後1時54分）
もちろん。ちなみにMackさんは、この土壇場での変更が私たちに無理強いをすることを認識していると言っていました。彼女は必ず私たちが何らかの方法で埋め合わせしてもらえるようにするつもりです。

Brenda Koster（午後1時55分）
彼女の思いやりはありがたいですね。

Brenda Koster（午後1時59分）
その便にはあと4席しか残っていません、Vince、ですから速やかに決断してください。

Vince Gayle（午後2時01分）
すみません、席を外さなければならなかったんです。はい、大丈夫だと思います。

Melvin Arocho（午後2時02分）
良かった。Brenda、どうぞ、すぐにその手配をしてください。

172 Why did Mr. Arocho contact his colleagues?

(A) To inform them of a change of plans
(B) To ask them about a recent meeting
(C) To go over a production schedule
(D) To discuss a merger the company is considering

Arochoさんはなぜ同僚に連絡したのですか。

(A) 彼らに予定の変更を知らせるため。
(B) 最近の会議について彼らに尋ねるため。
(C) 製造スケジュールを見直すため。
(D) 会社が検討している合併について話し合うため。

正解 A Arochoさんは❶で、自分たちの飛行機の手配をもう行ったかKosterさんに尋ねている。手配済みと知ったArochoさんは、❸でThe meeting with our Danish partners has been moved up one week, to next Wednesday.「デンマークの提携先との会議が1週間早まって、今度の水曜日になった」と述べているので、予定の変更を知らせるために同僚に連絡したと判断できる。inform ～ of …「～に…を知らせる」。

(B) ❸で、Arochoさんは会議の予定が早まったと伝えており、以前の会議について尋ねてはいない。
(C) ❸で、Arochoさんは開発のスピードを上げると述べているが、製造スケジュールを見直すとは言っていない。go over ～「～を見直す」。
(D) merger「合併」。

---

173 What is suggested about the company the writers work for?

(A) It organizes sporting activities for its employees.
(B) It sponsors cultural events in its community.
(C) It operates in a competitive market.
(D) It has its headquarters in Denmark.

書き手たちが働いている会社について何が分かりますか。

(A) 同社は自社の従業員向けのスポーツ活動を企画している。
(B) 同社は地元地域で文化的な催しを後援している。
(C) 同社は競争が激しい市場で事業を行っている。
(D) 同社はデンマークに本社がある。

正解 C Arochoさんは会議の予定変更の理由について、❸で「Arrownetic社が来年早々に新しいノートパソコンを発売すると今しがた分かったためだ。そして、それはつまり、当社はうちの新モデルの開発のスピードを上げなければならないということだ」と他社の発売予定に合わせて自社商品の開発を早める必要性に言及している。よって、Arochoさんたちが働く会社は競争の激しい市場で事業を行っていると考えられる。operate「事業を行う」、competitive「競争の激しい」。

(A) organize「～を企画する」。
(B) sponsor「～を後援する」、cultural「文化的な」。
(D) ❸でデンマークの提携先に言及があるが、自社の本社があるとは述べられていない。headquarters「本社」。

Words & Phrases

❶ make an arrangement 手配をする ❷ depart for ～ ～に向けて出発する ❸ actually 実は Danish デンマークの partners 提携会社 move up ～ 〈予定など〉を早める find out (that) ～ ～であることが分かる release ～を発売する laptop ノートパソコン ❺ sign up for ～ ～への参加登録をする amateur アマチュアの match 試合
❻ performance 公演 ballet company バレエ団 out of *one's* hand 〈人〉の手・管理を離れて rebook ～を再予約する ❼ check to see if ～ ～かどうか確認する ❾ incidentally ちなみに last-minute 土壇場の、ぎりぎりの時間の imposition 無理強い make sure (that) ～ 必ず～する compensate ～に埋め合わせる、～に補償する somehow 何らかの方法で ❿ considerate 思いやりのある
⓫ make *one's* mind up 決断する ⓬ step away from ～ ～から離れる ⓭ go ahead and *do* どうぞ～してください

174 Who most likely is Ms. Mack?

(A) A tournament organizer
(B) A company manager
(C) A travel agent
(D) A ballet dancer

Mackさんとは誰だと考えられますか。

(A) トーナメントの主催者
(B) 会社の管理職者
(C) 旅行代理店員
(D) バレエダンサー

正解 B Arochoさんが❾で、Ms. Mack said she realizes that this last-minute change is an imposition on us. She will make sure that we get compensated somehow.「Mackさんは、この土壇場での変更が私たちに無理強いをすることを認識していると言っていた。彼女は必ず私たちが何らかの方法で埋め合わせしてもらえるようにするつもりだ」と伝えている。急な日程変更により休暇の予定を変更せざるを得なくなったArochoさんら3人を気遣い、埋め合わせがされるよう対処する立場としてふさわしいのは彼らの会社の管理職の人物と考えられるので、(B)が正解。

(A) ❺でトーナメントへの言及はあるが、主催者については述べられていない。organizer「主催者」。

---

175 At 2:01 P.M., what does Mr. Gayle mean when he writes, "Yes, I suppose"?

(A) He will ask his family about the situation.
(B) He agrees to the suggested time.
(C) He believes four tickets are available.
(D) He thinks there are flights on Wednesday.

午後2時1分に、Gayleさんは "Yes, I suppose"という発言で、何を意味していますか。

(A) 彼は状況について自分の家族に尋ねるつもりだ。
(B) 彼は提案された時刻に同意している。
(C) 彼は4枚のチケットが入手可能だと考えている。
(D) 彼は水曜日に飛行機の便があると思っている。

正解 B ❻で飛行機の予約変更を依頼されたKosterさんは、❽でThere's a flight at 11:35 P.M. Is that time OK with both of you?「午後11時35分の便がある。その時間で2人とも大丈夫か」と尋ね、さらに⓫でVince, so make your mind up fast「Vince、ですから速やかに決断してほしい」とGayleさんに返事を急かしている。それに対してGayleさんは、下線部で「はい、だと思います」と応じているので、提示された飛行機の便の時刻に同意していると分かる。agree to ～「～に同意する」。

(C) available「入手可能な」。

Expressions

be supposed to *do* 「～することになっている、～するよう期待されている」(❹)

Nancy is supposed to be back in the office by noon.
Nancyは、正午までにはオフィスに戻ることになっています。

Questions 176-180 refer to the following schedule and e-mail.

1 予定表

Conference & Location	Dates	Presenter(s)	Presentation
❶ Adfinity Summit Sydney, NSW	1–4 June	Fergus Jones Martha Orr	Top Trends in Social Media Advertising Data Impact Revolution
❷ Overdrive Marketing Melbourne, VIC	4–7 June	Martha Orr Victor Voss	Visuals That Tell Your Story Product Launch: Seven Pitfalls to Avoid
❸ Pull Ahead Expo Brisbane, QLD	15–19 June	Fergus Jones Martha Orr	Effective Presentation Techniques Four Keys to Brand Loyalty
❹ Diaspawn Perth, WA	20–24 June	Martha Orr Alexa Rojas	Let Your Success Do the Talking Navigating the Marketing Labyrinth

2 Eメール

To: All Rowin Consulting team members

From: Tristan Fields, Manager

Re: June conference schedule

Date: 15 April

Dear Rowin Consulting team members,

❶ I need to bring several new developments regarding the conference schedule to your attention.

❷ First, Mr. Voss has just been asked to be the closing keynote speaker on the last day of the Adfinity Summit. Since this conflicts with his current schedule, Ms. Rojas will take over for him at the annual Overdrive Marketing conference.

❸ Secondly, Mr. Jones must go abroad in mid-June, so he cannot join Ms. Orr at the Pull Ahead Expo. We asked the conference organisers to drop his session from their schedule.

❹ Finally, Ms. Orr has been requested by Diaspawn to change her presentation topic for their conference. They would like her to address the theme of her recent book, so she should deliver her “Data Impact Revolution” talk there instead of her planned topic.

Thank you,

Tristan Fields

問題176-180は次の予定表とEメールに関するものです。

協議会と場所	日付	講演者	講演内容
Adfinityサミット シドニー、NSW	6月1～4日	Fergus Jones Martha Orr	ソーシャルメディア広告におけるトップトレンド データインパクト革命
Overdriveマーケティング協議会 メルボルン、VIC	6月4～7日	Martha Orr Victor Voss	あなたの話を伝えるビジュアル 製品の発売：避けたい7つの落とし穴
Pull Ahead博覧会 ブリスベン、QLD	6月15～19日	Fergus Jones Martha Orr	効果的なプレゼンテーションのテクニック ブランドロイヤルティーへの4つの鍵
Diaspawn協議会 パース、WA	6月20～24日	Martha Orr Alexa Rojas	成功に語らせよ マーケティングの迷宮を進む

受信者：Rowinコンサルティング社のチームメンバー各位
送信者：Tristan Fields、部長
件名：6月の協議会スケジュール
日付：4月15日

Rowinコンサルティング社のチームメンバーの皆さま

協議会スケジュールに関する新たな進展を皆さんにお伝えしておかなければなりません。

第一に、Vossさんはつい先ごろ、Adfinityサミット最終日の締めくくりの基調講演者を務めるように依頼されました。これは現在の彼のスケジュールとかち合うため、RojasさんがOverdriveマーケティング年次協議会で彼を代行します。

第二に、Jonesさんは6月中旬に海外に行かなければならないため、Pull Ahead博覧会でOrrさんと合流することができません。私たちは、彼のセッションを予定表から外すよう博覧会主催者に依頼しました。

最後に、OrrさんがDiaspawn協議会から、協議会での講演の題目を変更することを要請されました。彼らは、Orrさんに最近の自著のテーマを取り上げてもらいたいと希望しているので、Orrさんは予定されていた題目の代わりに、「データインパクト革命」の話をそこでするといいでしょう。

よろしくお願いいたします。

Tristan Fields

176 At what conference will attendees learn about creating brand loyalty?

(A) Adfinity Summit
(B) Overdrive Marketing
(C) Pull Ahead Expo
(D) Diaspawn

出席者はどの協議会で、ブランドロイヤルティーを生み出すことについて学びますか。

(A) Adfinityサミット
(B) Overdriveマーケティング協議会
(C) Pull Ahead博覧会
(D) Diaspawn協議会

正解 C 1の予定表を見ると、Presentation「講演内容」の欄に、ブランドロイヤルティーに関する記載があるのは❸の「Pull Ahead博覧会」。よって、(C)が正解。attendee「出席者」、create「〜を生み出す」。

---

177 Where will Mr. Voss give the closing presentation?

(A) In Sydney
(B) In Melbourne
(C) In Brisbane
(D) In Perth

Vossさんはどこで締めくくりの講演を行いますか。

(A) シドニー
(B) メルボルン
(C) ブリスベン
(D) パース

正解 A 2の❶より、Eメールは協議会スケジュールの最新情報を伝えているもの。同❷ 1〜2行目に、Mr. Voss has just been asked to be the closing keynote speaker on the last day of the Adfinity Summit「Vossさんはつい先ごろ、Adfinityサミット最終日の締めくくりの基調講演者を務めるように依頼された」とある。1のConference & Location「協議会と場所」の欄の❶を見ると、Adfinityサミットの開催場所はシドニーだと分かるので、(A)が正解。give a presentation「講演を行う」。

---

178 Why will a presentation be canceled?

(A) The presenter will be out of the country.
(B) Not enough people will attend.
(C) The presenter will be speaking at another conference.
(D) Someone else is already addressing the same topic.

ある講演はなぜ中止されますか。

(A) 講演者が国外にいるだろうから。
(B) 十分な数の人々が出席しないから。
(C) 講演者が別の会議で講演する予定だから。
(D) 他の誰かがすでに同じ題目を取り上げているから。

正解 A 2の❸ 1〜2行目に、Mr. Jones must go abroad in mid-June, so he cannot join Ms. Orr at the Pull Ahead Expo「Jonesさんは6月中旬に海外に行かなければならないため、Pull Ahead博覧会でOrrさんと合流することができない」とあり、続けてWe asked the conference organisers to drop his session from their schedule.「私たちは、彼のセッションを予定表から外すよう博覧会主催者に依頼した」と述べられている。よって設問の、中止される講演とはPull Ahead博覧会のJonesさんの講演を指すと分かり、Jonesさんは海外に行く予定なので(A)が正解。out of the country「国外に」。
(C) 2の❷ 1〜3行目に、VossさんがOverdriveマーケティング協議会での講演ができなくなったが、Rojasさんが代行するとあるので、この講演は中止されない。

179 What is indicated about the Rowin Consulting team?

(A) Each member is from a different city.
(B) Each member delivers presentations remotely.
(C) One of its members is a published author.
(D) One of its members presents topics with a partner.

Rowinコンサルティング社のチームについて何が示されていますか。

(A) 各メンバーは異なる都市の出身である。
(B) 各メンバーは中継で講演を行う。
(C) メンバーの1人は本を出版した著者である。
(D) メンバーの1人は仲間と一緒に題目について講演する。

正解 C Rowinコンサルティング社のチームメンバー宛てのEメールである2の❹ 2行目で、講演者の1人であるOrrさんについて、They would like her to address the theme of her recent book「彼らは、彼女に最近の自著のテーマを取り上げてもらいたいと希望している」と述べているので、Orrさんは出版している本の著者だと分かる。publish「～を出版する」、author「著者」。
(B) remotely「遠隔接続で、遠隔で」。

---

180 What presentation does Mr. Fields ask Ms. Orr to replace?

(A) Data Impact Revolution
(B) Visuals That Tell Your Story
(C) Four Keys to Brand Loyalty
(D) Let Your Success Do the Talking

FieldsさんはOrrさんに、どの講演内容を差し替えるよう頼んでいますか。

(A) データインパクト革命
(B) あなたの話を伝えるビジュアル
(C) ブランドロイヤルティーへの4つの鍵
(D) 成功に語らせよ

正解 D Fieldsさんは2のEメールの送信者。同❹ 1～2行目に、「OrrさんがDiaspawn協議会から、協議会での講演の題目を変更することを要請された」とあり、同2～3行目で、she should deliver her "Data Impact Revolution" talk there instead of her planned topic「Orrさんは予定されていた題目の代わりに、『データインパクト革命』の話をそこでするといいだろう」と述べているので、Fieldsさんは、OrrさんにDiaspawn協議会での講演内容を差し替えるよう頼んでいると判断できる。1の予定表の❹を見ると、Diaspawn協議会でのOrrさんの当初の講演内容はLet Your Success Do the Talkingなので、(D)が正解。replace「～を差し替える」。
(A) 2の❹ 2～3行目より、今後差し替えると思われる講演内容。

Words & Phrases

1 予定表 conference 協議会、会議　location 場所　❶ summit サミット、首脳会議　trend トレンド、動向　social media ソーシャルメディア　advertising 広告　impact インパクト、影響　revolution 革命　❷ visual ビジュアル、視覚情報　launch 発売　pitfall 落とし穴　avoid ～を避ける　❸ expo 〈expositionの略で〉博覧会　effective 効果的な　brand loyalty ブランドロイヤルティー(消費者が特定のブランドを購買し続けること)　❹ navigate ～を進む、～を航行する　labyrinth 迷宮

2 Eメール ❶ development 進展、動向　regarding ～に関する　❷ keynote speaker 基調講演者　conflict with ～ 〈スケジュールが〉～とかち合う　current 現在の　take over for ～ ～の仕事を代わってする　annual 年次の　❸ secondly 第二に　organiser 〈米国表記はorganizer〉主催者　drop ～ from … ～を…から外す　❹ request ～ to *do* ～に…することを要請する　topic 題目、トピック　address ～を取り上げる　deliver 〈講演など〉をする　instead of ～ ～の代わりに　planned 予定された

Expressions

bring ～ to *one's* attention 「～を…に知らせる」(2の❶ 1～2行目)

Thank you for bringing this to my attention.
このことを私に知らせていただき、ありがとうございます。

Questions 181-185 refer to the following letter and excerpt from a résumé.

1 手紙

January 15

Bernice J. Todd
Filvey Company
356 Main Street
Dearborn, MI 48124

Dear Ms. Todd,

❶ I am writing to apply for the position of production-line worker at Filvey Company. I currently work for an electronics manufacturer, but I previously worked at the Collins Corporation, and I am excited at the prospect of working in that field again. I have been employed in manufacturing for fourteen years and have broad knowledge of assembly equipment in many industries, including furniture and textiles. Supervisors consistently praise my attention to detail and ability to learn new processes quickly.

❷ As requested, I have enclosed my résumé and a list of references. I have also included my current supervisor's report from a course I led a few months ago. I had been asked to train new employees on our production-line assembly equipment, and my supervisor noted my effectiveness. In addition, I developed materials to teach about workplace cleanliness at my previous job, and I would be happy to discuss that experience with you.

Sincerely,

Andrew D. Chen

Andrew D. Chen

Enclosures

2 経歴書の抜粋

Andrew D. Chen • 2781 Moore Street • Ann Arbor, MI 48105

❶ **Overview:**
Production-line worker employed for many years in manufacturing plants of various sizes. Experienced trainer of new employees on assembly equipment.

❷ **Work experience:**
Kolpek, Inc., Ypsilanti, Michigan (current job, 5 years)
- Assemble electronic components for computers and communications equipment
- Assist in developing standards for safety and environmental compliance

❸ Collins Corporation, Detroit, Michigan (4 years)
- Worked on various components of a new line of energy-efficient automobiles
- Received quality assurance ratings in the top 10% of all production-line workers

問題181-185は次の手紙と経歴書の抜粋に関するものです。

1月15日

Bernice J. Todd
Filvey社
メイン通り356番地
ディアボーン、MI 48124

Todd様

Filvey社の製造ライン作業員の職に応募するためにお手紙を差し上げています。私は現在、電子機器製造会社に勤務しておりますが、以前はCollins社に勤務しておりましたので、再びその分野で働ける期待に心を躍らせています。私は製造業に14年間従事しており、家具と繊維産業を含む多くの産業における組立装置の幅広い知識があります。上司たちは一貫して、私の細部に至るまでの注意深さと新規工程を素早く習得する能力を称賛しています。

ご依頼いただいた通り、私の経歴書および身元照会先リストを同封いたしました。また、数カ月前に私が指導したコースに関する現上司の報告書も同封しました。製造ラインの組立装置について新規従業員を教育するよう頼まれたときのもので、上司は私の能力について記してくれました。さらに私は、前職で職場を清潔にすることを教示する教材を開発しており、その経験について喜んであなたとお話しさせていただきたいと思っています。

敬具
Andrew D. Chen（署名）
Andrew D. Chen

同封物あり

Andrew D. Chen／ムーア通り2781番地／アナーバー、MI 48105

概要：
さまざまな規模の製造工場で製造ライン作業員として、長年にわたり勤務。組立装置に関する新規従業員の経験豊かな指導者。

職歴：
Kolpek社、イプシランティ、ミシガン州（現職、5年間）
・コンピューターおよび通信機器の電子部品の組み立てに従事
・安全上および環境上のコンプライアンスの基準作成を支援

Collins社、デトロイト、ミシガン州（4年間）
・エネルギー効率の良い自動車の新シリーズの多様な部品を取り扱った
・品質保証の評定において、製造ライン全作業員の上位10パーセントとの評価を受けた

181 What does Filvey Company most likely manufacture?

(A) Automobiles
(B) Textiles
(C) Furniture
(D) Electronics

Filvey社は何を製造していると考えられますか。

(A) 自動車
(B) 繊維製品
(C) 家具
(D) 電子機器

正解 A 1の❶ 1行目より、この手紙はChenさんがFilvey社の職に応募するためのもの。同 2〜3行目に、「以前はCollins社に勤務していたので、再びその分野で働ける期待に心を躍らせている」とあることから、Filvey社は、Collins社と同じ分野の企業だと分かる。2の❸のCollins社におけるChenさんの職務内容の1点目にWorked on various components of a new line of energy-efficient automobiles「エネルギー効率の良い自動車の新シリーズの多様な部品を取り扱った」とあるので、Collins社は自動車製造関連の会社と判断でき、Filvey社も同業と考えられるので、(A)が正解。
(D) 1の❶ 2行目より、電子機器はChenさんの現在の会社の製造品。

---

182 In the letter, the word "broad" in paragraph 1, line 4, is closest in meaning to

(A) open
(B) spacious
(C) extensive
(D) variable

手紙の第1段落・4行目にある "broad" に最も意味が近いのは

(A) 開放された
(B) 広々とした
(C) 広範囲にわたる
(D) 変わりやすい

正解 C 1の手紙は応募書類に同封し、自分が採用されるよう企業にアピールしているものだと判断できる。broadを含む文では、製造業に14年間従事しているという経験に基づいて、broad knowledge of assembly equipment in many industries, including furniture and textiles「家具と繊維産業を含む多くの産業における組立装置の-------知識」があると自分の強みを述べていると考えられる。後ろのknowledgeを修飾して、幅広い知識を持つことを意味する(C)が適切。extensive「〈知識などが〉広範囲にわたる」。

---

183 In the letter, what does Mr. Chen mention as one of his qualifications for the job?

(A) He is good at repairing equipment.
(B) He learns new procedures easily.
(C) He writes very detailed reports.
(D) He has experience as a supervisor.

手紙の中で、Chenさんはその職に対する自身の適性の1つとして何を述べていますか。

(A) 彼は装置を修理するのが得意だ。
(B) 彼は新しい手順をたやすく覚える。
(C) 彼は非常に詳細な報告書を書く。
(D) 彼は管理者としての経験がある。

正解 B Chenさんは1の❶ 6〜7行目で、Supervisors consistently praise my attention to detail and ability to learn new processes quickly.「上司たちは一貫して、私の細部に至るまでの注意深さと新規工程を素早く習得する能力を称賛している」とその職に対する自身の強みを2つ挙げている。後者の「新規工程を素早く習得する能力」と一致する(B)が正解。qualification「適性」。procedure「手順」。
(A) 1の❷ 2〜4行目に組立装置の教育を担当したとあるが、装置の修理が得意とは述べていない。
(C) 1の❷ 1〜2行目で報告書について言及があるが、これはChenさんに関して上司が書いたもので、Chenさんの報告書作成能力に関する言及はない。detailed「詳細な」。

184 According to the letter, what did Mr. Chen NOT include with his application?

(A) A résumé
(B) A training evaluation
(C) Some references
(D) Some teaching materials

手紙によると、Chenさんが応募書類に含めなかったものは何ですか。

(A) 経歴書
(B) 研修の評価
(C) 身元照会先
(D) 教材

正解 D (A)「経歴書」と(C)「身元照会先」については、1の❷1行目で同封したと述べている。同1～2行目に「数カ月前に私が指導したコースに関する現上司の報告書も同封した」とあり、さらにChenさんの指導能力に関する上司の記載があると述べているので、(B)「研修の評価」についても同封されたと分かる。(D)「教材」については、同4～6行目に言及があるが同封したとは述べておらず、「その経験について喜んであなたと話したいと思っている」とあるので、Chenさんは教材を応募書類には含めずに、面接でその経験を説明するつもりだと分かる。よって、(D)が正解。application「応募書類」。
(B) evaluation「評価」。

---

185 What is suggested about Kolpek, Inc.?

(A) It often invests in new assembly equipment.
(B) It had problems with workplace cleanliness.
(C) It specializes in producing safety equipment.
(D) It recently hired production-line workers.

Kolpek社について何が分かりますか。

(A) 同社は頻繁に新しい組立装置に投資する。
(B) 同社は職場の清潔さに問題があった。
(C) 同社は安全装置の製造を専門にしている。
(D) 同社は最近、製造ラインの作業員を雇用した。

正解 D Chenさんの経歴書の2の❷2行目より、Kolpek社とはChenさんが現在勤務する会社だと分かる。1の❷2行目に、Chenさんが数カ月前にコースを指導したとあり、その内容について同2～4行目で、I had been asked to train new employees on our production-line assembly equipment「製造ラインの組立装置について新規従業員を教育するよう頼まれた」と述べている。よって、Kolpek社では最近、製造ラインの従業員が雇用されたと判断できる。
(A) invest in ～「～に投資する」。
(B) 1の❷4～5行目で職場を清潔にすることに言及があるが、これはChenさんの前職のCollins社での実績であり、Kolpek社に関するものではない。
(C) specialize in ～「～を専門にする」。

Words & Phrases

résumé 経歴書、履歴書

1 手紙
❶ apply for ～ ～に応募する　position 職　production-line 製造ラインの　currently 現在　electronics 電子機器　manufacturer 製造会社、メーカー　previously 以前は　prospect 期待、見通し　field 分野　be employed in ～ ～に従事する　knowledge 知識　assembly 組み立て　equipment 装置　industry 産業　textiles 繊維産業　supervisor 上司、管理者　consistently 一貫して　praise ～を称賛する　attention 注意　detail 細部　ability 能力　process 工程
❷ enclose ～を同封する　reference 身元照会先　include ～を同封する　train ～を教育する　note ～に特に言及する　effectiveness 有効性　in addition さらに　material 資料　workplace 職場　cleanliness 清潔にすること、清潔さ　enclosure 同封物

2 経歴書
❶ overview 概要　plant 工場　various さまざまな　experienced 経験豊かな　trainer 指導者
❷ assemble ～を組み立てる　electronic 電子の　component 部品　communications equipment 通信機器　assist in *doing* ～するのを補助する　standard 基準　environmental 環境の　compliance コンプライアンス、順守
❸ line 商品ライン　energy-efficient エネルギー効率の良い　automobile 自動車　quality assurance 品質保証(製品やサービスにおける望ましい質の維持)　rating 評定

Expressions

As requested, ～ 「ご依頼いただいた通り、～」(1の❷1行目)

As requested, we are sending you our latest catalog.
ご依頼いただいた通り、弊社の最新カタログをお送りします。

Questions 186-190 refer to the following flyer and e-mails.

1 チラシ

This Month at Office Flash

Our Top Deals

1
- Multipurpose white copy paper—normally $34.95 per box, now only $27.50
- Pro-Forda printer ink (color or black)—normally $24.95 per cartridge, now only $19.95
- Boligraph ballpoint pens (all colors)—normally $8.95 per box of 24, now only $6.50

2 **20% off All Antivirus Software**

Save with an instant in-store rebate on all leading brands!

3 **Free In-Store Workshops on Getting Yourself Organized**

Sign up for our popular weekly workshops! Cut the clutter, both at home and in the office. Space is limited, and the workshop is filling up fast, so register soon at www.officeflash.net/classes.

4

May 4	2:00–4:00 P.M.
May 11	8:30–11:30 A.M.
May 18	7:00–9:00 P.M.
May 25	12:30–2:30 P.M.

E-mail

2 Eメールの1通目

From: Deals <deals@officeflash.net>
To: Jae Choi <choi.j@bizmail.com>
Date: April 21
Subject: Correction

Dear Office Flash customer:

1 We regret to inform you that our latest flyer contained an error regarding an advertised item. The ballpoint pens are not available in all colors, only in black. To show our commitment to our customers, we are offering an e-coupon good for one box of blue or red pens at 50% off. The coupon can be used when our new shipment of colored pens arrives on April 28. Simply respond to this e-mail and request the coupon. Please note that this offer does not apply to the copy paper or printer ink because those items were in stock at the time the flyer was distributed. We thank you for your understanding and for being a loyal customer.

Sincerely,

The Office Flash Team

3 Eメールの2通目

From: Jae Choi <choi.j@bizmail.com>
To: Deals <deals@officeflash.net>
Date: April 22
Subject: RE: Correction

Hi,

1 I would definitely like to be sent the coupon you offered in your e-mail. Also, I no longer have a copy of the flyer, but I remember reading that you are offering workshops on organizing a home or office space. I am very interested in attending one, but I am only available in the evenings. Do you offer any classes that would fit my schedule?

Thanks,

Jae Choi

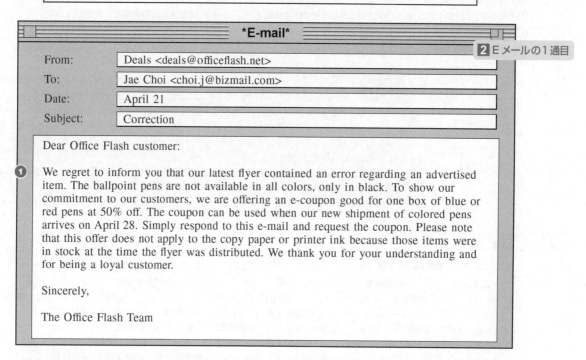

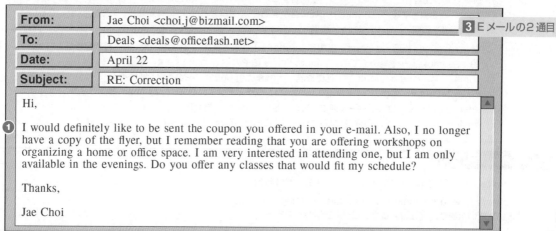

問題186-190は次のチラシと2通のEメールに関するものです。

今月のOffice Flashストア
最大のお買得品

・多目的用白色コピー用紙――通常1箱34.95ドルのところ、現在たったの27.50ドル
・Pro-Fordaプリンターインク（カラーまたは黒色）――通常1カートリッジ24.95ドルのところ、現在たったの19.95ドル
・Boligraphボールペン（全色）――通常24本入り1箱8.95ドルのところ、現在たったの6.50ドル

ウイルス対策ソフトウエア全品20パーセント引き
全ての有名銘柄の製品が店内即時の割り戻しでお得になります！

整頓上手になるための無料の店内ワークショップ
週に1度の人気のワークショップにお申し込みください！ 自宅でもオフィスでも、がらくたを減らしましょう。お席は限られており、このワークショップは即座に満員になるので、すぐにwww.officeflash.net/classesで登録してください。

5月4日	午後2:00－4:00
5月11日	午前8:30－11:30
5月18日	午後7:00－9:00
5月25日	午後12:30－2:30

送信者：お買得品担当 <deals@officeflash.net>
受信者：Jae Choi <choi.j@bizmail.com>
日付：4月21日
件名：訂正

Office Flashストアのお客さまへ

当店の最新のチラシに広告商品に関する誤りが含まれていたことをお詫びするとともに、お客さまにお知らせいたします。ボールペンは全色のご用意ではなく、黒色のみお求めいただけます。お客さまに対する当店の誠意を示すため、青色または赤色のペン1箱に有効の50パーセント引き電子クーポンをご提供いたします。クーポンは、4月28日にカラーペンが入荷する際にご利用になれます。本Eメールにご返信の上、クーポンを請求いただくだけです。この割引はコピー用紙やプリンターインクには適用されないことにご注意ください、と申しますのも、それらの商品はチラシが配布された時点では在庫があったためです。皆さまのご理解とごひいきに感謝いたします。

敬具

Office Flashストアチーム

送信者：Jae Choi <choi.j@bizmail.com>
受信者：お買得品担当 <deals@officeflash.net>
日付：4月22日
件名：RE: 訂正

こんにちは

貴店のEメールで案内されていたクーポンをぜひとも送っていただきたいです。また、もうチラシが手元にないのですが、貴店では、自宅やオフィススペースの整理整頓に関するワークショップを開催していると読んだ記憶があります。その1つへの参加にとても興味があるのですが、私は夜にしか都合がつきません。貴店は、私のスケジュールに合うような講座を開催していますか。

よろしくお願いします。

Jae Choi

186 What information is provided in the flyer?

(A) A list of discontinued items
(B) Changes to a class schedule
(C) Details about discounted products
(D) Instructions for downloading software

チラシではどんな情報が提供されていますか。

(A) 製造中止品目のリスト
(B) 講座スケジュールの変更点
(C) 割引品に関する詳細
(D) ソフトウエアをダウンロードするための説明

正解 C 1の見出しにOur Top Deals「最大のお買得品」とある。同❶では、コピー用紙、プリンターインク、ボールペンが特別価格で提供されていることが示され、同❷では、ソフトウエアの割引情報が記載されているので、(C)が正解。provide「～を提供する」。details「詳細」、discount「～を割引する」。
(A) discontinue「～を製造中止にする」。
(B) 1の❹にワークショップのスケジュール表があるが、変更点があるとは述べられていない。
(D) instructions「説明(書)」、download「～をダウンロードする」。

---

187 What is suggested about the classes?

(A) They are well attended.
(B) They are offered online.
(C) They require a small fee.
(D) They are held twice a week.

講座について何が分かりますか。

(A) それらは参加者が多い。
(B) それらはオンラインで提供される。
(C) それらは少額の料金を必要とする。
(D) それらは1週間に2度開かれる。

正解 A 1の❸には店内ワークショップの案内が記載されており、同❸ 2～3行目に、Space is limited, and the workshop is filling up fast「席は限られており、このワークショップは即座に満員になる」とあるので、参加者が多いと分かる。(A)が正解。well attended「参加者が多い」。
(B) online「オンラインで」。
(C) 1の❸ 1行目に、Free In-Store Workshops「無料の店内ワークショップ」とあるので、料金は不要。require「～を必要とする」、fee「料金」。
(D) 1の❸ 2行目に、weekly workshops「週に1度のワークショップ」とある。

---

188 What is the purpose of the first e-mail?

(A) To apologize for a mistake
(B) To introduce a new service
(C) To ask for customer feedback
(D) To promote an upcoming sale

1通目のEメールの目的は何ですか。

(A) 誤りを謝罪すること。
(B) 新しいサービスを紹介すること。
(C) 顧客の意見を求めること。
(D) 今度のセールを宣伝すること。

正解 A 1通目のEメールである2は、Office Flashストアチームが顧客宛てに送信したもので、件名にCorrection「訂正」とある。同❶ 1～2行目で、We regret to inform you that our latest flyer contained an error regarding an advertised item.「当店の最新のチラシに広告商品に関する誤りが含まれていたことをお詫びするとともに、お客さまに知らせる」と述べているので、(A)が正解。apologize for ～「～を謝る」。
(C) ask for ～「～を求める」、feedback「意見」。
(D) promote「～を宣伝する」、upcoming「今度の」。

189 What workshop date would be best for Mr. Choi?

(A) May 4
(B) May 11
(C) May 18
(D) May 25

どのワークショップの日程がChoiさんにとって最適と思われますか。

(A) 5月4日
(B) 5月11日
(C) 5月18日
(D) 5月25日

正解 C 3の「送信者」と「件名」の欄より、このEメールはOffice Flashストアチームが顧客宛てに送信した2のEメールに返信する形で、Choiさんが送ったものと分かる。Choiさんは3の❶1〜2行目で、もうチラシが手元にないが、そこでワークショップについて知ったと述べ、同❶3〜4行目で、ワークショップの参加に興味があると伝えて、I am only available in the evenings「私は夜にしか都合がつかない」と書いている。1のチラシの❹を見ると、夜間開催のワークショップは、5月18日午後7時から9時のもののみなので、(C)が正解。

---

190 What product does Mr. Choi suggest that he wants to buy?

(A) Copy paper
(B) Printer ink
(C) Software
(D) Pens

Choiさんはどの製品を買いたいと示唆していますか。

(A) コピー用紙
(B) プリンターインク
(C) ソフトウエア
(D) ペン

正解 D Choiさんは、3の❶1行目で、I would definitely like to be sent the coupon you offered in your e-mail.「Eメールで案内されていたクーポンをぜひとも送ってほしい」と述べている。ここでのクーポンについては、Office FlashストアチームからのEメールである2の❶3〜4行目で、we are offering an e-coupon good for one box of blue or red pens at 50% off「青色または赤色のペン1箱に有効の50パーセント引き電子クーポンを提供する」と述べられている。よって、Choiさんが買いたい製品はペンだと分かる。

Words & Phrases

flyer チラシ

1 チラシ
deal お買得品　❶ multipurpose 多目的の　copy paper コピー用紙　normally 通常は　per 〜につき　cartridge カートリッジ　ballpoint pen ボールペン　❷ antivirus ウイルス対策の　software ソフトウエア　instant 即座の　in-store 店内の　rebate 割り戻し　leading 一流の　brand 銘柄、ブランド　❸ workshop ワークショップ　get 〜 … 〜を…の状態にさせる　organize 〜を整理整頓する　sign up for 〜 〜に申し込む　clutter がらくた、散乱した物　limited 限られた　fill up いっぱいになる　register 登録する

2 Eメール
correction 訂正　❶ regret to *do* 残念ながら〜する　inform 〜に知らせる　latest 最新の　contain 〜を含む　error 誤り　regarding 〜に関して　advertised 広告された　item 商品　available 入手可能な　commitment 責任、約束　e-coupon 電子クーポン　good for 〜 〜に有効な　shipment 発送、出荷　colored カラーの　simply 単に　respond to 〜 〜に返事する　request 〜を要求する　note 〜に注意する　apply to 〜 〜に適用する　in stock 在庫の　distribute 〜を配布する　loyal customer 得意客

3 Eメール
❶ definitely 間違いなく　a copy of 〜 〜の1部　fit 〜に合う

Expressions

no longer 〜 「もはや〜でない」（3の❶1〜2行目）
We no longer have time to think about the matter.
私たちは、もはやその問題について考える時間がありません。

Questions 191-195 refer to the following cost estimate, notice, and e-mail.

1 費用見積書

Marlowe Movers ~ Your Choice for Ease and Security
Serving you from two convenient locations:
168 Roland Street, Brooklyn • 1422 Longway Avenue, Jersey City

1 **Moving Job Cost Estimate**

Prepared by	Date	Prices valid until
Denise Monteiro	March 15	April 30

2

Prepared for	Delivery from	Delivery to
Sri Lankan Imports, LLC	151 West 24th Street Suite 15 New York, NY 10011	240 Garrison Boulevard Floor 4, Suite 43 New York, NY 10013

3 **Items to be moved**

20 file-storage boxes, standard size
3 filing cabinets, 4-drawer vertical
1 desk, midsized
1 office chair, wheeled

4 **Cost estimate**

Labor: 2 crew members
Cost per hour per crew member: $30
Duration: 2 hours
Transport: Van rental, $35 flat fee
Estimated total: $155.00

5 **Inclusions and Exclusions:**
- Transport costs include fuel and tolls.
- Estimated labor fees *do not include* additional labor for pickups from or deliveries to buildings without elevator service. Where applicable, $3 per flight of stairs is added to the base hourly rate of each crew member.

2 お知らせ

Posted Tuesday, March 19

1 **Notice to All Residential and Commercial Tenants**

The elevator in this building will be out of service for routine maintenance on Wednesday, March 27.

2 Thank you,
Building Management
240 Garrison Blvd.

3 Eメール

To:	Ram Jeyakumar
From:	Dinesha Gamage
Date:	March 20
Subject:	Move

Dear Mr. Jeyakumar,

1 I wanted to provide you with an update about the transition to our new office suite on Garrison Boulevard. I learned today that the elevator there will be out of service on your scheduled move date. We cannot move you early because the Garrison location is not yet properly set up. But we also do not want to postpone the move because of your role in the stakeholder meeting on Tuesday, April 2. I understand that you want to have time to settle in before then and prepare your remarks.

2 Rather than reschedule your move, I have informed the movers about this complication, and they are willing to work with it. I just wanted you to know so that you will not be caught by surprise on the day of the move. I am in the process of alerting other staff members who will be affected.

Best,

Dinesha Gamage
Office Manager

問題191-195は次の費用見積書、お知らせ、Eメールに関するものです。

Marlowe引越会社 ～ 安心と安全のためのご選択
便利な場所にある2店舗で、あなたのお役に立ちます。
ローランド通り168番地、ブルックリン ／ ロングウェイ大通り1422番地、ジャージーシティ

引越作業費用見積書

作成者	日付	価格有効期限
Denise Monteiro	3月15日	4月30日

依頼者	配送元	配送先
スリランカ輸入会社	ウエスト24番通り151番地 15号室 ニューヨーク、NY 10011	ギャリソン大通り240番地 4階、43号室 ニューヨーク、NY 10013

移動する品目
ファイル保管用ボックス(標準サイズ) 20箱 書類整理棚(引き出し4段で縦長) 3台 机(中型サイズ) 1台 オフィス用椅子(車輪付き) 1脚

費用見積
労働力:作業員2名 **作業員1名分の時間当たりの費用**:30ドル **所要時間**:2時間 **運送代**:ワゴン車のレンタル、35ドル均一料金 **見積合計**:155.00ドル

含まれるものと含まれないもの:
・運送代には燃料費と通行料が含まれます。
・見積もりの労働力報酬には、エレベーター設備のない建物からの集荷、あるいはそこへの配送のために追加となる労働は含まれていません。該当する場合、階段一続きにつき3ドルが各作業員の基本時給に加算されます。

3月19日火曜日掲示

全ての居住テナントおよび商業テナントさまへのお知らせ

この建物のエレベーターは、3月27日水曜日に定期保守点検のため運転を休止します。

よろしくお願いいたします。
建物管理室
ギャリソン大通り240番地

受信者:Ram Jeyakumar
送信者:Dinesha Gamage
日付:3月20日
件名:引っ越し

Jeyakumar様

ギャリソン大通りにある私たちの新オフィスへの移動に関して、あなたに最新情報をお伝えしたいと思います。本日、そこのエレベーターが引越予定日に運転休止となることを知りました。ギャリソンのオフィスはまだきちんと整っていないため、あなたに早めに移っていただくことはできません。しかし、4月2日火曜日の出資者会議でのあなたの役割ゆえに、私たちは引っ越しを延期することも望みません。あなたがその前に新しい場所に落ち着いて、お話の準備をする時間を望んでいると承知しています。

あなたの引っ越しの予定を変更するのではなく、引越業者にこの複雑な状況を伝えましたところ、彼らは快くそれに対応してくれることになりました。私はただ、あなたが引っ越しの当日に驚くことがないよう、理解しておいていただきたかったのです。私は現在、影響を受けると思われる他のスタッフに知らせている最中です。

敬具

Dinesha Gamage
業務部長

191 According to the cost estimate, why would a client pay an extra fee?

(A) To reschedule a moving date
(B) To have movers climb stairs
(C) To get additional moving supplies
(D) To have large furniture transported

費用見積書によると、顧客はなぜ追加料金を払うと思われますか。

(A) 引越日を変更するため。
(B) 引越作業員に階段を上らせるため。
(C) 追加の引越用資材を得るため。
(D) 大型の家具を輸送してもらうため。

正解 B 1の費用見積書の❺ 2点目に、「見積もりの労働力報酬には、エレベーター設備のない建物からの集荷、あるいはそこへの配送のために追加となる労働は含まれていない」とあり、続けてそれに該当する場合の料金について、$3 per flight of stairs is added to the base hourly rate of each crew member「階段一続きにつき3ドルが各作業員の基本時給に加算される」と述べている。よって、引越作業員がエレベーターではなく階段を使うときには追加料金が発生すると分かるので、(B)が正解。have ~ *do*「~に…させる」。
(C) supply「必需品」。
(D) have ~ *done*「~を…してもらう」、transport「~を輸送する」。

---

192 What is the notice about?

(A) Scheduled maintenance
(B) Professional cleaning services
(C) A change in management
(D) A meeting of tenants

お知らせは何についてですか。

(A) 予定された保守点検
(B) 専門的な掃除サービス
(C) 管理者の変更
(D) 居住者の会合

正解 A 2のお知らせは、ギャリソン大通り240番地の建物管理室が、居住テナントと商業テナントに宛てて掲示したもの。同❶に、The elevator in this building will be out of service for routine maintenance on Wednesday, March 27.「この建物のエレベーターは、3月27日水曜日に定期保守点検のため運転を休止する」とあるので、(A)が正解。
(B) professional「専門的な」。
(C) 2の❷の掲示者名に管理室とあるが、管理者の変更は述べられていない。management「管理(者)」。

---

193 Where does Mr. Jeyakumar currently work?

(A) On Roland Street
(B) On Longway Avenue
(C) On West 24th Street
(D) On Garrison Boulevard

Jeyakumarさんは現在、どこで働いていますか。

(A) ローランド通り
(B) ロングウェイ大通り
(C) ウエスト24番通り
(D) ギャリソン大通り

正解 C Jeyakumarさんは、3のEメールの受信者である。同❶ 1~2行目に「ギャリソン大通りにある私たちの新オフィスへの移動に関して、あなたに最新情報を伝えたいと思う」とあり、その後も今後の新オフィスへの引っ越しに関する連絡が続いている。1の❷のDelivery to「配送先」の欄に240 Garrison Boulevardと住所の記載があることから、これがJeyakumarさんの執務室の引越先であり、Delivery from「配送元」の欄にある151 West 24th Streetが、Jeyakumarさんの現在の執務室がある場所だと考えられる。よって、(C)が正解。
(A)(B) 1の冒頭部分のMarlowe引越会社の2店舗の住所表記より、店舗の所在地。
(D) 1の❷の「配送先」の住所表記より、執務室の引越先の所在地。

194 What does Ms. Gamage suggest Mr. Jeyakumar will do in April?

(A) Contact a moving company
(B) Begin a new job
(C) Visit a client's office
(D) Make a presentation

Gamageさんは、Jeyakumarさんが4月に何をすると示唆していますか。

(A) 引越会社に連絡する。
(B) 新しい仕事を始める。
(C) 顧客の事務所を訪れる。
(D) 発表を行う。

正解 D Gamageさんが Jeyakumarさんに送ったEメールである3の❶ 4~6行目に、「4月2日火曜日の出資者会議でのあなたの役割ゆえに、私たちは引っ越しを延期することも望まない。あなたがその前に新しい場所に落ち着いて、話の準備をする時間を望んでいると承知している」とあるので、Jeyakumarさんは4月に出資者会議で話をすると判断できる。そのことをmake a presentation「発表を行う」と表している(D)が正解。

---

195 When will Mr. Jeyakumar's move take place?

(A) On March 19
(B) On March 20
(C) On March 27
(D) On April 2

Jeyakumarさんの引っ越しはいつ行われますか。

(A) 3月19日
(B) 3月20日
(C) 3月27日
(D) 4月2日

正解 C 3のEメールは宛先と件名から、Jeyakumarさんが引越予定の新オフィスで同僚となる業務部長から、Jeyakumarさんに宛てたもの。同❷ 1~2行目で、「あなたの引っ越しの予定を変更するのではなく、引越業者にこの複雑な状況を伝えたところ、彼らは快くそれに対応してくれることになった」と述べられているので、引っ越しは予定通りに行われると分かる。同❶ 2~3行目に、「本日、そのエレベーターが引越予定日に運転休止となることを知った」とあり、2の❶ 2~3行目より、エレベーターが運転を休止するのは3月27日と分かるので、(C)が正解。
(A) 2のお知らせの掲示日。
(B) 3のEメールの送信日。
(D) 3の❶ 4~5行目より、Jeyakumarさんが出資者会議に出席する日。

Words & Phrases

1 費用見積書
cost estimate 費用見積書
mover 引越会社　ease 安心　security 安全　serve ～の役に立つ　convenient 便利な
location 所在、立地　❶ prepare ～を準備する　valid 有効な　❷ delivery 配送
LLC 〈limited liability companyの略で〉有限責任会社　suite 〈一続きの〉部屋　❸ storage 保管
standard 標準の　filing cabinet 書類整理棚　drawer 引き出し　vertical 縦の　midsized 中規模の
wheeled 車輪の付いた　❹ labor 労働(力)　crew 〈仕事に従事する〉一団、クルー　per ～当たり
duration 継続時間　transport 運送　van ワゴン車、小型トラック　rental レンタル　flat fee 均一料金
❺ inclusion 含まれている物　exclusion 除外された物　fuel 燃料　toll 通行料　additional 追加の
pickup 集荷　where applicable 該当する場合　flight of stairs 一続きの階段(階と階の間の階段)
add ～ to … ～を…に加える　base 基本の　hourly rate 時間給

2 お知らせ
post ～を掲示する　❶ residential 居住の　commercial 商業の　tenant テナント、借用者
out of service 運転休止中で　routine 定期的な　maintenance 保守点検

3 Eメール
❶ provide ～ with … ～に…を提供する　update 最新情報　transition 移動　scheduled 予定された
properly きちんと　set up ～ ～を使える状態にする　postpone ～を延期する　role 役割
stakeholder 出資者、利害関係者　settle in 〈新居に〉落ち着く　remarks 言葉、文言
❷ rather than ～ ～ではなくて、～よりむしろ　reschedule ～の予定を変更する　complication 複雑な状況
be willing to *do* 快く～する　catch ～ by surprise ～を驚かせる　in the process of *doing* ～している最中で
alert ～に警告する　affect ～に影響を与える

Expressions

because of ～ 「～ゆえに、～のため」(3の❶ 4行目)

The charity marathon is expected to be postponed until next week because of bad weather.
チャリティーマラソンは、荒天のため来週まで延期される見込みです。

Questions 196-200 refer to the following editor's note, e-mail, and expense report.

1 編集後記

Transport Quarterly

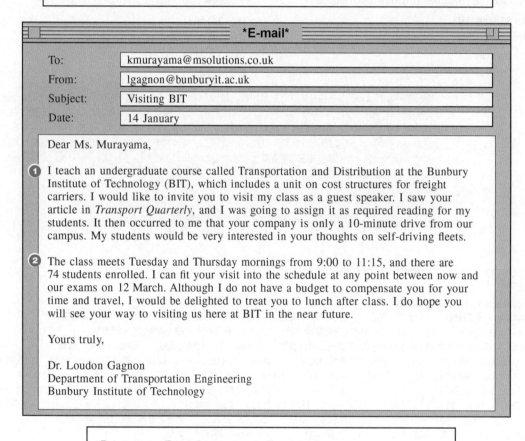

EDITOR'S NOTE:

❶ The news often talks about the use of driverless passenger cars in the near future, but self-directed trucks (SDTs) will likely be transporting deliveries on the country's roadways even sooner, perhaps within the next several years. In our autumn issue, we check in with industry experts for analysis on issues related to SDTs. Kimiko Murayama of Myeong Solutions talks about the economic factors that are making SDTs a reality. Telotin Technology's Jane Tilly takes a look at the technology that is literally "driving" SDTs. Leo Radosh of The Tapton Engineering Group describes advances in global positioning system (GPS) technology and the role that it will play in the acceptance of SDTs.

2 Eメール

E-mail

To: kmurayama@msolutions.co.uk
From: lgagnon@bunburyit.ac.uk
Subject: Visiting BIT
Date: 14 January

Dear Ms. Murayama,

❶ I teach an undergraduate course called Transportation and Distribution at the Bunbury Institute of Technology (BIT), which includes a unit on cost structures for freight carriers. I would like to invite you to visit my class as a guest speaker. I saw your article in *Transport Quarterly*, and I was going to assign it as required reading for my students. It then occurred to me that your company is only a 10-minute drive from our campus. My students would be very interested in your thoughts on self-driving fleets.

❷ The class meets Tuesday and Thursday mornings from 9:00 to 11:15, and there are 74 students enrolled. I can fit your visit into the schedule at any point between now and our exams on 12 March. Although I do not have a budget to compensate you for your time and travel, I would be delighted to treat you to lunch after class. I do hope you will see your way to visiting us here at BIT in the near future.

Yours truly,

Dr. Loudon Gagnon
Department of Transportation Engineering
Bunbury Institute of Technology

3 経費報告書

Bunbury Institute of Technology

Employee Expense Report

❶ **Name:** Dr. Loudon Gagnon
Department: Transportation Engineering
Date: 12 Feb
Amount: £40

❷ **Description of Purchase:**
Lunch at the Faculty Club hosting guest lecturer for course 316 (Transportation and Distribution)

❸ *Attach original receipts in order to receive reimbursement.*
All expenses above £200 must be preapproved by the dean of faculty.

Approved for payment by Frank Nadal on 19 February.

問題196-200は次の編集後記、Eメール、経費報告書に関するものです。

『*季刊誌　輸送*』
編集後記：

ニュースではよく、近い将来における自動運転の乗用車の利用について話題にするが、自律的なトラック（SDTs）の方がさらに早く、おそらく今後数年以内に、国内の車道で配達物を輸送することになりそうだ。秋季号でわれわれは、SDTsに関連する問題の分析のために業界の専門家と接触している。Myeong Solutions社のKimiko Murayamaは、SDTsを現実のものにしつつある経済的要因について言及している。Telotinテクノロジー社のJane Tillyは、SDTsを文字通り「動かしている」技術に注目している。Taptonエンジニアリンググループ会社のLeo Radoshは、全地球測位システム（GPS）技術の進歩と、SDTsが採用される際にそれが果たすであろう役割について述べている。

受信者：kmurayama@msolutions.co.uk
送信者：lgagnon@bunburyit.ac.uk
件名：BITへのご来校
日付：1月14日

Murayama様

私はBunbury工科大学（BIT）で、「輸送と流通」という学部学生向けのコースを受け持っており、本コースは貨物輸送業者の費用構造に関する単元を含んでいます。あなたに招待講演者として私のクラスを訪れていただきたくお招きします。私は『*季刊誌　輸送*』であなたの記事を拝見し、それを学生たちの必読文献に指定しようと思っていたところでした。そのとき、あなたの会社が当校のキャンパスから車でたった10分の所にあると気付きました。私の学生たちは自動運転の車両に関するあなたのお考えにとても興味を持つことでしょう。

当クラスは火曜日と木曜日の午前9:00から11:15にあり、74名の学生が登録しています。私はあなたのご来校を、今から3月12日の試験までの間でしたらいつでも、スケジュールに組み入れることができます。お時間と移動費に対して補償する予算はないのですが、クラスの後に昼食をごちそうさせていただければ大変うれしく存じます。あなたが近い将来、ここBITに私たちを訪ねてくださる見通しが立つことを強く願っています。

よろしくお願いいたします。

Loudon Gagnon博士
輸送工学部
Bunbury工科大学

Bunbury工科大学
従業員経費報告書

氏名：Loudon Gagnon博士
学部：輸送工学
日付：2月12日
金額：40ポンド

購入の詳細：
コース316（輸送と流通）の招待講師をもてなすための教職員クラブでの昼食

払い戻しを受けるには領収書の原本を添付すること。200ポンドを超える経費は全て、学部長により事前承認される必要がある。

Frank Nadalにより2月19日に支払い承認済み。

196 What is contained in the editor's note?

(A) A prediction about the future
(B) An analysis of GPS technology
(C) A summary of Ms. Tilly's career
(D) A description of driverless vehicles

編集後記には何が含まれていますか。

(A) 将来についての予測
(B) GPS技術の分析
(C) Tillyさんの略歴
(D) 自動運転の車両の説明

正解 A 1の編集後記では、❶ 1～3行目で、「ニュースではよく、近い将来における自動運転の乗用車の利用について話題にするが、自律的なトラック（SDTs）の方がさらに早く、おそらく今後数年以内に、国内の車道で配達物を輸送することになりそうだ」と将来についての予測をしており、同3行目以降では、秋季号に掲載されている業界専門家によるSDTs関連の分析を扱っていることに触れている。よって、(A)が正解。prediction「予測」。
(B) analysis「分析」。
(C) summary「概要」、career「経歴、職業」。
(D) 1の❶で自動運転の乗用車に言及があるが、それについての説明はされていない。vehicle「車両」。

---

197 What type of transportation is discussed in the fall issue of *Transport Quarterly*?

(A) Public mass transit
(B) Passenger railways
(C) Highway freight delivery
(D) Overseas cargo shipping

『*季刊誌　輸送*』の秋季号では、どんな種類の輸送が論じられていますか。

(A) 公共交通機関
(B) 旅客鉄道
(C) 幹線道路の貨物輸送
(D) 海外への貨物輸送

正解 C 『*季刊誌　輸送*』の編集後記である1の❶ 2～3行目に「自律的なトラック（SDTs）の方がさらに早く、おそらく今後数年以内に、国内の車道で配達物を輸送することになりそうだ」とあり、続く同3～4行目で、In our autumn issue, we check in with industry experts for analysis on issues related to SDTs.「秋季号でわれわれは、SDTsに関連する問題の分析のために業界の専門家と接触している」と説明されている。よって、秋季号では道路の貨物輸送について論じられていると考えられる。highway「幹線道路」、freight delivery「貨物輸送」。
(A) mass transit「交通機関、大量輸送機関」。
(B) railway「鉄道」。
(D) overseas「海外（へ）の」、cargo shipping「貨物輸送」。

---

198 What company is a short distance from Bunbury Institute of Technology?

(A) Myeong Solutions
(B) Telotin Technology
(C) The Tapton Engineering Group
(D) *Transport Quarterly*'s publisher

Bunbury工科大学から近い距離にあるのはどの会社ですか。

(A) Myeong Solutions社
(B) Telotinテクノロジー社
(C) Taptonエンジニアリンググループ会社
(D) 『*季刊誌　輸送*』の出版社

正解 A 2のEメールは、Bunbury工科大学のGagnon博士からMurayamaさんに宛てられたもの。2の❶ 5～6行目に、It then occurred to me that your company is only a 10-minute drive from our campus.「そのとき、あなたの会社が当校のキャンパスから車でたった10分の所にあると気付いた」と書かれている。1の❶ 4～5行目に、Kimiko Murayama of Myeong Solutions「Myeong Solutions社のKimiko Murayama」とあり、MurayamaさんはMyeong Solutions社に勤務していると分かるので、(A)が正解。
(D) publisher「出版社」。

199 What did Dr. Gagnon most likely do after reading the fall issue of *Transport Quarterly*?

(A) Write a letter to the editor
(B) Share it with his supervisor
(C) Encourage his students to submit articles to the publication
(D) Issue an invitation to a contributor

『*季刊誌 輸送*』の秋季号を読んだ後、Gagnon博士は何をしたと考えられますか。

(A) 編集者に手紙を書いた。
(B) 自分の上司とそれを共有した。
(C) その出版物に論文を投稿するよう、自分の学生に勧めた。
(D) 寄稿者に招待状を出した。

正解 D 1の❶ 3〜6行目より、『*季刊誌 輸送*』の秋季号にMurayamaさんの記事が掲載されていることが分かる。Murayamaさん宛てのEメールである2の❶ 3〜5行目で、Gagnon博士は「あなたに招待講演者として私のクラスを訪れていただきたくお招きする。私は『*季刊誌 輸送*』であなたの記事を見て、それを学生たちの必読文献に指定しようと思っていたところだった」と書いている。よって、Gagnon博士は秋季号を読んだ後に、その寄稿者であるMurayamaさんを自分のクラスに招待しようとEメールを送信したと考えられる。(D)が正解。issue an invitation「招待状を出す」、contributor「寄稿者」。
(B) supervisor「上司、監督者」。
(C) encourage ~ to *do*「~に…するように勧める」、submit「~を投稿する」、publication「出版物」。

---

200 What did Dr. Gagnon do at the Faculty Club on February 12?

(A) He stopped by to pay an annual membership fee.
(B) He hosted Ms. Murayama for a meal.
(C) He welcomed a new department member.
(D) He requested approval for a payment from Mr. Nadal.

Gagnon博士は2月12日に教職員クラブで何をしましたか。

(A) 彼は年会費を支払うために立ち寄った。
(B) 彼はMurayamaさんを食事でもてなした。
(C) 彼は新しい学部のメンバーを歓迎した。
(D) 彼はNadalさんからの支払いの承認を要請した。

正解 B 3の経費報告書の❶の氏名欄にGagnon博士の名があり、日付欄は2月12日、同❷に、「コース316の招待講師をもてなすための教職員クラブでの昼食」とある。Gagnon博士は1月14日付のEメールである2の❷ 4行目で、「クラスの後に昼食をごちそうできればうれしい」とMurayamaさんに伝えている。よって、2のEメール送信後、Murayamaさんが招待講師として博士のクラスを訪れ、博士は提案通りMurayamaさんを食事でもてなしたと考えられる。
(A) stop by「立ち寄る」、annual「毎年の」、membership fee「会費」。
(D) approval「承認」、payment「支払い」。

Words & Phrases

editor's note 編集後記　expense report 経費報告書

1 編集後記
transport 〈名詞で〉輸送、〈動詞で〉~を輸送する　quarterly 季刊誌　❶ driverless 自動運転の　passenger car 乗用車　in the near future 近い将来　self-directed 自律的な　likely ~しそうである　roadway 車道　issue 〈定期刊行物の〉号、問題点　check in with ~ ~に連絡を入れる　industry 業界　expert 専門家　analysis 分析　related to ~ ~に関連した　economic 経済的な　factor 要因　reality 現実(のもの)　take a look at ~ ~を見る　literally 文字通り　describe ~について述べる　advance 進歩、発展　global positioning system 全地球測位システム　play a role 役割を果たす　acceptance 受け入れること

2 Eメール
❶ undergraduate 学部学生の　transportation 輸送　distribution 流通　Institute of Technology 工科大学　structure 構造　freight 貨物　carrier 運送業者　assign ~を指定する　required 必須の　occur ふと気づく　drive 〈自動車で行く〉道のり　thought 考え　self-driving 自動運転の　fleet 全車両　❷ enroll ~に登録する　fit ~ into … ~を…に入れる　budget 予算　compensate ~ for … ~に…に対して補償する　be delighted to *do* 喜んで~する　treat ~にごちそうする　see *one's* way to *doing* ~する見通しが立つ　engineering 工学

3 経費報告書
❶ amount 金額　❷ description 説明　faculty 教職員　host ~をもてなす　lecturer 講師　❸ attach ~を添付する　original 原本の　receipt 領収書　in order to *do* ~するために　reimbursement 払い戻し　preapprove ~を事前に承認する　dean of faculty 学部長

TEST 2の正解一覧

リスニングセクション

問題番号	正解
Part 1	
1	B
2	D
3	C
4	A
5	B
6	A
Part 2	
7	A
8	B
9	B
10	A
11	C
12	B
13	A
14	A
15	B
16	B
17	A
18	C
19	A
20	A
21	B
22	A
23	B
24	C
25	C
26	B
27	C
28	C
29	B
30	C
31	C
Part 3	
32	D
33	B
34	A
35	C
36	D
37	D
38	D
39	B
40	A
41	B
42	A
43	C
44	A
45	C
46	A
47	C
48	D
49	B
50	A

問題番号	正解
51	B
52	D
53	A
54	D
55	D
56	A
57	C
58	D
59	A
60	B
61	D
62	B
63	D
64	D
65	D
66	C
67	C
68	C
69	A
70	A
Part 4	
71	A
72	D
73	B
74	D
75	B
76	A
77	C
78	A
79	D
80	C
81	A
82	A
83	B
84	C
85	A
86	D
87	C
88	B
89	A
90	C
91	B
92	A
93	C
94	B
95	C
96	B
97	C
98	D
99	A
100	B

リーディングセクション

問題番号	正解
Part 5	
101	C
102	D
103	C
104	A
105	A
106	B
107	A
108	D
109	D
110	C
111	A
112	B
113	A
114	B
115	D
116	D
117	C
118	B
119	D
120	D
121	A
122	B
123	A
124	C
125	D
126	A
127	A
128	C
129	B
130	A
Part 6	
131	C
132	D
133	B
134	A
135	C
136	A
137	D
138	A
139	D
140	B
141	D
142	C
143	C
144	B
145	B
146	D
Part 7	
147	A
148	C
149	A
150	B

問題番号	正解
151	C
152	D
153	B
154	D
155	B
156	B
157	D
158	C
159	D
160	A
161	B
162	A
163	C
164	A
165	B
166	A
167	C
168	C
169	B
170	B
171	D
172	A
173	D
174	B
175	C
176	C
177	A
178	B
179	B
180	D
181	D
182	C
183	B
184	B
185	C
186	A
187	D
188	A
189	D
190	C
191	D
192	B
193	B
194	D
195	A
196	C
197	D
198	C
199	C
200	A

PART 1

1

2

3

1 W

(A) They're shaking hands.
(B) He's holding a briefcase.
(C) They're hanging some artwork.
(D) She's turning on a light.

(A) 彼らは握手している。
(B) 彼は書類かばんを手に持っている。
(C) 彼らは美術品を掛けている。
(D) 彼女は明かりをつけている。

正解 B 右側にいる男性がbriefcase「書類かばん」を左手に持っている。hold「～を手に持つ」。
(A) 男性と女性は、握手しているところではない。shake hands「握手する」。
(C) hang「～を掛ける」、artwork「美術品」。
(D) turn on ～「〈明かり・電源など〉をつける」、light「明かり、照明」。

2 M

(A) She's taking off her jacket.
(B) She's sweeping the floor.
(C) She's closing a window.
(D) She's using exercise equipment.

(A) 彼女は上着を脱いでいるところである。
(B) 彼女は床を掃いている。
(C) 彼女は窓を閉めている。
(D) 彼女は運動器具を使用している。

正解 D 女性はサイクリングマシンのような器具を使って運動している。exercise「運動」、equipment「器具」。
(A) 女性は上着を身に着けており、それを脱いでいるところではない。take off ～「〈服など〉を脱ぐ」、jacket「ジャケット、ジャンパーなどの上着」。
(B) floor「床」は写っているが、女性はそれを掃除してはいない。sweep「～を掃く」。

3 M

(A) A woman is sealing an envelope.
(B) A woman is putting papers into a folder.
(C) A woman is talking on the telephone.
(D) A woman is arranging objects on a desk.

(A) 女性が封筒に封をしている。
(B) 女性が書類をフォルダーに入れている。
(C) 女性が電話で話している。
(D) 女性が机の上に物を並べている。

正解 C 女性は、電話の受話器を耳に当てて話している様子である。talk on the telephone「電話で話す」。
(A) seal「〈封筒や手紙など〉に封をする」、envelope「封筒」。
(B) folder「フォルダー」は机の上に置かれているが、女性はpapers「書類」をそれに入れているところではない。
(D) arrange「～をきちんと並べる」、object「物」。

4

5

6

4 M

(A) A man is filling a cup.
(B) A man is emptying a trash can.
(C) A woman is installing a light.
(D) A woman is carrying a tray of food.

(A) 男性がカップに注いでいる。
(B) 男性がごみ箱を空にしている。
(C) 女性が照明を取り付けている。
(D) 女性が食べ物が載ったトレーを運んでいる。

正解 A 男性はコーヒーサーバーのようなものから、カップに注いでいる。fill「～にいっぱいに注ぐ、～をいっぱいに満たす」。
(B) empty「～を空にする」、trash can「ごみ箱」。
(C) install「～を取り付ける」。
(D) 女性はカウンター前で立ち止まっており、tray「トレー」を運んではいない。carry「～を運ぶ」。

5 W

(A) One of the men is loading a truck.
(B) One of the men is stacking boxes.
(C) They're assembling some shelves.
(D) They're fixing some machinery.

(A) 男性の1人はトラックに荷を積み込んでいる。
(B) 男性の1人は箱を積み重ねている。
(C) 彼らは棚を組み立てている。
(D) 彼らは機械を修理している。

正解 B 手前の男性がbox「箱」を積み重ねている。stack「～を積み重ねる、～を積み上げる」。
(A) truck「トラック」は写っていない。load「〈車など〉に荷を積み込む」。
(C) assemble「～を組み立てる」。
(D) 機械類は写っているが、男性たちはそれらを修理しているところではない。fix「～を修理する」、machinery「機械(類)」。

6 M

(A) A message board has been placed between two benches.
(B) A walkway is covered with flowers.
(C) Some rocks are being removed from a garden.
(D) Some trees are being cut down.

(A) 1台の掲示板が2台のベンチの間に置かれている。
(B) 歩道が花で覆われている。
(C) 岩が庭から取り除かれているところである。
(D) 木が切り倒されているところである。

正解 A 奥の2台のベンチの間にmessage board「掲示板」が1台ある。〈have[has] been＋過去分詞〉で「～された状態である」という意味。place「～を置く」。
(B) walkway「歩道」は写っているが、花で覆われてはいない。cover「～を覆う」。
(C) remove「～を取り除く」。
(D) 木は写っているが、切り倒されているところではない。cut down ～「〈木など〉を切り倒す」。

7 W The accounting staff works on this floor, right?

M (A) Yes, their office is down the hall.
(B) That's not my invoice.
(C) A lot of renovation work.

経理の職員はこの階で働いているのですよね？
(A) はい、彼らのオフィスは廊下の先にあります。
(B) それは私の請求書ではありません。
(C) 多くの改修作業です。

正解 A 肯定文の文末に ~, right?を付けて「～ですよね」と、経理の職員はこの階で働いているのか確認している。これに対し、Yesと肯定して、「彼らのオフィスは廊下の先だ」と具体的な場所を伝えている(A)が正解。theirは質問にあるThe accounting staffを指す。accounting「経理、会計」、staff「職員」。down the hall「廊下の先に」。
(B) invoice「請求書」については尋ねられていない。
(C) renovation「改修」。

---

8 W I'm going to buy this cake.

M (A) Sugar and flour.
(B) Good choice.
(C) A famous chef.

私はこのケーキを買うつもりです。
(A) 砂糖と小麦粉です。
(B) いい選択ですね。
(C) 有名なシェフです。

正解 B 「このケーキを買うつもりだ」という発言に対し、「いい選択だね」と肯定的な意見で応じている(B)が正解。be going to *do*「～するつもりである」。choice「選択」。
(A) 質問にあるcakeと関連する名詞sugarやflour「小麦粉」が含まれるが、材料は尋ねられていない。
(C) ケーキの作り手については尋ねられていない。chef「シェフ」。

---

9 W When did the air conditioner arrive?

M (A) Thanks for sharing.
(B) It came yesterday.
(C) Yes, it's more efficient.

エアコンはいつ届きましたか。
(A) 話してくれてありがとう。
(B) それは昨日、到着しました。
(C) はい、それはもっと効率的です。

正解 B When ~?でエアコンがいつ届いたのかを尋ねているのに対し、「昨日、到着した」と具体的な到着日を答えている(B)が正解。air conditioner「エアコン」、arrive「届く」。
(A) 質問にあるairと似た音の動詞share「～に話す」に注意。
(C) efficient「効率的な」。

---

10 W Is Munich your final destination?

M (A) No, I'm flying to Berlin.
(B) A window seat, please.
(C) Did you purchase a ticket?

ミュンヘンがあなたの最終目的地ですか。
(A) いいえ、私はベルリンまで飛行機で行きます。
(B) 窓側の座席をお願いします。
(C) あなたはチケットを購入しましたか。

正解 A 「ミュンヘンがあなたの最終目的地か」と尋ねているのに対し、Noと否定して、「私はベルリンまで飛行機で行く」と具体的な行き先を伝えている(A)が正解。final「最終的な」、destination「目的地」。
(B) window seat「〈飛行機やバスなどの〉窓側の席」。
(C) purchase「～を購入する」。

---

11 W You already processed the refund, right?

M (A) Turn left at the corner.
(B) The processing plant is hiring.
(C) Yes, I did it this morning.

あなたはもう返金の手続きをしたのですよね？
(A) その角(かど)で左に曲がってください。
(B) その処理工場は人材を募集しています。
(C) はい、私は今朝それをしました。

正解 C 肯定文の文末に ~, right?を付けて、返金の手続きが済んだのか確認している。Yesと肯定して、「私は今朝それをした」と手続きの完了を伝えている(C)が正解。itは、返金の手続きをすることを表す。process「～の手続きをする」、refund「返金」。
(B) processing plant「処理工場」、hire「(～を)雇用する」。

12 M Please help yourself to some refreshments.

W (A) It wasn't helpful.
(B) Thanks, they look delicious.
(C) She's busy that night.

軽食をご自由に取って召し上がってください。
(A) それは役に立ちませんでした。
(B) ありがとう、おいしそうですね。
(C) 彼女はその夜忙しいです。

正解 B 軽食を自由に取って食べるよう勧めているのに対し、Thanksとお礼を言った上で、「おいしそうだ」と軽食についての肯定的な感想を述べている(B)が正解。help *oneself* to ～「～を自由に取って食べる」、refreshments「軽食」。
(A) 質問にあるhelpと似た音の形容詞helpful「役に立つ」に注意。
(C) Sheが誰を指すのか不明。

---

13 W Who's designing our next advertisement?

M (A) Check the meeting minutes.
(B) Our company style.
(C) No, it was last Saturday.

誰が当社の次の広告をデザインするのですか。
(A) 会議の議事録を確認してください。
(B) 当社の流儀です。
(C) いいえ、この前の土曜日でした。

正解 A Who ～?で次の広告をデザインする予定の人物を尋ねているのに対し、「会議の議事録を確認してください」とその情報が分かる書類を教えて、自分で確認するよう促している(A)が正解。design「～をデザインする」、advertisement「広告」。minutes「議事録」。
(B) style「流儀、スタイル」。
(C) 時期は尋ねられていない。

---

14 M When are you going to update Mr. Saleem's contact information?

W (A) By this Friday.
(B) In the filing cabinet.
(C) I don't have any to lend you.

あなたはSaleemさんの連絡先情報をいつ更新するつもりですか。
(A) 今週の金曜日までに。
(B) 書類整理棚の中に。
(C) 私は何もあなたに貸せるものはありません。

正解 A When ～?でSaleemさんの連絡先情報をいつ更新するつもりか尋ねているのに対し、「今週の金曜日までに」と具体的な時期を伝えている(A)が正解。update「～を更新する」、contact information「連絡先情報」。
(B) 場所は尋ねられていない。filing cabinet「書類整理棚」。
(C) anyが何を指すのか不明。

---

15 M Is this the two o'clock beginners' yoga class?

W (A) Just a mat and a towel.
(B) I teach the advanced level.
(C) These new lockers are nice.

こちらは2時の初心者向けヨガクラスですか。
(A) マットとタオルだけです。
(B) 私は上級レベルを教えています。
(C) これらの新しいロッカーはいいですね。

正解 B 「ここは2時の初心者向けヨガクラスか」と尋ねているのに対し、「私は上級レベルを教えている」と応じ、ここが初心者向けヨガクラスではないことを示唆している(B)が正解。beginner「初心者」。advanced「上級の」。
(A) 質問にあるyogaと関連する名詞matやtowelを含むが、使用する物は尋ねられていない。
(C) locker「ロッカー」。

---

16 M The printer's broken again.

W (A) Print it on both sides.
(B) Should we call a technician?
(C) I've already decided.

プリンターがまた故障しました。
(A) それを両面に印刷してください。
(B) 私たちは技術者に電話をした方がよいでしょうか。
(C) 私はもう決めました。

正解 B 「プリンターがまた故障した」という発言に対し、「私たちは技術者に電話をした方がよいか」と対処法の確認をしている(B)が正解。printer'sはprinter hasの短縮形。technician「技術者」。
(A) itが何を指すのか不明。質問にあるprinterと関連する動詞print「～を印刷する」に注意。

17 W Why can't they find someone to cover your shift?
M (A) Because everyone's busy now.
(B) Yes, the change will happen soon.
(C) I don't think so.

彼らは、なぜあなたのシフトの代わりを務める人を見つけられないのですか。
(A) 今、皆忙しいからです。
(B) はい、変化は間もなく起こるでしょう。
(C) 私はそう思いません。

正解 A Why ～?でシフトの代わりを務める人物がなぜ見つからないのかを尋ねているのに対し、Because ～を用いて、「今、皆忙しいからだ」と理由を述べている(A)が正解。cover「～の代わりを務める」、shift「シフト、(交代制の)勤務時間」。
(B) 理由を尋ねられているので、Yes、Noでは応答にならない。

18 M How did you like the movie last night?
W (A) Did you find the instructions online?
(B) Jim moved some over to his desk.
(C) I actually had to work late.

昨夜の映画はいかがでしたか。
(A) あなたはオンラインで説明書を見つけましたか。
(B) Jimは、幾つかを自分の机の方に移動させました。
(C) 実は、私は遅くまで仕事をしなければなりませんでした。

正解 C How did you like ～?「～はいかがでしたか」で昨夜の映画の感想を尋ねているのに対し、「私は遅くまで仕事をしなければならなかった」と答え、映画を見られなかったことを示唆している(C)が正解。
(A) instructions「説明書」。
(B) someが何を指すのか不明。質問にあるmovieと似た音の動詞movedに注意。

19 M Would you like to see the apartment that's available?
W (A) Sure, I'm free all weekend.
(B) He's the head of that department.
(C) Close to public transportation.

入居可能なアパートをご覧になりたいですか。
(A) もちろんです、私は週末ずっと空いています。
(B) 彼はその部署の責任者です。
(C) 公共交通機関の近くに。

正解 A Would you like to *do* ～?「～したいですか」は、丁寧に相手の意向を尋ねる表現。入居可能なアパートを見たいか尋ねているのに対し、Sureと肯定した上で、「私は週末ずっと空いている」と都合を伝えている(A)が正解。apartment「アパート(の1室)」、available「利用可能な」。
(B) head「責任者、長」、department「部署」。
(C) 立地は尋ねられていない。close to ～「～の近くに」、public transportation「公共交通機関」。

20 W This is where the leadership training is being held, right?
M (A) I had trouble finding the room, too.
(B) The train to Barcelona.
(C) At least ten boxes, please.

ここがリーダーシップ研修が行われる場所ですよね？
(A) 私も部屋を見つけるのに苦労しました。
(B) バルセロナ行きの電車です。
(C) 少なくとも10箱をお願いします。

正解 A 肯定文の文末に ～, right?を付けて「～ですよね」とリーダーシップ研修が行われる場所がこの部屋なのか確認している。これに対し、「私も部屋を見つけるのに苦労した」と伝えて、ここが研修の開催場所であることを示唆している(A)が正解。
(C) at least「少なくとも」。

21 W Did you pay for your hotel at the convention?
M (A) A convention about electronics.
(B) My company usually does that.
(C) We only take credit cards.

あなたは協議会で自分のホテル代の支払いをしましたか。
(A) 電子機器に関する協議会です。
(B) 私の会社が通常それをします。
(C) 私たちはクレジットカードのみ取り扱っております。

正解 B 協議会で自分のホテル代の支払いをしたのか尋ねているのに対し、会社が通常それをすると答えて、自分では代金の支払いをする必要がないことを示唆している(B)が正解。does thatは、協議会でホテル代を支払うことを指す。pay for ～「～の支払いをする」、convention「協議会、コンベンション」。
(A) electronics「電子機器」。
(C) 質問にあるpayと関連するcredit cardsが含まれるが、応答になっていない。

22 M What's the name of the new office manager?

W (A) I haven't met her yet.
(B) On the second floor, I think.
(C) They both want to go.

新しい事務所長の名前は何ですか。
(A) 私は彼女にまだ会ったことがありません。
(B) 2階だと思います。
(C) 彼らは2人とも行きたいと思っています。

正解 A What ～?で新しい事務所長の名前を尋ねているのに対し、「私は彼女にまだ会ったことがない」と答え、事務所長の名前を知らないことを示唆している(A)が正解。herは質問にある、the new office managerを指す。
(B) 場所は尋ねられていない。
(C) Theyが誰を指すのか不明。

---

23 W When's the deadline to sign the contract for maintenance service?

M (A) With someone from my department.
(B) Noon on Wednesday.
(C) Yes, I'd like one.

保守サービスの契約を結ぶための期限はいつですか。
(A) 私の部署の人と一緒に。
(B) 水曜日の正午です。
(C) はい、1つ頂きたいと思います。

正解 B When ～?で保守サービスの契約を結ぶための期限を尋ねているのに対し、「水曜日の正午だ」と時期を伝えている(B)が正解。deadline「期限」、sign a contract「契約を結ぶ、契約書に署名する」、maintenance「保守、整備」。
(C) oneが契約を指すとしても、時期を尋ねられているのに対し、応答になっていない。

---

24 W Which aisle are the paper plates in?

M (A) There's extra copy paper in the cabinet.
(B) You can set them on the table.
(C) We'll have more in stock tomorrow.

紙皿はどの通路にありますか。
(A) 戸棚に余分なコピー用紙があります。
(B) あなたはそれらをテーブルの上に置いていいですよ。
(C) 明日、もっと入荷します。

正解 C Which ～?で紙皿を保管しているのがどの通路かを確認しているのに対し、「明日、もっと入荷する」と予定を伝え、現在は紙皿の在庫が少なくなっていることを示唆している(C)が正解。aisle「通路」、paper plate「紙皿」。in stock「入荷して」。
(A) copy paper「コピー用紙」については尋ねられていない。extra「余分な」。
(B) set「～を置く、～を配置する」。

---

25 W How do I log on to this computer?

M (A) Building B.
(B) Yes, I know everyone here.
(C) I can help you.

このコンピューターにはどうやってログオンするのですか。
(A) B棟です。
(B) はい、私はここにいる皆を知っています。
(C) 私があなたをお手伝いできます。

正解 C How ～?でコンピューターにログオンする方法を尋ねているのに対し、「私がお手伝いできる」とログオンの手助けを申し出ている(C)が正解。log on to ～「～にログオンする、～にログインする」。
(A) 場所は尋ねられていない。
(B) 方法を尋ねられているのに対し、応答になっていない。

---

26 M Would you like to look at the report before I submit it?

W (A) I saw that play yesterday.
(B) Yes, just e-mail it to me.
(C) She's already been there.

私が提出する前に、その報告書を見ていただけませんか。
(A) 私は昨日、その演劇を見ました。
(B) はい、ちょっと私にそれをEメールで送ってください。
(C) 彼女はもうそこにいます。

正解 B Would you like to *do* ～?「～していただけませんか」と報告書を見てもらえないかと丁寧に頼んでいる。それに対し、Yesと肯定して、Eメールでそれを送るよう伝えている(B)が正解。itは質問にあるthe reportを指す。submit「～を提出する」。
(A) play「演劇」については尋ねられていない。
(C) Sheが誰を、thereがどこを指すのか不明。

27 M Does the conference call with our Japanese clients start at two or three?

W (A) A professional conference.
(B) Next year's automobile designs.
(C) They asked us to reschedule it.

日本の顧客との電話会議は2時に始まりますか、それとも3時ですか。
(A) 専門家の協議会です。
(B) 来年の自動車の設計です。
(C) 先方は、その日時を変更してほしいと私たちに頼んできました。

正解 C *A or B?*の形で、電話会議の開始時刻が2時か3時のどちらか尋ねている。これに対し、先方から電話会議の日時の変更依頼があったと伝えている(C)が正解。Theyは質問にあるour Japanese clientsを、itはthe conference callを指す。conference call「電話会議」、client「顧客」。reschedule「～の日時を変更する」。
(A) professional「専門家の」。
(B) 会議の議題は尋ねられていない。automobile「自動車」。

---

28 M Why has the restaurant freezer been moved?

W (A) On Thirty-First Street.
(B) Oh, that's a great café.
(C) Because it's being replaced.

レストランの冷凍庫はなぜ移動されたのですか。
(A) 31番街に。
(B) ああ、それは素晴らしいカフェです。
(C) それは交換されることになっているからです。

正解 C Why ～?でなぜレストランの冷凍庫が移動されたのかを尋ねているのに対し、Because ～を用いて、それが交換される予定だと理由を説明している(C)が正解。itは質問にあるfreezer「冷凍庫」を指す。replace「～を交換する」。
(A) 場所は尋ねられていない。

---

29 W Won't you be giving a presentation at the meeting?

M (A) I hope you like the gift.
(B) My project still needs some work.
(C) They just met last Thursday.

会議でプレゼンテーションをしてくれませんか。
(A) あなたがその贈り物を気に入ってくれればと思います。
(B) 私のプロジェクトはまだ作業が必要なのです。
(C) 彼らはこの前の木曜日に出会ったばかりです。

正解 B Won't you ～?「～してくれませんか」で会議でプレゼンテーションをするよう依頼しているのに対し、「私のプロジェクトはまだ作業が必要だ」と答えて、今は依頼に応じられないことを示唆している(B)が正解。
(A) 質問にあるgivingと関連する名詞gift「贈り物」が含まれるが、応答になっていない。
(C) Theyが誰を指すのか不明。

---

30 M Where should I park the truck after I unload these boxes?

W (A) A picnic in Hillside Park.
(B) I already downloaded the file.
(C) There's still one more delivery today.

私はこれらの箱を降ろしたら、どこにトラックを駐車するべきですか。
(A) Hillside公園でのピクニックです。
(B) 私はすでにそのファイルをダウンロードしました。
(C) 今日はまだもう1件配達があります。

正解 C Where ～?でトラックを駐車するべき場所を尋ねているのに対し、「今日はまだもう1件配達がある」と述べ、まだ駐車すべきではないことを示唆している(C)が正解。park「～を駐車する」、unload「〈荷物など〉を降ろす」。delivery「配達(物)」。
(B) 質問にあるunloadと似た音のdownload「～をダウンロードする」に注意。

---

31 M How far in advance should I make my appointment?

W (A) That's what I found, too.
(B) Yes, we require a cash payment.
(C) Well, this is our busiest time of year.

私はどれくらい前もって予約をするべきですか。
(A) それは私も見つけたものです。
(B) はい、私たちは現金での支払いをお願いしています。
(C) そうですね、今は私たちが一年で最も忙しい時期です。

正解 C 「どれくらい前もって予約すべきか」と尋ねているのに対し、Wellと間をつなぎ、「今は私たちが一年で最も忙しい時期だ」と繁忙期のため、早めに予約した方がよいことを示唆している(C)が正解。in advance「前もって」、make an appointment「予約する」。
(B) 支払い方法は尋ねられていない。require「～を求める」。

Questions 32 through 34 refer to the following conversation.

問題32-34は次の会話に関するものです。

M ❶Are you all set to pay, Ms. Rodriguez? Your new haircut looks really nice, by the way.

Rodriguezさん、お支払いの準備はよろしいでしょうか。ところで、あなたの新しいヘアスタイルはとても素敵ですよ。

W Thanks. As usual Marla did a really good job. Hmm… ❷I was wondering if I could apply this coupon to today's haircut... ❸it says it expired yesterday, but I just wanted to see if you'd accept it.

ありがとう。いつものように、Marlaが本当によくやってくれました。ええと…このクーポンを今日のヘアカットに適用できないかと思っていて…昨日で期限が切れたと書かれていますが、受け入れてくださるかどうかちょっと確かめたかったんです。

M Sure, we can take that. By the way, ❹we're also offering 50 percent off on all hair products until the end of next month.

もちろんです、お受けしますよ。ところで、当店では来月末まで全てのヘアケア製品に50パーセント引きも行っています。

W Oh, that's good to know, since I've run out of shampoo. ❺I'll take a look at what you have and see if there's something I'd like to buy.

ああ、それを知って良かったです、というのも私はシャンプーを切らしているので。どんなものがあるか見てみて、買いたいものがあるかどうか確かめてみます。

---

32 Where does the conversation most likely take place?

(A) At a department store
(B) At a photography studio
(C) At a health clinic
(D) At a hair salon

会話はどこで行われていると考えられますか。

(A) 百貨店
(B) 写真スタジオ
(C) 診療所
(D) 美容院

正解 D 男性は❶で、支払いの準備ができているか女性に尋ね、新しいヘアスタイルを褒めているのに対し、女性は❷で、今日のヘアカットにクーポンを適用できるかどうか確認している。さらに、男性は❹で、女性にヘアケア製品の割引を知らせているので、男性は美容院の店員で、女性はその顧客と考えられる。hair salon「美容院」。
(A) department store「百貨店」。
(B) photography「写真」。

---

33 What does the woman ask about?

(A) Receiving e-mail notifications
(B) Using a coupon
(C) Setting up an account
(D) Changing an appointment time

女性は何について尋ねていますか。

(A) Eメールの通知を受け取ること。
(B) クーポンを使用すること。
(C) 口座を開設すること。
(D) 予約時間を変更すること。

正解 B 女性は❷でクーポンを今日のヘアカットに適用できるか男性に尋ね、続けて❸「昨日で期限が切れたと書かれているが、受け入れてくれるか確かめたかった」と説明している。
(A) receive「～を受け取る」、notification「通知」。
(C) set up ～「～を開設する、～を設定する」、account「口座」。
(D) appointment「予約」。

---

34 What does the woman say she will do?

(A) Look at some products
(B) Complete some paperwork
(C) Write a review
(D) Come back another day

女性は何をするつもりだと言っていますか。

(A) 幾つかの製品を見る。
(B) 書類に全て記入する。
(C) レビューを書く。
(D) 別の日にまた来る。

正解 A 男性が❹で、全てのヘアケア製品を50パーセント引きで提供中だと知らせているのに対し、女性は❺「どんなものがあるか見てみて、買いたいものがあるかどうか確かめてみる」と言っている。
(B) complete「～に全て記入する」。
(C) review「レビュー、評価」。

Words & Phrases

be all set to *do* ～する準備がすっかりできている　haircut ヘアスタイル、ヘアカット
by the way ところで　as usual いつものように　apply ～ to … ～を…に適用する　coupon クーポン
expire 期限が切れる　see if ～ ～かどうか確かめる　accept ～を受け入れる　offer ～を提供する
run out of ～ ～を切らす、～がなくなる　shampoo シャンプー　take a look at ～ ～を見てみる

Questions 35 through 37 refer to the following conversation.

問題35-37は次の会話に関するものです。

W The Seafood Palace. How can I help you?

Seafood Palaceです。どんなご用件でしょうか。

M Hi. ❶I'm calling from Kinhex Corporation about a party we'd like to hold at your restaurant. We want to celebrate the grand opening of our company's new office here in town.

こんにちは。そちらのレストランで開催したいと思っているパーティーについて、Kinhex社から電話しています。この町での当社の新事務所の開設記念を祝いたいのです。

W Oh, yes. Congratulations on expanding your business!

ああ、はい。御社の事業拡大について心からお祝い申し上げます!

M Thanks! ❷I'm wondering about the capacity of your largest dining room. ❸Is it big enough to accommodate 100 people?

ありがとうございます。そちらの一番大きいダイニングルームの収容人数について知りたいと思っています。それは、100名を収容するのに十分広いでしょうか。

W Oh, definitely. And ❹if you'd like to reserve it for your party, we ask that you pay a small fee. ❺That's the only way we can guarantee it for you.

ええ、もちろんです。その部屋をパーティーのために予約なさりたい場合、当店は、少額の料金をお支払いいただくようお願いしています。それが、お客さまにその部屋を確約できる唯一の方法です。

35 What will Kinhex Corporation celebrate?

(A) The start of a holiday season
(B) The anniversary of its founding
(C) The opening of a new location
(D) The appointment of a company president

Kinhex社は何を祝いますか。

(A) 休暇シーズンの開始
(B) 創業記念日
(C) 新たな支社の開設
(D) 社長の任命

正解 C 男性は❶「そちらのレストランで開催したいと思っているパーティーについて、Kinhex社から電話している。この町での当社の新事務所の開設記念を祝いたい」と用件を伝えている。new officeをa new locationと表している(C)が正解。location「場所、用地」。
(B) anniversary「記念日」、founding「創業、設立」。
(D) appointment「任命」、president「社長、会長」。

36 What does the man ask about?

(A) The cost of a service
(B) Operating hours
(C) Entertainment options
(D) The size of a space

男性は何について尋ねていますか。

(A) サービスの費用
(B) 営業時間
(C) 娯楽の選択肢
(D) スペースの広さ

正解 D レストランに電話をしてきた男性は❷で、一番大きいダイニングルームの収容人数について知りたいと述べ、続けて❸「それは、100名を収容するのに十分広いか」と尋ねている。space「スペース、空間」。
(B) operating hours「営業時間」。
(C) entertainment「娯楽、エンターテインメント」、option「選択肢」。

37 What does the woman ask the man to do?

(A) Sample a menu item
(B) Look at a catalog
(C) Talk to a manager
(D) Make a payment

女性は男性に何をするよう求めていますか。

(A) メニューの品を試食する。
(B) カタログを見る。
(C) 支配人と話をする。
(D) 支払いをする。

正解 D 女性は男性に対して、❹「その部屋をパーティーのために予約したい場合、当店は、少額の料金を支払うようお願いしている」と述べた後、❺で、それが部屋を確約できる唯一の方法だと伝えている。よって、女性は男性に、パーティーの部屋を確保するために支払いをするよう求めていると分かる。
(A) sample「~を試食する」。
(C) manager「支配人、管理者」。

Words & Phrases

hold ~を開催する　celebrate ~を祝う　grand opening 開店記念、グランドオープン
Congratulations on ~ ~について心からお祝いします　expand ~を拡大する　business 事業
capacity 収容人数、定員　~ enough to *do* …するのに十分~　accommodate ~を収容する　reserve ~を予約する
fee 料金、費用　guarantee ~を確約する、~を保証する

Questions 38 through 40 refer to the following conversation.

W Hi, Joseph. ❶You know how our store does those workshops on home improvements? Well, ❷I'm supposed to lead one next month, but it turns out I have to go out of town.

M Well, ❸I could do it for you. ❹I'm finishing up a series of workshops on bathroom remodeling this month, so I'll have more time then. What's the topic of the workshop?

W It's about how to install light fixtures in your home. A lot of our customers are interested in that.

M OK, sure. But I haven't done that kind of workshop before. I'm not sure what materials I'll need.

W Don't worry. ❺I'll get all the materials ready so you'll have them beforehand.

問題38-40は次の会話に関するものです。

こんにちは、Joseph。当店が住宅リフォームに関するワークショップをどのように行っているかは知っていますよね。それで、私は来月に1つ主導することになっているのですが、町から離れなければならないことが分かりました。

なるほど、私が代わりにそれをしてもいいですよ。今月には浴室改装に関する一連のワークショップをやり終える予定なので、そのときにはもっと時間があるでしょう。ワークショップのテーマは何ですか。

自宅に照明器具を取り付ける方法に関してです。当店の多くのお客さまがそのことに興味を持っています。

いいですよ。ただ私は以前、その種のワークショップをしたことがありません。どんな資材が必要になるかよく分からないのです。

心配しないでください。私が全ての資材を準備して、事前にあなたが受け取れるようにします。

38 Where do the speakers most likely work?

(A) At a computer repair shop
(B) At a real estate firm
(C) At a restaurant
(D) At a home improvement store

話し手たちはどこで働いていると考えられますか。

(A) コンピューター修理店
(B) 不動産会社
(C) レストラン
(D) 住宅リフォーム店

正解 D 女性は❶「当店が住宅リフォームに関するワークショップをどのように行っているかは知っているよね」と男性に確認している。また男性は、❹「今月には浴室改装に関する一連のワークショップをやり終える予定だ」と述べているので、話し手たちは住宅リフォーム店で働いていると考えられる。
(A) repair「修理」。
(B) 住宅に関して話しているが、不動産についての言及はない。real estate「不動産」、firm「会社」。

39 What does the man offer to do?

(A) Wait on some customers
(B) Lead a workshop
(C) Take inventory
(D) Arrange a window display

男性は何をすることを申し出ていますか。

(A) 顧客の応対をする。
(B) ワークショップを主導する。
(C) 棚卸しをする。
(D) ショーウインドーの陳列を整える。

正解 B 女性が❷で、来月のワークショップを主導することになっているが、町から離れなくてはならないと説明しているのに対し、男性は、❸「私が代わりにそれをしてもいい」と申し出ている。
(A) wait on ～「〈顧客など〉の応対をする」。
(C) take inventory「棚卸しをする」。
(D) arrange「～を整える」。

40 What does the woman say she will do?

(A) Prepare some materials
(B) Call for transportation
(C) Return some merchandise
(D) Update a sign

女性は何をすると言っていますか。

(A) 資材を準備する。
(B) 乗り物を呼ぶ。
(C) 商品を返品する。
(D) 看板を新しくする。

正解 A ワークショップに必要な資材が分からないと言う男性に対し、女性は❺「私が全ての資材を準備して、事前にあなたが受け取れるようにする」と言っている。よって、get all the materials readyをPrepare some materialsと表している(A)が正解。
(B) call for ～「～を呼ぶ」、transportation「乗り物」。
(C) merchandise「商品」。
(D) update「～を新しくする」、sign「看板」。

Words & Phrases

workshop ワークショップ　improvement リフォーム、改良
be supposed to *do* ～することになっている　lead ～を主導する、～を指導する　it turns out (that) ～ ～であることが分かる
finish up ～ ～をやり終える　a series of ～ 一連の～　remodeling 改装　install ～を取り付ける
light fixture 照明器具　be interested in ～ ～に興味を持っている　material 材料　beforehand 事前に

Questions 41 through 43 refer to the following conversation.

M Hi, Francesca. ❶The graphic designer just sent us some sample logos for our camping company. ❷Since you'll be updating our company's Web site, I wanted to get your opinion on which one would look best.

W Let's see… I like the second one. The image and fonts are really clean, so it'll be easy for me to integrate it into our existing Web site. ❸But I don't like the color.

M I agree. A lot of other companies that make camping gear already use green logos.

W ❹What if we use orange instead?

M Good idea. ❺Let's get the team's opinion during tomorrow's meeting.

問題41-43は次の会話に関するものです。

こんにちは、Francesca。ちょうどグラフィックデザイナーが、うちのキャンプ用品会社のためのロゴ見本を幾つか送ってきました。あなたが当社のウェブサイトを更新することになっているので、どれが一番良さそうか意見を聞きたかったのです。

そうですね…私は2番目のものが好きです。画像とフォントがとても鮮明なので、私にとっては当社の既存ウェブサイトに統合しやすいでしょう。ただ、この色が好きではありません。

私も同意見です。キャンプ用具を製造する他の多くの会社が、すでに緑色のロゴを使用しています。

代わりにオレンジ色を使用したらどうでしょう？

いい考えですね。明日の会議中にチームの意見を聞きましょう。

41 Who most likely is the woman?

(A) A factory supervisor
(B) A Web site designer
(C) A financial planner
(D) A clothing manufacturer

女性は誰だと考えられますか。

(A) 工場の責任者
(B) ウェブサイトのデザイナー
(C) ファイナンシャルプランナー
(D) 衣料品製作者

正解 B 男性は女性に、❶で会社のロゴ見本が送られてきたと伝え、続けて❷「あなたが当社のウェブサイトを更新することになっているので、どれが一番良さそうか意見を聞きたかった」とウェブサイトの更新作業を担当する女性に意見を求めている。よって、女性はウェブサイトのデザイナーだと考えられる。
(A) supervisor「責任者」。
(C) financial「財務の」。
(D) manufacturer「製作者、メーカー」。

42 What does the woman suggest?

(A) Changing a color
(B) Replacing a machine
(C) Hiring a consultant
(D) Lowering a price

女性は何を提案していますか。

(A) 色を変えること。
(B) 機械を交換すること。
(C) コンサルタントを雇用すること。
(D) 価格を下げること。

正解 A 会社のロゴ見本について意見を求められた女性は❸で、ロゴ見本の一つについて色が好きではないと述べ、❹「代わりにオレンジ色を使用してはどうか」と提案している。
(B) 女性が換えることを提案しているのはロゴの色であって、機械ではない。replace「～を交換する」。
(D) lower「～を下げる」。

43 What will happen at tomorrow's meeting?

(A) New team members will be introduced.
(B) A product demonstration will take place.
(C) The speakers will gather feedback.
(D) A budget will be revised.

明日の会議で何が起こりますか。

(A) 新しいチームメンバーが紹介される。
(B) 製品の実演が行われる。
(C) 話し手たちが意見を集める。
(D) 予算が修正される。

正解 C ロゴ見本の色の代わりに、オレンジ色を使うという女性の提案に対し、男性は賛成して、❺「明日の会議中にチームの意見を聞こう」と述べている。このことをgather feedbackと表している(C)が正解。gather「～を集める」、feedback「意見」。
(A) introduce「～を紹介する」。
(B) demonstration「実演、デモ」。
(D) budget「予算」、revise「～を修正する」。

Words & Phrases

graphic designer グラフィックデザイナー　sample 見本　logo ロゴ
update ～を更新する　opinion 意見　image 画像　font フォント(文字の書体・大きさ)　clean 鮮やかな
integrate ～ into … ～を…に統合する　existing 既存の　agree 同意する　gear 用具　instead 代わりに

Questions 44 through 46 refer to the following conversation.

問題44-46は次の会話に関するものです。

W Patrick, do you have a minute? ❶I'm wondering if you could process my travel reimbursement forms.

Patrick、ちょっといいですか。私の旅費の払戻用紙を処理してくれませんか。

M Sure, no problem.

もちろん、問題ありません。

W Great. Just remember... ❷you'll need to make two copies—one for our records and one for me.

良かった。ちょっと覚えておいてほしいのですが…あなたはコピーを2部取る必要があります――1部は記録用で、もう1部は私用にです。

M Oh, thanks. ❸I didn't realize that was necessary.

ああ、ありがとうございます。それが必要だと認識していませんでした。

W Well, you're new here. ❹There's a lot to remember.

そう、あなたはここに来たばかりですね。覚えておくことがたくさんありますよね。

M That's true. By the way, ❺the copier is running low on paper. Can you show me where the supply closet is so I can get some more?

その通りです。ところで、コピー機の用紙が少なくなってきています。もう少し取ってこられるよう、備品収納室の場所を私に教えてもらえますか。

W Sure, I can do that now.

もちろん、今すぐにできますよ。

44 What does the woman want the man to do?

(A) Process some paperwork
(B) Attend a presentation
(C) Draft a proposal
(D) Rearrange a conference room

女性は男性に何をしてほしいと思っていますか。

(A) 書類を処理する。
(B) プレゼンテーションに参加する。
(C) 提案書の草案を書く。
(D) 会議室内の配列を変える。

正解 A 女性は男性に、❶「私の旅費の払戻用紙を処理してくれないか」と頼んでいる。travel reimbursement formsをsome paperworkと表している(A)が正解。
(B) attend「～に参加する」。
(C) draft「～の草案を書く」、proposal「提案(書)」。
(D) rearrange「～の配列を変える、～を並べ替える」、conference「会議」。

45 Why does the woman say, "you're new here"?

(A) To express surprise
(B) To give a compliment
(C) To show understanding
(D) To disagree with a suggestion

女性はなぜ"you're new here"と言っていますか。

(A) 驚きを表すため。
(B) 賛辞を述べるため。
(C) 理解を示すため。
(D) 提案に反対するため。

正解 C ❷でコピーを2部取ると教えてくれた女性に、男性は❸「それが必要だと認識していなかった」と言っている。それに対し、女性は下線部で「あなたはここに来たばかりだ」と述べ、❹「覚えておくことがたくさんある」と続けているので、女性は新人の男性がコピーが必要と認識していなかったことに理解を示していると判断できる。
(A) express「～を表す」。
(B) compliment「賛辞」。
(D) disagree with ～「～に反対する」。

46 What does the man ask about?

(A) Finding some supplies
(B) Delaying some training
(C) Submitting a time sheet
(D) Changing a password

男性は何について尋ねていますか。

(A) 備品を見つけること。
(B) 研修を延期すること。
(C) タイムシートを提出すること。
(D) パスワードを変更すること。

正解 A 男性は❺「コピー機の用紙が少なくなってきている。もう少し取ってこられるよう、備品収納室の場所を私に教えてくれるか」と女性に尋ねている。
(B) delay「～を延期する」、training「研修」。
(C) submit「～を提出する」、time sheet「タイムシート(勤務時間などを記録した用紙)」。

Words & Phrases

process ～を処理する　reimbursement 払い戻し　form 用紙
make a copy コピーを取る　record 記録　realize ～を認識する、～に気付く　copier コピー機
run low on ～ ～が少なくなる　supply 備品　closet 収納室、押し入れ

Questions 47 through 49 refer to the following conversation with three speakers.

問題47-49は3人の話し手による次の会話に関するものです。

W Excuse me, ❶I'm looking for a light jacket—something to keep me warm early in the morning when I go for a jog. It's been chilly the past few days.

すみません、軽いジャケットを探しています——早朝にジョギングに行くときに保温してくれるものです。ここ数日肌寒くて。

M Sure, ❷we have a selection of jackets right here. How about this one?

かしこまりました、ちょうどここにジャケットを取りそろえております。こちらのものはいかがですか。

W I like the style. But… ❸do you happen to have it in another color?

スタイルは好きです。ですが…ひょっとして他の色でこれがありますか。

M Hmm. They just came in today, and there might be more in the stockroom. ❹Hey, Antonio, do we have this jacket in any other colors back there in the stockroom?

うーん。それらは本日入荷したばかりなので、倉庫にはもっとあるかもしれません。なあ、Antonio、そっちの裏の倉庫にこのジャケットが他の色であるかい?

M ❺Yes, we do. It's available in blue and orange.

はい、あります。そちらは、青色とオレンジ色の在庫があります。

W Oh, ❻could I possibly see both?

なるほど、できたら両方とも見せていただけますか。

M Sure, ❼what size do you need?

もちろんです、どのサイズがご入用でしょうか。

47 Where most likely are the speakers?

(A) At a fitness center
(B) At a garden store
(C) At a clothing shop
(D) At a health food store

話し手たちはどこにいると考えられますか。

(A) フィットネスセンター
(B) 園芸店
(C) 衣料品店
(D) 健康食品店

正解 C 女性は❶「軽いジャケットを探している」と男性に声を掛け、続けてジャケットの希望と用途を伝えている。それに対し、1人目の男性は❷「ちょうどここにジャケットを取りそろえている。こちらのものはどうか」とジャケットの1つを女性に勧めている。よって、女性は客で、男性は衣料品店の店員と考えられるので、(C)が正解。

48 What does the woman want to purchase?

(A) Some running shoes
(B) Some organic tea
(C) A membership
(D) A jacket

女性は何を購入したいと思っていますか。

(A) ランニングシューズ
(B) 有機栽培の紅茶
(C) 会員権
(D) ジャケット

正解 D 女性は❶「軽いジャケットを探している」と用件を述べている。その後も女性は、勧められたジャケットについて❸で、他の色がないか尋ねている。purchase「～を購入する」。
(A) 女性は購入品の用途をジョギング用と説明しているが、シューズに言及はしていない。
(B) organic「有機栽培の、オーガニックの」。
(C) membership「会員(権)」。

49 What will Antonio probably do next?

(A) Check merchandise online
(B) Retrieve some items
(C) Call a different location
(D) Apply a discount

Antonioはおそらく次に何をしますか。

(A) 商品をオンラインで確認する。
(B) 幾つかの商品を取り出す。
(C) 別の店舗に電話する。
(D) 割引を適用する。

正解 B 女性に他の色のジャケットがあるか尋ねられた1人目の男性は、❹でAntonioに倉庫にあるか確認し、それに応答した2人目の男性が❺で、「青色とオレンジ色の在庫がある」と答えている。❻の両方を見たいという女性の求めにAntonioは、❼でサイズを尋ねているので、次に女性の希望サイズで両方の色のジャケットを倉庫から取り出すと考えられる。retrieve「～を取り出す」。
(C) location「店舗、場所」。(D) apply「～を適用する」。

Words & Phrases

look for ～ ～を探す　light 軽い、軽装の　go for a jog ジョギングに行く　chilly 肌寒い
selection 品ぞろえ、選択　happen to *do* 〈疑問文で〉ひょっとして～する、〈肯定文で〉偶然～する　come in 〈商品などが〉入荷する
stockroom 倉庫　available 在庫としてある、利用可能な　possibly 〈丁寧な依頼などで〉どうにかして、なんとかして

Questions 50 through 52 refer to the following conversation.

M Hi, Dr. Garcia. ❶That software program you ordered for our medical office just arrived—❷the one that will allow patients to schedule appointments online. Would you like me to install it today?

W Oh, good. Actually, ❸a service technician will be stopping by tomorrow to install it for us. But could you please let our patients know about this new option for making appointments?

M OK. ❹Once the program is ready tomorrow, I'll send an e-mail to our patients that will instruct them on how to use the scheduling system.

問題50-52は次の会話に関するものです。

こんにちは、Garcia医師。ちょうど、当診療所用にあなたが注文したあのソフトウエアプログラムが届きました——患者さんがオンラインで予約を入れるのを可能にするものです。私が今日、それをインストールしましょうか。

ああ、良かった。実は、サービス技術者が明日、当診療所のためにそれをインストールしに立ち寄ることになっています。でも、予約を行うこの新しい手段について、あなたから患者さんに知らせてくれますか。

分かりました。明日、プログラムの準備ができましたら、スケジュールシステムの使用方法について説明するEメールを私が患者さんに送ります。

50 What will the new software allow patients to do?

(A) Schedule appointments
(B) Request a prescription refill
(C) Ask the doctor a question
(D) Write a review

新しいソフトウエアは、患者が何をすることを可能にしますか。

(A) 予約を入れる。
(B) 処方薬の再調剤を依頼する。
(C) 医師に質問する。
(D) レビューを書く。

正解 A 男性は❶で、診療所用に注文したソフトウエアが届いたことを女性に知らせ、続けて❷で、そのソフトウエアについて「患者がオンラインで予約を入れるのを可能にするものだ」と説明している。
(B) prescription「処方（薬）」、refill「再調剤」。
(C) ソフトウエアは医師の女性が注文したとあるが、患者がそのソフトウエアを使って医師に質問できるとは述べられていない。

51 Who will be visiting the office tomorrow?

(A) A sales representative
(B) A service technician
(C) A pharmacist
(D) A building inspector

明日、誰が診療所を訪れることになっていますか。

(A) 営業担当者
(B) サービス技術者
(C) 薬剤師
(D) 建物検査員

正解 B ソフトウエアが届いたという報告を受けた女性は❸「サービス技術者が明日、当診療所のためにそれをインストールしに立ち寄ることになっている」と述べている。
(A) sales representative「営業担当者、販売員」。
(C) pharmacist「薬剤師」。
(D) inspector「検査員」。

52 What will the man include in an e-mail to patients?

(A) A list of specialists' phone numbers
(B) A reminder about required forms
(C) Directions to a new office
(D) Instructions on how to use a system

男性は患者へのEメールに何を含めるつもりですか。

(A) 専門家の電話番号リスト
(B) 必要書類についての通知
(C) 新しい診療所への道順
(D) システムの使用方法に関する説明

正解 D 男性は❹で「明日、プログラムの準備ができたら、スケジュールシステムの使用方法について説明するEメールを私が患者に送る」と言っている。include「～を含める」。instruction「説明、指示」。
(A) specialist「専門家」。
(B) reminder「〈思い出させるための〉通知」、required「必要な」、form「用紙」。
(C) directions「道順」。

Words & Phrases

order ～を注文する　medical office 診療所　arrive 届く、到着する
allow ～ to *do* ～が…することを可能にする　patient 患者　appointment 〈医師などとの〉予約
install ～をインストールする、～を設置する　technician 技術者　stop by 立ち寄る　option 選ぶべき手段、選択肢
once いったん～すると、～するやいなや　ready 準備された　instruct ～に教える、～に指示する

Questions 53 through 55 refer to the following conversation.

問題53-55は次の会話に関するものです。

W Welcome to the post office.

郵便局へようこそ。

M Hi. ❶I want to send this package to a colleague in London, and it needs to arrive within four days. ❷I guess I need to use express mail.

こんにちは。ロンドンの同僚にこの小包を送りたいのですが、4日以内に届く必要があるんです。速達郵便を利用しなければならないですよね。

W Well, <u>regular mail takes three or four days</u>.

ええと、<u>普通郵便にかかるのは3、4日ですよ</u>。

M Really? But ❸with regular mail can I get confirmation that the package arrived?

本当ですか。でも、普通郵便で私は、小包が届いたという確認通知を受け取ることはできますか。

W Well, ❹for an extra fee you can have your colleague in London sign for the package and you'll get an e-mail confirming that it's arrived.

そうですね、追加料金でロンドンのあなたの同僚の方に小包の受け取りの際に署名していただくことが可能で、あなたはそれが届いたことを知らせるEメールを受け取ることになります。

M Thanks. I'll do that then.

ありがとう。それなら、私はそのようにします。

53 Why is the man at the post office?

(A) To mail a package
(B) To buy some stamps
(C) To apply for a job
(D) To pick up some documents

男性はなぜ郵便局にいるのですか。

(A) 小包を郵送するため。
(B) 切手を購入するため。
(C) 職に応募するため。
(D) 書類を受け取るため。

正解 A 男性は❶「ロンドンの同僚にこの小包を送りたいのだが、4日以内に届く必要がある」と用件を述べ、続けて❷で、速達郵便を利用しなければならないと考えていることを伝えている。❶のsend this packageをmail a packageと表している(A)が正解。mail「～を郵送する」。
(C) apply for ～「～に応募する」。
(D) pick up ～「～を受け取る、～を入手する」、document「書類」。

54 Why does the woman say, "<u>regular mail takes three or four days</u>"?

(A) To offer an apology
(B) To express disappointment
(C) To explain a refund policy
(D) To correct a misunderstanding

女性はなぜ"<u>regular mail takes three or four days</u>"と言っていますか。

(A) 謝罪をするため。
(B) 失望を表すため。
(C) 返金方針を説明するため。
(D) 誤解を正すため。

正解 D 荷物を4日以内に届ける必要のある男性は、❷「速達郵便を利用しなければならないですよね」と確かめている。それに対し、女性は下線部で「普通郵便にかかるのは3、4日だ」と言っているので、女性は男性の誤解を正して、普通郵便でも4日以内に荷物を届けることができると伝えていると考えられる。correct「～を正す」、misunderstanding「誤解」。
(A) offer an apology「謝罪をする」。
(B) disappointment「失望」。
(C) refund「返金」、policy「方針」。

55 What will the man pay an additional fee for?

(A) Packaging materials
(B) Insurance
(C) A passport photo
(D) A confirmation notice

男性は何のために追加料金を支払いますか。

(A) 梱包材
(B) 保険
(C) パスポート写真
(D) 確認通知

正解 D ❸で、普通郵便で小包の受領確認ができるか尋ねる男性に対し、女性は❹「追加料金でロンドンのあなたの同僚に小包の受け取りの際に署名してもらうことが可能で、あなたはそれが届いたことを知らせるEメールを受け取る」と述べている。additional「追加の」。notice「通知」。
(A) packaging「梱包」、material「材料」。
(B) insurance「保険」。

Words & Phrases

post office 郵便局　package 小包　colleague 同僚　arrive 届く　within ～以内に
express mail 速達郵便　regular mail 普通郵便　confirmation 確認通知　extra fee 追加料金
sign for ～ ～を署名して受け取る　confirm that ～ ～ということを裏づける

Questions 56 through 58 refer to the following conversation with three speakers.

W Hi, Mr. Darren. I'm Jean Potter, and this is Shirley Olson. We're engineers here at Shellner Motors.

M ❶Thanks for agreeing to this interview. ❷The magazine I work for has assigned me to write an article on self-parking cars, and your company's the leader in this field. So, how does it work?

W ❸We're constantly improving the technology, but essentially what happens is the driver positions the car, sensors scan the parking space, and the car moves into that space.

M Wow—❹could you give me a demonstration so I can include some photos in the article?

W Sure—❺we have a car right outside. You can watch it park on its own.

問題56-58は3人の話し手による次の会話に関するものです。

どうもDarrenさん。私はJean Potter、こちらはShirley Olsonです。私たちはここShellner自動車社のエンジニアです。

このインタビューに応じていただきありがとうございます。私は仕事を受けている雑誌から、自動駐車式の車に関する記事を書くことを任されておりまして、御社はその分野の先導者です。さて、それはどのような仕組みなのでしょうか。

私たちは常にその技術を向上させていますが、基本的に何が起こるかというと、運転手が車の位置を定めると、センサーが駐車スペースを検知し、車がそのスペースに移動するのです。

すごい——記事に何枚か写真を掲載できるよう、実演をしていただけますか。

もちろんです——車はすぐ外にあります。それが独力で駐車するのをご覧になれますよ。

56 Who is the man?

(A) A journalist
(B) A taxi driver
(C) A laboratory assistant
(D) A parking garage attendant

男性は誰ですか。

(A) ジャーナリスト
(B) タクシー運転手
(C) 研究所の助手
(D) 駐車場の係員

正解 A 男性は❶で、インタビューに応じてくれたことに対し女性たちに感謝を述べている。続けて❷「私は仕事を受けている雑誌から、自動駐車式の車に関する記事を書くことを任されている」と言っている。
(C) laboratory「研究所」、assistant「助手」。
(D) 駐車スペースに言及はあるが、自動駐車の仕組みの説明として述べられている。parking garage「駐車場」、attendant「係員」。

57 What are the speakers mainly discussing?

(A) Updates to environmental regulations
(B) Effective magazine advertisements
(C) Self-parking technology for vehicles
(D) Cost estimates for a new project

話し手たちは主に何について話し合っていますか。

(A) 環境規制の最新情報
(B) 効果的な雑誌広告
(C) 車の自動駐車技術
(D) 新しいプロジェクトの費用見積もり

正解 C Shellner自動車社のエンジニアと言う女性たちに対し、男性は❷で、自動駐車式の車に関する記事を書くと伝え、その仕組みを尋ねている。女性はそれに応じて、❸で自動駐車の仕組みを説明している。vehicle「車、乗り物」。
(A) update「最新情報、更新」、environmental「環境の」、regulation「規制」。
(B) effective「効果的な」。
(D) estimate「見積もり」。

58 What will the man most likely do next?

(A) Fill out an insurance form
(B) Read an instruction manual
(C) Complete a purchase
(D) Watch a demonstration

男性は次に何をすると考えられますか。

(A) 保険用紙に記入する。
(B) 取扱説明書を読む。
(C) 購入を完了する。
(D) 実演を見る。

正解 D 自動駐車の仕組みを聞いた男性は、❹で記事に掲載する写真を撮るために実演を頼んでいる。了承した女性は❺「車はすぐ外にある。それが独力で駐車するのを見られる」と述べている。よって、男性は次にこの車の実演を見ると考えられる。
(A) fill out ～「～に記入する」、insurance「保険」。
(B) instruction manual「取扱説明書」。

Words & Phrases

agree to ～ ～に応じる、～に同意する　assign ～ to *do* ～に…することを任せる
self-parking 自動駐車式の　leader 先導者　field 分野　constantly 常に　improve ～を向上させる
essentially 基本的には　happen 起こる、生じる　position ～の位置を定める　sensor センサー
scan 〈電子機器などが〉～を検知する　demonstration 実演、デモ　on *one's* own 独力で

Questions 59 through 61 refer to the following conversation.

M Hey, Jo-Ellen. ❶I'm filling out the form for the supply order for our store. ❷I'm ordering new shelves for our home improvement section. Do we need anything else?

W Let's see… We're running low on plastic shopping bags. Can you add them to the supply order?

M You know, ❸I'm worried that we've been using too many plastic bags in our store…

W I've thought about that. ❹Why don't we offer a discount to customers who bring their own bags? That'll be good for the environment, and our store will save money, too!

問題59-61は次の会話に関するものです。

ねえ、Jo-Ellen。うちの店の補給品の注文用紙に記入しているところなんだ。僕は住宅リフォームコーナー用に新しい棚を注文するよ。何か他に必要なものはある？

そうね…。ビニールのレジ袋が少なくなっているわ。補給品の注文にそれを追加してくれる？

あの、うちの店ではビニール袋をたくさん使い過ぎていると、僕は心配しているんだ…。

私はそのことについて考えていたの。自分のバッグを持ってくるお客さまには割引を提供してはどうかしら？ そうすれば環境に良いだろうし、うちの店もお金を節約できるでしょう。

59 What is the man doing?

(A) Preparing an order form
(B) Putting labels on merchandise
(C) Checking employee time sheets
(D) Reading customer reviews

男性は何をしていますか。

(A) 注文用紙を準備している。
(B) 商品にラベルを貼っている。
(C) 従業員タイムシートを確認している。
(D) 顧客レビューを読んでいる。

正解 A 男性は❶「うちの店の補給品の注文用紙に記入しているところだ」と述べ、続けて❷で、自分が新しい棚を注文するが、他に必要なものがあるか女性に尋ねている。
(B) label「ラベル」。
(D) 顧客への言及はあるが、レビューについては述べられていない。review「レビュー、評価」。

60 Why does the man say he is worried?

(A) Too many products have been returned.
(B) Too many plastic bags are being used.
(C) A competing business has recently opened.
(D) An entrance is blocked by construction.

男性はなぜ心配していると言っていますか。

(A) あまりにも多くの製品が返品されたから。
(B) あまりにも多くのビニール袋が使用されているから。
(C) 最近、競合店がオープンしたから。
(D) 入り口が工事でふさがれているから。

正解 B 在庫が減ったビニールのレジ袋を注文するよう、女性から頼まれた男性は、❸「うちの店ではビニール袋をたくさん使い過ぎていると、僕は心配している」と述べている。
(A) return「～を返品する」。
(C) compete「競合する」。
(D) block「～をふさぐ」、construction「工事」。

61 What does the woman suggest doing?

(A) Changing business hours
(B) Starting a delivery service
(C) Hiring more staff
(D) Offering a discount

女性は何をすることを提案していますか。

(A) 営業時間を変更すること。
(B) 配達サービスを開始すること。
(C) もっと多数のスタッフを雇用すること。
(D) 割引を提供すること。

正解 D ❸で、店がビニール袋を使い過ぎていると心配する男性に対し、女性はそのことを考えていたと述べ、続けて❹「自分のバッグを持ってくる客には割引を提供してはどうか」と提案している。
(A) business hours「営業時間」。
(B) delivery「配達」。
(C) hire「～を雇用する」。

Words & Phrases

fill out ～ ～に記入する　supply 補給品、必需品　order 〈名詞で〉注文、〈動詞で〉～を注文する
shelf 棚　improvement リフォーム、改良　section 区画　else 他に　run low on ～ ～が少なくなる
plastic ビニール製の　shopping bag レジ袋、買い物袋　add ～ to … ～を…に加える
be worried (that) ～ ～を心配している　customer 顧客　environment 環境　save ～を節約する

Questions 62 through 64 refer to the following conversation and calendar.

問題62-64は次の会話と日程表に関するものです。

M Noriko, our new hires are doing well. ❶But there were a few mistakes in the database entries. ❷They might need some extra training on data entry.

Noriko、新入社員たちはよくやってくれていますね。ただ、データベース入力に数カ所ミスがありました。彼らはデータ入力に関して追加の研修が必要かもしれません。

W I have to go to a business conference this week. ❸But I'll make sure to schedule some training for the day after the conference.

私は今週、ビジネス協議会に行かなくてはならないのです。でも、私は必ず研修を協議会の翌日に予定するつもりです。

M Great. That'll definitely help them. Let me know if you'll need any equipment for the session.

素晴らしい。それは間違いなく彼らに役立つでしょう。研修会に何か機器が必要であれば、私に知らせてください。

W Actually, ❹could you reserve a projector for me? ❺Since I'll be in Singapore the day before, I won't have time to reserve it in advance.

実は、私のためにプロジェクターを1台予約してくださいませんか。その前日に私はシンガポールにいるでしょうから、事前にそれを予約しておく時間がないのです。

Mon 12	Brainstorming Meeting—2 P.M.
Tues 13	Client Consultation—10 A.M.
Wed 14	
Thurs 15	Singapore Conference
Fri 16	

月曜日 12日	ブレーンストーミング会議 —— 午後2時
火曜日 13日	顧客相談 —— 午前10時
水曜日 14日	
木曜日 15日	シンガポールの協議会
金曜日 16日	

62 What problem does the man point out?

(A) Some software needs to be updated.
(B) Some data were entered incorrectly.
(C) A conference room was not available.
(D) A project's due date needs to be extended.

男性はどんな問題を指摘していますか。

(A) 更新が必要なソフトウエアがある。
(B) 間違って入力されたデータがあった。
(C) 会議室が利用できなかった。
(D) プロジェクトの期日を延期する必要がある。

正解 B 男性は新入社員について、よくやっていると述べた後、❶「ただ、データベース入力に数カ所ミスがあった」と問題を指摘している。さらに新入社員について❷で、データ入力に関する追加研修が必要かもしれないと付け加えている。point out ～「～を指摘する」。enter「～を入力する」、incorrectly「間違って」。
(A) update「～を更新する」。
(C) available「利用できる」。
(D) due date「期日」、extend「～を延期する」。

---

63 Look at the graphic. What day will the woman most likely conduct the training?

(A) Monday
(B) Wednesday
(C) Thursday
(D) Friday

図を見てください。女性は何曜日に研修を行うと考えられますか。

(A) 月曜日
(B) 水曜日
(C) 木曜日
(D) 金曜日

正解 D 新入社員への追加研修が必要だと聞いた女性は、今週は協議会に行かなくてはならないと説明した後、❸「でも、私は必ず研修を協議会の翌日に予定するつもりだ」と男性に伝えている。また、女性は❺で、研修会の前日に自分はシンガポールにいるだろうと述べている。図を見ると、シンガポールの協議会があるのは木曜日。よって、女性はその翌日の金曜日に研修を行うと考えられる。conduct「～を行う」。

---

64 What does the woman ask the man to do?

(A) Contact a colleague
(B) Conduct an inspection
(C) E-mail some candidates
(D) Reserve some equipment

女性は男性に何をするよう求めていますか。

(A) 同僚に連絡する。
(B) 検査を行う。
(C) 何名かの候補者にEメールを送る。
(D) 機器を予約する。

正解 D 研修会に必要な機器があれば知らせるよう申し出た男性に対し、女性は❹「私のためにプロジェクターを1台予約してくれないか」と頼んでいる。この依頼をreserve some equipmentと表している(D)が正解。
(B) inspection「検査」。
(C) candidate「候補者」。

Words & Phrases

new hire 新入社員　mistake ミス　database entry データベース入力　extra 追加の　training 研修
conference 協議会、会議　make sure to *do* 必ず～するようにする　schedule ～ for … ～を…に予定する
definitely 間違いなく　equipment 機器　session 会合、セッション　reserve ～ for … …のために～を予約する
projector プロジェクター　in advance 事前に

日程表 brainstorming ブレーンストーミング　consultation 相談、協議

Questions 65 through 67 refer to the following conversation and map.

問題65-67は次の会話と地図に関するものです。

M Hi, Kate. ❶Would you be interested in helping me staff our table at the craft festival next Saturday? Our store sponsors the event, so ❷we get a booth in the sponsor's section to distribute promotional materials.

やあ、Kate。今度の土曜日の工芸祭で、うちのテーブルのスタッフとして手伝うことに興味はありますか。うちの店がその催しを後援しているので、スポンサーの区画にブースをもらっていて、販売促進用の資料を配布するんです。

W Of course! ❸What do I need to do?

もちろんです。私は何をする必要がありますか。

M ❹We've been assigned to booth number three. Here—it's on this map. I'll be there at nine o'clock to set up.

私たちには番号3のブースが割り当てられています。ここです——この地図にあります。私は準備のため9時にそこに行くつもりです。

W Thanks. ❺I can meet you there at nine o'clock.

ありがとう。9時にそこであなたと会えますよ。

M Sounds good. ❻Be sure to pick up your ID badge at the entrance before you come to our booth.

いいですね。うちのブースに来る前に、必ず入り口で自分のIDバッジを受け取ってください。

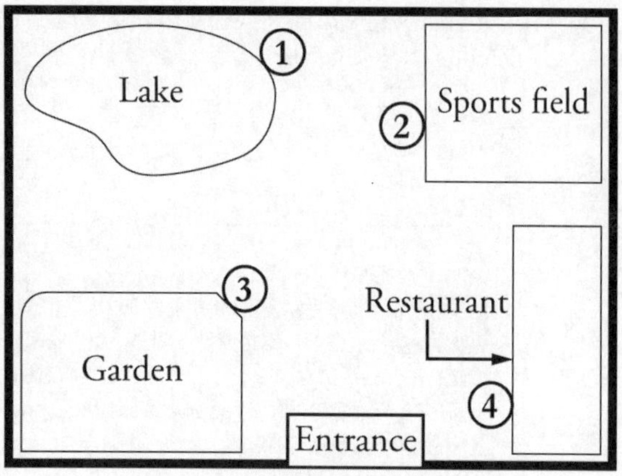

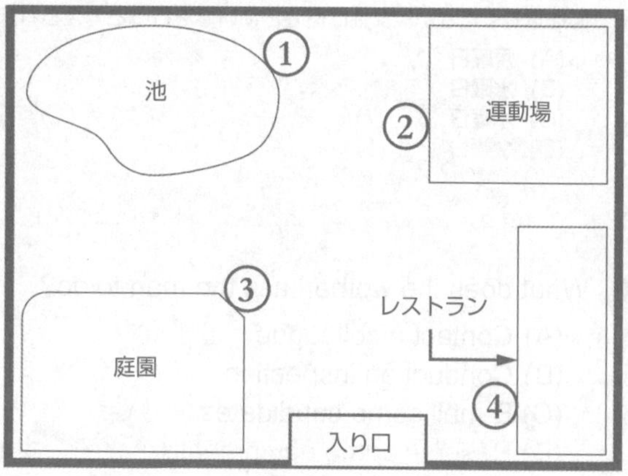

65 What are the speakers mainly discussing?

(A) Competing in a sports competition
(B) Planning a grand opening
(C) Attending an award ceremony
(D) Helping at a local festival

話し手たちは主に何について話し合っていますか。

(A) スポーツの競技会に参加すること。
(B) グランドオープンを企画すること。
(C) 授賞式に出席すること。
(D) 地元の催しで手伝うこと。

正解 D 男性は❶「今度の土曜日の工芸祭で、うちのテーブルのスタッフとして手伝うことに興味はあるか」と女性に尋ね、続けて❷で自分たちの店がブースで販売促進用の資料を配布すると伝えている。その誘いを了承した女性は、❸で自分がすることを尋ね、以降も話し手たちは、催しの手伝いについて話し合っている。local「地元の」。
(A) compete in ～「〈競技など〉に参加する」、competition「競技会」。
(C) award「賞」、ceremony「式典」。

---

66 Look at the graphic. Where will the woman meet her coworker?

(A) By the lake
(B) By the sports field
(C) By the garden
(D) By the restaurant

図を見てください。女性はどこで自分の同僚に会いますか。

(A) 池のそば
(B) 運動場のそば
(C) 庭園のそば
(D) レストランのそば

正解 C 催しでの手伝いを了承した女性に、男性が❹で、自分たちには番号3のブースが割り当てられていると述べ、その位置を地図上で示し、9時にそこに行く予定を伝えている。それに対し、女性は❺「9時にそこであなたと会える」と述べている。図を見ると、3番の番号が振られているのは庭園の近くなので、(C)が正解。coworker「同僚」。

---

67 According to the man, what should the woman pick up?

(A) Some brochures
(B) A training manual
(C) An identification badge
(D) Some refreshments

男性によると、女性は何を受け取るべきですか。

(A) パンフレット
(B) 研修マニュアル
(C) IDバッジ
(D) 軽食

正解 C 催しの手伝いをするため、9時にブースに行く意志を述べた女性に対し男性は、❻「うちのブースに来る前に、必ず入り口で自分のIDバッジを受け取ってください」と伝えている。
(A) 男性は販売促進用の資料に言及はしているが、女性にそれを受け取るよう伝えてはいない。brochure「パンフレット」。
(D) refreshments「軽食」。

Words & Phrases

be interested in ～ ～に興味がある　staff ～のスタッフを務める　craft 工芸　festival 祭、催し
sponsor 〈動詞で〉～を後援する、〈名詞で〉スポンサー　booth ブース　distribute ～を配布する
promotional 販売促進用の　material 資料　assign ～ to … ～に…を割り当てる　set up 準備する、据え付ける
sound ～のように思われる　be sure to *do* 必ず～する　pick up ～ ～を受け取る　ID 〈identificationの略で〉身元証明書
badge バッジ　entrance 入り口

地図　lake 池、湖　sports field 運動場

Questions 68 through 70 refer to the following conversation and pie chart.

問題68-70は次の会話と円グラフに関するものです。

W Hi, Paul. We need to discuss the budget before we present it at tomorrow's meeting with the company president. ❶Look what percentage of our expenses go to rent! I think we should suggest downsizing. I looked online at some office spaces, and ❷we could easily cut our rent expenses by five percent.

こんにちは、Paul。明日の社長との会議で予算案を提示する前に、私たちはそれについて話し合う必要があります。当社の経費のうちどのくらいの割合が賃料に回されているか見てください。私たちはスリム化を提案すべきだと思います。私がオンラインで幾つかのオフィススペースを調べたところ、当社は容易に賃料経費を5パーセント削減できる可能性があります。

M ❸That's a good point. Plus, ❹many employees have started to work remotely from their homes, so we really don't need an office this size any more.

いいことを言ってくれました。それに、多くの従業員が離れて家から勤務をし始めているので、もはやこの規模のオフィスは実際には必要ありません。

W I'm glad that you agree. ❺Why don't we adjust the presentation for tomorrow's meeting to include more information about this idea?

同意してくれてうれしいです。明日の会議向けのプレゼンテーションを調整して、この案に関する情報をもっと含めてはどうでしょうか。

M ❻Sounds good.

いいですね。

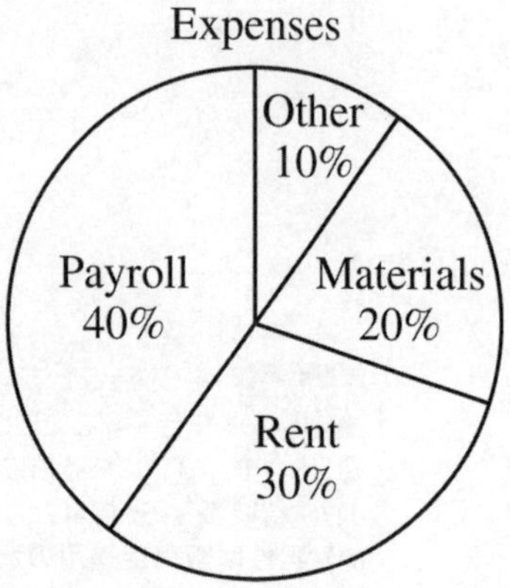

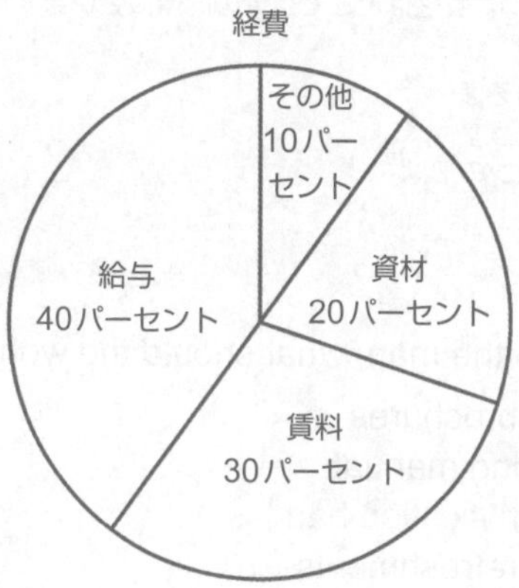

68 Look at the graphic. Which percentage do the speakers hope to reduce?

(A) 10%
(B) 20%
(C) 30%
(D) 40%

図を見てください。話し手たちはどの割合を削減することを望んでいますか。

(A) 10パーセント
(B) 20パーセント
(C) 30パーセント
(D) 40パーセント

正解 C 予算案について話し合う必要性を挙げた女性は❶で、賃料が経費の多くを占めていることを指摘し、スリム化を提案すべきだと主張している。さらに女性が、❷「当社は容易に賃料経費を5パーセント削減できる可能性がある」と述べているのに対し、男性は❸で同意している。図を見ると、Rent「賃料」は経費の30パーセントを占めているので(C)が正解。hope to *do*「～することを望む」、reduce「～を削減する」。

69 According to the man, what has changed at the company?

(A) Many employees now work from home.
(B) Several products are not selling well.
(C) The company is expanding into a new market.
(D) The company has updated its hiring policy.

男性によると、会社で何が変わりましたか。

(A) 多くの従業員が現在、在宅勤務をする。
(B) 幾つかの製品の売り上げがあまりよくない。
(C) 会社は新たな市場へ進出しようとしている。
(D) 会社は雇用方針を改訂した。

正解 A 会社の賃料経費の削減に関する提案を聞いた男性は、その案に同意し、❹「多くの従業員が離れて家から勤務をし始めている」と言っている。work from home「在宅勤務する」。
(C) expand into ～「～に進出する」。
(D) update「～を改訂して最新のものにする」、hiring「雇用の」。

70 What will the speakers do next?

(A) Update a presentation
(B) Speak with a consultant
(C) Check some inventory
(D) Make some travel reservations

話し手たちは次に何をしますか。

(A) プレゼンテーションを最新のものにする。
(B) コンサルタントと話をする。
(C) 在庫を確認する。
(D) 旅行の予約をする。

正解 A 賃料経費を削減する案について、女性が❺「明日の会議向けのプレゼンテーションを調整して、この案に関する情報をもっと含めてはどうか」と提案したのに対し、男性は❻で同意している。よって、話し手たちは次にプレゼンテーションを改訂して最新のものにすると考えられる。update「～を改訂して最新のものにする」。
(C) inventory「在庫」。
(D) reservation「予約」。

Words & Phrases

pie chart 円グラフ　budget 予算(案)　present ～を提示する　president 社長　percentage 割合
expense 経費、費用　rent 賃料、家賃　downsizing スリム化、経営合理化　look at ～ ～を調べる　easily 容易に
cut ～ by … ～を…削減する　That's a good point. 良いことを言ってくれた。　plus それに、加えて　employee 従業員
remotely 遠く離れて　agree 同意する　adjust ～を調整する　presentation プレゼンテーション、提示の仕方

円グラフ payroll 給与

トーク CD 2 63　問題 CD 2 64

Questions 71 through 73 refer to the following news report.

M

In local news, ❶we have a report from the Pine Brook Community Center, where activities are underway to plant a vegetable garden. ❷The project was started by Jessica Plank, the director of the center. Ms. Plank has been recognized for her work at the center before. ❸Just last month, she was honored for her commitment to community service at the town's outstanding citizens' awards ceremony. ❹All of the gardening tools for the project were donated by the Endo Company, one of the area's largest landscaping firms.

問題71-73は次のニュース報道に関するものです。

地方ニュースです。Pine Brookコミュニティーセンターからの報告で、そこでは菜園の種まき活動が進行中とのことです。そのプロジェクトは、センター長であるJessica Plankによって着手されました。Plankさんは以前、同センターでの自身の業績で表彰されたことがあります。ちょうど先月、優秀住民賞の町の表彰式で、彼女は地域奉仕活動への献身を称えられました。プロジェクトのための園芸用具は全て、地域大手の造園会社の一つであるEndo社によって寄贈されました。

71 Where does Jessica Plank work?

(A) At a community center
(B) At a radio station
(C) At a park
(D) At a restaurant

Jessica Plankはどこで働いていますか。

(A) コミュニティーセンター
(B) ラジオ放送局
(C) 公園
(D) レストラン

正解 A　話し手は❶で、Pine Brookコミュニティーセンターの菜園の種まき活動が進行中だと伝え、続けて❷「そのプロジェクトは、センター長であるJessica Plankによって着手された」と述べている。よって、Jessica Plankはコミュニティーセンターで働いていると分かる。
(B) radio station「ラジオ放送局」。

72 What took place last month?

(A) A store opening
(B) A job fair
(C) A landscaping contest
(D) An awards ceremony

先月、何が行われましたか。

(A) 店舗の開店
(B) 就職フェア
(C) 造園コンテスト
(D) 表彰式

正解 D　話し手は、Plankさんがセンターでの業績で表彰されたことがあると述べてから、❸「ちょうど先月、優秀住民賞の町の表彰式で、彼女は地域奉仕活動への献身を称えられた」と言っている。
(B) job fair「就職フェア」。
(C) 造園会社についての言及はあるが、造園コンテストについては述べられていない。

73 What did the Endo Company do?

(A) It started an internship program.
(B) It donated some tools.
(C) It created a new slogan.
(D) It opened a second location.

Endo社は何をしましたか。

(A) 同社はインターンシッププログラムを開始した。
(B) 同社は幾つかの用具を寄贈した。
(C) 同社は新しいスローガンを作った。
(D) 同社は2店舗目を開店した。

正解 B　話し手はコミュニティーセンターの菜園の種まき活動について、❹「プロジェクトのための園芸用具は全て、地域大手の造園会社の一つであるEndo社によって寄贈された」と述べている。
(A) internship「インターンシップ」。
(C) slogan「スローガン」。
(D) location「店舗、所在地」。

Words & Phrases

local 地方の　activity 活動　underway 進行中で　plant ～に種をまく、～に植え付ける　vegetable garden 菜園　director 所長　recognize ～を表彰する、～を認める　honor ～を称える　commitment 献身　community service 地域奉仕活動　outstanding 優れた　citizen 住民、市民　awards ceremony 表彰式　gardening 園芸　tool 用具、道具　donate ～を寄贈する　landscaping 造園　firm 会社

Questions 74 through 76 refer to the following advertisement. 問題74-76は次の広告に関するものです。

W

❶Come visit the new Regent Teahouse in Harden Mall. Get your favorite teas from all corners of the world. ❷We stock black tea, white tea, green tea, and every kind of fruit tea you can imagine. ❸To celebrate our grand opening, we're giving all customers a free teapot, which can be used to brew our delicious teas. And ❹don't forget to enroll in our customer loyalty program—you'll start earning benefits with your first purchase. Registration takes five minutes and ❺can be completed at the customer service desk.

Harden商店街にある、Regentティーハウスの新店にお越しください。世界の全ての地域からあなたのお好きなお茶を手に入れましょう。当店では、紅茶、白茶、緑茶、そして想像し得る限りのあらゆる種類のフルーツティーを取りそろえております。当店のグランドオープンを記念し、全てのお客さまに無料のティーポットを差し上げており、それは当店のおいしいお茶を入れるのにお使いいただけます。そして、当店のお得意さまプログラムに登録するのを忘れないでください——初回のご購入から特典を得られるようになります。登録にかかるのは5分で、お客さまサービスデスクにて完了することができます。

74 What does the speaker emphasize about the company's products?

(A) They are high quality.
(B) They are locally produced.
(C) Gift sets can be purchased online.
(D) A wide selection is available.

話し手は、会社の製品について何を強調していますか。

(A) それらは高品質である。
(B) それらは地元で生産されている。
(C) ギフトセットはオンラインで購入可能である。
(D) 幅広い品ぞろえがある。

正解 D 話し手は❶で、「Regentティーハウスを訪れて世界の全ての地域から好きなお茶を手に入れよう」と呼び掛けた後、❷「当店では、紅茶、白茶、緑茶、そして想像し得る限りのあらゆる種類のフルーツティーを取りそろえている」と店舗の幅広い品ぞろえを強調している。emphasize「～を強調する」。wide「幅広い」、selection「品ぞろえ、選択肢」、available「手元にある、在庫の」。
(A) quality「品質」。
(B) locally「地元で」。

75 What does the speaker say all customers will receive?

(A) A gift card
(B) A teapot
(C) Product samples
(D) Overnight delivery

話し手は、全ての顧客が何を受け取ると言っていますか。

(A) ギフトカード
(B) ティーポット
(C) 製品サンプル
(D) 翌日配達

正解 B 話し手は、❸「当店のグランドオープンを記念し、全てのお客さまに無料のティーポットを差し上げている」と述べている。
(D) overnight delivery「翌日配達」。

76 Why does the speaker say, "Registration takes five minutes"?

(A) To encourage participation in a program
(B) To apologize for a delay
(C) To volunteer to assist customers
(D) To invite customers to take a break

話し手はなぜ "Registration takes five minutes" と言っていますか。

(A) プログラムへの参加を促すため。
(B) 遅延したことを謝罪するため。
(C) 進んで顧客を手伝うと申し出るため。
(D) 顧客に休憩するよう勧めるため。

正解 A 話し手は❹で、当店のお得意さまプログラムに登録すると初回の購入から特典を得られると述べている。続けて、下線部で「登録にかかるのは5分だ」と手続きにかかる時間の短さを強調し、さらに❺で、お客さまサービスデスクで完了できると案内しているので、プログラムへの参加を促していると考えられる。encourage「～を促す」、participation「参加」。
(C) volunteer to *do*「進んで～しようと申し出る」。
(D) invite ～ to *do*「～に…するよう勧める」。

Words & Phrases

mall 商店街、モール　corner 地域　stock 〈商品〉を店に置く　black tea 紅茶
imagine ～を想像する　celebrate ～を記念する、～を祝う　grand opening グランドオープン、開店記念
teapot ティーポット　brew 〈お茶など〉を入れる　enroll in ～ ～に登録する
loyalty program 〈顧客をつなぎとめるためのポイントカードなどの〉お得意さまプログラム　earn ～を得る、～を受ける
benefit 特典、利点　complete ～を完了する

Questions 77 through 79 refer to the following announcement. 問題77-79は次のお知らせに関するものです。

W

All right, let's start our staff meeting. I met with the executive board yesterday, and after a lot of consideration, ❶they've decided to move our branch of Summerton Bank to a busier area of town in the spring. Our branch has been struggling for quite a while to attract new customers. ❷Our location on the edge of town is just too far away from people's homes and jobs. ❸We're not moving until spring, but we want to get the information out now. ❹Flyers will be mailed to all of our current customers to announce the change, but we'll also need you to hand them out to customers when they come in.

それでは、スタッフ会議を始めましょう。昨日、取締役会と会談したのですが、十分な検討の結果、彼らは春にSummerton銀行の当支店を町のもっと人通りの多い区域に移転させると決定しました。当支店は新規顧客を呼び込もうと、かなり長い間奮闘し続けてきました。町の外れにある当支店は、人々の家や職場から実に遠すぎるのです。われわれは春まで移転はしませんが、今から情報を外に発信したいと思います。この変更をお知らせするために、現在のお客さま全員にチラシが郵送されることになりますが、お客さまがご来行された際、あなた方からそれらをお客さまに配布してもらう必要もあるでしょう。

77 Where do the listeners most likely work?

(A) At a supermarket
(B) At a real estate agency
(C) At a bank
(D) At a print shop

聞き手はどこで働いていると考えられますか。

(A) スーパーマーケット
(B) 不動産会社
(C) 銀行
(D) 印刷店

正解 C 話し手は、スタッフ会議を始めようと呼び掛けてから、❶で昨日の取締役会との会談でSummerton銀行の当支店をもっと人通りの多い区域に移転させる決定がされたと伝えている。よって、聞き手は銀行に勤めていると判断できる。
(B) 移転について言及しているが、不動産会社だとは述べていない。

78 What is the speaker's announcement mainly about?

(A) A business relocation
(B) A sales promotion
(C) A budget cut
(D) A change in ownership

話し手のお知らせは、主に何についてですか。

(A) 店舗の移転
(B) 販売促進
(C) 予算の削減
(D) 所有権の変更

正解 A ❶で、取締役会が当支店の移転を決定したと伝えた話し手は、❷で現在は支店が町の外れにあるという移転理由に触れ、以降も顧客に移転を知らせる方法について言及している。よって、お知らせは主に店舗の移転についてだと分かる。relocation「移転」。
(D) ownership「所有権」。

79 What are the listeners asked to do?

(A) Adjust their work hours
(B) Participate in a staff training
(C) Renew an employment contract
(D) Pass out some informational flyers

聞き手は何をするよう求められていますか。

(A) 勤務時間を調整する。
(B) スタッフ研修に参加する。
(C) 雇用契約を更新する。
(D) 情報提供のチラシを配布する。

正解 D 話し手は聞き手に対し、❸「春まで移転はしないが、今から情報を外に発信したい」と述べ、❹「この変更を知らせるために、現在の顧客全員にチラシが郵送されることになるが、顧客が来行する際、あなた方からそれらを顧客に配布してもらう必要もあるだろう」と聞き手にチラシの配布を求めている。pass out ～「～を配布する」、informational「情報を提供する、情報の」。
(B) participate in ～「～に参加する」。
(C) renew「～を更新する」、employment「雇用」。

Words & Phrases

meet with ～ ～と会談する、(約束して)～と会う　executive board 取締役会
consideration 検討　move ～を移転させる　branch 支店　busy 人通りの多い、繁華な
struggle to *do* ～しようと奮闘する　for quite a while かなり長い間　attract ～を呼び込む　location 所在地、場所
edge 外れ、端　flyer チラシ　mail ～を郵送する　current 現在の　announce ～を知らせる
hand out ～ ～を配布する

Questions 80 through 82 refer to the following telephone message.

問題80-82は次の電話のメッセージに関するものです。

W

Hi, ❶this message is for Ms. Park of the *Glenn City Times*. This is Donna Silver calling from the Department of Agriculture. ❷I understand you're writing a newspaper article about farm production in the region and that you'd like to get a copy of our quarterly report. There's still some data in the report we're waiting to confirm. ❸In the meantime, I'd be happy to discuss any specific questions you have. ❹It's probably best to communicate by e-mail, as I'll be traveling for work next week.

こんにちは、*Glenn City Times*紙のParkさんへの伝言です。農業局のDonna Silverがお電話しています。私は、あなたが当地域の農産物に関する新聞記事を執筆されていて、当局の四半期報告書を1部ご希望だと承知しております。報告書には、まだ当局で確認待ちのデータが幾つかございます。それまでの間、具体的なご質問がありましたら何でも喜んで伺います。私は来週出張することになるので、おそらくEメールで連絡を取り合うのが最善でしょう。

80 Who is the message intended for?

(A) A farmworker
(B) A lawyer
(C) A journalist
(D) A supermarket owner

メッセージは誰に向けられていますか。

(A) 農場労働者
(B) 弁護士
(C) ジャーナリスト
(D) スーパーマーケットのオーナー

正解 C 話し手は、❶「*Glenn City Times*紙のParkさんへの伝言だ」と用件を述べ、❷で聞き手のParkさんが地域の農産物に関する新聞記事を執筆していることに言及している。よって、この電話のメッセージは新聞ジャーナリストであるParkさんに向けられたものであると分かる。be intended for ～「～に向けられている、～のために意図されている」。
(A) farmworker「農場労働者」。
(B) lawyer「弁護士」。

81 Why does the speaker say, "There's still some data in the report we're waiting to confirm"?

(A) To explain a delay
(B) To offer to help
(C) To show surprise about a conclusion
(D) To urge the listener to work quickly

話し手はなぜ "There's still some data in the report we're waiting to confirm" と言っていますか。

(A) 遅延について説明をするため。
(B) 手助けすると申し出るため。
(C) 結論に対する驚きを示すため。
(D) 聞き手に素早く仕事をするよう促すため。

正解 A 話し手は❷で、聞き手が農業局の四半期報告書の入手を希望している旨を承知していると伝えてから、下線部で「報告書には、まだ当局で確認待ちのデータが幾つかある」と述べ、報告書がまだ提供できないことを示唆している。よって、話し手はデータの一部が確認待ちのため報告書の提供が遅れていることを説明していると考えられる。delay「遅延」。
(C) conclusion「結論」。
(D) urge ～ to *do*「～に…するよう促す」。

82 Why does the speaker suggest communicating by e-mail?

(A) She will be out of town.
(B) She wants to keep a written record.
(C) She needs to send some pictures.
(D) She wants to include others in the discussion.

話し手は、なぜEメールで連絡を取り合うことを提案しているのですか。

(A) 自身が町を離れているだろうから。
(B) 自身が書面での記録を残したいから。
(C) 自身が写真を何枚か送る必要があるから。
(D) 自身が他の人たちを話し合いに含めたいから。

正解 A 話し手は❸で聞き手に対し、質問があれば応じると伝えた後、❹で「私は来週出張するので、Eメールで連絡を取り合うのが最善だろう」と述べている。よって、話し手は自身が出張で町を離れる予定なので、聞き手にEメールで連絡を取り合うことを提案していると分かる。out of town「町から離れて」。
(B) written「書面にした」、record「記録」。
(D) discussion「話し合い」。

Words & Phrases

department 局　agriculture 農業　article 記事　farm production 農産物
region 地域　a copy of ～ 1部の～　quarterly 四半期の　confirm ～を確認する
in the meantime それまでの間、その間に　specific 具体的な　communicate 連絡を取り合う

Questions 83 through 85 refer to the following excerpt from a meeting.

問題83-85は次の会議の抜粋に関するものです。

M

Next on the agenda, ❶I would like to discuss the prototype of our new refrigerator model, the Arctic Fox. ❷This is the first refrigerator we plan to manufacture using material that is extremely lightweight yet durable. Unfortunately, using this new special material could add to the production costs. So ❸I've invited everyone from the Manufacturing Department here to get your input on modifications we can make to the manufacturing process for this appliance. ❹I need your suggestions on ways we can reduce production costs.

次の議題では、当社冷蔵庫の新モデル、Arctic Foxの試作品について話し合いたいと思います。これは、極めて軽量ながら耐久性のある素材を使用して当社が製造を計画している初の冷蔵庫です。残念ながら、この新しい特殊素材の使用は製造費を増大させる可能性があります。そこで私は、この電化製品の製造工程において、われわれが変更可能な部分についてご意見を伺いたく、製造部より皆さんをここにお招きしました。製造費を削減できる方法についての皆さんのご提案が必要なのです。

83 What product is the speaker discussing?

(A) A car
(B) A refrigerator
(C) A computer
(D) An air conditioner

話し手は何の製品について話していますか。

(A) 車
(B) 冷蔵庫
(C) コンピューター
(D) エアコン

正解 B 話し手は❶「当社冷蔵庫の新モデル、Arctic Foxの試作品について話し合いたいと思う」と述べている。その後も、その新しい冷蔵庫の素材と製造費について話を続けている。
(D) 話し手は、電化製品の製造工程について言及しているが、エアコンの話はしていない。

84 What does the speaker say is different about the product?

(A) Its size
(B) Its color
(C) Its material
(D) Its energy usage

話し手は、この製品について何が異なっていると言っていますか。

(A) そのサイズ
(B) その色
(C) その素材
(D) そのエネルギー使用量

正解 C 話し手は会社の新製品となる冷蔵庫について、❷「これは、極めて軽量ながら耐久性のある素材を使用して当社が製造を計画している初の冷蔵庫だ」とその素材の特徴について説明している。
(D) usage「使用量」。

85 What does the speaker want suggestions about?

(A) Lowering production costs
(B) Finding qualified staff
(C) Reorganizing a department
(D) Responding to customer complaints

話し手は何についての提案を望んでいますか。

(A) 製造費を減らすこと。
(B) 有能なスタッフを見つけること。
(C) 部署を再編成すること。
(D) 顧客の苦情に対応すること。

正解 A 新しい特殊素材の使用による冷蔵庫の製造費増大の可能性に言及した話し手は❸で、製造工程の変更可能な点について聞き手の意見を聞きたいと伝え、さらに❹「製造費を削減できる方法についての皆さんの提案が必要だ」と述べている。lower「～を減らす、～を下げる」。
(B) qualified「有能な、資格のある」。
(C) reorganize「～を再編成する」。
(D) respond to ～「～に対応する」、complaint「苦情」。

Words & Phrases

agenda 議題　prototype 試作品　refrigerator 冷蔵庫
plan to *do* ～することを計画している　manufacture ～を製造する　material 素材　extremely 極めて
lightweight 軽量な　yet けれども、それにもかかわらず　durable 耐久性のある　unfortunately 残念ながら
add to ～ ～を増大させる　production 製造　department 部署　input 意見　make a modification 変更を加える
process 工程　appliance 電化製品　suggestion 提案　reduce ～を削減する

Questions 86 through 88 refer to the following broadcast.

問題86-88は次の放送に関するものです。

M

In local news, ❶the town council announced that they're considering increasing the fee to drive across the Ashington Bridge. ❷The additional funds would be used to repair roads in the area. ❸The council indicated that these repairs are necessary before the town hosts the statewide bicycle race next May. ❹Residents will be given the opportunity to express their opinions about the proposed bridge fee during next month's town hall meeting.

地方ニュースです。町議会は、Ashington橋の車両通行料の値上げを検討していると発表しました。増収となる財源は、同地域の道路を補修することに充てられるでしょう。町議会は、町が今度の5月に州全体にわたる自転車レースを主催する前に、これらの補修作業が必要だと述べました。住民には来月の対話集会の間、提案された橋の通行料に関する意見を表明する機会が与えられることになっています。

86 What is the broadcast mainly about?

(A) An update about a building renovation project
(B) A plan to encourage recycling
(C) A request for community volunteers
(D) A proposal for a fee increase

放送は主に何についてですか。

(A) 建物の改修プロジェクトに関する最新情報
(B) リサイクル促進計画
(C) 地域ボランティアの要請
(D) 料金値上げの提議

正解 D 話し手は❶「町議会は、Ashington橋の車両通行料の値上げを検討していると発表した」と述べ、続けて❷で、増収分は道路の補修に充てられると伝えている。その後も、道路の補修が必要な理由や、通行料に関する意見表明の機会について説明している。proposal「提議、提案」。
(A) 道路の補修に関する言及はあるが、建物の改修については述べられていない。
(B) encourage「～を促進する」、recycling「リサイクル」。

87 According to the broadcast, what will take place in May?

(A) A local election
(B) A park expansion
(C) A sporting event
(D) A town festival

放送によると、5月に何が行われますか。

(A) 地方選挙
(B) 公園の拡張
(C) スポーツイベント
(D) 町の祭り

正解 C 話し手は❷で、橋の車両通行料の値上げで得た財源を道路補修に充てると説明した後、❸「町議会は、町が今度の5月に州全体にわたる自転車レースを主催する前に、これらの補修作業が必要だと述べた」と伝えている。bicycle raceをa sporting eventと表している(C)が正解。
(A) election「選挙」。
(B) expansion「拡張」。
(D) 町が自転車レースを主催すると述べられているが、町の祭りに言及はない。

88 What will the listeners have an opportunity to do next month?

(A) Join a committee
(B) Provide some feedback
(C) Review a floor plan
(D) Purchase advance tickets

聞き手は来月、何をする機会を持ちますか。

(A) 委員会に加入する。
(B) 意見を提供する。
(C) 間取り図を再検討する。
(D) 前売り券を購入する。

正解 B この地方ニュースの聞き手である地域住民に対し、話し手は❹「住民には来月の対話集会の間、提案された橋の通行料に関する意見を表明する機会が与えられる」と伝えているので、(B)が正解。provide「～を提供する」、feedback「意見」。
(A) 対話集会で意見表明の機会があると述べられているが、committee「委員会」への加入に言及はない。
(C) review「～を再検討する」、floor plan「〈建物の〉間取り図」。
(D) advance ticket「前売り券」。

Words & Phrases

local 地方の　town council 町議会　consider *doing* ～することを検討する
increase ～を増やす　fee 料金　additional 追加の　funds 財源、所持金　repair ～を補修する
indicate ～と述べる、～を示す　repairs 補修作業　host ～を主催する　statewide 州全体にわたる
race 〈自転車などの〉レース　resident 住民　opportunity 機会　express 〈意見など〉を表明する　opinion 意見
proposed 提案された　town hall meeting 〈一般市民との〉対話集会

Questions 89 through 91 refer to the following talk.

W

Welcome to your first day of training. As you know, ❶our company specializes in commercial photography. We provide high-quality photographs that retailers can use in their advertisements. ❷Each image we take is uploaded to our database, and ❸today you will learn how to use this database to classify and sort these images. Since we're often dealing with thousands of files at a time, we have a strict classification system. ❹Right now, you'll each be partnered with an experienced employee who will work with you to show you how to use the system.

問題89-91は次の話に関するものです。

研修初日にようこそ。ご存じのように、当社は商業用写真を専門としています。私たちは、小売事業者の方々が広告用に使用できる高品質の写真を提供します。私たちが撮影したそれぞれの画像は、当社のデータベースにアップロードされます。そして本日皆さんには、これらの画像を分類して整理するためにこのデータベースをどのように使うか学んでもらいます。私たちはしばしば一度に数千ものファイルを扱うので、厳密な分類システムがあります。では今から、皆さんはそれぞれ、一緒に作業してシステムの使い方を教えてくれる経験豊かな従業員1名と組みになります。

89 What does the company specialize in?

(A) Photography
(B) Interior decorating
(C) Accounting
(D) Publishing

会社は何を専門としていますか。

(A) 写真
(B) 室内装飾
(C) 会計
(D) 出版

正解 A 話し手は❶で、「当社は商業用写真を専門としている。私たちは、小売事業者が広告用に使用できる高品質の写真を提供する」と会社の事業について説明している。
(B) interior「室内の」、decorating「装飾」。

90 What will the listeners be trained to do?

(A) Create a budget
(B) Write contracts
(C) Use a database
(D) Improve sales techniques

聞き手は何をすることを教わりますか。

(A) 予算を作成する。
(B) 契約書を書く。
(C) データベースを使う。
(D) 営業技術を向上させる。

正解 C 話し手は❶・❷で、自社が提供する広告用写真のために撮影した画像は、データベースにアップロードされると伝えている。続けて❸で「本日皆さんには、これらの画像を分類して整理するためにこのデータベースをどう使うか学んでもらう」と述べている。
(D) technique「技術、ノウハウ」。

91 What will the listeners do next?

(A) Watch an instructional video
(B) Work with a colleague
(C) Get some refreshments
(D) Read a printed manual

聞き手は次に何をしますか。

(A) 教育用の動画を見る。
(B) 1名の同僚と一緒に作業する。
(C) 軽食を取る。
(D) 印刷したマニュアルを読む。

正解 B 話し手は❹「では今から、皆さんはそれぞれ、一緒に作業してシステムの使い方を教えてくれる経験豊かな従業員1名と組みになる」と述べている。経験豊かな従業員のことをa colleague「同僚」と表している(B)が正解。
(A) 研修の中での話だが、動画については言及していない。instructional「教育の」。
(C) refreshments「軽食」。

Words & Phrases

specialize in ～　～を専門とする　commercial　商業の　photography　写真
provide　～を提供する　high-quality　高品質の　retailer　小売業者　image　画像　upload　～をアップロードする
database　データベース　classify　～を分類する　sort　～を整理する　deal with ～　～を扱う
thousands of ～　何千もの～　at a time　一度に　strict　厳密な　classification　分類
partner ～ with …　～を…と組ませる　experienced　経験豊かな

Questions 92 through 94 refer to the following broadcast.

問題92-94は次の放送に関するものです。

M

Welcome to Nutrition Talk on WKMN Radio! ❶Our guest today, Alexis Morris, is a nutritionist who recently released a mobile phone app. ❷The new app helps you track what you eat and gives you nutritional information about that food. Today we'll be talking with Ms. Morris about the importance of meal tracking. ❸I've kept records of my meal choices for years now, and I've tried a lot of other applications like this. ❹I can honestly say that this is the best one I've ever used. ❺We'll talk with Ms. Morris right after this commercial break.

WKMNラジオの『栄養学談義』へようこそ! 本日のゲスト、Alexis Morrisは、つい最近携帯電話用アプリを発表した栄養士です。その新しいアプリは、あなたが食べたものを記録する手助けをし、その食べ物の栄養に関する情報を教えてくれます。本日は、食事記録の大切さについてMorrisさんとお話します。私は今まで何年もの間、自分が選択した食事を記録して、これと同じような他の多くのアプリを試してきました。これは私が今まで使用してきた中で一番のものだと率直に申し上げることができます。次のコマーシャル放送の後すぐにMorrisさんとお話します。

92 Who is Alexis Morris?

(A) A nutrition expert
(B) A gardener
(C) A chef
(D) A supermarket owner

Alexis Morrisとは誰ですか。

(A) 栄養学の専門家
(B) 園芸家
(C) シェフ
(D) スーパーマーケットのオーナー

正解 A 話し手はラジオ番組のゲストについて、❶「本日のゲスト、Alexis Morrisは、つい最近携帯電話用アプリを発表した栄養士だ」と紹介している。nutritionistをnutrition expertと表している(A)が正解。expert「専門家」。
(B) gardener「園芸家」。

93 What does the speaker imply when he says, "I've tried a lot of other applications like this"?

(A) He wants to try other applications.
(B) He is offering to work with a colleague.
(C) The listeners can trust his opinion.
(D) The listeners should call the station.

話し手は "I've tried a lot of other applications like this"という発言で、何を示唆していますか。

(A) 話し手は他のアプリを試したいと思っている。
(B) 話し手は同僚と働くことを申し出ている。
(C) 聞き手は話し手の意見を信頼できる。
(D) 聞き手は放送局に電話すべきである。

正解 C 話し手は、❷でゲストのMorrisさんが発表した食事記録用アプリについて説明している。さらに❸「私は今まで何年もの間、自分が選択した食事を記録している」と言い、下線部で「これと同じような他の多くのアプリを試してきた」と続け、❹でMorrisさんが発表したアプリが一番だと意見を述べている。よって話し手は、長年同種の食事記録用アプリを多数使用してきた自分の意見には信頼性があることを示唆していると考えられる。trust「～を信頼する」。
(D) station「放送局」。

94 According to the speaker, what will listeners hear next?

(A) A weather report
(B) A commercial break
(C) A traffic update
(D) A news bulletin

話し手によると、聞き手は次に何を耳にしますか。

(A) 天気予報
(B) コマーシャル放送
(C) 最新の交通情報
(D) 臨時ニュース

正解 B 話し手は❺「次のコマーシャル放送の後すぐにMorrisさんと話す」と、以降の放送の流れについて予告している。
(A) weather report「天気予報」。
(C) traffic「交通」、update「最新情報」。
(D) news bulletin「臨時ニュース、ニュース速報」。

Words & Phrases

nutrition 栄養(学)　nutritionist 栄養士　recently つい最近
release ～を発表する、～を公開する　app 〈applicationの略で〉アプリ　track ～を記録する、～を追跡する
nutritional 栄養の　importance 大切さ、重要性　meal 食事　tracking 追跡　keep a record of ～ ～の記録を付ける
choice 選択　for years 何年もの間　honestly 率直に、正直に　commercial break コマーシャル休憩

Questions 95 through 97 refer to the following tour information and map.

問題95-97は次のツアー情報と地図に関するものです。

W

Welcome to Southridge National Park, everyone! ❶Today's hike will take us to Diamond Sand Lake. It isn't the shortest trail in the park, but it is a pretty easy one. I'm glad you all brought your binoculars ❷because it's migration season, so we're likely to see lots of interesting birds along the way. Now, today's forecast calls for a chance of showers. ❸If you have a raincoat, I suggest you put it on. We'll be leaving in about fifteen minutes.

皆さん、Southridge国立公園へようこそ！ 本日のハイキングで私たちは、Diamond Sand湖まで向かいます。公園内で最短のコースではありませんが、かなり楽なものです。皆さん全員が双眼鏡をご持参くださって良かったです。というのも、今は鳥の渡りの時季なので、私たちは道中で興味深い鳥をたくさん見る可能性が高いからです。さて、今日の予報では、にわか雨の可能性があると伝えています。レインコートをお持ちでしたら、着用することをお勧めします。私たちは約15分後に出発します。

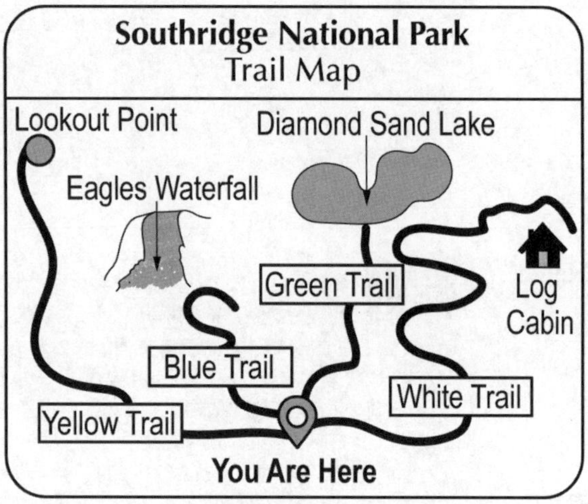

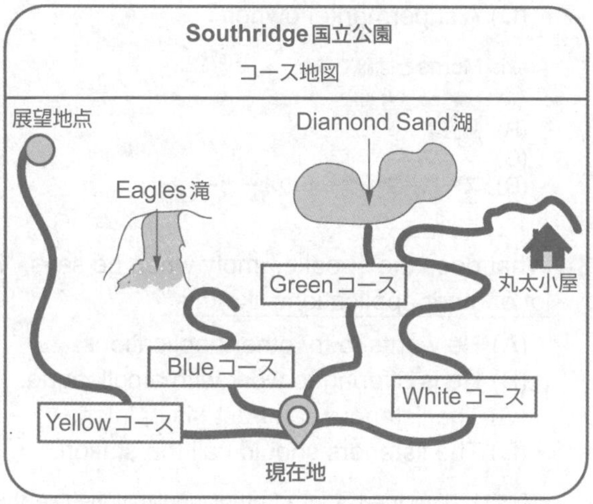

95 Look at the graphic. Which trail does the speaker plan on taking?

(A) Yellow Trail
(B) Blue Trail
(C) Green Trail
(D) White Trail

図を見てください。話し手はどのコースを進む予定ですか。

(A) Yellowコース
(B) Blueコース
(C) Greenコース
(D) Whiteコース

正解 C 話し手は❶「本日のハイキングで私たちは、Diamond Sand湖まで向かう」と行動予定を伝えている。図を見ると、Diamond Sand湖に至るコースはGreenコースのみなので(C)が正解。

---

96 What does the speaker say the listeners are likely to see during the hike?

(A) Historic ruins
(B) Migrating birds
(C) Camping sites
(D) Wildflowers

話し手は、聞き手がハイキングの間に何を見る可能性が高いと言っていますか。

(A) 歴史的遺跡
(B) 渡り鳥
(C) キャンプ場
(D) 野草

正解 B 話し手は聞き手が皆、双眼鏡を持参したことを良かったと言った後、その理由について❷で、「というのも、今は鳥の渡りの時季なので、道中で興味深い鳥をたくさん見る可能性が高いからだ」と述べている。migrate「〈鳥などが〉渡る、移住する」。
(A) historic「歴史的な」、ruins「遺跡」。
(C) site「場所、用地」。
(D) wildflower「野草」。

---

97 What does the speaker suggest the listeners do?

(A) Pose for a photograph
(B) Bring healthy snacks
(C) Wear a raincoat
(D) Sign a visitors' book

話し手は聞き手に何をすることを提案していますか。

(A) 写真撮影のためにポーズを取る。
(B) 健康的な軽食を持ってくる。
(C) レインコートを着用する。
(D) 来訪者名簿に署名する。

正解 C 話し手は、天気予報でにわか雨の可能性が伝えられていることに言及し、❸「レインコートを持っていたら、着用することを勧める」と聞き手に提案している。wear「～を着用する」。
(A) pose for ～「〈絵・写真など〉のためにポーズを取る」。
(B) healthy「健康的な」、snack「軽食」。
(D) sign「～に署名する」、visitors' book「来訪者名簿」。

Words & Phrases

national park 国立公園　hike ハイキング　trail 〈ハイキングや登山などの〉コース、小道　pretty かなり
binoculars 双眼鏡　migration 〈鳥の〉渡り、移住　be likely to *do* ～する可能性が高い、～しそうである
along the way 道中　forecast 〈天気の〉予報　call for ～ ～を予報する　chance 可能性　shower にわか雨
raincoat レインコート　put on ～ ～を着用する
地図 lookout 眺望、見晴らし　waterfall 滝　log cabin 丸太小屋

Questions 98 through 100 refer to the following telephone message and schedule.

問題98-100は次の電話のメッセージと予定表に関するものです。

M

Hello, Regina. It's Ezra. I wanted to give you an update about our client Wang Sporting Goods. ❶They want to meet with us to discuss the artwork for their upcoming advertising campaign. ❷They like what we've done so far, but they have some other ideas they want to share with us. ❸Representatives from Wang Sporting Goods will be in town on Wednesday. ❹I reserved Conference Room A, the one with the large screen, for a couple of hours. ❺Could you please bring your laptop computer to the meeting to show our work?

もしもし、Regina。Ezraです。当社の顧客であるWangスポーツ用品社についての最新情報をあなたにお伝えしたかったのです。先方は今度の広告キャンペーン用のアートワークについて話し合うために、私たちと会うことを望んでいます。先方は私たちがこれまで行ってきたことを気に入ってくれていますが、私たちと共有したいと考えている他のアイデアを幾つかお持ちです。Wangスポーツ用品社の担当者たちは、水曜日に町を訪れるでしょう。私は、大型スクリーンがある会議室Aを２時間予約しました。私たちの作品をお見せするため、その会議にあなたのノートパソコンを持ってきていただけますか。

Conference Room A Schedule

Wednesday, May 14

10:00 A.M.	Wang Sporting Goods
1:00 P.M.	Open
2:00 P.M.	Department Meeting
4:00 P.M.	Freeman Incorporated

会議室Aの予定表

5月14日、水曜日

午前10時	Wangスポーツ用品社
午後1時	空き
午後2時	部署会議
午後4時	Freeman社

98 What does the speaker say will be discussed at the meeting?

(A) An office renovation project
(B) A company merger
(C) A quarterly budget
(D) An advertising campaign

話し手は、会議で何について話し合われると言っていますか。

(A) 事務所の改修プロジェクト
(B) 企業の合併
(C) 四半期予算
(D) 広告キャンペーン

正解 D 話し手は、顧客であるWangスポーツ用品社について、❶「先方は今度の広告キャンペーン用のアートワークについて話し合うために、私たちと会うことを望んでいる」と言っている。また、❷で顧客が共有したいと考えているアイデアがあると述べ、❹で会議室の手配について伝えている。よって、今後顧客との会議で広告キャンペーンについて話し合われると分かる。
(A) renovation「改修」。
(B) merger「合併」。
(C) quarterly「四半期ごとの」、budget「予算」。

---

99 Look at the graphic. At what time will the meeting take place?

(A) 10:00 A.M.
(B) 1:00 P.M.
(C) 2:00 P.M.
(D) 4:00 P.M.

図を見てください。その会議は何時に行われますか。

(A) 午前10時
(B) 午後1時
(C) 午後2時
(D) 午後4時

正解 A 話し手は会議を希望しているWangスポーツ用品社について、❸で、担当者たちが水曜日に来訪すると述べ、❹「私は、大型スクリーンがある会議室Aを2時間予約した」と伝えている。会議室Aの5月14日水曜日の予定を示した図を見ると、午前10時にWangスポーツ用品社と記載がある。よって、(A)が正解。
(C)(D) 図では、午後2時に部署会議、午後4時にFreeman社とある。

---

100 What does the speaker ask the listener to do?

(A) Take some measurements
(B) Bring a computer
(C) Prepare some slides
(D) Make a list of questions

話し手は聞き手に何をするよう求めていますか。

(A) 測定をする。
(B) コンピューターを持ってくる。
(C) スライドを準備する。
(D) 質問リストを作成する。

正解 B 話し手は顧客との会議のために部屋を予約したと伝えた後、❺「私たちの作品を見せるため、その会議にあなたのノートパソコンを持ってきてくれるか」と聞き手に頼んでいる。
(A) take measurements「測定する」。
(C) slide「スライド」。

TEST 2 PART 4

Words & Phrases

update 最新情報　client 顧客　goods 用品、商品
artwork 〈印刷物上の挿絵･写真･グラフなどを指して〉アートワーク、図版　upcoming 今度の、もうすぐ来る
advertising 広告　campaign キャンペーン　so far これまでのところ　share ~ with … ~を…と共有する
representative 担当、代表　reserve ~を予約する　conference 会議　a couple of ~ 2つの~、2、3の~
laptop computer ノートパソコン
予定表 open 空き　department 部署　incorporated 〈会社名の終わりに付けて〉~社

101 Mr. Lang has been running ------- carpet store for more than twenty years.

(A) himself
(B) him
(C) his
(D) he

Langさんは、自身のカーペット店を20年以上経営しています。

(A) 彼自身
(B) 彼を
(C) 彼の
(D) 彼は

正解 C 選択肢は全て人称代名詞。空所の前は述語動詞has been running「～を経営している」で、後ろはその目的語となる名詞句carpet storeが続いているので、名詞を修飾する所有格の(C) hisが適切。run「～を経営する」。
(A) 再帰代名詞。
(B) 人称代名詞の目的格。
(D) 人称代名詞の主格。

---

102 When designing the conference poster, be sure to ------- the company logo at the top.

(A) manage
(B) refer
(C) reach
(D) place

その会議のポスターをデザインする際には、必ず最上部に会社のロゴを配置してください。

(A) ～を管理する
(B) ～に参照させる
(C) ～に着く
(D) ～を配置する

正解 D 選択肢は全て動詞の働きを持つ語。空所はbe sure to ～「必ず～してください」に続いている。at the top「最上部に」と位置を表す語句があるので、(D) place「～を配置する」を入れて「必ず最上部に会社のロゴを配置してください」とすると、ポスターをデザインする際の注意点を伝える内容となり、文意が通る。conference「会議」、logo「ロゴ」。

---

103 The hotel ballroom was ------- decorated for the wedding of the mayor's daughter.

(A) beauty
(B) beautiful
(C) beautifully
(D) beautify

ホテルの大宴会場は、市長の娘の結婚式のために美しく装飾されました。

(A) 美しさ
(B) 美しい
(C) 美しく
(D) ～を美しくする

正解 C 文の主語はThe hotel ballroom「ホテルの大宴会場」、述語動詞はwas decorated「装飾された」で、空所に何も入れなくても文が成立している。よって、述語動詞was decoratedを修飾する副詞の(C) beautifully「美しく」が適切。ballroom「〈ホテルなどの〉大宴会場」、decorate「～を装飾する」、wedding「結婚式」、mayor「市長」。
(A) 名詞。
(B) 形容詞。
(D) 動詞beautify「～を美しくする」の原形。

104 The city completed its annual financial report ------- the state deadline.

(A) before
(B) between
(C) beside
(D) below

市は、州の締め切り期限の前に年次会計報告書を完成させました。

(A) ～の前に
(B) ～の間に
(C) ～のそばに
(D) ～の下に

正解 A 選択肢は全て前置詞の働きを持つ語。空所の後ろのthe state deadline「州の締め切り期限」を目的語として続けられる前置詞で文意に合うのは、(A) before「～の前に」。complete「～を完成させる」、annual「年次の」、financial report「会計報告書」、state「州」、deadline「締め切り期限」。

---

105 Guests at the Homer Hotel can expect ------- service from every member of our staff.

(A) attentive
(B) attention
(C) attentively
(D) attentiveness

Homerホテルのお客さまは、当スタッフ全員からの心遣いの行き届いたサービスをご期待いただけます。

(A) 心遣いの行き届いた
(B) 心遣い
(C) よく気を配って
(D) 注意深さ

正解 A 空所の前に述語動詞can expect「～を期待できる」があり、後ろに名詞serviceが続いているので、空所には名詞を修飾する形容詞の(A) attentiveが適切。guest「〈ホテルの〉宿泊客」。
(B)(D) 名詞。動詞の後ろに続けられるが、文意に合わない。
(C) 副詞。前の動詞を修飾できるが、文意に合わない。

---

106 YLT Supply Company offers its customers a 10 percent discount ------- they pay for their lumber order in cash.

(A) also
(B) if
(C) but
(D) and

YLT供給会社は、顧客が材木の注文に対して現金で支払いをする場合には、10パーセント引きを提供しています。

(A) また
(B) ～の場合には
(C) しかし
(D) そして

正解 B 空所の前後は共に〈主語+動詞〉の形を含む文なので、空所には両方の文をつなぐ接続詞が入る。空所の後ろは「顧客が材木の注文に対して現金で支払いをする」という意味で、空所の前の「YLT供給会社は10パーセント引きを提供する」の条件となるので、(B) if「～の場合には」が適切。supply「供給」、lumber「材木」、order「注文」、in cash「現金で」。
(A) 副詞。2つの文をつなぐことができないので不適切。
(C)(D) 接続詞だが、文意に合わない。

107 Carolyn Fanner will speak about her new memoir at the next ------- at the Delville Public Library.

(A) lecture
(B) lecturer
(C) lecturing
(D) lectured

Carolyn Fannerは、Delville公立図書館での次回の講演において、自身の新たな回顧録について話します。

(A) 講演
(B) 講演者
(C) 講演をしている
(D) 講演をした

正解 A 選択肢は、動詞lecture「講演をする」と、その形が変化したものや派生語。空所の前の形容詞next「次回の」と、後ろのat the Delville Public Library「Delville公立図書館での」によって修飾される名詞が入る。文意から(A) lecture「講演」が適切。memoir「回顧録」。
(B) 名詞だが、文意に合わない。
(C) 現在分詞、または動名詞。
(D) 過去形、または過去分詞。

108 The number 17 bus is the quickest ------- to get from the rail station to the business district.

(A) style
(B) direction
(C) control
(D) way

17番バスが、列車の駅から商業地区に行く最も速い手段です。

(A) 様式
(B) 方向
(C) 制御
(D) 手段

正解 D 選択肢は全て名詞の働きを持つ語。空所には、形容詞の最上級のthe quickestによって修飾される名詞が入る。後ろのto不定詞「列車の駅から商業地区に行くための」を続けて文意に合うのは、特定のやり方・方法を表す(D) way「手段」。rail「鉄道」、business district「商業地区」。

109 Ms. Cho ------- the Busan office in the coming months in Ms. Kim's absence.

(A) to supervise
(B) supervised
(C) has been supervising
(D) will be supervising

Kimさんが不在のこれからの数カ月間、Choさんが釜山のオフィスを監督します。

＊選択肢の訳は省略

正解 D 選択肢は全て動詞supervise「～を監督する」の変化した形。この文には述語動詞がないため、空所に必要。in the coming months「これからの数カ月間」と未来を表す語句があるので、未来進行形の(D) will be supervisingが適切。in *one's* absence「～のいないときに」。
(A) to不定詞。
(B) 過去形。未来を表す語句があるので、不適切。
(C) 現在完了進行形。

110 A special ------- of porcelain sculptures by Riku Ohtani is being shown at the Vanport Art Museum.

(A) outlook
(B) function
(C) exhibit
(D) event

Riku Ohtaniによる磁器彫刻品の特別展示が、Vanport美術館において公開されています。

(A) 見通し
(B) 機能
(C) 展示
(D) 催し物

正解 C 空所の後ろにofが続くので、空所に入るのは名詞。前のspecialは形容詞で、この名詞を修飾している。文の主語は「Riku Ohtaniによる磁器彫刻品の特別な-------」で、述語動詞is being shown以降は「美術館で公開されている」という意味なので、文意から(C) exhibit「展示」が適切。porcelain「磁器」、sculpture「彫刻」、show「～を見せる、～を展示する」。
(D) 述語動詞is being shown「公開されている」が続くので、文意に合わない。

---

111 ------- who has not read the new information protection policy must do so today.

(A) Anyone
(B) Another
(C) Any
(D) Anything

情報保護に関する新しい方針を読んでいない人は皆、本日それを行わなければなりません。

(A) どの人も
(B) もう1人
(C) 誰でも
(D) 何でも

正解 A 選択肢は全て代名詞の働きを持つ語。述語動詞はmust doで、空所の後ろにwhoで始まる関係代名詞節があるので、空所にはwhoの先行詞となる(A) Anyoneが適切。do soは、情報保護の新しい方針を読むことを表している。protection「保護」、policy「方針」。
(B) 2つを対照させる場合に用いるが、対照するものがないので、不適切。
(C) 肯定文で「誰でも」を表すが、後ろに関係代名詞は続かないので、不適切。

---

112 Aapo Systems is ------- to be our distributor when we begin exporting to Finland.

(A) ahead
(B) likely
(C) over
(D) finely

当社がフィンランドに輸出を開始する際には、Aapoシステムズ社がうちの販売代理店になりそうです。

(A) 有利な立場に立ちつつある
(B) ありそうな
(C) 終わって
(D) 素晴らしく

正解 B 空所の前にbe動詞があり、後ろにはto不定詞が続いている。be likely to *do*で「～しそうな」という意味になる、形容詞の(B) likelyが適切。distributor「販売代理店」、export「輸出する」。
(A) 形容詞、または副詞。aheadにto不定詞を続けて「～するのに一歩先にいる」という意味は表さない。
(C) 形容詞。文の意味が通らない。
(D) 副詞。

113 The creation of the new park was only possible with the ------- of the town council.

(A) support
(B) supportive
(C) supported
(D) supportable

新しい公園の創設は、町議会の支持があって初めて可能でした。

(A) 支持
(B) 支持している
(C) 支持された
(D) 支持できる

正解 A 空所の前に冠詞theがあり、後ろに前置詞句of the town council「町議会の」が続いているので、空所には名詞の(A) supportが適切。creation「創設」、town council「町議会」。
(B) 形容詞。
(C) 動詞support「～を支持する」の過去分詞。後ろに名詞がないので不適切。
(D) 形容詞。

---

114 The pay increase for Lansuli Fishery employees is ------- from April 15.

(A) permissive
(B) effective
(C) collective
(D) objective

Lansuli水産会社の従業員の賃上げは、4月15日から実施されます。

(A) 許された
(B) 実施されている
(C) 集合的な
(D) 客観的な

正解 B 選択肢は全て形容詞の働きを持つ語。文の主語に当たるのはThe pay increase for Lansuli Fishery employees「Lansuli水産会社の従業員の賃上げ」で、空所の後ろには、from April 15「4月15日から」と具体的な起点日が示されているので、(B) effective「実施されている、効力のある」を入れると文意が通る。effective from ～「～から実施されている」。pay increase「賃上げ」、fishery「水産会社」。
(A) 「〈言葉・態度が〉許された」という意味であり、文意に合わない。

---

115 Patient reviews of Dunleavy Dental's staff and facility are ------- positive.

(A) consist
(B) consistent
(C) consisting
(D) consistently

Dunleavy歯科医院のスタッフと設備に関する患者からの評価は、一貫して肯定的なものです。

(A) 成り立つ
(B) 一貫した
(C) 成り立っている
(D) 一貫して

正解 D 文の主語はPatient reviews「患者からの評価」、述語動詞はareで、空所に何も入れなくても文が成立している。空所には後ろの形容詞positiveを修飾する副詞の(D) consistentlyが適切。review「評価」、dental「歯科の」、facility「設備、施設」、positive「肯定的な」。
(A) 動詞consist「成り立つ」の原形。
(B) 形容詞。
(C) 現在分詞。

116 The training program for new flight attendants ------- over the course of three weeks.

(A) insists
(B) protects
(C) allows
(D) extends

新しい客室乗務員向けの研修プログラムは、3週間にわたります。

(A) 主張する
(B) ～を保護する
(C) ～を許す
(D) わたる

正解 D 選択肢は全て動詞の三人称単数現在形。空所の後ろにover the course of three weeks「3週間の間」という語句が続いているので、文意よりextend「〈期間が～にまで〉わたる」の三人称単数現在形の(D) extendsが適切。training「研修」、flight attendant「〈旅客機の〉客室乗務員」、over the course of ～「～の間」。
(A)(B)(C) いずれも文意に合わない。それぞれinsist、protect、allowの三人称単数現在形。

117 We would like to thank employees ------- ideas led to recent departmental improvements.

(A) whichever
(B) whom
(C) whose
(D) whatever

私たちは、最近の部署の改善につながったアイデアを出してくれた従業員の方々に感謝したいと思います。

(A) ～するどちらでも
(B) ～するところの…
(C) その人の～が…する
(D) ～するものは何でも

正解 C 空所の前後は共に〈主語＋動詞〉の形を含む文なので、空所には両方の文をつなぐ関係代名詞が入る。空所の前の名詞employeesを先行詞として受け、後ろの関係代名詞節の主語のideasを修飾できる所有格の関係代名詞(C) whoseが適切。lead to ～「～につながる」、recent「最近の」、departmental「部署の」、improvement「改善」。
(A)(D) 複合関係代名詞。先行詞なしで用いるので不適切。
(B) 目的格の関係代名詞。空所の後ろの節には目的語があるので、不適切。

118 The Pimasoft four-person tent is light, strong, and ------- to tearing and ripping.

(A) resist
(B) resistant
(C) resisted
(D) resistance

Pimasoft社の4人用テントは軽くて丈夫で、また、裂けと破れに強いです。

(A) 耐える
(B) 耐性がある
(C) 耐えられた
(D) 耐性

正解 B 空所の前にlight, strong「軽くて丈夫な」と形容詞が列挙され、さらに並列を表す接続詞andが続いているので、空所には形容詞が入る。resistant to ～で「～に耐性がある」という意味になる(B)が適切。tear「裂ける」、rip「破れる」。
(A) 動詞resist「耐える」の原形。
(C) 動詞の過去分詞。
(D) 名詞。

119 ------- those at yesterday's meeting, Mr. Swartz has been with the company the longest.

(A) Around
(B) Despite
(C) Inside
(D) Among

昨日の会議に出席した人々の中で、Swartzさんが最も長くその会社に勤務しています。

(A) ～の周りに
(B) ～にもかかわらず
(C) ～の内側に
(D) ～の中で

正解 D 選択肢は全て前置詞の働きを持つ語。文末に副詞の最上級the longestがあり、その会社でのSwartzさんの勤務期間を他者のものと比較している。空所の後ろでthose (who were) at yesterday's meeting「昨日の会議に出席した人々」と比較対象が示されているので、3者以上の場合に用いて「～の中で」を表す(D) Amongが適切。those「人々」。

---

120 The estate-planning position requires some ------- knowledge of finance or customer service.

(A) prompt
(B) constant
(C) equal
(D) prior

資産計画の職には、財務または顧客サービスに関する幾らかの予備知識が必要です。

(A) 迅速な
(B) 一定の
(C) 等しい
(D) 事前の

正解 D 選択肢は全て形容詞の働きを持つ語。空所に続く名詞句knowledge of finance or customer service「財務または顧客サービスに関する知識」を修飾する形容詞として文意に合うのは、(D) prior「事前の」。prior knowledgeで「予備知識」という意味。estate-planning「資産計画、相続計画」、position「職」、require「～を必要とする」、finance「財務」。

---

121 The CEO's opening remarks were rewritten to place more ------- on welcoming new employees.

(A) emphasis
(B) emphasize
(C) emphatic
(D) emphatically

最高経営責任者の開会のあいさつは、新しい従業員を歓迎するということをもっと強調するために書き直されました。

(A) 強調
(B) ～を強調する
(C) 強調された
(D) 強調して

正解 A to以降は目的を表すto不定詞句で、「新しい従業員を歓迎するということをもっと-------するために」と開会のあいさつを書き直した目的を述べている。place emphasis on ～で「～を強調する」という意味になる(A)が適切。CEO「最高経営責任者」、opening remarks「開会のあいさつ」、rewrite「～を書き直す」、welcome「～を歓迎する」。
(B) 動詞emphasize「～を強調する」の原形。
(C)(D) どちらもmoreで修飾できるが、前後とつながらない。

122 Although concrete is one of the most durable construction materials, some form of maintenance work will ------- be needed.

(A) already
(B) eventually
(C) correctly
(D) further

コンクリートは最も耐久性のある建設資材の一つですが、いつかは何らかの形の保守作業が必要になります。

(A) すでに
(B) いつかは
(C) 正確に
(D) さらに

正解 B 選択肢は全て副詞の働きを持つ語。カンマの前は、譲歩を表す接続詞Althoughで始まる節で、「コンクリートは最も耐久性のある建設資材の一つだが」という意味で、カンマの後ろは「何らかの形の保守作業が必要になる」と前と相反する内容になっている。(B) eventually「いつかは」を入れると文意が通る。concrete「コンクリート」、durable「耐久性のある」、construction「建設」、material「資材、材料」、maintenance「保守」。

---

123 All shareholders of Techtraco Ltd. ------- to attend the upcoming annual meeting.

(A) are invited
(B) have been inviting
(C) had invited
(D) will be inviting

Techtraco社の全株主が、今度の年次総会に出席するよう招待されています。

＊選択肢の訳は省略

正解 A 選択肢は全て動詞invite「～を招待する」の変化した形。「今度の年次総会」とあり、主語のAll shareholders「全株主」は年次総会に招待される側なので、現在形の受動態の(A) are invitedが文意にも合い適切。shareholder「株主」、invite ～ to *do*「～を…するよう招待する」、attend「～に出席する」、upcoming「今度の、来る」、annual「年次の」。
(B) 現在完了進行形。(C) 過去完了形。(D) 未来進行形。

---

124 Of the new features at the Portview Gym, the rock-climbing wall is ------- members use most.

(A) close to
(B) other than
(C) the one
(D) one time

Portviewジムの新しい目玉の中で、ボルダリング用の壁は会員たちが最も利用しているものです。

(A) ～に近い
(B) ～の他に
(C) もの
(D) 1回

正解 C 空所の後ろはmembersを主語、useを動詞とする節だが、目的語に当たる名詞がない。名詞句の(C) the oneを入れると、the one (that) members use most「会員たちが最も利用するもの」と、the oneを目的語として後ろから説明する関係代名詞節の形になり、文意が通る。the oneはジムの新しい目玉の１つを表している。feature「目玉、特徴」、rock-climbing wall「ボルダリング用の壁」。

125 ------- the Sandmore Hotel is located in the city center, the Madrugada Inn is situated just outside of the city limits.

(A) Only if
(B) In case
(C) When
(D) While

Sandmoreホテルが市の中心部に位置している一方で、Madrugadaホテルは市境のすぐ外側に位置しています。

(A) ～の場合に限り
(B) 万一～の場合には
(C) ～のときは
(D) ～する一方で…

正解 D 選択肢は全て接続詞の働きを持つ語句。カンマの前後では、2つのホテルの対照的な立地が述べられている。よって、対照を表す(D) While「～する一方で…」を入れると、両ホテルの立地の特徴を対比して説明する文となり、適切。be located「位置している」、inn「ホテル、旅館」、be situated「位置している」、limits「〈地域や範囲の〉境界」。

---

126 Before the training, Mr. Bonnay was ------- unaware of recent developments in automated delivery systems.

(A) largely
(B) closely
(C) faintly
(D) finally

研修前には、Bonnayさんは自動配送システムにおける最近の事情を大部分認識していませんでした。

(A) 大部分は
(B) 密接に
(C) かすかに
(D) 最終的に

正解 A 選択肢は全て副詞。空所の後ろのunaware of recent developments「最近の事情を認識していない」を修飾し、文意に合うのは、(A) largely「大部分は」。be unaware of ～「～を認識していない」、development「新事情、新事実」、automated「自動化された」、delivery「配送」。

---

127 ------- weeks, it was clear that the long-term sponsorship deal with basketball star Joe Littleton would be successful.

(A) Within
(B) Several
(C) Just
(D) During

数週間以内に、バスケットボールのスター選手のJoe Littletonとの長期スポンサー契約が成功するであろうことが、明らかになっていました。

(A) ～以内に
(B) 幾つかの
(C) わずか
(D) ～の間に

正解 A カンマの後ろには〈主語＋動詞〉の形があり、文として成り立っているので、カンマの前の------- weeksは副詞句と分かる。期間を表すweeksを続けて文意に合うのは、前置詞の(A) Within「～以内に」。long-term「長期の」、sponsorship deal「スポンサー契約」、successful「成功した」。
(B) 形容詞。weeksを修飾できるが、カンマまでとその後ろの文をつなぐことができないので不適切。(C) 副詞。
(D) 前置詞。後ろに特定の期間を表す語句が続いていないので不適切。

128 The ideal job candidate will quickly be able to become ------- with software packages that are designed in-house.

(A) compatible
(B) possible
(C) proficient
(D) fortunate

理想的な求職候補者は、社内で設計されるソフトウエア一式に素早く熟達できる人です。

(A) 両立できる
(B) 可能な
(C) 熟達した
(D) 幸運な

正解 C 選択肢は全て形容詞。主語はThe ideal job candidate「理想的な求職候補者」、空所の前はbecomeで、後ろはwith software packagesで手段・対象を示しているので、文意に合うのは(C) proficient「熟達した」。ideal「理想的な」、candidate「候補者」、design「～を設計する」、in-house「社内で」。
(A) be compatible with ～で「～と両立できる」という意味。文意に合わない。

---

129 The retirement party surprised Mr. Rheims, who could not ------- his gratitude for his colleagues' thoughtfulness.

(A) be concealed
(B) conceal
(C) concealing
(D) to conceal

その退職パーティーはRheimsさんを驚かせ、彼は同僚たちの思いやりに対して感謝の気持ちを隠すことができませんでした。

＊選択肢の訳は省略

正解 B 動詞conceal「～を隠す」の適切な形を選ぶ。カンマの後ろはMr. Rheimsを先行詞に取る関係代名詞節。助動詞could notの後ろに置いて、目的語のhis gratitudeを続けられるのは、原形の(B)。retirement「退職」、gratitude「感謝(の念)」、colleague「同僚」、thoughtfulness「思いやり」。
(A) 受動態。関係代名詞節中の主語は動作の主体であるMr. Rheimsなので、不適切。
(C) 現在分詞、または動名詞。(D) to不定詞。

---

130 ------- on the age of the computer's operating system, the program may run more slowly than expected.

(A) Depending
(B) Focused
(C) Relying
(D) Centered

コンピューターのオペレーティングシステムの経年数次第で、プログラムは思っているより低速で作動する可能性があります。

(A) 次第で
(B) ～の焦点が合わせられて
(C) 当てにして
(D) 集中させて

正解 A カンマまではonで始まる前置詞句のみなので、後ろの文を修飾できる、分詞構文の形にする。depend on ～で「～次第である」という意味なので、(A) Dependingを入れると文意が通る。age「経年数」、run「作動する」。
(B) 動詞focus「～の焦点を合わせる」の過去分詞。
(C) 動詞rely「当てにする」の現在分詞。
(D) 動詞center「集中する」の過去分詞。

Questions 131-134 refer to the following advertisement.

Corporate Team-Building Workshops

❶ Strong teams with members that collaborate effectively are at the heart of any business organization. What better way to improve your employees' productivity and your company's profits than by strengthening team skills? -------. (131.) The result? Improved performance for your employees and increased ------- (132.) for your company!

❷ We work with groups of all sizes to facilitate creative team activities that ------- (133.) to be fun and inspiring. However, there is a serious purpose ------- (134.) every activity — generating team spirit! Contact Plainfield Solutions at 512-555-0121 for a free consultation.

問題131-134は次の広告に関するものです。

企業のチーム構築に関する講習会

効果的に協力し合うメンバーを有する強力なチームは、どんな事業組織においても核心にあるものです。従業員の生産性と会社の利益を向上させる上で、チーム力を強化することよりも優れた方法があるでしょうか。*チーム構築に関する当社の講習会は、信頼を築き上げ、コミュニケーションを改善するのに役立ちます。その成果ですか？従業員にとっての業績の向上、そして会社にとっての収入の増加です！

当社の講習会では、あらゆる規模のグループで作業して、楽しくてやる気を起こさせること請け合いの創造的なチームアクティビティーを促進します。しかしながら、どのアクティビティーの背後にも真剣な目的があります――チーム精神を生み出すことです。無料のご相談については、512-555-0121までPlainfield Solutions社にご連絡ください。

*問題131の挿入文の訳

Words & Phrases

corporate 企業の　workshop 講習会　❶ collaborate 協力する　effectively 効果的に　organization 組織
improve ～を向上させる　productivity 生産性　profit 利益　strengthen ～を強化する　skill 能力、力量
result 成果、結果　improved 向上した　performance 業績　increased 増加した　❷ facilitate ～を促進する
creative 創造的な　inspiring やる気を起こさせる　serious 真剣な、重大な　purpose 目的　generate ～を生み出す
contact ～に連絡する　consultation 〈専門家との〉相談

Expressions

be at the heart of ～ 「～の核心にある、～の中心にある」（❶ 1行目）

Several start-up companies are at the heart of the city's economy.
数社の新興企業がその都市の経済の中心にあります。

131 (A) Many employees are reluctant to participate in team-building activities.
(B) Most companies lack the time and resources for a team-building program.
(C) Our team-building workshops help build trust and improve communication.
(D) Team building is not just for established companies.

(A) 多くの従業員は、チーム構築に関するアクティビティーに参加したがりません。
(B) ほとんどの会社は、チーム構築に関するプログラムのための時間と資源を欠いています。
(C) チーム構築に関する当社の講習会は、信頼を築き上げ、コミュニケーションを改善するのに役立ちます。
(D) チーム構築は、定評のある会社のためだけのものではありません。

正解 C 空所の直前の文では、チーム力の強化が従業員の生産性と会社の利益を向上させる最善の方法だと述べられている。また、空所の後ろでは、講習会の成果として「従業員の業績向上と会社の-------の増加」が得られると説明されているので、空所ではこの成果を得るために必要なチーム力の強化方法が紹介されていると考えられる。よって、チーム構築に関する自社の講習会を紹介している(C)を入れると流れとして自然。
(A) be reluctant to *do*「～したがらない、～するのに気が進まない」、participate in ～「～に参加する」。
(B) lack「～を欠く」、resources「資源」。
(D) established「定評のある、確立した」。

132 (A) property
(B) advertising
(C) competition
(D) revenue

(A) 資産
(B) 広告
(C) 競争
(D) 収入

正解 D この文書はチーム力構築の講習会の広告。チーム力の強化が必要な理由として❶2行目に、improve your employees' productivity and your company's profits「従業員の生産性と会社の利益を向上させる」とある。また、空所の文の直前にThe result?「その成果ですか?」とあり、Improved performance for your employeesとincreased ------- for your companyという成果を2つ挙げている。よって空所では、チーム力強化により実際に得られる成果の2つ目が述べられていると分かる。1つ目の成果の「従業員にとっての向上した業績」と並んで、2つ目の「会社にとっての増加した-------」という文意に合うのは(D) revenue「収入」。

133 (A) guarantees
(B) are guaranteed
(C) guaranteeing
(D) had been guaranteeing

＊選択肢の訳は省略

正解 B 選択肢は全て動詞guarantee「～を請け合う、～を保証する」が変化した形。thatの前までに〈主語＋動詞〉の形があり、文として成立しているので、that以降は直前の名詞activitiesを説明する節と考えられる。guarantee ～ to *do*で「～が…すると請け合う、～が…すると保証する」という意味。アクティビティーを伴う講習会を提供するのは広告主の会社なので、activitiesを先行詞とする関係代名詞のthat節は、「楽しくてやる気を起こさせることが保証された(アクティビティー)」という受動態になる。よって、(B) are guaranteedが適切。
(A) 三人称単数現在形。(C) 現在分詞。(D) 過去完了進行形。

134 (A) behind
(B) after
(C) above
(D) along

(A) ～の背後に
(B) ～の後に
(C) ～の上に
(D) ～に沿って

正解 A 選択肢は全て前置詞の働きを持つ語。直前の文で、「楽しくてやる気を起こさせること請け合いの創造的なチームアクティビティー」に言及した後、However「しかしながら」と対照を表す表現を挟んで、there is a serious purpose ------- every activityと続けている。よって、空所を含む文ではアクティビティーについて直前の文とは対照的な特長を述べていると考えられる。(A) behind「～の背後に」を入れると、楽しいアクティビティーの裏に真剣な目的がある、という意味になり文意が通る。

Questions 135-138 refer to the following letter.

February 5

Dr. Jenna E. Delphin
671 South Prince Street
Missoula, MT 59804

Dear Dr. Delphin:

❶ Thank you for ------- (135.) a proposal for the Atelic Chemical Association conference. I am delighted to confirm that your proposal has been approved. We have tentatively scheduled your presentation for the morning of July 25, which is the second full day of the conference. ------- (136.).

❷ Dr. Henry Knecht ------- (137.) you with a list of guidelines for speakers, the preferred format for each presentation, and our logo and marketing materials. If you do not receive that e-mail by February 15, please feel free to reach out to him ------- (138.) at hknecht@atelicca.org.

❸ I look forward to seeing you in July.

Best wishes,

Randall Antoun, Conference Manager

問題135-138は次の手紙に関するものです。

2月5日

Jenna E. Delphin博士
サウスプリンス通り671番地
ミズーラ、MT 59804

Delphin博士

Atelic化学協会の協議会に提案書をご提出いただきありがとうございます。あなたの提案書が承認されたことを喜んでお知らせいたします。私どもは、あなたのプレゼンテーションを暫定的に7月25日の午前に予定しており、この日は協議会の終日開催日の2日目です。*これがご了承いただけるかどうかお知らせください。

Henry Knecht博士が講演者のための指針リスト、各プレゼンテーションに推奨される形式、そして当協会のロゴとマーケティング資料をあなたに提供することになっております。2月15日までにあなたがそのEメールを受信されていない場合は、ご遠慮なくhknecht@atelicca.orgまで彼と直接連絡をお取りください。

7月にあなたとお会いできることを心待ちにしております。

敬具

Randall Antoun、協議会管理者

*問題136の挿入文の訳

Words & Phrases

❶ proposal 提案(書)　chemical 化学の　association 協会　conference 協議会、会議
be delighted to *do* 喜んで～する　confirm ～とはっきり述べる　approve ～を承認する　tentatively 暫定的に
schedule ～ for … ～を…に予定する　full day 終日　❷ guidelines 指針　speaker 講演者　preferred 好ましい
format 形式　logo ロゴ　material 資料　reach out to ～ ～と連絡を取ろうとする
❸ look forward to *doing* ～することを心待ちにする　manager 管理者

135 (A) studying
(B) changing
(C) submitting
(D) reviewing

(A) ～を熟読すること
(B) ～を変更すること
(C) ～を提出すること
(D) ～を再検討すること

正解 C この手紙の差出人は、最後の記名より協議会管理者のAntounさんで、受取人は、冒頭の宛先よりDelphin博士。空所の文ではDelphin博士に対し、Atelic化学協会の協議会への提案書に関して「提案書を------- くれてありがとう」と礼を述べている。空所直後の2文でDelphin博士に、提案書が承認されたこととプレゼンテーションの暫定日時を伝え、また❷で、講演者の指針とプレゼンテーションの形式などの詳細が説明されているので、Delphin博士は協議会で発表を行うと分かる。よって、Delphin博士は協議会を主催するAtelic化学協会に提案書を提出したと判断できるので、(C)が適切。
(A)(B)(D) 後ろの文脈と合わない。

---

136 (A) Please let me know if this is acceptable to you.
(B) Instead, a list of speakers is included with this letter.
(C) For this reason, the association's membership fees have increased.
(D) You should be prepared to join us here next week.

(A) これがご了承いただけるかどうかお知らせください。
(B) 代わりに、講演者リストを本状に同封しております。
(C) このような理由で、当協会の会費は上がりました。
(D) 来週あなたは、こちらに加わる用意をした方がよいでしょう。

正解 A 空所直前の文に「あなたのプレゼンテーションを暫定的に7月25日の午前に予定した」とあるので、(A)を入れると、その暫定的な予定をthisと受け、その日時で問題がないかを尋ねる内容が続くこととなり、流れとして自然。acceptable「受け入れられる」。
(D) be prepared to *do*「～する用意がある」。

---

137 (A) provides
(B) provided
(C) used to provide
(D) will be providing

＊選択肢の訳は省略

正解 D 動詞provide「～を提供する」の適切な形を選ぶ。空所を含む文は「Henry Knecht博士が講演者のための指針リスト、各プレゼンテーションに推奨される形式、そして当協会のロゴとマーケティング資料をあなたに-------」という意味。直後の文で、この内容をthat e-mail「そのEメール」と受け、2月15日までに受信しない場合は彼と連絡を取るよう伝えられている。冒頭の手紙の日付が2月5日なので、そのEメールはこれから送信されると判断できることから、空所を含む文の時制は未来。未来進行形の(D) will be providingが適切。provide ～ with …で「～に…を提供する」という意味。
(A) 三人称単数現在形。(B) 過去形。(C) used to *do*「〈過去の習慣・状態を表して〉よく～していた」。

---

138 (A) directly
(B) directed
(C) directs
(D) director

(A) 直接に
(B) 管理された
(C) ～を管理する
(D) 管理者

正解 A 空所を含む文は、空所の語がなくても文として成立するので、副詞が入る。(A) directly「直接に」が適切。Knecht博士が送信する予定のEメールが期日までに届かない場合には、本人と直接連絡を取るよう伝えている文となり、流れとしても自然。
(B) 動詞direct「～を管理する」の過去分詞。
(C) 動詞directの三人称単数現在形。
(D) 名詞。

Expressions

feel free to *do* 「遠慮なく～する、気軽に～する」(❷ 3行目)
Please feel free to drop by our showroom if you are interested in our new products.
当社の新製品に関心がおありでしたら、どうぞお気軽に当社のショールームにお立ち寄りください。

Questions 139-142 refer to the following letter.

May 6

Fenella Hornstein
4099 Unison Street
Tampa, FL 33601

Dear Ms. Hornstein,

❶ It has been brought to our attention that many of our customers ------- (139.) more options for paying their Tampa Bank credit card bill. ------- (140.), we are offering an option called Auto Pay starting on June 1.

❷ With this new payment option, your credit card balance is automatically paid in full on the first day of each month with funds from your checking account. It's so ------- (141.) !

❸ If you do not wish to use Auto Pay, there is no need to do anything. ------- (142.). If you would like to give Auto Pay a try, however, simply visit any Tampa Bank branch to get it set up.

❹ Thank you for banking with Tampa Bank.

Ken Rhys
Customer Service Manager

問題139-142は次の手紙に関するものです。

5月6日

Fenella Hornstein様
ユニゾン通り4099番地
タンパ、FL 33601

Hornstein様

当行のお客さまの多くが、タンパ銀行のクレジットカード請求の支払い方法に、より多くの選択肢を求めていらっしゃることに当行は注目してまいりました。それゆえ、当行は6月1日より、Auto Payという選択肢をご提供いたします。

この新たな支払い方法では、お客さまのクレジットカードの利用残高が、毎月１日にお客さまの当座預金口座の預金から自動的に全額支払われます。非常に便利です！

Auto Payの利用を希望されない場合は、何もする必要はございません。*お客さまには従来通り、お手続きによって引き続きお支払いをしていただけます。一方、Auto Payをお試しになりたい場合は、タンパ銀行のいずれかの支店にお越しいただき、Auto Payの設定をお申し付けください。

タンパ銀行とお取引いただきありがとうございます。

Ken Rhys
顧客サービス責任者

*問題142の挿入文の訳

Words & Phrases

❶ option 選択肢、選ぶべき方法　bill 請求額、請求書　❷ balance 差引残高　automatically 自動的に　in full 全額　funds 銀行預金　checking account 当座預金口座　❸ give ～ a try ～を試してみる　simply ただ　branch 支店　set up ～ ～を設定する　❹ bank with ～ 〈銀行〉と取引する

139 (A) to like
(B) had liked
(C) are liking
(D) would like

＊選択肢の訳は省略

正解 D 空所を含む文は、Itが形式主語でthat以下の内容を指し、「当行のお客さまの多くが、タンパ銀行のクレジットカード請求の支払い方法に、より多くの選択肢を------- ことに当行は注目してきた」という意味。直後の文で、「当行は6月1日より、Auto Payという選択肢を提供する」と顧客の要望に対応することが述べられており、その後も新サービスのAuto Payについての説明が続いているので、空所には願望を表す(D) would like「～が欲しい」が適切。
(A) to不定詞。(B) 過去完了形。that節を導く文の時制は過去ではないので、不適切。
(C) 現在進行形。動詞likeは通常現在進行形にしない。

140 (A) Instead
(B) Therefore
(C) Regretfully
(D) Nevertheless

(A) その代わりに
(B) それゆえ
(C) 残念ながら
(D) それにもかかわらず

正解 B 選択肢は全て副詞。直前の文で、銀行の顧客がクレジットカード請求の支払い方法についてより多くの選択肢を求めていることが述べられ、空所の後ろには「当行は6月1日より、Auto Payという選択肢を提供する」と続いている。よって、2つの文をつなぎ、因果関係を表す接続副詞の(B) Therefore「それゆえ」を入れると、顧客の要望に応じて新たな選択肢を提供するという流れになり、文意が通る。
(D) 2つの文をつなぐ接続副詞の働きを持つが、反意的な意味を持つので、文意に合わない。

141 (A) close
(B) familiar
(C) memorable
(D) convenient

(A) 近い
(B) よく知られた
(C) 記憶すべき
(D) 便利な

正解 D 選択肢は全て形容詞の働きを持つ語。直前の文で、Auto Payという新たな支払い方法について、「お客さまのクレジットカードの利用残高が、毎月1日にお客さまの当座預金口座の預金から自動的に全額支払われる」と手間がかからないことが説明されている。Auto PayをItで受け、形容する語として適切なのは、文意から(D) convenient「便利な」。

142 (A) Our customer service department is available 24 hours a day.
(B) Many customers save 5 percent of their monthly income.
(C) You can continue making payments manually as usual.
(D) You can receive a $50 gift certificate for recommending our bank to a friend.

(A) 当社の顧客サービス部は1日24時間対応しております。
(B) 多くのお客さまは月収の5パーセントを貯蓄しています。
(C) お客さまには従来通り、お手続きによって引き続きお支払いをしていただけます。
(D) 当行をご友人に推薦していただくことで、50ドルの商品券をお受け取りになれます。

正解 C ❷では、新たな支払い方法であるAuto Payについて、カードの請求額が毎月自動的に口座から支払われる仕組みが説明されている。空所の直前の文に、Auto Payの利用を希望しない場合について、「何もする必要はない」とある。一方、空所の後ろの文には「対照」を表すhoweverに続けて、Auto Payを試したい場合について「タンパ銀行のいずれかの支店を訪れ、Auto Payの設定を申し付けてください」とある。よって空所の文では、その前文で述べられているAuto Payを利用しない場合の説明が続くと考えられるので、従来通りの支払い方法を希望する顧客に対する説明の(C)が適切。(C)のmanuallyは、「手動で、人力を要して」という意味だが、ここでは顧客が小切手を使うなどの何らかの手続きを行って支払いをすることを表している。as usual「いつものように」。
(D) gift certificate「商品券」、recommend「～を推薦する」。

Expressions

bring ～ to *one's* attention　「～を人に注目させる、～を人に指摘する」（❶ 1行目）
Thank you for bringing this mistake in the invoice to our attention.
請求書におけるこの誤りをご指摘いただきありがとうございます。

Questions 143-146 refer to the following e-mail.

To: Laura Moreno <lm54@spotmail.ca>
From: Jack Chen <genmanager@qualityautosspringfield.ca>
Date: 3 March
Subject: Survey

Dear Ms. Moreno,

❶ Thank you for ------- **143.** Quality Autos of Springfield for your recent car purchase. We would greatly appreciate feedback on your experience. Please follow the link below to answer a brief survey. Responses are anonymous. To show our appreciation, ------- **144.** who complete the survey will receive an exclusive offer. After you click "submit" at the end of the survey, a ------- **145.** will appear. This may be redeemed for three oil changes for $43.99 — or just under $15.00 per oil change. ------- **146.**. If you find a better price for any maintenance service elsewhere, we will match it.

❷ Survey link: www.qualityautosspringfield.ca/survey

Best regards,

Jack Chen, General Manager

問題143-146は次のEメールに関するものです。

受信者：Laura Moreno <lm54@spotmail.ca>
送信者：Jack Chen <genmanager@qualityautosspringfield.ca>
日付：3月3日
件名：アンケート調査

Moreno様

先日の車のご購入にQuality自動車スプリングフィールド店をお選びいただき、ありがとうございました。ご購入体験に関してお客さまのご意見を頂ければ大変ありがたく存じます。下記にあるリンクに沿って簡単なアンケート調査にお答えください。回答は匿名です。当店の感謝の印といたしまして、アンケート調査に全てご記入いただいた方々は限定特別サービスをお受け取りになれます。アンケート調査の最後に「提出する」をクリックすると、クーポンが表示されます。こちらは、43ドル99セントでの3回分のオイル交換に換えることができます——つまり、オイル交換1回分につきわずか15ドル足らずということです。*これ以上お得な待遇はどこでも見つけられないでしょう。お客さまが他の所での何らかの整備サービスで、よりお得な価格を見つけられた場合、当店はそれに合わせます。

アンケート調査リンク：www.qualityautosspringfield.ca/survey

敬具

Jack Chen、支店長

*問題146の挿入文の訳

Words & Phrases

survey アンケート調査　❶ auto 〈automobileの略で〉自動車　recent 最近の　greatly 大いに　feedback 意見
follow ～をたどる、～に従う　below 〈本・ページの〉下記に　brief 簡単な、簡潔な　response 回答
anonymous 匿名の　appreciation 感謝　complete ～に全て記入する　exclusive 限定の　offer 特別サービス
submit ～を提出する　appear 表示される　redeem 〈クーポンなど〉を商品に換える　or つまり　per ～につき
maintenance 整備　elsewhere 他の場所で　match ～に釣り合わせる　❷ general manager 支店長

143 (A) chose
(B) choose
(C) choosing
(D) chosen

＊選択肢の訳は省略

正解 C 動詞choose「～を選ぶ」の適切な形を選ぶ。空所を含む文はThank you for ～「～してくれてありがとう」の形になっており、前置詞forの後ろには名詞(句)が続くので、動名詞の(C) choosingが適切。
(A) 過去形。
(B) 原形。
(D) 過去分詞。

144 (A) their
(B) those
(C) theirs
(D) that

(A) 彼らの
(B) 人々
(C) 彼らのもの
(D) それ

正解 B 空所を含む文には主語がないため、空所には直後のwho complete the surveyの先行詞となり主語の働きをする名詞が必要。those who ～の形で「～する人々」という意味を表す代名詞の(B) thoseが適切。
(A) 代名詞の所有格。
(C) 所有代名詞。
(D) 指示代名詞。

145 (A) report
(B) coupon
(C) license
(D) preview

(A) 報告書
(B) クーポン
(C) 許可証
(D) プレビュー

正解 B ❶ 1～2行目で、車の購入体験に関するアンケート調査への回答を依頼されており、同3～4行目で、感謝の印に回答者には限定特別サービスが提供されると述べられている。空所を含む文に「アンケート調査の最後に『提出する』をクリックすると、-------が表示される」とあるので、空所にはアンケート送信完了後に提供される限定特別サービスに関して表示されるものが入ると分かる。さらに直後の文に「これは、43ドル99セントでの3回分のオイル交換に換えることができる」とあるので、文意に合うのは(B) coupon「クーポン」。

146 (A) We have just expanded our Springfield location.
(B) The terms of your purchase agreement are attached.
(C) You can pick up your purchase at the dealership.
(D) You will not find a better deal anywhere.

(A) 当社は、スプリングフィールドの店舗を拡張したばかりです。
(B) お客さまの購入契約の条件が添付されています。
(C) お客さまはその販売代理店でご購入品を受け取ることができます。
(D) これ以上お得な待遇はどこでも見つけられないでしょう。

正解 D ❶ 3～5行目で、アンケート調査の全問回答者は、43ドル99セントでオイル交換3回分が行えるクーポンをもらえると説明されており、続けて「つまり、オイル交換1回分につきわずか15ドル足らずということだ」と、クーポンによってオイル交換サービスをお得な価格で受けられることが強調されている。よって、この後ろに(D)を入れると、(D)のbetter deal「より良い待遇」がクーポン利用による特別価格を上回る条件を表し、特別価格のお得さをさらに強調する文が続くこととなり、流れとして自然。deal「待遇、取引」。
(A) expand「～を拡張する」、location「店舗、場所」。
(B) terms「条件」、agreement「契約」。
(C) pick up ～「～を受け取る」、dealership「販売代理店」。

TEST 2 PART 6

Expressions

would appreciate 「～を頂けるとありがたく思う」(❶ 1～2行目)

I would appreciate your continued support.
引き続きご支援を頂ければ幸いです。

Questions 147-148 refer to the following e-mail.

E-mail

To: All Staff
From: Enid Barton
Date: August 18
Subject: Invitation

My fellow Grand Investment Trust employees:

❶ It has been 25 years since our company was founded. Please join us for a luncheon to mark the occasion.

❷ The event will take place at L'Espoir Restaurant from noon until 2:30 p.m. on Friday, November 12. Attendees will receive commemorative desk clocks as gifts.

❸ To ensure that we have an accurate count of attendees, please respond to llewis@grandit.com to confirm your attendance.

We hope to see you there.

Enid Barton

❹ Social Events Coordinator

問題147-148は次のEメールに関するものです。

受信者：全従業員
送信者：Enid Barton
日付：8月18日
件名：招待

同僚のGrand投資信託会社従業員の皆さん

当社が設立されてから25年になります。その出来事を記念する昼食会にお越しください。

イベントは11月12日金曜日の正午から午後2時30分まで、L'Espoirレストランで行われます。出席者は、進呈品として記念の卓上時計を受け取ります。

私たちが正確な出席者数を確実に把握できるよう、llewis@grandit.comに返信して出席を知らせてください。

皆さんとそこでお会いできることを願っています。

Enid Barton

社交行事まとめ役

147 What is the purpose of the event?

(A) To celebrate a company's anniversary
(B) To observe the retirement of a company officer
(C) To honor a founder's birthday
(D) To announce important changes in a company

イベントの目的は何ですか。

(A) 会社の記念日を祝うこと。
(B) 会社の役員の退職を祝うこと。
(C) 創立者の誕生日をたたえること。
(D) 会社における重要な変更を知らせること。

正解 A ❶に、It has been 25 years since our company was founded. Please join us for a luncheon to mark the occasion.「当社が設立されてから25年になる。その出来事を記念する昼食会にお越しください」と昼食会への案内があるので、イベントとは昼食会のことで、その目的は会社の設立25周年を祝うことだと分かる。よって、(A)が正解。celebrate「～を祝う」、anniversary「記念日」。
(B) observe「〈祝祭日など〉を祝う」、retirement「退職」、officer「役員」。
(C) honor「～の名誉をたたえる」、founder「創立者」。

---

148 What are employees asked to do?

(A) Bring lunch
(B) Invite a friend
(C) Send an e-mail
(D) Buy a gift

従業員たちは何をするよう求められていますか。

(A) 昼食を持参する。
(B) 友人を招待する。
(C) Eメールを送信する。
(D) 贈り物を買う。

正解 C Eメールは従業員全員に宛てたもの。❶・❷で会社の25周年記念の昼食会に招待して日時などを案内した後、❸でplease respond to llewis@grandit.com to confirm your attendance「llewis@grandit.comに返信して出席を知らせてください」と、従業員にEメールを送信することで出席を明らかにするよう求めている。
(A) ❶・❷より、従業員はレストランでの昼食会に招待されているのであり、昼食を持参するよう求められてはいない。
(D) ❷に、出席者は進呈品として卓上時計を受け取るとあるが、従業員たちは贈り物を買うよう求められてはいない。

Words & Phrases

invitation 招待　fellow 同僚、仲間　investment 投資　trust 信託　❶ found ～を設立する
join ～ for … …に～と一緒に参加する　luncheon 昼食会　mark ～を記念する、～を祝う　occasion 出来事、機会
❷ take place 行われる　attendee 出席者　commemorative 記念の　desk clock 卓上時計
❸ ensure that ～ 確実に～する　accurate 正確な　count 総数　confirm ～を正式に認める　attendance 出席
❹ social event 社交行事　coordinator まとめ役、コーディネーター

Expressions

respond to ～ 「～に返信する、～に反応する」(❸ 1行目)

We would like you to respond to this e-mail if you're interested in answering the survey.
アンケートへの回答にご興味があれば、このEメールに返信していただきたいと思います。

Questions 149-150 refer to the following notice.

Western Regional Rail—Changes to Train Schedule

❶ Maintenance on the train lines begins mid-July. Repairs are expected to take six weeks, so please plan for the revised schedule to remain in force through August.

❷ **Tips for Passengers**

- All trains will run on reduced frequency. Please consult the schedule posted in the station and on our Web site for specific times.
- Allow an extra 20 to 45 minutes per trip, depending on the route, day of the week, and time of day.
- Adjust your commute to avoid the peak times of 7 to 9 A.M. and 5 to 7 P.M., which will be more crowded than usual.
- Space for bicycles and baby strollers aboard trains will be more limited than usual.
- Use alternate transportation when possible.

問題149-150は次のお知らせに関するものです。

西部地域鉄道——列車時刻表の変更

7月中旬より、鉄道路線の保守作業が始まります。修繕作業には6週間かかる見込みですので、8月の終わりまで有効の改定時刻表に対応して計画を立ててください。

乗客の皆さまへのお役立ち情報

・全ての列車は、本数を減らして運行します。具体的な時刻につきましては、駅構内や当社ウェブサイトに掲示されている時刻表をご覧ください。
・経路や曜日、時間帯により、1回の乗車につき20分から45分の余裕を見ておいてください。
・ピーク時の午前7時から9時および午後5時から7時を避けるよう、通勤通学を調整してください。この時間帯は通常より混雑すると思われます。
・列車内の自転車やベビーカーのためのスペースは、通常よりも限られるでしょう。
・可能であれば、代替の交通機関をご利用ください。

Words & Phrases

regional 地域の　rail 鉄道　schedule 時刻表、スケジュール　❶ maintenance 保守作業、メンテナンス
train line 鉄道路線　repairs 修繕(作業)　plan for ～ ～に対する計画を立てる　revise ～を改定する
remain ～のままである　in force 有効な　through ～ ～の終わりまで　❷ tip 役に立つ情報、ヒント
passenger 乗客　reduce ～を減らす　frequency 回数、頻度　consult ～を見る、～を調べる　post ～を掲示する
specific 具体的な　allow ～を見込んでおく　extra 余分な　per ～ ～につき　trip 移動、旅行
depending on ～ ～によって　day of the week 〈週の中の〉曜日　time of day 〈一日の中の〉時間(帯)
adjust ～を調整する　commute 通勤、通学　avoid ～を避ける　peak ピークの　crowded 混雑した
baby stroller ベビーカー　aboard ～に乗って　limited 限られた、制限された　alternate 代替の
transportation 交通機関

149 What is indicated about the trains?

(A) They will not run as often as usual.
(B) They will be available earlier than usual.
(C) They will not have as many stops as usual.
(D) Their routes will be different than usual.

列車について何が示されていますか。

(A) それらは通常ほど頻繁に運行しないだろう。
(B) それらは通常より早い時間に利用できるだろう。
(C) それらは通常より停車駅が少ないだろう。
(D) それらの経路は通常とは異なるだろう。

正解 A ❷の「乗客へのお役立ち情報」の1点目に、All trains will run on reduced frequency.「全ての列車は、本数を減らして運行する」とある。この内容を、比較表現のas ～ as …を用いてwill not run as often as usual「通常ほど頻繁に運行しないだろう」と表している(A)が正解。not as ～ as …「…ほど ～ ではない」。
(B) available「利用できる」。
(C) stop「停車駅」。

150 What is indicated in the notice that might concern passengers?

(A) The schedule has not yet been posted.
(B) There will be less room on the trains.
(C) The Web site is temporarily down.
(D) The ticket prices will increase.

お知らせでは、乗客を懸念させる可能性があることとして何が示されていますか。

(A) 時刻表はまだ掲示されていない。
(B) 列車内のスペースが少なくなるだろう。
(C) ウェブサイトは一時的にダウンしている。
(D) 切符の値段が上がるだろう。

正解 B ❷の「乗客へのお役立ち情報」の4点目に、Space for bicycles and baby strollers aboard trains will be more limited than usual.「列車内の自転車やベビーカーのためのスペースは、通常よりも限られるだろう」とある。concern「～を心配させる」。room「スペース」。
(A) ❷ 2～3行目に「駅構内や当社ウェブサイトに掲示されている時刻表を見てください」とあるので、時刻表はすでに掲示されていると考えられる。
(C) temporarily「一時的に」、down「ダウンした、作動不能状態の」。

Expressions

be expected to *do* 「～する見込みである、～する見通しである」(❶ 1行目)
The furniture is expected to arrive tomorrow afternoon.
家具は明日の午後、届く見込みです。

Questions 151-152 refer to the following card.

Harper's Gym

Guest Membership

❶ One of our valued members has invited you to Harper's Gym! As our guest, enjoy a complimentary membership for one month. Bring this card to Harper's Gym and an attendant at the front desk will activate your membership.

❷ The guest membership entitles you to unlimited use of our facilities and equipment. You can also sign up for fitness classes and personal training sessions; extra charges may apply. This guest membership program is limited to first-time visitors.

---

❸ For the member: complete the information below and give the card to your invitee. You will be entered into our drawing for fitness clothing.

Guest: Maria Zoranski

Member: Rick Armstrong

問題151-152は次のカードに関するものです。

Harper'sジム
ゲスト会員資格

当ジムの大切な会員のお一人が、あなたをHarper'sジムに招待しました！私どものゲストとして1カ月間、無料の会員資格をお楽しみください。このカードをHarper'sジムにお持ちくだされば、受付の係員があなたの会員資格を有効にいたします。

ゲスト会員資格により、あなたには当ジムの施設や器具を制限なしで使用する権利が与えられます。また、フィットネスのクラスや個人向けトレーニング・セッションに申し込むこともできます。その場合、追加料金が適用される可能性がございます。このゲスト会員プログラムは、初回のお客さま限定とさせていただいております。

会員の方へ：下記の情報に全て記入して、ご招待者さまにカードをお渡しください。あなたはフィットネスウエアの抽選に登録されます。

ゲスト： Maria Zoranski

会員： Rick Armstrong

Words & Phrases

membership 会員(資格)　❶ valued 大切な　complimentary 無料の　attendant 係員　front desk 受付
activate ～を有効にする　❷ unlimited 制限のない　facility 施設　equipment 器具　sign up for ～ ～に申し込む
personal 個人に向けられた　session セッション、授業　extra 追加の　charge 料金　apply 適用される
be limited to ～ ～に限定されている　first-time 初めての　❸ complete ～に全て記入する　below 〈本・ページの〉下記の
invitee 招待される人　enter ～を登録する　drawing 抽選　clothing ウエア、衣類

151 What is indicated about the offer?

(A) It is good for one year.
(B) Guests may use only certain equipment.
(C) Some activities may cost extra.
(D) A regular member must accompany the guest.

提示内容について何が示されていますか。

(A) それは1年間有効である。
(B) ゲストは特定の器具のみを利用できる。
(C) 幾つかのアクティビティーは追加で料金がかかる可能性がある。
(D) 正規の会員がゲストに同行しなければならない。

正解 C カードの見出しの下に「ゲスト会員資格」とあり、❶1～2行目より、このカードはジムの会員からの招待によって、ゲストとしてジムを無料で利用できる会員資格を提示していると分かる。❷2行目の「フィットネスのクラスや個人向けトレーニング・セッションに申し込むこともできる」に続き、セミコロン(;)を挟んで、extra charges may apply「その場合、追加料金が適用される可能性がある」と補足しているので、(C)が正解。offer「提示、申し出」。activity「アクティビティー、活動」、cost「〈料金が〉かかる」。
(A) ❶1～2行目に無料会員資格は1カ月有効とある。be good for ～「～の間有効である」。
(B) ❷1行目に、施設や器具は制限なしで使用できるとある。certain「特定の」。
(D) regular「正規の」、accompany「～に同行する」。

---

152 What is suggested about Ms. Zoranski?

(A) She is a personal trainer.
(B) She won some fitness clothing.
(C) She is Mr. Armstrong's supervisor.
(D) She has never been to Harper's Gym before.

Zoranskiさんについて何が分かりますか。

(A) 彼女は個人向けのトレーナーである。
(B) 彼女はフィットネスウエアを獲得した。
(C) 彼女はArmstrongさんの上司である。
(D) 彼女は以前、Harper'sジムに行ったことがない。

正解 D Zoranskiさんの名前は❸の「ゲスト」の欄に書かれているので、招待されてゲスト会員資格を与えられた人物だと分かる。❷3行目にThis guest membership program is limited to first-time visitors.「このゲスト会員プログラムは、初回の客限定だ」とあることから、Zoranskiさんはこれまで Harper'sジムに行ったことがないと判断できる。
(A) trainer「トレーナー、教官」。
(B) ❸1行目のFor the member「会員の方へ」という記載の後、カードを記入するとウエアの抽選に登録されるとあるので、抽選の対象者は会員であり、ゲストのZoranskiさんは抽選でウエアを獲得できないと分かる。win「〈賞品など〉を獲得する」。
(C) supervisor「上司」。

Expressions

entitle ～ to … 「～に…の権利を与える」(❷1行目)
This ticket entitles you to free admission to the Digital Content Expo.
このチケットは、あなたにデジタルコンテンツ博覧会への無料入場の権利を与えます。

Questions 153-155 refer to the following article.

Burwell's Garage Celebrates Half-Century Mark

❶ (May 11)—Many things have changed on Ridgeford's Main Street in recent years, but one thing has remained constant. Burwell's Garage, still in its original location at the north end of the street, continues to see a steady stream of customers.

❷ When Roy Burwell first started his car repair shop, he worked on very few foreign cars and had never used a computer. Mr. Burwell, whose son Dean became chief mechanic at the shop two years ago, said, "Computers changed everything. We used to just look at the engine to see what the trouble was. Now we also need a lot of expensive equipment."

❸ The full-service garage, which celebrates its fiftieth anniversary this month, offers services including oil changes, motor overhauls, and tire replacements. The younger Mr. Burwell will add towing services to the list next month.

❹ When asked the secret to the continued success of the business, Roy Burwell's answer is straightforward. "We charge a fair price for honest work. We can fix any kind of car out there. And all our work is guaranteed."

問題153-155は次の記事に関するものです。

Burwell's自動車修理工場が半世紀の節目を祝う

(5月11日)――リッジフォードのメイン通りでは近年多くのものが変化したが、1つ不変のものがある。Burwell's自動車修理工場は、今なお通りの北端という創業時の場所にあり、絶え間ない顧客の流れが続いている。

Roy Burwellが最初に自分の自動車修理店を始めたとき、外国車に対応することはほとんどなく、コンピューターを使用したことは一度もなかった。2年前にBurwell氏の息子のDeanが店の主任整備士になった。「コンピューターが全てを変えました。以前は、何が問題なのかを調べるためにエンジンを見るだけでした。今や私たちは、多数の高価な機器も必要です」とBurwell氏は述べた。

この全サービスに対応する自動車修理工場は、今月50周年を迎え、オイル交換、モーターのオーバーホール、タイヤ交換を始めとするサービスを提供している。息子の方のBurwell氏は、来月レッカー移動サービスをそのリストに追加するつもりだ。

事業が成功し続けている秘訣を尋ねられたとき、Roy Burwellの答えは明快だった。「私たちは、誠実な作業の対価として適正な価格をご請求しています。私たちは、世の中にあるどんな種類の車でも直すことができます。そして、私たちの作業は全て保証付きです」。

Words & Phrases

garage 自動車修理工場　celebrate ～を祝う、～を記念する　half-century 半世紀　mark 目印、標識
❶ remain ～のままである　constant 不変の　original 元の　see (出来事などの)場になる　steady 絶え間のない
stream 〈人・物などの〉絶え間ない流れ　❷ work on ～ ～に取り組む　chief mechanic 主任整備士
used to *do* 以前は～していた　expensive 高価な　equipment 機器
❸ full-service フルサービスの、包括的業務を提供する　anniversary ～周年、記念日　overhaul オーバーホール、分解修理
replacement 交換　towing service レッカー移動サービス　❹ continued 継続する
straightforward 明快な、単刀直入な　charge ～を請求する　fair 適正な　honest 誠実な　fix ～を直す
out there 世の中にある　guarantee ～を保証する

153 What is suggested about Roy Burwell?

(A) He specializes in repairing imported cars.
(B) He had to gain experience using computers.
(C) He no longer owns Burwell's Garage.
(D) He recently moved his business.

Roy Burwellについて何が分かりますか。

(A) 彼は輸入車の修理を専門にしている。
(B) 彼は、コンピューターを使用する経験を積まなければならなかった。
(C) 彼はもはやBurwell's自動車修理工場を所有していない。
(D) 彼は最近、店を移転した。

正解 B ❷ 1～3行目で、Roy Burwellが自動車修理店を始めた当初はコンピューターを使用したことが一度もなかったと述べられている。さらに同5～6行目で、Computers changed everything.「コンピューターが全てを変えた」とBurwellさんの発言が引用され、以前はエンジンを見るだけで良かったが、今では多数の高価な機器も必要になったと、以前と現在の状況の違いが述べられている。よって、Roy Burwellは必要に迫られてコンピューターを使用する経験を積まなければならなかったと考えられる。gain experience「経験を積む」。
(A) specialize in ～「～を専門にしている」、imported car「輸入車」。
(C) ❷ 3～5行目にRoy Burwellの息子のDeanが主任整備士になったとあるが、店の所有権についての言及はない。no longer ～「もはや～でない」、own「～を所有している」。
(D) ❶ 3～4行目に、Burwell's自動車修理工場は創業時と同じ場所にあると述べられている。move「～を移転する」。

154 The word "trouble" in paragraph 2, line 7, is closest in meaning to

(A) drawback
(B) effort
(C) amount
(D) problem

第2段落・7行目にある "trouble" に最も意味が近いのは

(A) 欠点
(B) 努力
(C) 量
(D) 問題

正解 D ❷では、Burwellさんの自動車修理工場について説明されており、同6～7行目でWe used to just look at the engine「以前は、エンジンを見るだけだった」とBurwellさんの発言が引用され、to see what the trouble wasとエンジンを見る目的が述べられている。自動車修理工場でエンジンを見る目的は自動車の故障なので、(D) problem「問題、支障」が適切。
(A) drawbackは「欠点、不利益」という意味で、状況・商品などの短所や難点を示す。記事中のtroubleは車の不調を示しているので、不適切。

155 What service will Burwell's Garage soon offer?

(A) Tire replacements
(B) Vehicle towing
(C) Oil changes
(D) Vehicle loans

Burwell's自動車修理工場は間もなく、どんなサービスを提供しますか。

(A) タイヤ交換
(B) 車のレッカー移動
(C) オイル交換
(D) 車のローン

正解 B ❸ 1～4行目で、Burwell's自動車修理工場が提供するサービスが列挙されており、続けて同4～5行目でThe younger Mr. Burwell will add towing services to the list next month.「息子の方のBurwell氏は、来月レッカー移動サービスをそのリストに追加するつもりだ」と、前文で列挙されたサービスリストに、来月からレッカー移動サービスが追加されると説明されている。よって、(B)が正解。vehicle「車」。
(A)(C) ❸ 1～4行目に、タイヤ交換やオイル交換サービスは現在すでに提供しているとある。
(D) loan「ローン、貸し付け」。

Expressions

continue to *do* 「～し続ける」(❶ 5行目)
After remodeling, Pete's Teashop will continue to serve the area.
改装後も、Pete'sティーショップは引き続き地域に貢献してまいります。

Questions 156-157 refer to the following text-message chain.

1 **Amihan Mendoza [1:31 p.m.]**
Can you meet me for coffee this afternoon?

2 **Gavino Andrada [1:32 p.m.]**
Sure. What's up?

3 **Amihan Mendoza [1:32 p.m.]**
I want to talk with you about the Dunhume account. I just heard I'll be taking it over.

4 **Gavino Andrada [1:33 p.m.]**
Good idea. They keep changing their minds about the number of software packages they want to purchase. But this is not unusual for them. You'll need to be careful in working with them.

5 **Amihan Mendoza [1:34 p.m.]**
How about 2:30 at Cha Cha Grill?

6 **Gavino Andrada [1:35 p.m.]**
Sounds good. If you haven't already, you should ask Thomas to give you any information he has on that account. He was the lead salesperson before you, and I'm sure he can fill you in on the challenges he faced.

7 **Amihan Mendoza [1:36 p.m.]**
OK. I'll see you there.

問題156-157は次のテキストメッセージのやりとりに関するものです。

Amihan Mendoza [午後1時31分]
今日の午後、会ってコーヒーを飲まない？

Gavino Andrada [午後1時32分]
いいよ。どうしたの？

Amihan Mendoza [午後1時32分]
得意先のDunhume社の件であなたと話がしたいの。ちょうど、私がそれを引き継ぐことになると聞いたところよ。

Gavino Andrada [午後1時33分]
いい考えだね。彼らはソフトウエアのセットの購入希望数について、ころころ考えを変えるんだ。だけど、これは彼らには珍しくないさ。君が彼らと仕事をする際には気を付ける必要があるだろうね。

Amihan Mendoza [午後1時34分]
Cha Chaグリルで2時30分はどう？

Gavino Andrada [午後1時35分]
いいね。もしまだならThomasに、あの取引先に関して彼が持っているどんな情報でも教えてほしいと頼んだ方がいいよ。彼は君の前の営業主任だったので、彼が直面した難題について、きっと君に情報を提供できると思うよ。

Amihan Mendoza [午後1時36分]
分かったわ。では、そこで会いましょう。

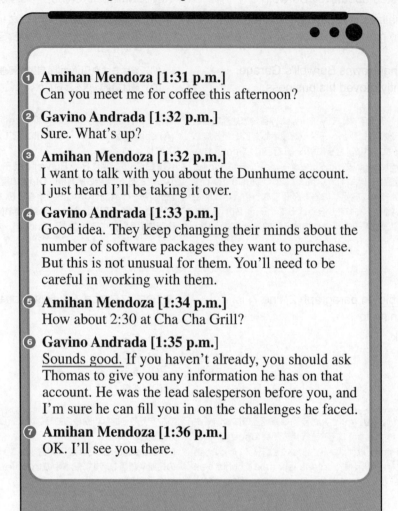

156 In what department does Ms. Mendoza most likely work?

(A) Personnel
(B) Sales
(C) Accounting
(D) Product Design

Mendozaさんはどんな部署で働いていると考えられますか。

(A) 人事部
(B) 営業部
(C) 経理部
(D) 製品設計部

正解 B Mendozaさんは❸で、得意先のDunhume社を引き継ぐことになったと述べている。それに対し、Andradaさんは❹で、Dunhume社はソフトウエアのセットの購入希望数を変更ばかりしていると仕事上の注意点を説明し、さらに❻で、Mendozaさんの前任の営業主任のThomasという人物に言及している。よって、Mendozaさんは営業部で働いていると判断できる。sales「営業(部)」。
(A) personnel「人事部」。

---

157 At 1:35 P.M., what does Mr. Andrada most likely mean when he writes, "Sounds good"?

(A) He likes a restaurant's chef.
(B) He agrees to represent his coworker Thomas at a luncheon.
(C) He thinks a client will like a restaurant.
(D) He agrees that he and Ms. Mendoza should meet.

午後1時35分に、Andradaさんは "Sounds good"という発言で、何を意味していると考えられますか。

(A) 彼はレストランのシェフを気に入っている。
(B) 彼は、昼食会で自分の同僚であるThomasの代理を務めることに同意している。
(C) 彼は、顧客がレストランを気に入るだろうと思っている。
(D) 彼は、自分とMendozaさんが会うことに同意している。

正解 D ❶の今日の午後に会えないかというMendozaさんの依頼に対し、Andradaさんは❷で快諾している。その後、❺でMendozaさんが「Cha Chaグリルで2時30分はどうか」と会う場所と時間を提案したのに対し、Andradaさんは下線部で「いいね」と応答していることから、提示された場所と時間にMendozaさんと会うことに同意を示していると考えられる。agree「～に同意する」。
(B) represent「～の代理を務める」、luncheon「昼食会」。

Words & Phrases

❷ What's up? どうしたの?、何かあったの?　❸ account 得意先、顧客　❹ keep *doing* ～し続ける
change *one's* mind about ～ ～に関して考えを変える　purchase ～を購入する　unusual 珍しい
❺ grill グリル料理を出すレストラン　❻ lead 指導的な、リーダー株の　salesperson 営業担当者
fill ～ in on … ～に…について情報を与える　challenge 難題　face ～に直面する

Expressions

take over ～ 「～を引き継ぐ」(❸)

I decided to take over the family business instead of starting my own company.
私は自分の会社を立ち上げるのではなく、家業を継ぐことを決心しました。

Questions 158-160 refer to the following e-mail.

E-Mail Message

To: Lila Mendham
From: Alcott Appliances Ltd.
Date: 10 May
Subject: Contract Number 09803

Dear Ms. Mendham,

❶ This is a follow-up to our service call of 9 May at your restaurant located at 601 Elms Lane, Wembley, to confirm that you elected to have the ice maker repaired rather than replaced. To arrange a day and time for this service, the refrigeration technician assigned to your contract will be calling you in the next 1 to 3 business days. On the day of the service, please turn the device off and clear all ice and water from it before the technician arrives.

❷ If you have any questions about the work, please telephone Alcott Appliances at 020-7946-9430 and make reference to the contract number given above. You may also visit our Web site, alcottappliances.co.uk, at any time for information regarding our prices and services.

問題158-160は次のEメールに関するものです。

受信者：Lila Mendham
送信者：Alcott電気器具社
日付：5月10日
件名：契約番号 09803

Mendham様

このEメールは、ウェンブリーのエルムズ通り601番地にあるあなたのレストランにおける、5月9日の当社の修理サービス訪問に関するフォローアップのご連絡であり、製氷機を交換するのではなく修理をするというあなたの決定を確認するためのものです。この修理サービスの日時を取り決めるために、あなたの契約を担当する冷凍技術者が1～3営業日中にお電話いたします。修理サービス当日は、技術者が到着する前に製氷機の電源を切って、中の氷と水を全て取り除いておいてください。

作業に関して何かご質問がございましたら、Alcott電気器具社に020-7946-9430までお電話いただき、上記の契約番号をお伝えください。また、当社の価格やサービスに関する情報については、当社ウェブサイトalcottappliances.co.ukにいつでもアクセスしてください。

Words & Phrases

appliance 電気器具　contract 契約　❶ follow-up フォローアップ、続き　service call 〈修理などのための〉業務訪問
lane 小道　confirm ～を確認する　elect to *do* ～することに決める　ice maker 製氷機　repair ～を修理する
replace ～を交換する　arrange ～を取り決める　refrigeration 冷凍　technician 技術者
assign ～ to … ～を…に割り当てる　business day 営業日　turn off ～ ～の電源を切る　device 機器
clear ～を取り除く　❷ telephone ～に電話する　make reference to ～ ～に言及する　regarding ～に関して

Expressions

A* rather than *B 「*B*ではなくて*A*、*B*よりもむしろ*A*」（❶ 2～3行目）

This educational software was developed for adults rather than children.
この教育ソフトウエアは、子どもではなく大人向けに開発されました。

158 What is the purpose of the e-mail?

(A) To recommend that Ms. Mendham purchase a new appliance
(B) To provide instructions for using a new ice maker
(C) To alert Ms. Mendham that a repair will be scheduled
(D) To explain why an ice maker should be repaired

Eメールの目的は何ですか。

(A) Mendhamさんに新しい電気器具を購入するよう勧めること。
(B) 新しい製氷機の使用説明書を提供すること。
(C) 修理の予定が組まれるとMendhamさんに注意を促すこと。
(D) 製氷機の修理がなぜ必要かを説明すること。

正解 C ❶1〜3行目に「このEメールは、あなたのレストランにおける、5月9日の当社の修理サービス訪問に関するフォローアップの連絡であり、製氷機を交換するのではなく修理をするというあなたの決定を確認するためのものだ」とあり、続く同3〜4行目で、担当の技術者が修理日時を決めるためにMendhamさんに電話をすると伝えている。よって、Eメールの目的は、これから製氷機の修理の予定が組まれるとMendhamさんに知らせることだと分かる。alert「〜に自覚させる、〜に警告する」。
(A) ❶1〜3行目に、Mendhamさんは製氷機を交換するのではなく修理してもらうことに決めたとあるので、不適切。recommend「〜を勧める」。
(B) instructions「使用説明書」。

---

159 What will most likely happen next?

(A) Ms. Mendham will visit Alcott Appliances.
(B) Ms. Mendham will have an ice maker delivered to her restaurant.
(C) A technician will remove ice and water from a faulty ice maker.
(D) A technician will telephone Ms. Mendham.

次に何が起こると考えられますか。

(A) MendhamさんがAlcott電気器具社を訪れる。
(B) Mendhamさんが、製氷機を自分のレストランへ配達してもらう。
(C) 技術者が、欠陥のある製氷機から氷と水を取り除く。
(D) 技術者がMendhamさんに電話する。

正解 D Mendhamさんのレストランの製氷機の修理に関して、❶3〜4行目にTo arrange a day and time for this service, the refrigeration technician assigned to your contract will be calling you in the next 1 to 3 business days.「この修理サービスの日時を取り決めるために、あなたの契約を担当する冷凍技術者が1〜3営業日中に電話する」とあるので、(D)が正解。
(A) ❶1〜4行目に、このEメールは5月9日の修理サービス訪問について確認するためのものとあり、次回の訪問の話も出ているが、Mendhamさんが電気器具社を訪れるという記載はない。
(C) ❶4〜6行目で、Mendhamさんに対して、技術者の到着前に製氷機から氷と水を取り除く依頼がされているので不適切。remove「〜を取り除く」、faulty「欠陥のある」。

---

160 According to the e-mail, why would a customer visit Alcott Appliances' Web site?

(A) To find out how much products cost
(B) To review information about a contract
(C) To select a repair technician
(D) To schedule a service visit

Eメールによると、顧客はなぜAlcott電気器具社のウェブサイトにアクセスすると思われますか。

(A) 製品の値段が幾らか調べるため。
(B) 契約に関する情報を見直すため。
(C) 修理技術者を選ぶため。
(D) 訪問サービスの予定を組むため。

正解 A このEメールはAlcott電気器具社から送られたもの。❷2〜4行目に「当社の価格やサービスに関する情報については、当社ウェブサイトalcottappliances.co.ukにいつでもアクセスしてください」とある。よって、ウェブサイトでは製品の価格を確かめられると分かるので、(A)が正解。find out 〜「〜を調べる」。
(B) review「〜を見直す」。

Questions 161-164 refer to the following letter.

Opus 27 Ltd.
3241 Tupper Avenue
Vancouver BC Canada V5K 1A6
Telephone: 778-555-0134
www.opus27.ca

July 6

Julia Demers
Serano 455
C1026ABF CABA, Argentina

Dear Ms. Demers,

❶ Thank you for booking a trip with Opus 27, the finest tour boat company in the North Island region. You will be traveling aboard the *Salty Mist*, our newest and most modern ship. Your reservation is for two adults and one child on a sight-seeing cruise leaving from Port McNeill, traveling to Sointula and Alert Bay, and returning to Port McNeill. Departure is on August 4 at 10 A.M. The duration of the trip is ten hours, including shore time at each destination.

❷ Opus 27 has been in business for over twenty years, and we pride ourselves on creating an excellent passenger experience. The *Salty Mist* features comfortable seating, an outdoor deck, and a variety of dining options.

❸ Please arrive at the Port McNeill terminal one hour before your departure time, and make sure you have identification for each passenger. Do not hesitate to contact me with any questions or concerns.

Sincerely,

Felix Li

Felix Li, Booking Agent
felix.li@opus27.ca

問題161-164は次の手紙に関するものです。

Opus 27社
タッパー大通り3241番地
バンクーバー BC カナダ V5K 1A6
電話番号：778-555-0134
www.opus27.ca

7月6日

Julia Demers様
セラーノ455番地
C1026ABF CABA、アルゼンチン

Demers様

ノースアイランド地域随一の遊覧船会社であるOpus 27社での旅行をご予約いただき、ありがとうございます。お客さまには、当社の最も新しくかつ最新式の船である『海の霧号』に乗船してご旅行いただきます。お客さまのご予約は、大人2名、子ども1名の観光クルーズで、ポート・マクニールを出港し、ソイントゥラとアラートベイを経由して、ポート・マクニールに帰港します。出発は8月4日午前10時です。旅行の所要時間は、各目的地での上陸時間も含めて10時間です。

Opus 27社は20年以上営業しており、乗客の皆さまに極上の体験をご提供することを誇りとしております。『海の霧号』は、座り心地の良い座席や屋外デッキ、さまざまなお食事の選択肢を目玉にしています。

出発時刻の1時間前にポート・マクニールのターミナルにご到着ください。また、乗船するお客さま各自の身元証明書を忘れずにお持ちください。ご質問やご心配事がございましたら、ご遠慮なく私にご連絡ください。

敬具

Felix Li（署名）
Felix Li、予約係
felix.li@opus27.ca

Words & Phrases

❶ book ～を予約する　region 地域　aboard ～に乗って　modern 最新式の、現代的な　reservation 予約　sight-seeing 観光の　duration 持続時間　including ～を含めて　shore 陸の　destination 目的地
❷ be in business 営業している　pride *oneself* on *doing* ～することを誇る　feature ～を目玉にする、～を特長とする　comfortable 心地よい　seating 座席　outdoor 屋外の　deck デッキ　a variety of ～ さまざまな～　dining 食事　option 選択肢
❸ identification 身元証明書　hesitate to *do* ～するのをためらう　contact ～に連絡する　concern 心配事、懸念　agent 係員

161 Why did Mr. Li send the letter?

(A) To request payment of a bill
(B) To confirm travel arrangements
(C) To ask for additional identification
(D) To describe sight-seeing attractions

Liさんはなぜ手紙を送ったのですか。

(A) 請求書の支払いを求めるため。
(B) 旅行の手配を確認するため。
(C) 追加の身元証明書を求めるため。
(D) 観光名所について説明するため。

正解 B 文末より、Liさんとは手紙の差出人でOpus27 社の予約係。Liさんは❶1行目で、Opus 27 社で旅行の予約をしてくれたことについてお礼を述べ、同 3～6 行目では、予約人数、旅行の行程などを確認している。また、❸1～2行目で、当日の集合時刻や持参すべきものについて伝えている。よって、Liさんは旅行の手配を確認するために手紙を送ったと考えられる。arrangement「手配」。
(C) ❸2行目で身元証明書を持参するよう伝えられているが、追加分は求められていない。ask for ～「～を求める」、additional「追加の」。
(D) ❶3～5 行目に観光クルーズの旅程の説明があるが、観光名所への言及はない。attraction「名所、人を引き付けるもの」。

---

162 What is suggested about Opus 27?

(A) It operates more than one ship.
(B) It recently changed management.
(C) It is the most popular way to visit the region.
(D) It is an inexpensive travel option.

Opus 27社について何が分かりますか。

(A) 同社は2隻以上の船を運航している。
(B) 同社は最近、経営陣を変更した。
(C) 同社は、その地域を訪れるには最も人気のある手段である。
(D) 同社は安価な旅行の選択肢である。

正解 A ❶1～2行目のOpus 27, the finest tour boat company in the North Island region「ノースアイランド地域随一の遊覧船会社であるOpus 27 社」より、Opus 27 社とは遊覧船を運航する会社であると分かる。また、同2～3行目で、the *Salty Mist*, our newest and most modern ship「当社の最も新しくかつ最新式の船である『海の霧号』」と紹介していることから、同社はこの船の他に複数の船を所有していることが分かる。よって、(A)が正解。operate「～を運行する」。
(B) management「経営陣」。
(D) inexpensive「安価な」。

---

163 How many seats have been reserved?

(A) One
(B) Two
(C) Three
(D) Four

座席は何席予約されていますか。

(A) 1席
(B) 2席
(C) 3席
(D) 4席

正解 C ❶3～4行目に、Your reservation is for two adults and one child on a sight-seeing cruise「お客さまの予約は、大人2名、子ども1名の観光クルーズだ」とあり、計3名分の座席が予約されていると分かる。

---

164 What time should Ms. Demers arrive at the departure terminal?

(A) At 9:00 A.M.
(B) At 10:00 A.M.
(C) At 1:00 P.M.
(D) At 2:00 P.M.

Demersさんは何時に出発ターミナルに到着すべきですか。

(A) 午前9時
(B) 午前10時
(C) 午後1時
(D) 午後2時

正解 A Demersさんとはこの手紙の受取人。❸1行目に、Please arrive at the Port McNeill terminal one hour before your departure time「出発時刻の1時間前にポート・マクニールのターミナルにご到着ください」とある。❶5行目で、Departure is on August 4 at 10 A.M.「出発は8月4日午前10時だ」と述べられているので、Demersさんは出発時刻の1時間前の午前9時にターミナルに到着すべきだと分かる。
(B) ❶5行目より、『海の霧号』の出発時刻。

Expressions

make sure (that) ～ 「必ず～する」（❸2行目）
Make sure that the handouts arrive at the venue by the day before the meeting.
配布資料は、必ず会議の前日までに会場に届くようにしてください。

Questions 165-167 refer to the following article.

❶ SACRAMENTO (August 1)—After receiving unwelcome attention in the press for its low levels of employee satisfaction, technology giant Sundale Systems is making changes. — [1] —. The company has hired Angela Lyons as its new chief culture officer, a position designed to address both human resources functions and employee morale.

❷ Ms. Lyons is a renowned workplace wellness expert. — [2] —. As Hundrigen Health's Human Resources director, she reduced employee turnover by over 25 percent in just under three years. — [3] —.

❸ "I look forward to addressing Sundale's challenges," said Ms. Lyons. "My team and I will do our best to meet staff expectations as quickly as possible."

❹ Ms. Lyons has a stellar reputation in management circles. She authors the popular blog *Satisfy Your Staff* and teaches classes in human resource management at Sutter University. — [4] —.

問題165-167は次の記事に関するものです。

サクラメント（8月1日）――低い従業員満足度によりマスコミからありがたくない注目を集めた後、テクノロジー大手のSundaleシステムズ社は変革を起こしている。同社は、人事機能と従業員の士気の両方に対応することを目的とした職位である新規の文化最高責任者として、Angela Lyonsを雇用したのだ。

Lyonsさんは、職場における健康推進に関する著名な専門家である。Hundrigen Health社の人事部長として、彼女はわずか３年足らずで従業員の離職率を25パーセント以上減少させた。*彼女はSundaleシステムズ社で同じことをするつもりだ。

「Sundale社の課題に取り組むのを心待ちにしています」とLyonsさんは述べた。「できるだけ速やかに従業員の期待に応えるよう、私はチームと共に最善を尽くします」。

Lyonsさんは、経営関係者の間で非常に高い評判を得ている。彼女は人気ブログ『*社員を満足させよう*』を執筆し、Sutter大学で人的資源管理の講座を教えている。

*問題167の挿入文の訳

Words & Phrases

❶ receive ～を受ける　unwelcome ありがたくない　attention 注目　the press マスコミ　level 度合い
employee 従業員　satisfaction 満足　technology テクノロジー、技術　giant 大手企業
make a change 変化をもたらす　position 職、地位　address ～に取り組む、～を扱う
human resources 人事部、人的資源　function 機能　morale 士気　❷ renowned 有名な　workplace 職場
wellness 健康推進、心身が健康な状態　expert 専門家　turnover 離職率
❸ look forward to *doing* ～することを心待ちにする　challenge 課題　do *one's* best 最善を尽くす
meet 〈要求など〉に応える　expectation 期待　as ～ as possible できるだけ～　❹ stellar 素晴らしい、優れた
reputation 評判　circle 仲間、集団　author ～を執筆する　satisfy ～を満足させる

165 What is the purpose of the article?

(A) To announce a corporate merger
(B) To report on a hiring decision
(C) To explain the origins of a company
(D) To advertise an upcoming event

記事の目的は何ですか。

(A) 企業合併を知らせること。
(B) 雇用の決定について報道すること。
(C) 会社の起源を説明すること。
(D) 今度のイベントを宣伝すること。

正解 B ❶ 1～4行目に「低い従業員満足度によりマスコミからありがたくない注目を集めた後、テクノロジー大手のSundaleシステムズ社は変革を起こしている」とあり、続く同5～6行目でThe company has hired Angela Lyons as its new chief culture officer「同社は新規の文化最高責任者として、Angela Lyonsを雇用した」と変革の具体例が述べられている。その後、Lyonsさんについての紹介が続いているので、記事の目的は、Sundaleシステムズ社がLyonsさんを雇用したと報じることだと分かる。
(A) corporate「企業の」、merger「合併」。(C) origin「起源」。
(D) advertise「～を宣伝する」、upcoming「今度の、近づいている」。

166 What is indicated about Ms. Lyons?

(A) She is a university instructor.
(B) She is skilled at software programming.
(C) She has written several books.
(D) She runs her own business.

Lyonsさんについて何が示されていますか。

(A) 彼女は大学の講師である。
(B) 彼女はソフトウエアのプログラミングに熟練している。
(C) 彼女は本を数冊執筆した。
(D) 彼女は自分の会社を経営している。

正解 A Lyonsさんについて、❹ 2～5行目に、She ...... teaches classes in human resource management at Sutter University.「彼女はSutter大学で人的資源管理の講座を教えている」とあるので、(A)が正解。instructor「講師」。
(B) be skilled at ～「～に熟練している」。
(C) ❹ 2～3行目に、Lyonsさんがブログを執筆しているとあるが、本の執筆については述べられていない。

167 In which of the positions marked [1], [2], [3], and [4] does the following sentence best belong?

"She plans on doing the same thing at Sundale Systems."

(A) [1]
(B) [2]
(C) [3]
(D) [4]

[1]、[2]、[3]、[4]と記載された箇所のうち、次の文が入るのに最もふさわしいのはどれですか。

「彼女はSundaleシステムズ社で同じことをするつもりだ」

正解 C ❶で、会社の変革に着手したSundaleシステムズ社にLyonsさんが雇用されたことが述べられ、❷ 2～5行目で「Hundrigen Health社の人事部長として、彼女はわずか3年足らずで従業員の離職率を25パーセント以上減少させた」とLyonsさんの過去の業績が挙げられている。この後ろの(C) [3]に挿入文を入れると、Lyonsさんが Sundaleシステムズ社でも同様に離職率を減少させるつもりだ、という意味になり、流れとして自然。plan on *doing*「～するつもりである」。

Expressions

design ～ to *do* 「～を…するよう意図する」(❶ 7行目)
This event is designed to raise awareness of environmental issues.
このイベントは、環境問題の意識を高めることを目的としています。

Questions 168-171 refer to the following e-mail.

To:	rsetlur@okboxmail.com.au
From:	emontowski@montowskiandassociates.com.au
Date:	23 August
Subject:	Estimate

Dear Ms. Setlur,

1 Thank you for allowing me to examine the building you own in Perth. — [1] — . I would be happy to undertake the rehabilitation project. You were correct to assume that it will require extensive restoration work. — [2] —. Below is an approximate breakdown of costs, including all the major components of the work. — [3] —.

2 • Restoring the wood flooring, $3,000 to $5,000 (Labour cost depends on whether you would prefer laminate or wood flooring. Wood flooring would need to be polished and painted.)

3 • Replacing the plaster on the ceiling, $800

4 • Repainting the walls, $1,200

5 • Recreating the fireplace, $2,900 (Based on the photographs you provided, we could build it exactly to size in the spot where it was originally located.)

6 If you have any questions or prefer to talk over the phone, please call my office at (08) 5550 0177. Also, it is in your best interest to schedule as soon as possible. — [4] —. I look forward to hearing from you.

Sincerely,

Edward Montowski
Montowski & Associates

問題168-171は次のEメールに関するものです。

受信者：rsetlur@okboxmail.com.au
送信者：emontowski@montowskiandassociates.com.au
日付：8月23日
件名：お見積もり

Setlur様

あなたがパースに所有する建物を弊社が検査することを許可していただき、ありがとうございます。私は喜んで修復プロジェクトをお引き受けいたします。広範囲に及ぶ修復作業を必要とするだろうという、あなたのご推測は正しいものでした。以下は、主な作業項目を全て含めた費用の概算内訳です。

・木製床の修復、3,000ドル～5,000ドル（人件費は、積層床材と木質床材のどちらをあなたがお選びになるかによって決まります。木質床材は研磨および塗装の必要があります。）

・天井のしっくいの塗り替え、800ドル

・壁の再塗装、1,200ドル

・暖炉の再形成、2,900ドル（ご提供いただいた写真に基づき、元々設置されていた場所に全く同じ大きさに作ることができるでしょう。）

ご質問がある場合、もしくは電話でお話しされたい場合には、私の事務所まで(08) 5550 0177にお電話ください。また、できるだけ早くご予定をお決めになった方がよろしいかと存じます。*私のチームは今後4週間にわたって予約が入っており、間もなくさらに依頼が入る見込みです。ご連絡をお待ちしております。

敬具

Edward Montowski
Montowski & Associates社

*問題171の挿入文の訳

168 Why did Mr. Montowski write the e-mail?

(A) To schedule an inspection
(B) To inquire about the size of a project
(C) To offer renovation services
(D) To explain how payment should be made

Montowskiさんはなぜ E メールを書いたのですか。

(A) 検査の日程を決めるため。
(B) プロジェクトの規模について尋ねるため。
(C) 改修サービスを提供するため。
(D) 支払方法を説明するため。

正解 C Eメールの送信者であるMontowskiさんは、❶ 1～2 行目で建物の検査を自社に許可してくれたことに謝意を表し、建物の修復プロジェクトを引き受けると伝えている。さらに、同2～3行目でit will require extensive restoration work「広範囲に及ぶ修復作業を必要とする」と述べ、❷～❺に、その修復作業の費用の概算内訳を記載している。よって、Montowskiさんは、建物の修復を引き受けて、そのサービス内容と見積金額を提示するためにEメールを書いたと分かるので、(C)が正解。restorationを(C)ではrenovation「改修」と言い換えている。offer「～を提供する」。
(A) inspection「検査」。
(B) Montowskiさんは、すでに建物の検査を終え、修復の規模を把握しているので不適切。inquire about ～「～について尋ねる」。
(D) ❷～❺に修復作業の費用の記載があるが、支払方法の説明はしていない。

---

169 According to the e-mail, what information will Ms. Setlur have to provide?

(A) Where the plaster should be replaced
(B) What flooring material she prefers
(C) What color she wants the walls painted
(D) Where she wants photographs to be taken

Eメールによると、Setlurさんはどんな情報を提供する必要がありますか。

(A) どこの場所のしっくいが塗り替えられるべきか。
(B) 自身がどんな床材を好むか。
(C) 自身が何色に壁を塗ってほしいか。
(D) 自身がどこで写真を撮ってほしいか。

正解 B SetlurさんとはこのEメールの受信者。❷～❺に、建物の修復作業の内容と概算費用が記載されている。❷ 1～2 行目にRestoring the wood flooring, $3,000 to $5,000 (Labour cost depends on whether you would prefer laminate or wood flooring.「木製床の修復、3,000ドル～5,000ドル（人件費は、積層床材と木質床材のどちらをあなたが選ぶかによって決まる」とある。つまり、床の修復費用は床材の材質によって決まるので、Setlurさんはどちらの床材を希望するか知らせる必要があると分かる。よって、(B)が正解。

Words & Phrases

estimate 見積もり ❶ allow ～ to *do* ～に…することを許可する examine ～を検査する own ～を所有する
be happy to *do* 喜んで～する undertake ～を引き受ける、～を請け負う rehabilitation 修復、復旧 correct 正しい
assume ～と推測する require ～を必要とする extensive 広範囲に及ぶ restoration 修復 approximate 概算の
breakdown 内訳 cost 費用 major 主要な component 構成要素 ❷ restore ～を修復する
flooring 床(材) labour 〈米国表記はlabor〉労働 depend on ～ ～によって決まる prefer ～を選ぶ、～の方を好む
laminate 薄板状の、ラミネート状の polish ～を磨く ❸ replace ～を取り換える plaster しっくい ceiling 天井
❹ repaint ～を塗り直す ❺ recreate ～を再形成する fireplace 暖炉 based on ～ ～に基づく
provide ～を提供する exactly ぴったりと to size 適切な大きさに spot 場所 originally 元々
locate ～を設置する ❻ as soon as possible できるだけ早く look forward to *doing* ～することを心待ちにする

170 What is indicated about the fireplace?

(A) It is ready for use.
(B) It has been removed.
(C) It needs to be repainted.
(D) It will be expensive to maintain.

暖炉について何が示されていますか。

(A) それは使える状態である。
(B) それは取り払われている。
(C) それは再塗装する必要がある。
(D) それは維持に費用がかかるだろう。

正解 B ❺ 1行目にRecreating the fireplace「暖炉の再形成」とあり、同 1〜2 行目で、we could build it exactly to size in the spot where it was originally located「元々設置されていた場所に全く同じ大きさに作ることができるだろう」と述べられている。よって、古い暖炉は以前あった場所から取り払われていると考えられるので、(B)が正解。remove「〜を取り払う」。
(A) ready for use「使える状態で」。
(D) maintain「〜を維持する」。

---

171 In which of the positions marked [1], [2], [3], and [4] does the following sentence best belong?

"My team is booked for the next four weeks, and we expect more requests soon."

(A) [1]
(B) [2]
(C) [3]
(D) [4]

[1]、[2]、[3]、[4]と記載された箇所のうち、次の文が入るのに最もふさわしいのはどれですか。

「私のチームは今後4週間にわたって予約が入っており、間もなくさらに依頼が入る見込みです」

正解 D 挿入文はMontowskiさんのチームの今後の仕事の予約状況について述べているので、今後の予定について言及している文の前後に入ると考えられる。❻ 2行目にit is in your best interest to schedule as soon as possible「できるだけ早く予定を決めた方が良い」とあり、この後ろに続けると、早急に修復予定を決めるよう促している理由を挿入文で説明する形になり、流れとして自然。よって、(D)が正解。book「〜を予約する」、expect「〜を見込む」。

Expressions

be in *one's* best interest to *do* 「〜することは最も〈人〉のためになる」(❻ 2行目)
It will be in your best interest to find a good lawyer.
優秀な弁護士を見つけることが、最もあなたのためになるでしょう。

Questions 172-175 refer to the following text-message chain.

[1] **Marty Johnson (2:15 P.M.)**
Thank you for sending the information to me today. I looked it over, and I am interested in viewing the property on Forest Avenue tomorrow.

[2] **Kendra Gomez (2:17 P.M.)**
I could arrange a tour for tomorrow at 10 A.M. Would that work?

[3] **Kendra Gomez (2:18 P.M.)**
Also, my colleague just mentioned that two other potential buyers are looking at it today.

[4] **Marty Johnson (2:18 P.M.)**
I am available after 11:30 A.M. tomorrow or any time on Wednesday.

[5] **Kendra Gomez (2:20 P.M.)**
Tomorrow at 11:30 is fine. Unless you would like to see it today, considering the interest it is generating.

[6] **Marty Johnson (2:22 P.M.)**
Have you had any offers yet?

[7] **Kendra Gomez (2:24 P.M.)**
Not yet.

[8] **Marty Johnson (2:25 P.M.)**
OK. Then I'll be there tomorrow at 11:30 A.M.

問題172-175は次のテキストメッセージのやりとりに関するものです。

Marty Johnson（午後2時15分）
今日は情報を送っていただき、ありがとうございます。私はそれに目を通しまして、明日、Forest大通りの物件を見たいと考えています。

Kendra Gomez（午後2時17分）
明日の午前10時に見学を手配できます。それでご都合に合うでしょうか。

Kendra Gomez（午後2時18分）
また、ご購入を検討中の方が他に2名、今日その物件を見る予定だと、私の同僚がつい今しがた申しておりました。

Marty Johnson（午後2時18分）
明日の午前11時30分以降、もしくは水曜日ならば何時でも都合がつきます。

Kendra Gomez（午後2時20分）
明日の午前11時30分で構いません。同物件が関心を集めていることをご考慮なさって、お客さまが本日ご覧になりたい場合は別ですが。

Marty Johnson（午後2時22分）
すでに申し込みはありましたか。

Kendra Gomez（午後2時24分）
まだありません。

Marty Johnson（午後2時25分）
そうですか。それでは、明日の午前11時30分に現地に伺います。

Words & Phrases

[1] look ～ over　～に目を通す　view　～を見る　property　物件　[2] arrange　～を手配する　tour　見学　work　好都合である、うまくいく　[3] colleague　同僚　potential　潜在的な、可能性のある　buyer　買い手　[4] available　都合がつく、利用できる　[5] unless　もっとも～ならば話は別だが、～でない限りは　consider　～を考慮する　interest　関心　generate　～を生み出す　[6] offer　〈売買の〉申し込み

172 Why did Mr. Johnson write to Ms. Gomez?

(A) To schedule an appointment
(B) To place an advertisement
(C) To arrange a sales call
(D) To make an offer

Johnsonさんはなぜ Gomezさんにメッセージを書いたのですか。

(A) 予約を入れるため。
(B) 広告を出すため。
(C) 営業訪問を手配するため。
(D) 提案をするため。

正解 A Johnsonさんが❶で、I am interested in viewing the property on Forest Avenue tomorrow「明日、Forest大通りの物件を見たいと考えている」と伝えているのに対し、Gomezさんは❷で日時を提案しており、以降でも内見の日時についてやりとりが続いている。(A)が正解。appointment「予約」。
(B) place an advertisement「広告を出す」。
(C) sales call「営業訪問」。
(D) make an offer「提案をする」。

173 What most likely is Ms. Gomez' job?

(A) Interior designer
(B) Residential architect
(C) Building inspector
(D) Real estate agent

Gomezさんの職業は何だと考えられますか。

(A) インテリアデザイナー
(B) 住宅建築家
(C) 建築検査官
(D) 不動産業者

正解 D ❶で、明日に物件の内見をしたいと述べるJohnsonさんに対し、Gomezさんは❷でI could arrange a tour「見学を手配できる」と述べてから、具体的な時刻を提示し、都合がつくかどうか尋ねている。続く❸では同僚からの補足情報として、その物件に興味を持つ他の顧客について言及している。よって、Gomezさんは不動産業者であると判断できる。

174 What does Ms. Gomez suggest about the property?

(A) It is not very old.
(B) It may sell quickly.
(C) It is in a good location.
(D) It is not well-known.

Gomezさんは物件について何を示唆していますか。

(A) それはそれほど古くない。
(B) それはすぐに売れるかもしれない。
(C) それは立地が良い。
(D) それはあまり知られていない。

正解 B Gomezさんは❸で、my colleague just mentioned that two other potential buyers are looking at it today「購入を検討中の方が他に2名、今日その物件を見る予定だと、私の同僚がつい今しがた言っていた」と述べている。また❺でも、同物件に関心が集まっていることに言及している。よって、Gomezさんはその物件が間もなく売れる可能性があると示唆していると考えられる。(B)が正解。
(D) well-known「よく知られた」。

175 At 2:17 P.M., what does Ms. Gomez most likely mean when she writes, "Would that work"?

(A) She doubts that a plan will be successful.
(B) She is confirming the details of an assignment.
(C) She wants to know whether a time is convenient.
(D) She is unsure that there is enough time for a tour.

午後2時17分に、Gomezさんは"Would that work"という発言で、何を意味していると考えられますか。

(A) 彼女は計画が成功しないだろうと思っている。
(B) 彼女は業務の詳細を確認している。
(C) 彼女は時間が都合が良いかどうか知りたいと思っている。
(D) 彼女は見学の時間が十分にあるか確かでない。

正解 C ❶の明日物件を内見したいというJohnsonさんの希望に対し、Gomezさんは❷でI could arrange a tour for tomorrow at 10 A.M.「明日の午前10時に見学を手配できる」と書いている。その後に下線部の発言が続いているので、下線部中のthatは午前10時という提示時間を指し、Gomezさんは下線部の発言でその時間で良いかJohnsonさんに都合を尋ねていると考えられる。(C)が正解。convenient「都合のよい」。
(A) doubt「～ではないと思う」、successful「成功した」。
(B) confirm「～を確認する」、assignment「業務、割り当て」。
(D) unsure「確かでない」。

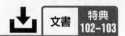

Questions 176-180 refer to the following e-mail and Web page.

1 Eメール

To:	Martine Depas <mdepas@imail.com>
From:	Anita Eckert <aeckert@fenogliotimes.com>
Date:	June 27
Subject:	Reader Campaign

Dear Ms. Depas:

❶ Thank you for being a loyal reader of *Fenoglio Times*. As one of the few remaining news outlets that does not require a subscription fee for access to our content, we proudly provide news that is accessible to all.

❷ To support our valuable investigative journalism, we have depended almost entirely on a single revenue source, the sale of advertising. However, we have added three new features over the past year in response to reader feedback, and our primary source of revenue is no longer enough. It takes a lot of money to conduct interviews, compile reports, and produce well-researched stories that interest our readers around the globe.

❸ Please consider making a contribution before our fiscal year ends on June 30. A contribution of $250 or more will put your name on our Silver Sponsors list, which will appear prominently on our Web site. But even a gift of $25 would go a long way toward meeting our goal of $10,000. If every reader pitches in, we can ensure the continued high-quality content that you have come to expect from us over the past decade.

❹ Starting in January, watch for our special weekly news summaries geared toward school-age children.

Sincerely,

Anita Eckert, Managing Editor

2 ウェブページ

❶ **Donor Name:** Martine Depas

Donation Amount: $300

Comments:

❷ After receiving an e-mail from the managing editor of *Fenoglio Times* yesterday, I went online first thing this morning to make my donation. *Fenoglio Times* produces some of the best journalism out there. Your articles are lengthy and thorough—I can tell how much effort has gone into each story. This news source is worth supporting.

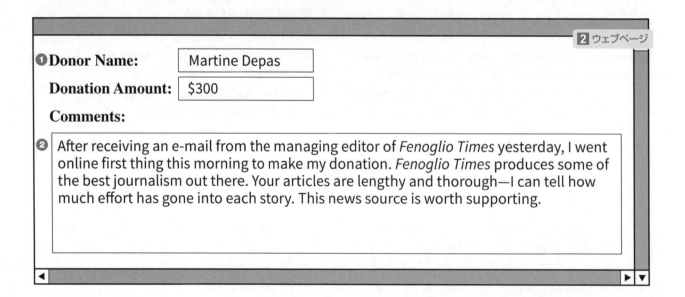

問題176-180は次のEメールとウェブページに関するものです。

受信者：Martine Depas <mdepas@imail.com>
送信者：Anita Eckert <aeckert@fenogliotimes.com>
日付：6月27日
件名：読者キャンペーン

Depas様

*Fenoglio Times*紙をご愛読いただき、ありがとうございます。コンテンツの利用に購読料を必要としない、残り少ない報道機関の一つとして、私たちは全ての人に利用可能なニュースを誇りを持ってご提供しております。

価値ある調査報道を維持するために、私たちは唯一の収入源である広告の売り上げにほぼ完全に依存してまいりました。しかしながら、私たちはこの1年で、読者の皆さまのご意見にお応えして3つの新たな特集記事を追加し、主要収入源ではもはや十分ではありません。取材を行い、報道をまとめ、世界中の読者の関心を引く綿密に調査されたニュース記事を制作するには、多額のお金がかかります。

私たちの会計年度が6月30日に終わる前に寄付を行うことについて、どうかご検討ください。250ドル以上の寄付をしていただくと私たちのシルバー賛助者リストにお名前が掲載され、そのリストは当ウェブサイト上で目立つように表示されます。ですが、たとえ25ドルの贈与であっても、1万ドルという私たちの目標額達成に大変役立ちます。読者の皆さまお一人お一人が援助してくださるなら、過去10年を通じて私たちにご期待いただけるようになった高品質なコンテンツを継続することを保証できます。

1月から開始する、学齢期の子ども向けの特別な週刊ニュース概要にご注目ください。

敬具

Anita Eckert、編集長

寄付者名：Martine Depas
寄付額：300ドル
コメント：
昨日*Fenoglio Times*紙の編集長からのEメールを受信した後、私は、寄付をするために今朝一番にインターネットに接続しました。*Fenoglio Times*紙は、世の中で最良の報道記事を生み出しています。貴紙の記事は長くて緻密です――各記事にどれだけ労力が注がれているかが見て取れます。この情報源は支援に値します。

176 What is indicated in the e-mail about *Fenoglio Times*?

(A) It specializes in financial journalism.
(B) It has been in operation for 20 years.
(C) It does not charge a fee to its readers.
(D) It has increased its readership by 30 percent.

Eメールで、*Fenoglio Times*紙について何が示されていますか。

(A) 同紙は金融報道を専門にしている。
(B) 同紙は20年間運営されている。
(C) 同紙は読者に料金を請求しない。
(D) 同紙は読者数を30パーセント増やした。

正解 C 1の❶ 1行目に「*Fenoglio Times*紙を愛読してくれて、ありがとう」とあり、また文末の記名より、このEメールは*Fenoglio Times*紙の編集長から各読者に宛てたものと分かる。同❶ 1～2行目に、As one of the few remaining news outlets that does not require a subscription fee for access to our content「コンテンツの利用に購読料を必要としない、残り少ない報道機関の一つとして」と述べられているので、*Fenoglio Times*紙は読者に料金を請求していないと分かる。
(A) specialize in ～「～を専門にする」。
(B) in operation「運営中で」。
(D) readership「読者数、読者層」。

---

177 Why does Ms. Eckert mention advertising?

(A) To identify a source of funding
(B) To attract new businesses
(C) To announce the launch of a marketing campaign
(D) To urge readers to buy promoted products

Eckertさんはなぜ広告について述べていますか。

(A) 資金源を明らかにするため。
(B) 新たな企業を引き付けるため。
(C) マーケティングキャンペーンの開始を発表するため。
(D) 販売促進中の製品を買うよう読者に促すため。

正解 A Eメールの送信者であるEckertさんは1の❷ 1～2行目で、we have depended almost entirely on a single revenue source, the sale of advertising「私たちは唯一の収入源である広告の売り上げにほぼ完全に依存してきた」と述べ、同2～5行目で、広告売上だけではもはや十分ではない現状を説明している。よってEckertさんは、*Fenoglio Times*紙の制作資金不足の現状を説明する上で、現在の資金源を明らかにするために、現時点で唯一の収入源である広告について述べていると分かる。(A)が正解。identify「～を明らかにする」、funding「資金」。
(C) 1の件名に「読者キャンペーン」とあるが、同❸より、寄付を呼び掛けるキャンペーンだと分かるので、不適切。launch「開始」。
(D) urge ～ to *do*「～に…するよう促す」、promote「～を販売促進する」。

---

178 According to the e-mail, what does *Fenoglio Times* plan to do in the future?

(A) Conduct more interviews
(B) Attract younger readers
(C) Expand its reporting staff
(D) Merge with another publication

Eメールによると、*Fenoglio Times*紙は今後何をする予定ですか。

(A) より多くの取材を行う。
(B) より若年の読者層を引き付ける。
(C) 報道スタッフを増員する。
(D) 別の出版物と統合する。

正解 B 1の❹ 1～2行目に、Starting in January, watch for our special weekly news summaries geared toward school-age children.「1月から開始する、学齢期の子ども向けの特別な週刊ニュース概要に注目してください」とあることから、*Fenoglio Times*紙はより若年の読者層を取り込もうと計画を進めていると分かる。よって、(B)が正解。attract「～を引き付ける」。
(A) 1の❷ 4～5行目に、多額の費用がかかることの一例として取材を行うことが挙げられているが、今後取材を増やすとの記載はない。
(C) expand「～を増す、～を拡張する」。
(D) merge with ～「～と統合する、～と合併する」、publication「出版物」。

179 When did Ms. Depas post her comment?

(A) On June 27
(B) On June 28
(C) On June 29
(D) On June 30

Depasさんはいつコメントを投稿しましたか。

(A) 6月27日
(B) 6月28日
(C) 6月29日
(D) 6月30日

正解 B Depasさんは**2**のウェブページのコメント欄の❷ 1～2行目で、After receiving an e-mail from the managing editor of *Fenoglio Times* yesterday, I went online first thing this morning to make my donation.「昨日*Fenoglio Times*紙の編集長からのEメールを受信した後、私は、寄付をするために今朝一番にインターネットに接続した」と述べている。*Fenoglio Times*紙の編集長から送信されたEメールである**1**の日付は6月27日なので、Depasさんが**2**のウェブページにコメントを投稿したのは翌28日と判断できる。post「～を投稿する」。
(A) **1**の送信日付より、Eメールが送信された日。
(D) **1**の❸ 1行目より、*Fenoglio Times*紙の会計年度の最終日。

---

180 What can Ms. Depas expect to receive from *Fenoglio Times*?

(A) A gift in the mail
(B) A tour of the newsroom
(C) Access to the archives
(D) Public recognition

Depasさんは*Fenoglio Times*紙から何を受けることを期待できますか。

(A) 郵便での贈り物
(B) ニュース編集室の見学
(C) アーカイブの利用
(D) 世間の認知

正解 D **2**の❶「寄付者名」と「寄付額」の欄から、Depasさんは*Fenoglio Times*紙に300ドルを寄付したことが分かる。**1**の❸ 1～3行目で、A contribution of $250 or more will put your name on our Silver Sponsors list, which will appear prominently on our Web site.「250ドル以上の寄付をするとシルバー賛助者リストに名前が掲載され、そのリストは当ウェブサイト上で目立つように表示される」と説明されているので、300ドルを寄付したDepasさんの名前は*Fenoglio Times*紙のウェブサイト上に掲載され、寄付した事実が一般に認知されると判断できる。よって、(D)が正解。public「世間の、一般の」、recognition「認知」。
(C) archive「アーカイブ、保存資料」。

Words & Phrases

1 Eメール
❶ loyal 忠実な　remaining 残りの　news outlet 報道機関　subscription fee 購読料　access to ～ 〈情報など〉の利用の権利　content コンテンツ、中身　proudly 誇りを持って　accessible 利用可能な　❷ support ～を維持する　valuable 価値ある　investigative 調査の　journalism 報道、報道記事　depend on ～ ～に依存する　entirely 完全に　single たった一つの、単一の　revenue 収益　source 源　feature 特集記事　feedback 意見　primary 主要な　no longer ～ もはや～でない　conduct ～を行う　interview 取材　compile ～を収集してまとめる　report 報道、記事　interest ～の関心を引く　globe 世界、地球　❸ consider ～を検討する　make a contribution 寄付する　fiscal year 会計年度　appear 現れる　prominently 目立つように　gift 贈与　go a long way toward *doing* ～することにとても役立つ　meet a goal 目標を達成する　pitch in 〈寄付やボランティアで〉援助する　ensure ～を保証する　continued 継続した　high-quality 高品質な　come to *do* ～するようになる　decade 10年間　❹ watch for ～ ～に注目する　summary 概要　geared toward ～ ～向きである　school-age 学齢期の　managing editor 編集長

2 ウェブページ
❶ donor 寄付者　donation 寄付　❷ go online インターネットに接続する　first thing 真っ先に　out there 世の中で　article 記事　lengthy 長い　thorough 綿密な、徹底的な　effort 努力　worth *doing* ～することに値する

Expressions

in response to ～ 「～に応えて、～に対する応答として」（**1**の❷ 3行目）
Starting next month, online ticket reservation will be available in response to customers' needs.
来月より、顧客の皆さまのご要望にお応えして、オンラインチケット予約が可能となります。

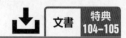

Questions 181-185 refer to the following information and e-mail.

http://www.wheelsaway.com

1 案内

❶ Thank you! Your payment has been successfully processed, and your booking at www.wheelsaway.com is now complete. Your confirmation number is #SEA52411.

❷ Notes about this reservation: The reservation holder is the only authorized driver on this reservation. You may authorize a second driver with one of our representatives at no cost when you pick up your vehicle. Your reservation is for our Seattle-Tacoma branch, conveniently located at 17203 Pacific Highway, just minutes from the airport. Our complimentary airport shuttle stops at each terminal.

❸ Changes and cancellations: If you need to make a change to your vehicle type, reservation date, or pickup or drop-off location, please fill out a change request form at www.wheelsaway.com/changes. A $20 change fee will be assessed for changes requested less than 24 hours in advance. If you reduce the length of your reservation or change to a lower-cost vehicle, you will be refunded the difference immediately upon returning the vehicle. If you need to cancel your reservation, you must do so at least 48 hours in advance, or you will incur a $30 cancellation fee.

2 Eメール

To: Jun Hong <junhong@tomail.com>
From: Madison Hurley <customercare@wheelsaway.com>
Subject: Reservation change for booking #SEA52411
Date: May 12

Dear Mr. Hong,

❶ We have received and processed your reservation change request. The details are as follows:

❷ **Booking change request:**
Product: 1 midsize sedan **Dates:** May 16–May 19
Pickup location: 17203 Pacific Hwy, SeaTac **Drop-off location:** 17203 Pacific Hwy, SeaTac

❸ If you owe an additional fee because of this change, we will charge your credit card within the next 24 hours.

❹ The details of your original booking are below for your records.

❺ **Original booking:**
Product: 1 midsize sedan **Dates:** May 16–May 20
Pickup location: 17203 Pacific Hwy, SeaTac **Drop-off location:** 17203 Pacific Hwy, SeaTac

❻ Please do not hesitate to contact us if you have any questions.

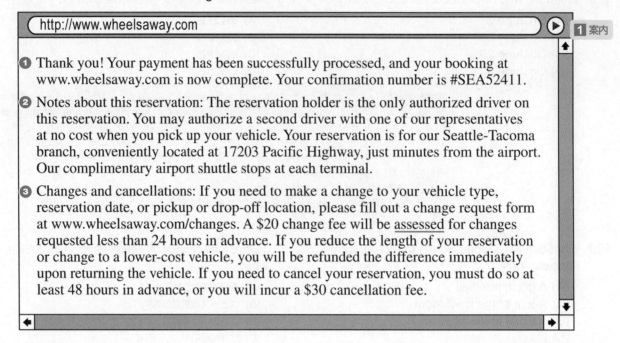

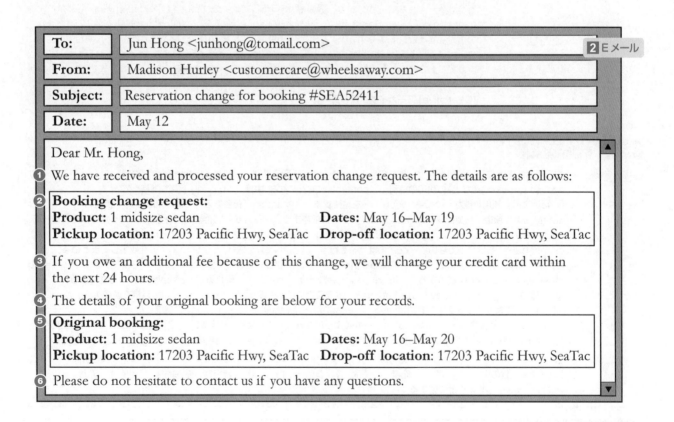

問題181-185は次の案内とＥメールに関するものです。

http://www.wheelsaway.com

ありがとうございます！お客さまのお支払いは正常に処理され、www.wheelsaway.comでのご予約がただいま完了しました。お客さまの予約確認番号は#SEA52411です。

当予約に関する注意事項：当予約においては、予約者ご本人さまのみが運転者の権限を付与されています。車を受け取る際に、担当者のいずれかにお申し付けいただくことで、お客さまは無料で２人目の運転者に権限を付与することも可能です。お客さまのご予約は当社のシアトル・タコマ支店のもので、同支店はパシフィック幹線道路17203番地という、空港からわずか数分の便利な場所にあります。当社の無料空港シャトルバスは各ターミナルに停車いたします。

変更とキャンセル：車種、ご予約日、受け取りまたは乗り捨て場所を変更する必要がある場合は、www.wheelsaway.com/changesにて変更依頼フォームにご入力ください。ご利用日時の24時間前以降に依頼された変更に対しては、20ドルの変更料が請求されます。ご予約の利用期間を短縮したり、より低価格の車に変更したりなさる場合は車を返却次第、差額が返金されます。ご予約をキャンセルする必要がある場合は少なくとも48時間前までにキャンセルしなければならず、そうでない場合は30ドルのキャンセル料をご負担いただきます。

受信者：Jun Hong <junhong@tomail.com>
送信者：Madison Hurley <customercare@wheelsaway.com>
件名：予約#SEA52411に関する予約変更
日付：5月12日

Hong様

お客さまの予約変更依頼を受理し、処理いたしました。詳細は以下の通りです。

予約変更依頼：
商品：中型セダン車１台　**日にち：**5月16日～5月19日
受け取り場所：パシフィック幹線道路17203番地、シアトル・タコマ
乗り捨て場所：パシフィック幹線道路17203番地、シアトル・タコマ

この変更により追加料金をご負担いただく場合には、24時間以内にお客さまのクレジットカードにご請求いたします。

お客さま控えとして、元のご予約の詳細は以下の通りです。

元の予約内容：
商品：中型セダン車１台　**日にち：**5月16日～5月20日
受け取り場所：パシフィック幹線道路17203番地、シアトル・タコマ
乗り捨て場所：パシフィック幹線道路17203番地、シアトル・タコマ

ご質問がありましたら、ご遠慮なく当社までご連絡ください。

181 What type of business is Wheelsaway.com?

(A) A hotel
(B) An airline
(C) A holiday resort
(D) A car-rental company

Wheelsaway.comはどのような業種ですか。

(A) ホテル
(B) 航空会社
(C) リゾート産業
(D) レンタカー会社

正解 D Wheelsaway.comの案内である1の❷ 1～2行目にThe reservation holder is the only authorized driver「予約者本人のみが運転者の権限を付与されている」とあり、同❷ 3行目には「車を受け取る際に」、同❸ 1～2行目にはIf you need to make a change to your vehicle type, reservation date, or pickup or drop-off location「車種、予約日、受け取りまたは乗り捨て場所を変更する必要がある場合は」などとあるので、Wheelsaway.comとはレンタカー会社であると考えられる。よって、(D)が正解。
(C) resort「リゾート地」。

---

182 According to the information, how can a customer add a person to a reservation?

(A) By visiting a Web site
(B) By paying an administrative fee
(C) By speaking with a representative
(D) By e-mailing a change request form

案内によると、顧客はどうすれば予約に1名追加できますか。

(A) ウェブサイトにアクセスすることによって。
(B) 事務手数料を支払うことによって。
(C) 担当者と話をすることによって。
(D) 変更依頼フォームをEメールで送信することによって。

正解 C 1の案内に2人目の運転者の追加への言及がある。同❷ 1～2行目に、予約者本人のみに運転者の権限が付与されているとあるが、続く文にYou may authorize a second driver with one of our representatives at no cost when you pick up your vehicle.「車を受け取る際に、担当者のいずれかに伝えることで、お客さまは無料で2人目の運転者に権限を付与することも可能だ」と述べられている。よって、レンタカーの受け取り時に、担当者と話をすることで、車を運転できる人数を1名追加できると分かるので(C)が正解。
(A)(D) 1の❸ 1～3行目で、車種、予約日、受け取りや乗り捨て場所の変更が必要な場合は、ウェブサイトにアクセスして変更依頼フォームに入力するよう案内しているが、人数の追加についての言及はない。
(B) administrative fee「事務手数料」。

---

183 In the information, the word "assessed" in paragraph 3, line 3, is closest in meaning to

(A) graded
(B) charged
(C) evaluated
(D) discounted

案内の第3段落・3行目にある"assessed"に最も意味が近いのは

(A) 格付けされる
(B) 請求される
(C) 評価される
(D) 値引きされる

正解 B 1の❸ 1行目にChanges and cancellations「変更とキャンセル」とあり、同1～2行目で、変更が必要な場合の手順が述べられている。それに続く該当の語を含む文は、「利用日時の24時間前以降に依頼された変更に対しては、20ドルの変更料が-------」という意味で、予約変更に対して料金がかかる場合についての説明と考えられるので、charge「～を請求する」の過去分詞である(B) chargedが正解。
(A) grade「～を格付けする、～に成績をつける」の過去分詞。
(C) evaluate「～を評価する」の過去分詞。
(D) discount「～を値引きする」の過去分詞。

184 What did Mr. Hong ask to have changed?

(A) The address of his destination
(B) The length of his reservation
(C) His payment method
(D) His arrival date

Hongさんは何を変更してもらうよう頼みましたか。

(A) 自身の目的地の住所
(B) 自身の予約の期間
(C) 自身の支払いの方法
(D) 自身の到着日

正解 B Hongさん宛てのEメールの2の❶ 1行目に、「お客さまの予約変更依頼を受理し、処理した」とあるので、Hongさんは予約内容の変更を頼んでいたと分かる。同❷ではその変更後の予約内容が、❺では元の予約内容がそれぞれ記載されている。両者のDates「日にち」の項目を見てみると、当初の利用は5月20日までだったが、5月19日までに変更されていることが分かるので、(B)が正解。have ～ *done*「～を…してもらう」。
(A) destination「目的地」。
(C) method「方法」。
(D) arrival「到着」。

---

185 When will Mr. Hong probably receive his refund?

(A) On May 12
(B) On May 16
(C) On May 19
(D) On May 20

Hongさんはいつ返金を受けると思われますか。

(A) 5月12日
(B) 5月16日
(C) 5月19日
(D) 5月20日

正解 C 1の❸ 4～6行目に、If you reduce the length of your reservation ...... you will be refunded the difference immediately upon returning the vehicle.「予約の利用期間を短縮した……場合は車を返却次第、差額が返金される」とある。2の❷・❺より、Hongさんは利用期間を1日短縮したので、差額が返金されると分かる。同❷より、予約変更後の利用最終日は5月19日になっているので、Hongさんには5月19日に車の返却直後に差額が返金されると考えられる。よって、(C)が正解。
(A) 2のEメールの日付。
(B) 2の❷より、Hongさんが車を受け取る日付。
(D) 2の❺より、Hongさんが予約変更前に予定していた車を返却する日付。

Words & Phrases

1 案内
❶ successfully うまく　process ～を処理する　booking 予約　confirmation 確認　❷ note 注記　holder 所有者　authorize ～に権限を与える、～を許可する　representative 担当者　at no cost 無料で　pick up ～ ～を受け取る　vehicle 車　branch 支店　conveniently 便利に　complimentary 無料の　shuttle シャトルバス　❸ cancellation キャンセル　make a change 変更する　pickup 受け取り　drop-off 乗り捨て、降車　fill out ～ ～に記入する　in advance 前もって　reduce ～を減らす　length 期間、長さ　refund ～ … ～に…を払い戻す　difference 差額　immediately すぐに　upon ～ ～のすぐあとで　incur ～を負担する

2 Eメール
❶ details 詳細　as follows 次の通りで　❷ midsize 中型の　sedan セダン車　❸ owe ～を支払う義務がある　❹ original 元の　record 記録

Expressions

Please do not hesitate to *do* 「ご遠慮なく～してください」(2の❻ 1行目)

If you have any questions about our photocopiers, please do not hesitate to call our office.
当社のコピー機に関するご質問がございましたら、どうぞご遠慮なく当営業所にお電話ください。

Questions 186-190 refer to the following Web page, order form, and e-mail.

1 ウェブページ

www.faonebakery.com/wholesale

Desserts to Delight

❶ Faone Bakery's wholesale division creates delicious cakes, pies, cookies, and specialty products that are sure to leave your customers smiling and coming back for more. Our bakery in Baltimore allows us to service the greater mid-Atlantic region of the United States and we hope to expand nationwide soon. (Check back in March of next year!)

❷ In order to set up a wholesale account with us, create a username and password. Once your registration is confirmed (within two days of your initial account sign-up), simply log in to the Web-based ordering system and begin making your selections!

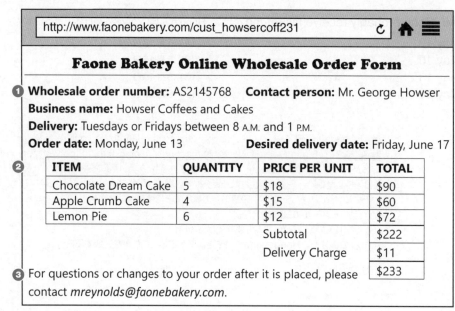

2 注文書

http://www.faonebakery.com/cust_howsercoff231

Faone Bakery Online Wholesale Order Form

❶ **Wholesale order number:** AS2145768 **Contact person:** Mr. George Howser
Business name: Howser Coffees and Cakes
Delivery: Tuesdays or Fridays between 8 A.M. and 1 P.M.
Order date: Monday, June 13 **Desired delivery date:** Friday, June 17

❷

ITEM	QUANTITY	PRICE PER UNIT	TOTAL
Chocolate Dream Cake	5	$18	$90
Apple Crumb Cake	4	$15	$60
Lemon Pie	6	$12	$72
		Subtotal	$222
		Delivery Charge	$11
			$233

❸ For questions or changes to your order after it is placed, please contact *mreynolds@faonebakery.com*.

3 Eメール

To: mreynolds@faonebakery.com
From: management@howsercoffee.com
Date: Tuesday, June 14
Re: Re: Order

Dear Ms. Reynolds,

❶ We have been very pleased with our customers' responses to your desserts and are considering increasing our selections. We are interested in offering the carrot cake but are concerned about how long it will stay moist. We would like to test it out—would you be able to send a couple of slices with Friday's delivery?

❷ We would also like to add an additional pie to our June 13 order to accommodate a special request from one of our customers.

Thanks for your help.

George Howser, Owner
Howser Coffees and Cakes

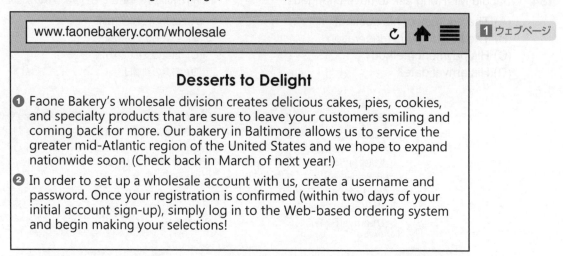

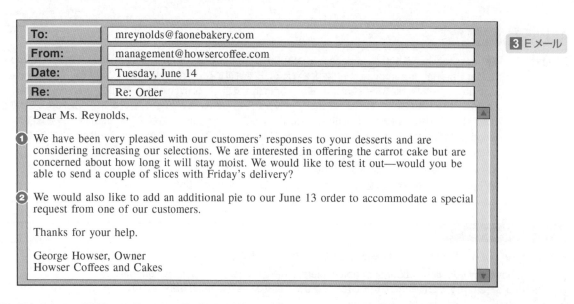

問題186-190は次のウェブページ、注文書、Eメールに関するものです。

www.faonebakery.com/wholesale

喜びを生むデザート

Faoneベーカリー卸売部門では、必ず貴店のお客さまを笑顔にし、またご来店いただけるようなおいしいケーキ、パイ、クッキーや自慢の品を生み出しています。ボルチモアにある当社のパン製造所は、当社がアメリカ合衆国の中部大西洋地域圏にサービス提供することを可能にしており、近々全国に拡大したいと考えております。(来年3月にまた確認してください!)

当社の卸売アカウントを設定するために、ユーザー名とパスワードを作成してください。登録が確認されましたら(最初のアカウント登録から2日以内に)、ウェブベースの注文システムにログインして商品選択を開始してください!

---

www.faonebakery.com/cust_howsercoff231

Faoneベーカリー　オンライン卸売注文書

卸売注文番号:AS2145768　**ご担当者**:George Howser様
店名:Howser Coffees and Cakes
配達:火曜日または金曜日の午前8時と午後1時の間
注文日:6月13日、月曜日　**希望配達日**:6月17日、金曜日

商品	数量	単価	合計
チョコレートドリームケーキ	5	18ドル	90ドル
アップルクラムケーキ	4	15ドル	60ドル
レモンパイ	6	12ドル	72ドル
		小計	222ドル
		配送料	11ドル
			233ドル

ご質問またはご注文後の変更につきましては、mreynolds@faonebakery.comにご連絡ください。

受信者:mreynolds@faonebakery.com
送信者:management@howsercoffee.com
日付:6月14日、火曜日
件名:Re:注文

Reynolds様

当店は御社のデザートに対するうちのお客さまの反応にとても満足しており、種類を増やすことを検討しています。キャロットケーキを提供したいと思っていますが、どのくらいの時間しっとりした状態を保てるかが気になります。それを試したいと思っています——金曜日の配達品と一緒に2、3切れを送っていただくことは可能でしょうか。

また、うちのお客さまの1人からの特別なご要望にお応えし、6月13日の注文にパイをもう1個追加したいと思っています。

どうぞよろしくお願いいたします。

George Howser、オーナー
Howser Coffees and Cakes

186 Where does Faone Bakery deliver?

(A) Within the mid-Atlantic region only
(B) Within Baltimore only
(C) Throughout the United States
(D) Throughout various countries

Faoneベーカリーはどこに配達していますか。

(A) 中部大西洋地域内のみ
(B) ボルチモア内のみ
(C) アメリカ合衆国全域
(D) さまざまな国の至る所

正解 A Faoneベーカリーのウェブページである1の❶ 3～4行目に、Our bakery in Baltimore allows us to service the greater mid-Atlantic region of the United States「ボルチモアにある当社のパン製造所は、当社がアメリカ合衆国の中部大西洋地域圏にサービス提供することを可能にしている」とあるので、(A)が正解。
(C) 1の❶ 4～5行目にwe hope to expand nationwide soon「近々全国に拡大したいと考えている」と今後の拡大の希望が述べられているが、現状に関しては中部大西洋地域外のサービスへの言及はない。
(C)(D) throughout「～の全体にわたって、～の至る所」。

---

187 What is indicated about Faone Bakery?

(A) It has opened another retail store.
(B) It offers a full breakfast menu.
(C) It opened in March.
(D) It is planning to grow.

Faoneベーカリーについて何が示されていますか。

(A) 同社はもう1軒小売店をオープンした。
(B) 同社はフル・ブレックファストのメニューを提供している。
(C) 同社は3月にオープンした。
(D) 同社は拡大する計画である。

正解 D 1の❶ 3～4行目で、Faoneベーカリーは現在、アメリカ合衆国の中部大西洋地域圏でサービスを提供していると述べられている。同4～5行目に、we hope to expand nationwide soon「近々全国に拡大したいと考えている」とあり、続けて来年3月にウェブページを再確認するよう促しているので、同社は来年3月に拡大する計画だと分かる。grow「〈規模などが〉拡大する」。
(A) retail store「小売店」。
(B) full breakfast「フル・ブレックファスト〈イギリスの伝統的な朝食で、卵やベーコンなどを含むたっぷりしたもの〉」。

---

188 What did Mr. Howser most likely do before June 13?

(A) He created an online account.
(B) He added sandwiches to his menu.
(C) He visited Faone Bakery to taste a product.
(D) He sent a promotional link to customers.

Howserさんは6月13日以前に何をしたと考えられますか。

(A) 彼はオンラインのアカウントを作った。
(B) 彼はサンドイッチをメニューに加えた。
(C) 彼は製品を試食するためにFaoneベーカリーを訪れた。
(D) 彼は顧客に販売促進のリンクを送った。

正解 A オンラインの注文書である2の❶ Contact person「担当者」、Order date「注文日」の欄より、Howserさんは6月13日にFaoneベーカリーにオンラインで注文をしたと分かる。1の❷ 1～2行目で、オンライン注文するためにFaoneベーカリーの卸売アカウントを作成する手順が説明されており、続けて「登録が確認されたら（最初のアカウント登録から2日以内に）、ウェブベースの注文システムにログインして商品選択を開始してください」とある。よって、Howserさんは6月13日以前にオンラインのアカウントを作成したと考えられる。
(C) 3の❶ 2～4行目で、Howserさんはキャロットケーキを試したいと送付を頼んでいるが、このEメールの送信日は6月14日。また、ベーカリーを訪問するとも述べていない。taste「～を試食する」。
(D) promotional「販売促進の」。

189 What is one reason why Mr. Howser sent the e-mail?

(A) To cancel a delivery
(B) To complain about a cake
(C) To invite Ms. Reynolds to his business
(D) To request samples from Faone Bakery

HowserさんがEメールを送った1つの理由は何ですか。

(A) ある配達をキャンセルすること。
(B) ケーキについて不満を言うこと。
(C) Reynoldsさんを自分の店に招くこと。
(D) Faoneベーカリーに試食品を依頼すること。

正解 D Howserさんは3のEメールの❶ 2～3行目で、「キャロットケーキを提供したいと思っているが、どのくらいの時間しっとりした状態を保てるかが気になる」と述べた後、同3～4行目で、それを試したいと伝えて、would you be able to send a couple of slices with Friday's delivery「金曜日の配達品と一緒に2、3切れを送ってもらうことは可能か」と尋ねている。(D)が正解。sample「試供品」。
(B) 3の❶ 1～2行目より、HowserさんはFaoneベーカリーのデザートに対する客の反応に満足していると分かるので不適切。complain about ～「～について不満を言う」。

---

190 How many pies will Mr. Howser most likely receive on June 17?

(A) Five
(B) Six
(C) Seven
(D) Nine

Howserさんは6月17日に、パイを何個受け取ると考えられますか。

(A) 5個
(B) 6個
(C) 7個
(D) 9個

正解 C Howserさんは3の❷ 1～2行目で、We would also like to add an additional pie to our June 13 order「また、6月13日の注文にパイをもう1個追加したいと思っている」と述べている。6月13日付の注文書である2の❶「希望配達日」の欄に「6月17日」とあり、同❷ Lemon Pie「レモンパイ」の数量は6なので、Howserさんは6月17日に計7個のパイを受け取ると分かる。

Words & Phrases

order form　注文書

1 ウェブページ
dessert　デザート　delight　～を喜ばせる　❶ bakery　ベーカリー、パン製造所　wholesale　卸売り
division　部門　create　～を作る　specialty product　自慢の品、特産品　be sure to *do*　必ず～する
leave ～ …　～に…させる　service　～にサービスを提供する、～の役に立つ　greater　(近郊を含む)～圏
mid-Atlantic　中部大西洋の　region　地域　expand　拡大する　nationwide　全国的に
❷ set up ～　～を設定する　account　〈インターネットなどの〉アカウント　once　いったん～すると
registration　登録　confirm　～を確認する　initial　最初の　sign-up　登録
log in to ～　～にログインする　-based　～ベースの、～を用いた　make a selection　選択をする

2 注文書
❶ contact person　担当者、連絡窓口　business　店　desired　望ましい　❷ quantity　数量
per unit　単位当たり　subtotal　小計　delivery charge　配送料　❸ place　〈注文〉を出す
contact　～に連絡する

3 Eメール
❶ be pleased with ～　～に満足している　response　反応　consider　～を検討する
increase　～を増やす　selection　〈選ばれた〉種類　be concerned about ～　～を心配している
moist　しっとりした　test ～ out　～を試す　a couple of ～　2、3の～　slice　〈パンなどの〉ひと切れ
❷ accommodate　〈要求など〉に応じる

Expressions

allow ～ to *do*　「～が…するのを可能にする」(1の❶ 3行目)
Please allow me to ask one more question.
私にもう1つ質問をさせてください。

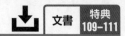

Questions 191-195 refer to the following e-mail, job summaries, and Web page.

1 Eメール

To:	Regional managers
From:	Mie Ichikawa <m.ichikawa@kiraku.co.jp>
Subject:	Western Canada
Date:	July 10

Regional Managers,

❶ As you know, Kiraku is planning an expansion to Western Canada. A top priority this quarter is to fill several staff positions in this region, including a new midlevel position being created to strengthen communication with sales teams. Please send an e-mail to Maya Janit, our National Director (Canada), if you are interested in being on the hiring team for this expansion.

Warm regards,
Mie Ichikawa

2 職務概要

Kiraku Japanese Furniture

Western Canada Region—Available Positions

❶ **Regional Manager** (Winnipeg; reports to the National Director)

- researches and recruits new corporate clients and retailers; maintains client relationships
- coordinates with the logistics team to make sure merchandise is available
- travels regularly to all locations within the region

❷ **District Supervisor** (Saskatoon and Vancouver; reports to the Regional Manager)

- assists Regional Manager in maintaining client relationships
- attends conferences and trade shows to stay up-to-date on industry trends
- builds and maintains ongoing communication with sales teams

❸ **Sales Associate** (Calgary, Saskatoon, Vancouver, and Winnipeg; reports to the District Supervisor)

- delivers presentations to clients
- attends conferences and trade shows to maintain design skills
- works evenings and weekends as necessary
- must have background in interior design

❹ **Delivery Associate** (Calgary, Saskatoon, Vancouver, and Winnipeg; reports to the District Supervisor)

- provides customer service
- must have commercial driver's license and be able to carry 25 kilograms

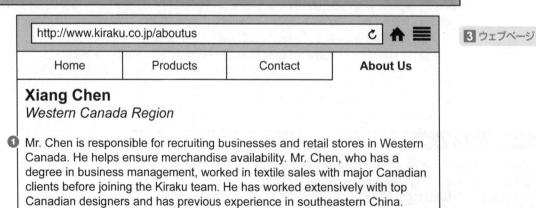

3 ウェブページ

http://www.kiraku.co.jp/aboutus

Home | Products | Contact | **About Us**

Xiang Chen

Western Canada Region

❶ Mr. Chen is responsible for recruiting businesses and retail stores in Western Canada. He helps ensure merchandise availability. Mr. Chen, who has a degree in business management, worked in textile sales with major Canadian clients before joining the Kiraku team. He has worked extensively with top Canadian designers and has previous experience in southeastern China.

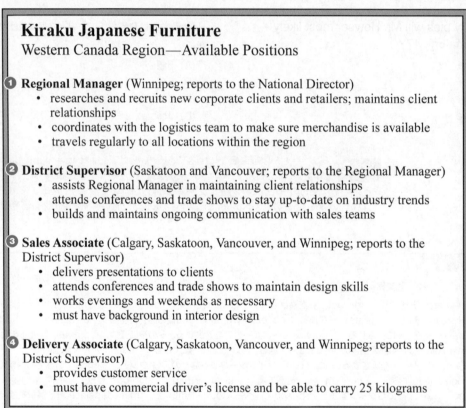

問題191-195は次のEメール、職務概要、ウェブページに関するものです。

受信者：地域担当マネージャー
送信者：Mie Ichikawa <m.ichikawa@kiraku.co.jp>
件名：カナダ西部
日付：7月10日

地域担当マネージャー各位

ご存じの通り、Kiraku社はカナダ西部への拡大を計画しています。今四半期の最優先事項は、販売チームとのコミュニケーション強化のために設けられる新たな中間職を含め、この地域の幾つかの社員の職を埋めることです。この拡大に向けての採用チームに入ることに興味があれば、当社の国内責任者（カナダ）のMaya JanitにEメールを送ってください。

よろしくお願いいたします。
Mie Ichikawa

Kiraku日本家具社
カナダ西部地域――募集中の職

地域担当マネージャー（ウィニペグ。国内責任者に直属）
・新規の法人顧客や小売業者を調査し、勧誘する。すなわち、顧客との関係を維持する
・確実に商品の在庫があるように物流管理チームと連携する
・地域内の全店舗を定期的に訪問する

地区監督者（サスカトゥーンおよびバンクーバー。地域担当マネージャーに直属）
・顧客との関係維持において地域担当マネージャーを支援する
・業界動向に関する最新情報を常に把握するために、協議会や見本市に参加する
・販売チームとの継続的なコミュニケーションを構築、維持する

販売員（カルガリー、サスカトゥーン、バンクーバー、ウィニペグ。地区監督者に直属）
・顧客にプレゼンテーションを行う
・デザインスキルを維持するために、会議や見本市に参加する
・必要に応じて夜間や週末に勤務する
・インテリアデザインにおける経歴が必須

配達員（カルガリー、サスカトゥーン、バンクーバー、ウィニペグ。地区監督者に直属）
・顧客サービスを提供する
・営業用自動車免許を所持し、25キログラムを運べることが必須

---

http://www.kiraku.co.jp/aboutus

ホーム　製品　お問い合わせ　スタッフ紹介

Xiang Chen
カナダ西部地域

Chen氏は、カナダ西部で事業所や小売店を勧誘する責任者。彼は、商品の在庫を確実にするよう支援する。Chen氏は経営管理の学位を有し、Kiraku社への入社前は、カナダの大手顧客に対する織物販売業務に従事した。彼はカナダのトップデザイナーたちと共に幅広く仕事をしてきており、中国南東部での経験を有する。

191 What is the purpose of the e-mail?

(A) To report on quarterly sales
(B) To share regional data
(C) To thank salespeople
(D) To provide plans for staffing

Eメールの目的は何ですか。

(A) 四半期の売上高を報告すること。
(B) 地域のデータを共有すること。
(C) 販売員に謝意を述べること。
(D) 人員配置の計画を提供すること。

正解 D 1のEメールの❶ 1行目で、Kiraku社の拡大計画について述べられ、続けてA top priority this quarter is to fill several staff positions in this region「今四半期の最優先事項は、この地域の幾つかの社員の職を埋めることだ」と説明されている。また、同❶ 3〜5行目では、採用チームへの参加に興味がある場合には国内責任者にEメールを送るよう伝えている。よって、Eメールの目的は、今後の人員の採用や配置の計画を知らせることだと分かるので、(D)が正解。staffing「人員配置」。
(A) 1の❶ 1〜3行目で、四半期の最優先事項に言及しているが、売上高については述べられていない。quarterly「四半期の」。
(C) salespeople「販売員」。

---

192 What position was recently created?

(A) Regional manager
(B) District supervisor
(C) Sales associate
(D) Delivery associate

最近、どんな職が設けられましたか。

(A) 地域担当マネージャー
(B) 地区監督者
(C) 販売員
(D) 配達員

正解 B 1の❶ 2〜3行目に、採用が必要な職についてincluding a new midlevel position being created to strengthen communication with sales teams「販売チームとのコミュニケーション強化のために設けられる新たな中間職を含め」とあるので、販売チームとのコミュニケーション強化のための中間職が新設されたと分かる。2の職務概要の❷のDistrict Supervisor「地区監督者」の職務内容の3点目の、builds and maintains ongoing communication with sales teams「販売チームとの継続的なコミュニケーションを構築、維持する」が、前述の新たな中間職の職務内容と一致するので、最近設けられたのは、地区監督者の職と考えられる。

---

193 What is required of a Kiraku sales associate?

(A) Providing training in interior design
(B) Working outside of regular business hours
(C) Organizing trade shows
(D) Delivering furniture to client work sites

Kiraku社の販売員には何が求められていますか。

(A) インテリアデザインの研修を提供すること。
(B) 通常の営業時間外に働くこと。
(C) 見本市を企画すること。
(D) 顧客の職場に家具を配達すること。

正解 B Kiraku社のsales associate「販売員」の職務内容は、2の❸にある。箇条書きの3点目にworks evenings and weekends as necessary「必要に応じて夜間や週末に勤務する」とあるので、(B)が正解。require ～ of …「…に～を要求する」。outside of ～「～以外に」、regular「通常の」、business hours「営業時間」。
(A) 2の❸箇条書きの4点目に「インテリアデザインの経歴が必須」とあるが、研修を行うとの言及はない。
(C) 2の❸箇条書きの2点目に「見本市に参加する」とあるが、「企画する」とは述べられていない。organize「～を企画する」。
(D) 2の❹箇条書きの2点目にある運搬に関する記載は、配達員の条件。work site「職場」。

194 In what city is Mr. Chen most likely based?

(A) Calgary
(B) Saskatoon
(C) Vancouver
(D) Winnipeg

Chenさんはどの都市に拠点を置いていると考えられますか。

(A) カルガリー
(B) サスカトゥーン
(C) バンクーバー
(D) ウィニペグ

正解 D 3の❶ 1〜2行目に、Mr. Chen is responsible for recruiting businesses and retail stores in Western Canada. He helps ensure merchandise availability.「Chen氏は、カナダ西部で事業所や小売店を勧誘する責任者。彼は、商品の在庫を確実にするよう支援する」とある。この職務内容は、2の❶箇条書きの1点目のresearches and recruits new corporate clients and retailers「新規の法人顧客や小売業者を調査し、勧誘する」と一致し、2点目のcoordinates with the logistics team to make sure merchandise is available「確実に商品の在庫があるように物流管理チームと連携する」と一致するため、Chenさんは地域担当マネージャーと分かる。地域担当マネージャーの拠点は、同❶ 1行目にWinnipegとあるので、(D)が正解。be based in 〜「〜に拠点を置く」。

---

195 According to the Web page, what is true about Mr. Chen?

(A) He studied business.
(B) He designs furniture.
(C) He owns textile companies in China.
(D) He works in human resources.

ウェブページによると、Chenさんについて正しいことは何ですか。

(A) 彼は経営について学んだ。
(B) 彼は家具をデザインしている。
(C) 彼は中国に織物会社を所有している。
(D) 彼は人事部で働いている。

正解 A 3のウェブページの❶ 2〜3行目で、Mr. Chen, who has a degree in business management「Chen氏は経営管理の学位を有する」と紹介されているので、(A)が正解。
(B) 3の❶ 4〜5行目で、Chenさんがトップデザイナーたちと仕事をした経験に言及があるが、Chenさん自身がデザインを行うとは述べられていない。
(C) 3の❶ 3〜5行目で、以前Chenさんは織物販売の業務に従事しており、中国での経験があると述べられているが、会社の所有についての言及はない。
(D) human resources「人事部」。

Words & Phrases

summary 概要

1 Eメール
regional 地域の ❶ expansion 拡大 top priority 最優先事項 quarter 四半期
fill 〈仕事の空きなど〉を埋める position 職 including 〜を含めて midlevel 中間の
strengthen 〜を強化する national 国内の director 責任者 hiring 採用

2 職務概要
furniture 家具 available 入手できる、利用できる ❶ report to 〜 〜に直属する research 〜を調査する
recruit 〜を勧誘する corporate 法人の retailer 小売業者 maintain 〜を維持する
relationship 関係 coordinate with 〜 〜と連携する logistics 物流管理
make sure (that) 〜 〜を確実にする merchandise 商品 regularly 定期的に location 店舗、所在地
❷ district 地区 supervisor 監督者 assist 〜を支援する trade show 見本市
stay 〈ある状態〉にとどまる up-to-date 最新の情報を採り入れた industry 業界 trend 動向、トレンド
ongoing 継続中の ❸ sales associate 販売員 deliver 〈講義・演説など〉をする skill スキル、技能
background 経歴 interior design インテリアデザイン ❹ delivery associate 配達員
commercial 営業用の、商業の driver's license 運転免許

3 ウェブページ
❶ retail store 小売店 ensure 〜を確実にする availability 利用できること degree 学位
business management 経営管理 textile 織物 major 主要な extensively 幅広く
previous 以前の

Expressions

as necessary 「必要に応じて」(2の❸ 5行目)
Passengers can adjust the seat height as necessary.
乗客は、必要に応じて座席の高さを調節できます。

Questions 196-200 refer to the following Web site, form, and e-mail.

1 ウェブサイト

https://www.humstellhotel.com

About | Rooms | Dining | **Meeting Spaces** | Contact

❶ Humstell Hotel is a great place to host events, conferences, or meetings. Spaces can be arranged in rows of individual chairs or with tables seating groups of 4 to 8 persons. Please refer to the chart below for pricing and room capacities.

❷ **Room Specifications**

Room	Price per day	Capacity (If seated in rows)	Capacity (If seated in groups)
Blue Room	$800	200 persons	160 persons
Green Room	$650	100 persons	72 persons
Yellow Room	$500	50 persons	32 persons
Purple Room	$350	25 persons	16 persons

❸ All rooms with the exception of the Purple Room are equipped with audio capabilities and a computer. Additional equipment is available on-site at the prices listed below.

❹ **Equipment Rental Costs (NOT included in room prices):**
Microphone: $25 Screen: $45
LCD Projector: $100 Projector and screen package: $130

To reserve equipment or a meeting space at Humstell Hotel, fill out our Event Space Request Form at https://www.humstellhotel.com/event.

2 フォーム

❶ **Humstell Hotel–Event Space Request Form**

A member of our staff will contact you within 24 business hours to confirm availability.

❷ **Name:**	Samuel Ma	**Event type:**	Meetings
Job title:	Manager	**Event date(s):**	September 19
Phone:	541-555-0157	**Equipment needed:**	1 LCD Projector and screen
Email:	samma@corgetinsurance.com	**Room(s) requested:**	Purple Room, Green Room
Company name:	Corget Insurance	**Set-up request:**	Rows

❸ Please note that we offer on-site catering. If you are interested in offering meal or beverage services for your event, please contact our Kitchen Manager, Cooper Blackley, directly at cblackley@humstellhotel.com.

3 Eメール

E-mail

To: Carissa Stanley
From: Samuel Ma
Subject: Change of rooms
Date: June 12

Hello, Ms. Stanley:

❶ I submitted an Event Space Request Form yesterday, but I am hoping to make a change. We will be running a number of small meetings and presentations in our two rooms throughout the day, but we now expect over 120 employees to attend our all-staff meeting. So while the Purple Room should be suitable for the small meetings, I don't think the Green Room will be adequate. Could you please let me know if the larger room is still available for September 19?

❷ I apologize for the confusion and thank you in advance for your help.

Samuel Ma, Corget Insurance

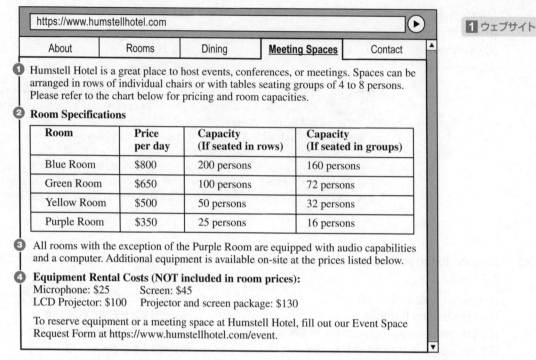

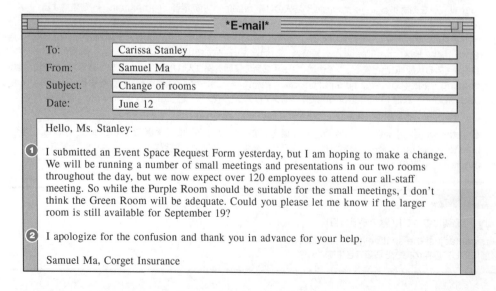

問題196-200は次のウェブサイト、フォーム、Eメールに関するものです。

https://www.humstellhotel.com

当ホテルについて　部屋　食事　<u>会議スペース</u>　お問い合わせ

Humstellホテルは、イベント、協議会、会議を開催するのに最適な場所です。スペースには、個々の椅子を数列に、もしくは4～8名のグループごとに着席するテーブルを配置させることができます。価格設定と部屋の収容人数については以下の表を参照してください。

部屋の仕様

部屋	1日当たりの価格	収容人数（列で着席する場合）	収容人数（グループで着席する場合）
青の間	800ドル	200名	160名
緑の間	650ドル	100名	72名
黄色の間	500ドル	50名	32名
紫の間	350ドル	25名	16名

紫の間を除く全ての部屋には、オーディオ機能とコンピューター1台が備え付けてあります。追加の機材は、以下に記載されている価格にて現地でご利用になれます。

機材レンタル費用（部屋の価格には含まれません）:
マイク：25ドル　スクリーン：45ドル
液晶プロジェクター：100ドル　プロジェクターとスクリーンのセット：130ドル

Humstellホテルで機材や会議スペースを予約するには、https://www.humstellhotel.com/eventでイベントスペース依頼フォームにご記入ください。

Humstellホテル――イベントスペース依頼フォーム

当ホテルのスタッフが、空き状況を確認するため24営業時間内にお客さまにご連絡いたします。

氏名：	Samuel Ma	**イベントの種類：**	会議
役職名：	部長	**イベントの日程：**	9月19日
電話：	541-555-0157	**必要な機材：**	液晶プロジェクターとスクリーン1セット
Eメール：	samma@corgetinsurance.com	**希望の部屋：**	紫の間、緑の間
会社名：	Corget保険会社	**希望の配置：**	列

当ホテルが会場内でのケータリングを提供していることにご留意ください。イベント用の飲食物のサービスのご提供にご興味がおありでしたら、当ホテルのキッチン管理者のCooper Blackleyにcblackley@humstellhotel.comまで直接ご連絡ください。

受信者：Carissa Stanley
送信者：Samuel Ma
件名：部屋の変更
日付：6月12日

Stanley様

私は昨日イベントスペース依頼フォームを提出しましたが、変更したいと思っています。私どもは終日を通して2つの部屋で小さな会議とプレゼンテーションを数多く行うつもりですが、目下のところ全スタッフ会議に120名を超える従業員が参加すると見込んでいます。そのため、紫の間の方は小さな会議用に適しているのですが、緑の間の方は十分ではないだろうと考えています。もっと広い部屋が9月19日にまだ利用可能かどうか教えていただけますか。

混乱を招いてしまい申し訳ありませんが、ご協力のほどよろしくお願いいたします。

Samuel Ma、Corget保険会社

196 What is indicated about the meeting rooms?

(A) All are on the same hotel floor.
(B) All can seat more than 50 people.
(C) All can be set up for groups.
(D) All are equipped with a computer.

会議室について何が示されていますか。

(A) 全てがホテルの同じフロアにある。
(B) 全てが50名を超える人の着席が可能である。
(C) 全てがグループ用の設置が可能である。
(D) 全てにコンピューターが1台備え付けてある。

正解 C 1のウェブサイトでは、「会議スペース」のタブが選択されており、同❶ 1～2行目に、Spaces can be arranged in rows of individual chairs or with tables seating groups of 4 to 8 persons.「スペースには、個々の椅子を数列に、もしくは4～8名のグループごとに着席するテーブルを配置させることができる」とあり、同❷「部屋の仕様」の表に「収容人数(グループで着席する場合)」の欄があり、いずれの部屋の項目にも人数が記載されているので、全ての会議室はグループ用の設置が可能と分かる。(C)が正解。
(B) 1の❷の一番下の行より、紫の間は50名の着席はできないと分かる。
(D) 1の❸ 1～2行目より、紫の間にはコンピューターが備え付けられていない。

197 How much will Mr. Ma pay for equipment?

(A) $25
(B) $45
(C) $100
(D) $130

Maさんは機材に幾ら支払いますか。

(A) 25ドル
(B) 45ドル
(C) 100ドル
(D) 130ドル

正解 D 2の❷ Name「氏名」の欄にMaさんの名前があるので、このフォームはMaさんによって入力されたもの。同❷右欄3段目のEquipment needed「必要な機材」に、1 LCD Projector and screen「液晶プロジェクターとスクリーン1セット」とある。また1の❹「機材レンタル費用」に、Projector and screen package: $130「プロジェクターとスクリーンのセット:130ドル」とあるので、Maさんは、液晶プロジェクターとスクリーンのセットのレンタル料金として130ドル支払うと分かる。(D)が正解。
(A) 1の❹より、マイクのレンタル費用。
(B) 1の❹より、スクリーンのみのレンタル費用。
(C) 1の❹より、液晶プロジェクターのみのレンタル費用。

198 According to the form, why should a customer contact Mr. Blackley?

(A) To change a booking
(B) To make a payment
(C) To order food for an event
(D) To schedule an equipment pickup

フォームによると、顧客はなぜBlackleyさんに連絡しますか。

(A) 予約を変更するため。
(B) 支払いをするため。
(C) イベント用に食べ物を注文するため。
(D) 機材受け取りの予定を入れるため。

正解 C 2のフォームの❸ 1行目で、ホテルが会場内のケータリングを提供していると述べられ、同1～2行目に、If you are interested in offering meal or beverage services for your event, please contact our Kitchen Manager, Cooper Blackley「イベント用の飲食物のサービスの提供に興味があれば、当ホテルのキッチン管理者のCooper Blackleyに連絡してください」とあるので、(C)が正解。
(A) booking「予約」。
(D) pickup「受け取り」。

199 Who most likely is Ms. Stanley?

(A) A presenter
(B) A friend of Mr. Ma
(C) A Humstell Hotel employee
(D) A manager at Corget Insurance

Stanleyさんとは誰だと考えられますか。

(A) 講演者
(B) Maさんの友人
(C) Humstellホテルの従業員
(D) Corget保険会社の部長

正解 C 3はMaさんからStanleyさんに宛てたEメール。Eメールの件名にChange of rooms「部屋の変更」とあり、3の❶ 1行目で、イベントスペース依頼フォームで予約した部屋の変更を希望していることが伝えられ、以降ではその詳細が説明されている。Eメールの送信者のMaさんの名前が2の❷「氏名」の欄に記載されているので、Maさんは2のHumstellホテルのイベントスペース依頼フォームで部屋の予約を行った後、3でStanleyさんにその予約の変更を依頼していると分かる。よって、StanleyさんとはHumstellホテルの従業員だと考えられる。(C)が正解。
(D) 2の❷「役職名」と「会社名」の欄より、Corget保険会社の部長はMaさん。

200 Where will Corget Insurance most likely hold its all-staff meeting?

(A) In the Blue Room
(B) In the Green Room
(C) In the Yellow Room
(D) In the Purple Room

Corget保険会社は、どこで全スタッフ会議を開くと考えられますか。

(A) 青の間
(B) 緑の間
(C) 黄色の間
(D) 紫の間

正解 A 2の❷ Name「氏名」とCompany name「会社名」の欄より、Corget保険会社はMaさんが所属している会社と分かる。Maさんは、3で部屋の予約の変更希望を伝えている。同❶ 3～4行目に、「目下のところ全スタッフ会議に120名を超える従業員が参加すると見込んでいる」とあり、続く4～6行目で「そのため、緑の間は十分ではないだろうと考えている。もっと広い部屋が9月19日にまだ利用可能かどうか教えてもらえるか」と尋ねている。各部屋の仕様を示す1の❷の表を見ると、緑の間よりも収容人数が多く、120名を超える人数を収容可能なのは青の間である。よって、Corget保険会社は全スタッフ会議を青の間で行うと考えられる。

Words & Phrases

1 ウェブサイト ❶ host ～を開催する　arrange ～を配置する　in rows 幾つも列をなして　individual 個々の、1名用の　seat ～を座らせる　refer to ～ ～を参照する　chart 表　pricing 価格設定　capacity 収容人数　❷ specifications 仕様　❸ with the exception of ～ ～を除いて　be equipped with ～ ～が備え付けてある　capability 性能　additional 追加の　equipment 機材　available 利用できる　on-site 現地で、その場で　list ～を記載する　❹ microphone マイク　screen スクリーン　LCD projector 液晶プロジェクター　package セット　reserve ～を予約する　fill out ～ ～に記入する

2 フォーム ❶ business hours 営業時間　confirm ～を確認する　availability 空き具合　❷ job title 役職名　insurance 保険　❸ note ～を覚えておく　catering ケータリング　beverage 飲み物　directly 直接

3 Eメール ❶ submit ～を提出する　run ～を管理する、～を切り回す　a number of ～ たくさんの～　throughout ～を通して　expect ～ to *do* ～が…すると見込む　while ～である一方で　be suitable for ～ ～に適している　adequate 十分な、適切な　❷ apologize for ～ ～を謝る　confusion 混乱　in advance 前もって

Expressions

Could you (please) let me know if ～? 「～かどうか知らせていただけますか」(3の❶ 5～6行目)

Could you let me know if this Friday is convenient for you?
今週金曜日があなたにとってご都合がよいかお知らせいただけますか。

CDトラック・特典音声ファイル 一覧表

● CD1

Test	Track No.	Contents
サンプル問題	1	タイトル
	2	Listening Test Directions/ Part 1 Directions
	3	Q1
	4	Part 2 Directions
	5	Q2, Q3
	6	Part 3 Directions
	7	Q4-6
	8	Q7-9
	9	Part 4 Directions
	10	Q10-12
TEST 1	11	Test 1
	12	Listening Test Directions/ Part 1 Directions
	13	Q1
	14	Q2
	15	Q3
	16	Q4
	17	Q5
	18	Q6
	19	Part 2 Directions
	20	Q7
	21	Q8
	22	Q9
	23	Q10
	24	Q11
	25	Q12
	26	Q13
	27	Q14
	28	Q15
	29	Q16
	30	Q17
	31	Q18
	32	Q19
	33	Q20
	34	Q21
	35	Q22
	36	Q23
	37	Q24
	38	Q25
	39	Q26
	40	Q27
	41	Q28
	42	Q29
	43	Q30
	44	Q31
	45	Part 3 Directions

Test	Track No.	Contents
TEST 1	46	Part 3 Q32-34 会話
	47	Q32-34 問題
	48	Q35-37 会話
	49	Q35-37 問題
	50	Q38-40 会話
	51	Q38-40 問題
	52	Q41-43 会話
	53	Q41-43 問題
	54	Q44-46 会話
	55	Q44-46 問題
	56	Q47-49 会話
	57	Q47-49 問題
	58	Q50-52 会話
	59	Q50-52 問題
	60	Q53-55 会話
	61	Q53-55 問題
	62	Q56-58 会話
	63	Q56-58 問題
	64	Q59-61 会話
	65	Q59-61 問題
	66	Q62-64 会話
	67	Q62-64 問題
	68	Q65-67 会話
	69	Q65-67 問題
	70	Q68-70 会話
	71	Q68-70 問題
	72	Part 4 Directions
	73	Q71-73 トーク
	74	Q71-73 問題
	75	Q74-76 トーク
	76	Q74-76 問題
	77	Q77-79 トーク
	78	Q77-79 問題
	79	Q80-82 トーク
	80	Q80-82 問題
	81	Q83-85 トーク
	82	Q83-85 問題
	83	Q86-88 トーク
	84	Q86-88 問題
	85	Q89-91 トーク
	86	Q89-91 問題
	87	Q92-94 トーク
	88	Q92-94 問題
	89	Q95-97 トーク
	90	Q95-97 問題
	91	Q98-100 トーク
	92	Q98-100 問題

● CD2

Test	Track No.	Contents
TEST 2	1	Test 2
	2	Listening Test Directions/ Part 1 Directions
	3	Q1
	4	Q2
	5	Q3
	6	Q4
	7	Q5
	8	Q6
	9	Part 2 Directions
	10	Q7
	11	Q8
	12	Q9
	13	Q10
	14	Q11
	15	Q12
	16	Q13
	17	Q14
	18	Q15
	19	Q16
	20	Q17
	21	Q18
	22	Q19
	23	Q20
	24	Q21
	25	Q22
	26	Q23
	27	Q24
	28	Q25
	29	Q26
	30	Q27
	31	Q28
	32	Q29
	33	Q30
	34	Q31
	35	Part 3 Directions
	36	Q32-34 会話
	37	Q32-34 問題
	38	Q35-37 会話
	39	Q35-37 問題
	40	Q38-40 会話
	41	Q38-40 問題
	42	Q41-43 会話
	43	Q41-43 問題
	44	Q44-46 会話
	45	Q44-46 問題
	46	Q47-49 会話

次ページの「音声を使った学習例の紹介」を参考に、問題に解答した後の学習用教材としてもご活用ください。

音声ダウンロードの手順▶本誌 p.3　音声を使った学習例▶別冊 p.200

Test	Track No.	Contents
TEST 2	47	Part 3 Q47-49 問題
	48	Q50-52 会話
	49	Q50-52 問題
	50	Q53-55 会話
	51	Q53-55 問題
	52	Q56-58 会話
	53	Q56-58 問題
	54	Q59-61 会話
	55	Q59-61 問題
	56	Q62-64 会話
	57	Q62-64 問題
	58	Q65-67 会話
	59	Q65-67 問題
	60	Q68-70 会話
	61	Q68-70 問題
	62	Part 4 Directions
	63	Q71-73 トーク
	64	Q71-73 問題
	65	Q74-76 トーク
	66	Q74-76 問題
	67	Q77-79 トーク
	68	Q77-79 問題
	69	Q80-82 トーク
	70	Q80-82 問題
	71	Q83-85 トーク
	72	Q83-85 問題
	73	Q86-88 トーク
	74	Q86-88 問題
	75	Q89-91 トーク
	76	Q89-91 問題
	77	Q92-94 トーク
	78	Q92-94 問題
	79	Q95-97 トーク
	80	Q95-97 問題
	81	Q98-100 トーク
	82	Q98-100 問題

● 特典（ダウンロード）

Test	File No.	Contents
TEST 1	01	Part 5 Q101 問題
	02	Q102 問題
	03	Q103 問題
	04	Q104 問題
	05	Q105 問題
	06	Q106 問題
	07	Q107 問題
	08	Q108 問題
	09	Part 5 Q109 問題
	10	Q110 問題
	11	Q111 問題
	12	Q112 問題
	13	Q113 問題
	14	Q114 問題
	15	Q115 問題
	16	Q116 問題
	17	Q117 問題
	18	Q118 問題
	19	Q119 問題
	20	Q120 問題
	21	Q121 問題
	22	Q122 問題
	23	Q123 問題
	24	Q124 問題
	25	Q125 問題
	26	Q126 問題
	27	Q127 問題
	28	Q128 問題
	29	Q129 問題
	30	Q130 問題
	31	Part 6 Q131-134 問題
	32	Q135-138 問題
	33	Q139-142 問題
	34	Q143-146 問題
	35	Part 7 Q147-148 文書
	36	Q149-150 文書
	37	Q151-152 文書
	38	Q153-154 文書
	39	Q155-157 文書
	40	Q158-160 文書
	41	Q161-163 文書
	42	Q164-167 文書
	43	Q168-171 文書
	44	Q172-175 文書
	45-46	Q176-180 文書
	47-48	Q181-185 文書
	49-51	Q186-190 文書
	52-54	Q191-195 文書
	55-57	Q196-200 文書
TEST 2	58	Part 5 Q101 問題
	59	Q102 問題
	60	Q103 問題
	61	Q104 問題
	62	Q105 問題
	63	Q106 問題
	64	Q107 問題
	65	Part 5 Q108 問題
	66	Q109 問題
	67	Q110 問題
	68	Q111 問題
	69	Q112 問題
	70	Q113 問題
	71	Q114 問題
	72	Q115 問題
	73	Q116 問題
	74	Q117 問題
	75	Q118 問題
	76	Q119 問題
	77	Q120 問題
	78	Q121 問題
	79	Q122 問題
	80	Q123 問題
	81	Q124 問題
	82	Q125 問題
	83	Q126 問題
	84	Q127 問題
	85	Q128 問題
	86	Q129 問題
	87	Q130 問題
	88	Part 6 Q131-134 問題
	89	Q135-138 問題
	90	Q139-142 問題
	91	Q143-146 問題
	92	Part 7 Q147-148 文書
	93	Q149-150 文書
	94	Q151-152 文書
	95	Q153-155 文書
	96	Q156-157 文書
	97	Q158-160 文書
	98	Q161-164 文書
	99	Q165-167 文書
	100	Q168-171 文書
	101	Q172-175 文書
	102-103	Q176-180 文書
	104-105	Q181-185 文書
	106-108	Q186-190 文書
	109-111	Q191-195 文書
	112-114	Q196-200 文書

＊CDに収録の問題音声は全て、*TOEIC*®公式スピーカーによるものです。
＊特典音声は、CDとは別に収録したもので、標準的な北米発音を採用しています。

スマホやPCを使ってさらにひと学習！

音声を使った学習例の紹介

『公式 *TOEIC*® Listening & Reading 問題集6』は、付属CDの音声の他、特典としてTEST 1、2のリーディングセクションの一部の音声を、スマートフォンやPCにダウンロードしてお聞きいただけます。以下に音声を使った公式問題集の学習法の一例をご紹介しますので、学習の参考になさってください。

準備するもの：別冊「解答・解説」（本書）、音声をダウンロードしたスマートフォンまたはPC

＊ Part 1～4の音声は付属CDでも聞くことができます。Part 5～7の特典音声を含む全ての音声の利用は、abceedへの会員登録（無料）とダウンロードが必要です。本誌p. 3の「音声ダウンロードの手順」に従ってサイトにアクセスし、『公式 *TOEIC*® Listening & Reading 問題集6』をダウンロードしてください。リーディングの特典音声のスピードが速くて聞き取りが難しいと感じる方は、abceedのアプリなどのスピード調整機能を利用しましょう。初めのうちは0.8～0.9倍などで聞くことをお勧めします。

Part 1、2

1. 「解答・解説」で正解の英文の意味内容を正しく理解する。
2. 音声を聞き、発音やイントネーションを真似て音読する（リピーティング）。最初はスクリプトを見ながら行い、慣れてきたらスクリプトを見ずに行う。

Part 1では写真を見ながら正解の描写文だけを、Part 2では質問と正解の応答を、音読してみましょう。自分が発話しているつもりで音読すると、表現が定着しやすくなります。

Part 3、4

1. 「解答・解説」でスクリプトの英文と訳を確認。知らない語の意味や英文の内容を把握する。
2. スクリプトを見ながら会話やトークを聞く。発話と同じスピードで英文を目で追い、即座に意味を理解できるようになるまで繰り返す。
3. スクリプトを見ずに会話やトークを聞く。聞き取りづらい箇所や意味が理解できない箇所をスクリプトで確認し、再び音声だけで理解できるか挑戦する。

Part 3ではスピーカー同士の関係や会話の目的、Part 4では場面やトークの趣旨をまず把握し、徐々に理解できる範囲を増やしていくつもりで、細部の情報を聞き取るようにしましょう。

Part 5、6

1. 「解答・解説」で英文と訳を確認。知らない語の意味や英文の内容を把握する。
2. 本書のTEST 1、2の該当ページ(p.42-48とp.84-90)のコピーを取り、音声を聞いて空所の語や文を書き取る。知っている語彙や文法の知識も用いて空所を埋め、書き取ったものと実際の英文を比較する。最後に、もう一度音声を聞く。

聞き取れない箇所は、飛ばしたりカタカナで書いたりしても構いません。音声だけに頼らず、語彙力や文法の知識を用いて挑戦してみましょう。Part 5は短い文なので、ディクテーションするのもよいでしょう。

Part 6、7

1. 「解答・解説」で英文と訳を確認。知らない語の意味や英文の内容を把握する。その際、読み方に迷った箇所に印を付けておく。
2. 音声を聞きながら英文を目で追い（初めはスピードを遅めにしても可）、英語の語順のまま理解できるようになることを目指す。分からなかった箇所は、適宜訳を確認する。
3. 1.で印を付けた、読み方に迷った箇所の言い方を確認する。
   例：数字や記号の言い方（日付、住所、飛行機の便名、価格、URL）など。

1は構文や語彙の学習、2は速読の学習です。2では意味のまとまりを意識しながら英文を読み進めていくようにすると、取り組みやすいでしょう。3は、実際の会話の際にも役立つので積極的に覚えるとよいでしょう。